The First Cold Warrior

THE FIRST COLD WARRIOR

Harry Truman, Containment, and the
Remaking of Liberal Internationalism

ELIZABETH EDWARDS SPALDING

THE UNIVERSITY PRESS OF KENTUCKY

Publication of this volume was made possible in part by a grant
from the National Endowment for the Humanities.

Scholarly publisher for the Commonwealth,
serving Bellarmine University, Berea College, Centre
College of Kentucky, Eastern Kentucky University,
The Filson Historical Society, Georgetown College,
Kentucky Historical Society, Kentucky State University,
Morehead State University, Murray State University,
Northern Kentucky University, Transylvania University,
University of Kentucky, University of Louisville,
and Western Kentucky University.

Editorial and Sales Offices: The University Press of Kentucky
663 South Limestone Street, Lexington, Kentucky 40508-4008
www.kentuckypress.com

08 09 10 11   6 5 4 3

Library of Congress Cataloging-in-Publication Data

Spalding, Elizabeth Edwards, 1966–
The first cold warrior : Harry Truman, containment, and the remaking of
liberal internationalism / Elizabeth Edwards Spalding.
  p. cm.
Includes bibliographical references and index.
ISBN-13: 978-0-8131-2392-9 (hardcover : alk. paper)
ISBN-10: 0-8131-2392-5 (hardcover : alk. paper)
1. Truman, Harry S., 1884–1972. 2. United States—Foreign relations—1945–1953.
3. Internationalism—History—20th century. 4. Liberalism—United States—
History—20th century. 5. Cold War. I. Title.
E814.S63 2006
973.918092—dc22
2006002564

Manufactured in the United States of America.

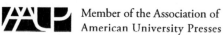

Member of the Association of
American University Presses

To Whittle Johnston

Contents

Acknowledgments

I would like to express my appreciation to those who have helped me with this project. Among those who read all or part of the manuscript, I am especially grateful to Patrick Garrity, Robert Kaufman, and Michael Warner. Pat, in particular, challenged me to clarify general themes and specific points, and the book is better for his suggestions. I am indebted to the Earhart Foundation for providing me with a generous grant, which enabled me to travel to and research at several libraries and archives. And so I thank the staffs of the Harry S. Truman, Seeley G. Mudd, George C. Marshall, and Clemson University libraries and of the Library of Congress for their assistance while I was researching in their manuscript collections. Anyone writing on the Cold War also owes gratitude to the Cold War International History Project of the Woodrow Wilson Center. For publication, I have been fortunate to work with Steve Wrinn—always interested, thorough, and efficient—and his excellent staff at the University Press of Kentucky.

My family has been indispensable. My parents, Lee and Anne Edwards, introduced me to the study of the Cold War, and I first did archival research for one of my father's writing projects when I was in high school. With skill and good humor, my mother helped me research at the libraries in Lexington, Virginia, and Princeton, New Jersey. Joseph and Catherine created temporary office space next to their mother's while pretending to write their own books, and they delighted in manning the printer. Above all, my husband Matthew has been loving and supportive and has never grown bored listening to comments about Harry Truman, George F. Kennan, and the centrality of the Cold War to both U.S. foreign policy and the remaking of liberal internationalism in the modern era.

Introduction

"I suppose that history will remember my term in office as the years when the 'cold war' began to overshadow our lives," Harry S. Truman speculated in his presidential farewell address of January 1953. "I have had hardly a day in office that has not been dominated by this all-embracing struggle—this conflict between those who love freedom and those who would lead the world back into slavery and darkness. And always in the background there has been the atomic bomb."

From the moment he became president of the United States in April 1945, Truman made hard decisions under acutely trying circumstances, steering the United States between what he saw as the shoals and reefs of military conflict with the Soviet Union, on the one hand, and acquiescence to Communist ideology, on the other. "But when history says that my term of office saw the beginning of the cold war, it will also say that in those eight years we have set the course that can win it," Truman continued. "We have succeeded in carving out a new set of policies to attain peace—positive policies, policies of world leadership, policies that express faith in other free people. We have averted World War III up to now, and we may already have succeeded in establishing conditions which can keep that war from happening as far ahead as man can see."[1] These policies—notably, the Truman Doctrine, the Marshall Plan, and the North Atlantic Treaty Organization—and the geopolitical conditions they created made up what is called the strategy of containment.

It is often said that George F. Kennan—author of the Long Telegram in 1946 and "The Sources of Soviet Conduct," better known as the X article that appeared anonymously in *Foreign Affairs* in 1947—was the father of containment. "In these circumstances it is clear," he wrote in the latter work, "that the main element of any United States policy toward the Soviet Union must be that of a long-term, patient but firm and vigilant containment of Russian expansive tendencies."[2] Yet while Kennan was a key intellectual figure of the post–World War II era, and contributed significantly to U.S. foreign policy in the 1940s, it was, in the end,

1

President Truman who conceived, enunciated, and directed the strategy of containment. In crucial ways—ways that would form and determine American policy—Truman's and Kennan's ideas differed. Containment, as implemented by the United States, was Truman's containment; the alternative, what we may term Kennan's containment, was never policy in the Truman years.

Truman's beliefs, assumptions, judgment, and policies not only gave rise to and defined containment's content but also shaped America's understanding of the Cold War. Because of his fundamental role, it is right to say that Harry Truman was the first cold warrior.

Truman's containment strategy also provided the grounds for a new liberal internationalism, which departed from that of both Woodrow Wilson and Franklin D. Roosevelt and became the core of a postwar bipartisan consensus on U.S. foreign policy maintained by almost every president since the end of World War II. There is a scholarly as well as journalistic tendency to lump together Wilson, FDR, and Truman with respect to liberal internationalism, especially since they were all Democrats. A more nuanced argument suggests that Truman either amended or fused aspects of Wilsonian idealism and Rooseveltian realism.[3] But Truman ultimately went beyond these interpretations in forging a new view in the context of the Cold War. For Wilson, international meant universal. He wanted the international organization of the League of Nations to become a permanent, universal institution. For Roosevelt, international meant the United Nations (UN) would legitimate decisions made by the great powers in an increasingly interdependent postwar world. He expected the UN to appear as a universal, Wilsonian institution and to serve as cover for the realist policies of the most important countries in terms of power, influence, and hegemony. For Truman, by contrast, international meant that American leadership was central and that many, though not necessarily all, nations were concerned, whether working together (loosely or in alliances) or through the United Nations. Free peoples and free governments were always more essential to him than any specific international organization, although he never hid his hope that free men and open regimes could build a future world community of lasting depth. Truman regarded the United Nations and Bretton Woods entities as international organizations—not universal institutions—in which the countries of the world would make good-faith efforts to prevent or stop conflict and to promote free markets. As well, he gave equal weight in the Cold War to the Atlantic Alliance, a regional organization based on collective defense, in opposition to Wilson's League of Nations and its dependence on collective security. In these theoretical and practical ways, all of the major post–World War II international and regional organizations were precisely neither Wilsonian nor Rooseveltian.

Truman's liberal internationalism also differed from Wilson's progressive internationalism and partly from FDR's version of liberal internationalism in terms of educating and moving both congressional and public opinion. To keep his League of Nations pure, Wilson determined that he had to be in charge of all debate about the international organization during and after the First World War. He not only fought his main Republican Party opponents—famously, Senator Henry Cabot Lodge, regarding reservations to the Versailles Treaty—but he also alienated potential GOP allies, especially former president William Howard Taft. At the same time, Wilson lost many of his progressive Democratic Party supporters, who were excluded from his inner circle and found the League of Nations insufficiently idealistic and the peace treaty too punitive. Avoiding such mistakes during the Second World War, Roosevelt made use of private organizations such as the Council on Foreign Relations and the United Nations Association to help mobilize public opinion. FDR did not permit any resolution for a postwar international organization into Congress until 1943, at which point the language was kept deliberately vague in order to win votes; when the terms had to be made more concrete, he bypassed issues that would cause opposition, even though this resulted in ambiguity in terms of U.S. commitments.[4] Truman did not follow this lead, but—in private meetings and in public statements, and with the help of well-chosen people in his administration—he obtained a broad bipartisan consensus for his containment policies. (His previous career in the Senate also aided him in executive-legislative relations.) While he did not place Republicans in his cabinet as Roosevelt strategically had, Truman was effective in appointing public servants, such as General George C. Marshall, Averell Harriman, and Robert Lovett, who were acceptable to or had close friendships with GOP leaders. Much as FDR had relied on Wendell Willkie to deliver Republican backing for liberal internationalism, Truman would depend on Senator Arthur Vandenberg to foster GOP support for his new internationalism. Like Roosevelt with respect to the United Nations, Truman never forgot about forming public support for the strategy of containment that animated his liberal internationalism.

Truman rooted his policies in common-sense assumptions regarding man, the state, freedom, and tyranny—and therefore about the United States and the Soviet Union. He believed that what he sometimes called the "war of nerves" was dominated by tyranny's ideological assault on human freedom, and that the nature of the East-West conflict transcended both partisanship and domestic political opinions.[5] His ideas and policies stemmed from a multifaceted definition of peace, composed of freedom, justice, and order. Yet for all his clarity and directness, there seemed to be a contradiction in his thinking: Truman longed for a permanent peace and held that the United Nations was the best vehicle by which to attain this goal; at the same time, he realized that the components of peace and the practical requirements of American foreign policy were more profound and immediate. In the end, his moral convictions and religious beliefs helped him resolve the tension in his political thought.

Many of Truman's contemporaries attacked his articulation and implementation of containment. One segment of opinion at the time blamed the president for being too soft on communism; this view reached its height after the fall of China in 1949 and during the morass of the Korean War. Nonetheless, those who criticized Truman in the 1940s and early 1950s for being easy on the Communists largely endorsed the president's policies of containment; they may have wanted more on particular issues and particular points, but they approved his strategy of pursuing peace through the demonstration and application of strength and the defense and promotion of freedom. The best-remembered, most-analyzed foils to Truman are not those who censured him for being weak but those—such as George Kennan, Henry Wallace, and Walter Lippmann—who found him to be blinded by anticommunism. On the whole, these contemporary opponents faulted the president for being too hard on the Communists, for construing the conflict as a clear-cut ideological struggle rather than as a complicated balancing relationship, and for missing opportunities to ameliorate or better manage U.S.-Soviet relations. It is no coincidence that these critics presaged the modern academic schools of thought that continue to analyze and, usually, denounce Truman's containment.

Today, four views dominate the academic study of the Cold War: realism, revisionism, postrevisionism, and corporatism. Rejecting what is perceived as the idealism of the interwar period and critical of Truman's "universalism" replacing professional diplomacy and carefully calibrated policy statements, realism depicts a power struggle between two great nation-states that acted alike in global politics, starting with the inevitable move to fill the vacuum caused by the end of World War II.[6] Revisionism—an outgrowth of Marxist and neo-Marxist thought of the New Left movement in American protest politics and the academy of the late 1950s and 1960s—holds that the East-West clash was caused by democratic capitalism and leaders who were motivated by economic imperialism when they should have been more accommodating to the Soviet Union.[7] Established in the 1970s and 1980s, postrevisionism accepts the essence of realist power politics but contends that mutual misunderstandings and mirror-imaging by the United States and the Soviet Union both generated and sustained the Cold War.[8] Gaining strength in the late 1980s and 1990s, corporatism combines the struggle for power with economic determinism to characterize the U.S.-Soviet conflict.[9]

While not the focus of this book, it must be noted that these schools of thought, despite having roots in political theory and having become mostly academic abstractions, grow out of practical politics, in particular, the contemporary debate over the Truman administration's policies concerning the Soviet Union and the Cold War. Kennan—primarily and with help from Lippmann—and Wallace, secondarily, laid the groundwork for each of these modern paradigms. Diplomat and high-level State Department official Kennan was the central figure, since he not only contributed to the development of containment but also provided one of the first commentaries on Truman's Cold War approach. His critique rose out of and defined a realist outlook on the subject, although revisionists and corporatists, as well as realists, came to appreciate his views on nuclear disarmament and what he termed the egotism of American moralism. Former vice president Wallace, the leading progressive political leader of the 1940s, was also an important participant in the public debate about the Cold War's meaning and America's role in the conflict; as such, he was the first revisionist on the subject. His contention that the United States was forsaking its status as a revolutionary power in its Cold War foreign policy and his call for multilateral UN action in place of U.S. unilateralism have been crucial to revisionists and, lately in policy circles, to progressives. A longtime observer of the American political scene, journalist and essayist Lippmann (who popularized the term Cold War) exhibited in his appraisal mostly realist tendencies with a residue of Wilsonianism, due to his government service under President Wilson and a past commitment to progressivism. Lippmann offered a version of realism with early revisionist undertones and was a consistent antagonist of Truman.[10] His indictment of what he regarded as the ideological and military excesses of Truman's containment, along with his endorsement of General Marshall's position on China and equilibrium with the USSR in Europe, resonated with both realists and postrevisionists. While some have relied heavily on Kennan (such as postrevisionist historian John Lewis Gaddis) and others have drawn much from Wallace (such as revisionist historians William Appleman Williams and, more recently, Arnold Offner), most academic writers on the Cold War and containment are the intellectual heirs of Kennan, Lippmann, and Wallace rather than Harry Truman.

Here, by contrast, I examine the political thought and action of Truman's approach to the war of nerves and how, ultimately, that approach both infused and was subsumed in a new postwar liberal internationalism. The argument and structure in this book illuminate the fundamental differences between Truman's and Kennan's views through an explication of each man's thought about the Cold War and U.S. foreign policy in the East-West conflict. The first chapter traces the beginnings of Truman's internationalism and containment strategy, including biographical background, his first months as president in 1945, and the effect of Kennan's Long Telegram early the following year. Along with events in Europe and the Near East, Winston Churchill's 1946 Fulton address, and Henry Wallace's disputations, the development of Truman's containment is followed through the 1946 Clifford memorandum in the second chapter. That development is then elaborated from the 1947 Truman Doctrine in the third chapter through the Marshall Plan (announced in 1947 and passed in 1948) in the fourth chapter, all against the backdrop of ongoing challenges in world and, where pertinent, domestic politics. George Kennan and his conflicting presentation of containment from 1946 into 1948 receive thorough attention in the fifth chapter, as does journalist Walter Lippmann's critique of aspects of Truman's and Kennan's containments. Truman's commitment to the North Atlantic Treaty, starting in 1948 and 1949, and to Western Europe is juxtaposed in the sixth chapter with Kennan's objections to NATO and his suggestions for the settlement of the German question. In the seventh chapter, the new postwar notion of national security is examined, as are the creation of the National Security Council (NSC) in 1947 and the institutionalization of Truman's containment in early NSC papers. The culmination of Truman's containment in NSC 68 of 1950 and the conclusion of Kennan's alternative containment are analyzed in the eighth chapter. In the ninth chapter, Truman's study of history and his religious beliefs are related to his understanding of the Cold War and the duties of American leadership in meeting the conflict. A brief conclusion assesses the lasting significance of Truman's approach to the Cold War.

For this work I rely first on primary documents, especially Truman's writings, letters, words, and speeches,[11] and, second, on other primary sources found in archives, manuscript collections, and official government documents. Secondary sources are used in light of the primary documents; in this way, I do not subscribe to a particular methodology, and the book is not a piece of formal Cold War historiography. Nor is it a biography or a complete assessment of Truman's intellectual and political thought. I do not address Truman's domestic policies, except as they intersect with his foreign policy. As I am largely concerned with the period from 1945 through the first part of 1950, the themes in the text precede the Korean War. And since the practical focus is on U.S.-Soviet relations, I do not deal with the conflict in China. Instead, this work is a study of the primary American actor in the early postwar period of the Cold War, and I seek to understand the man as he understood not only himself but also the individuals, events, and arguments around him concerning the central political question of his day.

How Truman approached the central political question of his day can help us think about the central political question of our day. It is standard for historians and political scientists to point out the perils of conflating the past and present. But many scholars would also be the first to say that we must not forget history's lessons. The most appropriate parallel we have to the war on terrorism, to this point, is the early part of the Cold War. There are important differences between then and now, to be sure: no surprise attack on the United States occurred in 1945, and so Truman could take a short but valuable time to devise his strategy; the Communists of the mid-1940s were either located in or swore allegiance to a particular regime, the Union of Soviet Socialist Republics (USSR), not a supranational extremist movement based on a perverted interpretation of a major world religion; and it is unclear at this point if the war on terrorism will be of the magnitude and duration of the Cold War. But the similarities are striking. In both cases, the United States has faced an ideological enemy implacably opposed to liberal democracy generally and America specifically. In both cases, the war was unexpected by most people. Truman had expressed his distaste for both Nazi and Soviet tyranny in the years before he became president, but he had not supposed he would regard the USSR as an enemy while the Grand Alliance was still fighting the Second World War. In both cases, the presidents at the time had to define the meaning of the war for their fellow citizens. As well, the Cold War and the war on terrorism each became worldwide in scope with local hot battles: Korea under the Truman administration and Afghanistan and Iraq on George W. Bush's watch.

Notable similarities also exist at the levels of politics and foreign policy. In both instances, the presidents followed popular predecessors who were inspiring communicators respected for their displays of wide-ranging intelligence. Before their presidencies, neither Truman nor Bush was known for his foreign policy acumen; before and during their respective terms in office, neither was praised for his eloquence, a quality that is prized in politics, especially during times of crisis. Both men came to be associated with their blunt statements about the main conflicts of their day. Conceiving and directing a new U.S. foreign policy, too, is a noteworthy point of comparison between the time periods: from creating new government institutions—such as the National Security Council, the Department of Defense, and the Central Intelligence Agency—to putting his belief in freedom and democracy, as well as his religious faith, at the center of his foreign policy, Truman has much to teach in relation to the presidency of George W. Bush.

Here our purpose is to understand what Truman said and did: how well he expressed his principles and applied them, how quickly and deeply he came to grasp the challenges of the war of nerves, how securely he constructed new institutions and policies in order to fight the East-West conflict, and how effectively he left a legacy to his successors in the Oval Office—perhaps, as we see now, even after the end of the Cold War. Many have argued that, even with or because of the war on terrorism, the Wilsonian project has more currency these days. When reading his second inaugural address and other speeches, it has become popular to refer to the "Wilsonianism" of George W. Bush. But the promotion of democratic principles was neither the original nor the sole province of Wilson. The Truman era provides a better model: through the correct blend of political, moral, military, and economic strength, the United States should articulate and promote the principles of the liberal democratic regime; discourage the spread of despotism (which, in today's world, would mean opposing terrorists as well as tyrants); and encourage the establishment and maintenance of healthy, democratic, constitutional states.

1

"I'm tired babying the Soviets"

The Beginnings of Truman's Internationalism

When Harry Truman became president in April 1945, liberal internationalism was little more than an intellectual concept and by no means a common expression. For the first part of the twentieth century, politicians spoke in terms of being nationalists or internationalists, but they tended not to add modifiers such as liberal, conservative, or progressive. As World War II came to a close, the two great presidential expositors of internationalism—Woodrow Wilson and Franklin Roosevelt—were gone, but their presence still dominated American politics. Facing a global conflict with the Soviet Union, an ally during the Second World War, Truman could have taken up the mantle of either one of these leaders; he could have pursued a fusion of their approaches, much as Secretary of State James Byrnes advocated in 1945 and 1946. But Truman, while admiring his predecessors, chose neither Wilson nor FDR nor a combination of their international theories as his model. Instead, he fashioned a unique postwar liberal internationalism that applied broadly held domestic principles to the nation's foreign policy. It was inclusive, bipartisan, and informed by the ideals of the United States rather than a particular philosophy of international relations or the agenda of a political party. Built on a foundation of strength and an understanding of freedom, this liberal internationalism first found voice in Truman's policies and statements toward the Soviet Union on such topics as Trieste, Iran, and Berlin.

Making the World Safe for Democracy

When he was twenty-eight years old, Harry Truman followed with interest the 1912 Democratic Party convention, which took many days and ballots to determine a presidential nominee. Although initially for native Missourian and representative Champ Clark, Truman and his father came to favor New Jersey governor Woodrow Wilson. It was renowned Populist William Jennings Bryan's endorsement of Wilson that changed the Truman men's minds.[1] In his early thirties, Truman answered President Wilson's call to fight in World War I—finagling his way out of several eye exams in order to be accepted by the military—not only because of his patriotism but also to test himself under the rigors and deprivations of war. From the beginning and, eventually, through his command of a field artillery battery, he excelled at both his self-imposed trial of character and the combat-tested challenge of leadership. In addition to the discipline and habits of the military life, he learned how to direct people of different minds and diverse backgrounds, by both decision and example.[2] Captain Truman served as an officer in the army reserves for over thirty years, retiring in 1945 as a full colonel when he became the nation's commander in chief. His men respected and admired him during the war and after, actively supporting him as captain, judge, senator, and president; for his part, Truman always remained close to his battery through correspondence and in person.

Truman carried away from the Great War and its immediate aftermath a deeper understanding of world politics. He liked to say that America owed it to the Marquis de Lafayette, who had crossed the Atlantic to serve under General George Washington in the Revolutionary War, to help the French fight the Germans. Although he perceived that European politics and wars derived from beliefs and customs other than those of the American experience, Truman held that the United States could not retreat from the world arena. In his estimation, World War I had been America's initiation into world leadership. In explaining the First World War and the interwar period, he eschewed isolationism, which, he believed, contributed to the Second World War. During his senatorial and presidential years, he repeatedly exhorted the American people and the U.S. Congress to exercise the global leadership they had refused to assume in 1919.

Truman did not refer much to Wilson in his World War I letters to his future wife, Bess, noting in 1919 that he—and "every A.E.F. [American

Expeditionary Force] man feels the same way"—wanted to come home after helping to beat the Germans and did not "give a whoop" about either the League of Nations or the situation in Russia.[3] In time and with distance from his fighting days, he wrote in 1954 that he "became one of [Wilson's] great admirers" after the 1912 nomination and was pleased with his reelection in 1916; in 1953, Truman placed Wilson in company with Buddha, Jesus, Cincinnatus, George Washington, and Abraham Lincoln as makers of history; after seventy-five historians ranked American presidents in a 1962 poll in *Time* magazine, Truman reordered the first five from Lincoln, Washington, FDR, Wilson, and Thomas Jefferson to Washington, Jefferson, Wilson, Lincoln, and Roosevelt.[4] Despite such laudatory comparisons, Truman's internationalism differed significantly from that of Woodrow Wilson.

Wilson's worldview stressed the primacy of peace as the fulfillment of progressive history. In 1916, the same year that he campaigned for reelection on the theme that he kept the United States out of war, Wilson focused on the world after the Great War and urged that "we must move forward to the thought of the modern world, the thought of which peace is the very atmosphere." After adding that "[o]ur interest is only in peace and its future guarantees," he expressed "the confidence I feel that the world is even now upon the eve of a great consummation," which would result not only in some sort of international security organization but also in coercion being put only "to the service of a common order, a common justice, and a common peace." Wilson based these comments on the proposition that "[t]he interests of all nations are our own also." In making all states' interests interchangeable, he acknowledged the rights of individual peoples and nations and of small states, but emphasized that the world had an overarching right, specifically to be free from "every disturbance of its peace that has its origin in aggression and disregard of the rights of peoples and nations."[5]

To secure the primacy of peace, Wilson called for "peace without victory" in 1917, several months before the United States entered World War I. To him, this memorable phrase meant that only a postwar "peace between equals" would "win the approval of mankind" and last. While arguing that the United States and the other peoples of the New World would have a special role in guaranteeing peace and justice, Wilson contended that the "organized major force of mankind," seemingly in the form of a global policeman and an all-encompassing concert of power, was the key to an enduring peace. Rejecting the mechanisms of realpolitik, he proposed new procedures in another one of his most famous phrases: "There must be, not a balance of power, but a community of power; not organized rivalries, but an organized common peace." In fact, Wilson took the opportunity to repudiate the main elements of international relations before the Great War, such as entangling alliances and hegemony, and to advance instead self-determination, freedom of the seas, and military power used only as a tool to maintain order. Although he stressed that his new procedures and processes of peace were essential, he believed that "[t]he right state of mind, the right feeling between nations, is as necessary for a lasting peace." Wilson knew that he was advocating a different way of engaging in world politics, but submitted its principles were both American and "forward looking," "modern," and "enlightened."[6]

"We are at the beginning of an age," Wilson said in presenting the declaration of war against Germany in April 1917, "in which it will be insisted that the same standards of conduct and of responsibility for wrong done shall be observed among nations and their governments that are observed among the individual citizens of civilized states." Equating progress with his view of civilization (and arguing that civilization hung in the balance in the war), he planted the seeds for a League of Nations by emphasizing that a "steadfast concert for peace" could only be maintained by a partnership of democratic nations. "The world," he proclaimed, "must be made safe for democracy."[7]

In the Fourteen Points speech of January 1918, Wilson set forth the "processes of peace" by which all peoples and nations, Germany included, would take their place in "the new world in which we now live." Once more, he spurned what he saw as old ways, such as conquest, aggrandizement, and secret covenants, and praised the acceptance of new methods "now clear to the view of every public man whose thoughts do not still linger in an age that is dead and gone, which makes it possible for every nation whose purposes are consistent with justice and the peace of the world to avow now or at any other time the objects it has in view."[8] Following these themes in the presentation of the Covenant of the League of Nations in February 1919, Wilson termed the covenant a "belated document" and remarked that "the conscience of the world has long been prepared to express itself in some such way." In the end, "the moral force of the public opinion of the world"—with armed force in the background as a last resort—would secure and sustain peace.[9] Wilson viewed himself as specially equipped, if not chosen, to help others see that politics could now operate according to an open and democratic process and that the power politics of realism had given way to the inevitable forces of history.[10]

Woodrow Wilson pursued what many have termed liberal internationalism, but what should more accurately be termed progressive internationalism.[11] By the end of World War I, he viewed democracy and freedom ultimately as tools to obtain an organized peace through the vehicle of the League of Nations. Wilson's progressive internationalism inhered in his Presbyterianism, the childhood impression the Civil War left on him, his belief in democracy, his conviction that the United States had a special role in world politics, and his aspirations to create a new world order. The last was inspired, in part, by Wilson's correspondence and interaction with the progressive leaders of his day, who renounced militarism, imperialism, and balance of power politics. In foreign policy and international relations, Wilson wanted a community of power and nations.

Truman did not speak in such language, although he too rejected militarism, imperialism, and balance of power politics as unethical and outdated. In his political thought, free peoples and a community of free nations were the goals. In place of Wilson's expectations for collective security through a single international organization, Truman placed his trust in collective defense, most notably in the North Atlantic Treaty Organization (NATO), an arrangement that would have been impossible and illegal in Wilson's world under the League of Nations. He concluded that international organizations could achieve good global effects, but, unlike Wilson, he did not predict universal results. Truman's liberal internationalism relied on the combined strength of the free nations of the world—led by the United States—to defend and further freedom, promote justice and order, and result in peace of a durable sort. Wilson's progressive internationalism assumed that peace was inevitable and the world community of nations would practice moderation, seek peace and justice, and be able to thwart the actions of potential aggressor states through the strength of their moral power and, only as a last resort, their military power. Truman was attracted to Wilson's affirmation of the need for the United States to be involved in world politics and his belief in international organization. Any other Wilsonian influence on Truman was deflected to a large extent by the realities of the Cold War.[12]

Where Truman might be the most indebted to Wilson is in the latter's view of the executive power in foreign affairs, even though it is unclear whether Truman (like other modern presidents) fully grasped this legacy. In his 1911 *Constitutional Government in the United States*, Wilson argued for the president's "control, which is very absolute, of the foreign relations of the nations," and added that the "initiative in foreign affairs, which the President possesses without any restriction whatever, is virtually the power to control them absolutely." And although Americans (including most earlier presidents) were only beginning to regard the presidency in this light, it would increasingly be the case that the office and its inhabitant would be viewed, for all intents and purposes, as absolute in foreign policy. Because "it has risen to the first rank in power and resources," wrote Wilson, the United States "can never hide our President again as a mere domestic officer."[13] While also believing in a strong presidency and acting with dispatch and boldness in the Korean War, Truman never echoed Wilson's general comments about the virtual absolute primacy of the president in international relations, and he chose as a matter of course to involve Congress in foreign policymaking such as the Truman Doctrine, the Marshall Plan, and NATO.

To the Presidency

Once he was elected in 1934 to represent Missouri in the U.S. Senate, Truman consistently articulated his belief that tyranny must be defeated in world politics and that a real peace required strength, freedom, and international commitment. As early as the latter part of 1937, he was dissatisfied with the policies of neutrality, and, in 1939, he wanted American legislation revised in order to permit arms and munitions aid to Great Britain; in 1941, he was one of the few Democrats who joined Republicans in an effort to repeal all neutrality provisions. In his September 1939 letters to Bess, Truman expressed his concern that, if not stopped, the Soviet Union and Nazi Germany would take over Europe, defeat France and England, and then "we'll have a Nazi, or nasty, world."[14] He explained to a Missouri audience in October that the current neutrality policy penalized American allies because "we should not help the thugs among nations by refusing to sell arms to our friends."[15] While he hoped that the United States might be able to escape entry into the Second World War, he believed that the country could not sit by idly and permit a worldwide catastrophe.

Truman did not suffer tyrants gladly. In October 1939, he said that the "three dictators, Russian, German, and Italian," had returned to "a code little short of cave-man savagery," and that he saw their exploitation of "this magnificent machine age of ours" as an effort to destroy civilization. Without a moral reawakening, he thought another dark age was possible.[16] His most controversial public remark on the subject of despotic aggression came after the Nazi invasion of the Soviet Union in June 1941: "If we see that Germany is winning we ought to help Russia and if Russia is winning we ought to help Germany and that way let them kill as many as possible, although I don't want to see Hitler victorious under any circumstances. Neither of them think anything of their pledged word."[17] Truman's immediate criticism of the two powers stemmed from his understanding of the 1939 Molotov-Ribbentrop pact, the nonaggression treaty between the USSR and Germany. While recognizing that the United States had to accept the Soviet Union as an ally against Hitler, Truman did not think that the Kremlin could be trusted as a friend.

In aiming to change matters and prepare the United States for war, Senator Truman was practical. Having been reelected in 1940 without FDR's endorsement (and having supported favorite-son candidate Missouri Senator Bennett Clark for the Democratic presidential nomination), Truman returned to the Senate with a reputation as an anti-Roosevelt Democrat.[18] In summer 1940, he had noticed that the American defense buildup was handicapped by wasteful expenditures and the failure to award more competitive contracts. After briefing Roosevelt in February 1941 on his preliminary findings (in which FDR showed no interest), Truman introduced a Senate resolution creating the Special Committee to Investigate the National Defense Program, which he then headed until August 1944. Popularly known as the Truman Committee, it uncovered evidence of extensive economic improprieties, carelessness, and corruption in defense spending, which, once corrected, saved the nation both money and the lives of American soldiers.[19] The committee, which the administration had tried to suspend, proved Truman's independence and willingness to stand up against the FDR loyalists. Assessing the committee's importance in its first years, *Time* described the Truman Committee in 1943 as a "billion dollar watchdog" and "the closest thing yet to a domestic high command," and reported the assessment of one Washington insider: "There's only one thing that worries me more than the present state of the war effort. That's to think what it would be like by now without TRUMAN."[20]

Truman was also an acknowledged driving force behind the drafting of the congressional resolution for the establishment of a postwar international organization. In summer 1943, he traveled the Midwest as part of a bipartisan congressional team to explain why internationalism and the United Nations would be essential after World War II.[21] Although he had high expectations for these postwar plans, Truman maintained that the United States would first have to prosecute the current war and secure peace terms. In a spring 1942 letter to Bess, he conveyed his concern about a return to isolationism because of the Nazi peace initiatives: "That German peace offensive worries me. If Britain were to run out on us, or if China should suddenly collapse, we'd have all that old isolation fever again and another war in twenty years. We must take this one to its conclusion and *dictate* peace terms from Berlin and Tokyo. Then we'll have Russia and China to settle afterwards."[22] It was this sort of man, with this sort of opinions and background in foreign policy, who became the Democratic vice presidential candidate in 1944.

Many accounts depict Harry Truman as a nonentity in foreign policy before April 12, 1945. He was best known and chosen to be vice president for his reliable New Deal voting and his Missouri political connections, not to mention the desire of the moderate and anti–New Deal Democrats to prevent Henry A. Wallace from succeeding the now ailing President Roosevelt. As vice president, he was only twice alone with Franklin Roosevelt before the latter's death, and they discussed little of international significance. In terms of the most important technological development of the day, Truman was not fully informed about the near completion of the atomic bomb until he became president.[23] Yet he was a man of clearly formed convictions, had deep experience as a legislator and as an administrator, and was an astute student of world history.[24] From his earliest writings about global affairs, Truman voiced a desire for a world that was characterized by peace—the teaching of the Sermon on the Mount was his touchstone—while admitting the difficulty of achieving it. No fuzzy idealist, he advocated the use of strength if required to achieve or sustain world peace. And as long as fallible men ran the world, strength was needed to defend the cause of freedom.

When he became president, Truman was thrust into harsh global circumstances, in which many key decisions—or, at minimum, the parameters for those decisions—had been made for him. Given his commitment to the use of firmness and strength when necessary, his disagreement with British Prime Minister Winston Churchill regarding troop disposition in

Europe in spring 1945—one of his earliest command decisions—must have made him uneasy. Indeed, the president soon regretted the decision, writing several years after the fact: "We were about 150 miles east of the border of the occupation zone line agreed to at Yalta. I felt that agreements made in the war to keep Russia fighting should be kept and I kept them to the letter. Perhaps they should not have been adhered to so quickly."[25] Churchill had been concerned about Kremlin intentions and actions in Europe since the Soviet victory at Stalingrad; by the end of March 1945, troubled by Soviet violations of the Yalta agreements, he entreated the Anglo-American military leadership to take Berlin, in order to have a stronger bargaining position vis-à-vis the Kremlin. With Roosevelt's approval, however, Generals George C. Marshall and Dwight D. Eisenhower had defined the "single objective" as "quick and complete victory." In pursuance of this "single objective," Eisenhower made the decision to stop at the Elbe River just as FDR died. When implored by Churchill to advance on April 17, Truman stood by the Roosevelt-Marshall agreement—and, by default, supported Eisenhower's tactical decision—that strategy should be determined according to the occupation agreements reached by the European Advisory Commission in 1944.[26]

It is a partial explanation to say that Truman was hampered by American public opinion, for it would have been almost impossible to order troops to oppose an ally that had been critical in the fight against Nazi Germany.[27] During the crucial month of April 1945, moreover, Truman was influenced by Generals Marshall (whom he greatly esteemed) and Eisenhower. They urged the president not to confuse political, postwar matters with the agreed-upon military objective of winning the war against the Nazis.

Throughout the rest of April and May, Truman cabled back and forth between Stalin and Churchill in an attempt to stave off the USSR from taking more territory.[28] In late May, he thought that presidential advisor Harry Hopkins had conveyed American displeasure with Soviet actions, especially in Poland, in a Moscow meeting with Stalin.[29] Yet Truman abided by the American military command when Pilsen and Karlsbad, rather than Prague, were chosen as the goals for U.S. troops in Czechoslovakia. When the time came in June 1945 to make a decision about American troop removal from the Soviet zone in Germany, he told Churchill that he was "unable to delay the withdrawal of American troops from the Soviet zone in order to use pressure in the settlement of other problems" because "it would be highly disadvantageous to our relations with the Soviet to postpone action in this matter until our meeting in July." But when the president sent Stalin his message about the withdrawal, he incorporated all of the prime minister's suggested language about a strong Anglo-American stance on Austria.[30] In fact, less than a week later, Truman stressed that he intended to take more of an initiative at subsequent meetings in San Francisco and at Potsdam.[31]

Churchill wanted the democratic allies to change course immediately, but Truman believed that he could not be more assertive at the time.[32] In early June 1945, it was unclear if the American economy would remain robust as a result of the war, but it was clear that American soldiers were war-weary and would be reluctant to fight another conflict. Besides, the war in the Pacific continued and was in need of additional American troops. Further, the president thought—in his contradictory wish for peace and simultaneous grasp of the political realities—that the Soviet Union would honor its commitments at Yalta.[33] Although he maintained that the Soviets had an edge that would be hard to counter in disputed territories, he hoped that the Kremlin would reciprocate American acts of good faith.[34]

Truman was not passive, however, concerning America's role in the emerging postwar world. His experience at Potsdam disabused him of the notion of Stalin's goodwill.[35] Thus Truman made several comments as early as 1945 about the need to rehabilitate Europe, showing that his attention was focused on the postwar picture and the part that economic well-being would play in reinvigorating the region's peoples and politics. In October 1945, at a moment when many others wanted to retreat and American opinion overwhelmingly favored releasing men from the armed services, he advocated universal military training.[36] The president stressed that only strength would deter future aggressors from threatening peace or liberty and that the United States must quickly rebuild its strength before further postwar erosion. In this sense, Truman understood that victory in World War II would not end grave, global threats, as many had anticipated after World War I.

In the Shadow of FDR

It is commonplace to observe that Truman walked in the shadow cast by Franklin Delano Roosevelt.[37] Shortly after becoming president, Truman himself wrote toward the end of a letter to Eleanor Roosevelt that "I never think of anyone as the President but Mr. Roosevelt."[38] In October 1946, Truman drafted a speech (that was never delivered) about various post-war conversion issues, in which he reprimanded his opponents for having "forgotten the ideals for which we fought under Franklin Roosevelt" and having vision dimmed "by greed, by selfishness, by a thirst for power."[39] Truman had known FDR personally in a way he had not Wilson, and the relationship contributed to his perception of Roosevelt's character and ideas. Yet he was never overwhelmed (personally or politically) by Roosevelt's aura and charm. In reference to the Truman Committee in 1941, Senator Truman wrote Bess that he would tell FDR "to go to hell" if the president failed to meet with him, and added, "He's so damn afraid that he won't have all the power and glory that he won't let his friends help as it should be done."[40] Nor was vice presidential candidate Truman impressed by Roosevelt's flattery in 1944 on one of their rare meetings.[41] And criticizing FDR in 1946 on grounds that would be echoed by some scholars in later years, he told Bess: "It seems the late President had a positive genius for picking inefficient administrators. His Court appointments are somewhat disgraceful too. I've about come to the conclusion that he wanted to do everything himself and get all the acclaim for successful accomplishment and then have a dumb cluck to take the blame for what failed."[42]

Truman's praise and criticism of Roosevelt remained consistent after he left the presidency: he described FDR as a "great, great president" who brought the United States out of the Depression and was a "first-rate executive," but whose "principal defect" was "that growing ego of his" and who "wasn't a good administrator because he just wasn't able to delegate authority to anybody else."[43] In Truman's opinion, Roosevelt "wanted to be in a position where he could say yes or no to everything without anyone's ever arguing with him or questioning him, and of course you can't do that in our system of checks and balances." Every president ought to have restraints, wrote Truman, and "I sometimes argued with [FDR] myself when he wanted to go too far or when he set out to do something strictly on his own and without the argument or help of others."[44] Truman benefited from and partially used Wilson's institutional expansion of the presidency, at the same time that he explicitly rejected what he saw as Roosevelt's unwarranted personal expansion of presidential powers.

The question remains, though, as to whether Truman followed FDR's version of liberal internationalism, which borrowed from and amended

Wilson's progressive internationalism. Roosevelt believed that an association of the great powers would be necessary after World War II to prevent future world wars and was willing to include as many nations as possible to obtain the core arrangement. As a result, Roosevelt planned to reconstruct the global balance of power while describing it in Wilsonian language as a community of power and nations; and he aimed to achieve this end by embracing and compromising with potentially troublesome great powers—such as the Soviet Union—in order to make them part of the postwar order, restraining them only as a last resort. In September 1944, FDR wrote to Churchill that the USSR would have to be a "fully accepted and equal member" of any international organization intended to prevent world war, and that "[i]t should be possible to accomplish this by adjusting our differences through compromise by all the parties concerned and this ought to tide things over for a few years until the child learns how to toddle."[45] Like Wilson, Roosevelt thought that the basis of procedures and collective security would be personal diplomacy and control, especially by the United States and with him as president (although he perhaps exceeded Wilson in the trust he placed in personal diplomacy).

Wilson and Roosevelt were both more intellectual and elitist than Truman. But FDR was more pragmatic and practical, and less philosophical, than Wilson—prompting some to call Roosevelt an instrumental Wilsonian. This assessment is helpful: FDR was not empty of idealism, but in him realism came to the forefront; and he wanted to be perceived as Wilson's heir in a theoretical sense, but succeed where Wilson had failed in the creation of a postwar world order.[46] In Roosevelt's view, progressive internationalism, the engine of Wilsonian universalism, had resonated with the American people before the Great Depression, and he aimed to resurrect its rhetoric and ideals in order to depress what he saw as isolationist tendencies in the 1930s and 1940s. FDR's commitment to the United Nations stemmed less from a confidence in Wilsonian collective security and more from a belief that an international organization was needed to reflect the reality of global interdependence in the twentieth century.[47] For the postwar era, he thought that the United Nations would serve four additional ends: regulating the control of geographic spheres around the world by the great powers; drawing the Soviet Union into extended cooperation with the West; involving the United States permanently in world politics; and satisfying American idealism by cloaking the realpolitik that would actually characterize international relations.[48]

It is difficult to discern Roosevelt's final thoughts about the shape of the postwar order, let alone the Cold War, because he did not make public pronouncements or inform his vice president and top advisors of his intentions in his dying days. But in the years leading up to his well-known, brief, last message of April 11, 1945, to British Prime Minister Winston Churchill, we can see the outline and substance of Roosevelt's framework for an enduring postwar peace. "In the future days, which we seek to make secure," FDR said in January 1941, "we look forward to a world founded upon four essential human freedoms." And so began his articulation of what came to be called the Four Freedoms: freedom of speech and expression; freedom of worship; freedom from want; and freedom from fear, which later he also referred to as freedom from terror. If the first two freedoms were not ambitious enough to achieve "everywhere in the world," the third freedom promised "economic understandings which will secure to every nation a healthy peacetime life for its inhabitants—everywhere in the world," and the fourth freedom meant "a world-wide reduction of armaments to such a point and in such a thorough fashion that no nation will be in a position to commit an act of physical aggression against any neighbor—anywhere in the world." Roosevelt believed that the Four Freedoms were "no vision of a distant millennium" but "a definite basis for a kind of world attainable in our time and generation."[49] Before the United States had even entered World War II, FDR committed the United States to a new world order that, in certain respects, had first been limned by Wilson.

Also before the United States entered the Second World War, Roosevelt and Churchill jointly issued the Atlantic Charter in August 1941, "to make known certain common principles in the national policies of their respective countries on which they base their hopes for a better future for the world." Some of the principles were straightforward, such as the United States and Great Britain stating that they sought no territorial or other aggrandizement, promoting self-government and freely made choices about territory and government by the concerned peoples, and furthering equal access to trade and raw materials for all states after the war. Other points seemed to bear FDR's imprint more than Churchill's and to be perhaps intentionally beholden to Woodrow Wilson. The charter's fifth point called for improved labor standards and economic advancement, as had Wilson's Fourteen Points and the Covenant of the League of Nations, to which was added the New Deal promise of "social security." Although the first of the

Four Freedoms was partially absent and the second completely missing from the Atlantic Charter, the charter's sixth point specifically described a postwar peace guaranteeing "that all the men in all the lands may live out their lives in freedom from fear and want." The Atlantic Charter's seventh point, like Wilson's Fourteen Points, stated that the postwar peace "should enable all men to traverse the high seas and oceans without hindrance." The eighth and final principle of the Atlantic Charter started with Wilson but went beyond the Fourteen Points and the Covenant of the League of Nations, holding "that all nations of the world, for realistic as well as spiritual reasons must come to the abandonment of the use of force."[50]

But Roosevelt was both Wilsonian and realist. Acknowledging in late 1943 the possibility that the use of force would be necessary to preserve world peace after World War II, he said that "international force" should then be applied. To make effective the use of international force, FDR set forth his concept of what came to be known as the Four Policemen. After the Teheran and Cairo conferences, he reported to the American people that he "got along fine" with Stalin, whom he saw as "truly representative of the heart and soul of Russia," and that he believed "we are going to get along very well with him and the Russian people." Then Roosevelt promoted the role of the great powers by stressing that Great Britain, Russia, China, and the United States and their allies represented more than three-quarters of the global population. If these "four Nations with great military power stick together in determination to keep the peace," he said, "there will be no possibility of an aggressor Nation arising to start another world war." Although he mentioned the freedom-loving peoples of Europe, Asia, Africa, and the Americas, as well as the need to guard the rights of all nations, his accent was on the primacy of the great powers in international relations.[51] While advancing what amounted rhetorically to a Wilsonian edifice for the United Nations, FDR built in a realist foundation of power politics and spheres of influence.

After his final wartime conference at Yalta in 1945, Roosevelt once more spoke about his plans and hopes for the postwar world. Contrasting the founding of the United Nations to that of the League of Nations, he said that this time the "machinery of peace" was being set up during the war and that the April 1945 UN conference in San Francisco would result in a "definite charter of organization under which the peace of the world will be preserved and the forces of aggression permanently outlawed." But while the "structure of world peace" would rest on the cooperative effort of the whole world, the settlement in liberated Nazi territory would be the province of Russia, Great Britain, and the United States; Roosevelt thought the Yalta agreements would bring a "more stable political Europe than ever before." He asserted the advantages of "planning," as opposed to the "tragic mistakes" that had been made before and during the Great Depression "by reason of lack of planning," and predicted that the domestic improvements accomplished by such planning would now be "true in relations between Nations."[52] What Wilson had failed to achieve in world affairs, FDR claimed could now be done through better planning and a combination of great power cooperation and Wilsonian ideals.

In the closing passages of his congressional address concerning Yalta, Roosevelt used Wilsonian language to depict the "permanent structure of peace upon which we can begin to build, under God, that better world in which our children and grandchildren—yours and mine, the children and grandchildren of the whole world—must live, and can live." FDR stated that the Crimea Conference "ought to spell the end of the system of unilateral action, the exclusive alliances, the spheres of influence, the balances of power, and all the other expedients that have been tried for centuries—and have always failed." In their place, he proposed "a universal organization in which all peace-loving Nations will finally have a chance to join."[53] Wilson had made much the same plea after World War I, and Roosevelt updated his ideas for the post–World War II era. But in blending realism and Wilsonianism, FDR altered the latter; he believed that this mixture would pacify the Soviet Union through deals of power politics (in his personal diplomacy he used expedients such as spheres of influence and the balance of power) and satisfy Americans and other freedom-loving peoples with Wilsonian goals of peace and justice. From the vantage of 1919, Wilson did not realize what radical ideology would do in the twentieth century and thought that global politics after World War I would make war obsolete and all men into pluralist peacemakers; in 1945, after experience with Nazi tyranny and in light of Soviet actions since 1939, Roosevelt believed that his politics of planning along with compromise (first) and containment (last) would prevent war and allow for reasonable accommodation. Both presidents presumed moderation on the part of their adversaries, which proved to be a costly error and one that Truman would avoid.

Truman strongly endorsed a theme of one of FDR's most famous fireside chats during World War II: "The present great struggle has taught us increasingly that freedom of person and security of property anywhere in the world depend upon the security of the rights and obligations of liberty and justice everywhere in the world."[54] To Truman, Roosevelt's words were evidence of the primacy of freedom and the necessity of protecting freedom wherever possible; in addition, they showed the connection between political and economic freedom. Truman also applauded FDR's promises in spring 1945 to press Stalin on honoring the Yalta Conference agreements with respect to Poland. But within two weeks of becoming president, he departed from what Roosevelt on his deathbed conveyed to Churchill, "I would minimize the general Soviet problem as much as possible because these problems, in one form or another, seem to arise every day and most of them straighten out as in the case of the Bern meeting." Instead, Truman expanded FDR's final line of the message: "We must be firm, however, and our course thus far is correct." Roosevelt apparently meant that firmness to be limited to the position that Churchill and he had taken with Stalin on Poland, but Truman would use firmness as part of the foundation of his Cold War strategy of containment.[55]

There was a small part of Harry Truman in 1945 that was convinced he should carry on with FDR's policies since he was serving out his predecessor's term. There was another, larger part of Truman that was convinced that he should maintain and extend the New Deal because he believed in its substance and goals. In foreign policy, Truman continued Roosevelt's wartime policies—from tactical decisions on troop dispositions to maintaining the Grand Alliance in order to defeat the Nazis and the Japanese—but he had little idea what FDR had intended for American foreign policy beyond the United Nations. Some FDR advisors, like Harry Hopkins, stressed to Truman that Roosevelt had meant to carry over a friendly relationship with the USSR into the postwar era. But even if Truman briefly toyed with such an idea, he quickly formed his own opinion of the Soviet Union, its intentions, and its actions, and he rejected what FDR insiders told him Roosevelt had wanted.

Truman Sets His Own Course

In neither his private nor public positions did Truman replicate FDR's policies in his early months in office. Through his personal diplomacy, Roosevelt had expected postwar liberal internationalism—and, by extension, world peace—to be characterized by spheres of influence and a balance of power maintained by the Four Policemen: the United States, Great Britain, the Soviet Union, and China. In FDR's mind, the USSR would feel secure in such an arrangement and act like a traditional great power. From the beginning, Truman rejected this interpretation of world politics and the Soviet Union. Records of Soviet foreign minister Vyacheslav Molotov's visit in April 1945 reveal a president already committed to a policy of firmness with respect to the Kremlin. Long before the expression "patience and firmness" was associated with future secretary of state James Byrnes, U.S. Ambassador to the Soviet Union Averell Harriman recommended "standing firm" on issues of importance to the United States. Truman's own resolve to be firm with the USSR emerged as the theme of an April 20 conversation among the president, Secretary of State Edward Stettinius, and Harriman. As State Department official Charles Bohlen recorded in the official notes of the conversation, "The President again repeated that he intended to be firm with the Russians and make no concessions from American principles or traditions for the fact of winning their favor." Truman underscored that he would tell Molotov "in words of one syllable" that the Polish question must be settled in order to fulfill the Yalta agreements.[56]

In conversations with Molotov, Truman made clear that the Soviets must uphold their wartime agreements. In particular, he stated that "the Polish question had become for our people the symbol of the future development of our international relations." Told of Molotov's repeated attempts to gain the advantage by applying the Yugoslavian "model" to Poland, thus essentially acquiring another sphere of influence, Truman said that the agreements with the USSR so far had been a "one way street" and that if the Soviets did not want to commit properly to the United Nations "they could go to hell." Face to face with Molotov, the president spoke sharply of his displeasure with the Soviet failure to honor its agreements.[57]

The president's private writings at the time reveal a man who was growing in his new position. Although not a daily diarist, Truman frequently wrote longhand notes in order to clarify his thoughts—and, sometimes, to blow off steam. In spring and summer 1945, he went back and forth in his notes about Europe's future and America's relations with its wartime allies. At times, the president's views on communism were a reaction to his good or bad opinion of the person who was speaking to him. As a result, scholars debate if and when in 1945 and 1946 Truman believed the Soviets were truly a threat. But what emerges is that although he did not want to alienate the USSR in negotiations, the president was worried about the

Kremlin and its movements. By avoiding what he termed the appearance that the United States and Great Britain were "ganging up" on the Soviet Union, he hoped that Stalin would be less belligerent. Nevertheless, a substantive, overriding theme developed in the president's longhand notes: clarity about the nature and goals of the regime that Stalin controlled, and the fact that communism and democracy were in fundamental opposition. "I've no faith in any Totalitarian State be it Russian, German, Spanish, Argentinian, Dago, or Japanese," he wrote, adding that these states "all start with a wrong premise—that lies are justified and that the old disproven Jesuit formula—the end justifies the means is right and necessary to maintain the power of government."[58]

Truman's public declarations reflected in more polished tones what he said privately and further separated him from Roosevelt's policies. They marked the beginning of his efforts as president to educate the American people about the realities of the postwar world. Often overlooked in this sense is Truman's first major foreign policy statement, his September 1945 radio speech on the surrender of Japan. He told the American people that the victory in World War II was of more than arms alone; it was a triumph of liberty over tyranny—the main theme of Truman's end-of-the-war assessment. "It was the spirit of liberty which gave us our armed strength and which made our men invincible in battle," he said. "We now know that that spirit of liberty, the freedom of the individual, and the personal dignity of man, are the strongest and toughest and most enduring forces in all the world." The president also maintained that the same liberty that had sustained the nation in battle would provide the bedrock for peacetime and, through democratic constitutionalism, meet the challenges of everyday living: "Liberty does not make all men perfect nor all society secure. But it has provided more solid progress and happiness and decency for more people than any other philosophy of government in history. And this day has shown again that it provides the greatest strength and the greatest power which man has ever reached."[59]

More significant was Truman's Navy Day speech of October 1945, which is often seen as an affirmation of FDR's policy by a new and insecure president who chose to maintain the status quo. In the context of the September statement, however, the Navy Day remarks embodied his intention to sustain American internationalism. Since Truman made few statements about world affairs in 1945, both the September radio message and the October Navy Day address provide insights into the president's thinking prior to 1946 and 1947, and how he came to believe that American foreign policy had to oppose world communism.

Although the Navy Day address retained some fidelity to President Roosevelt, it tellingly revealed the beginnings of Truman's distinctive strategy of containment. In setting forth twelve points of foreign policy, the president was, at times, rhetorically faithful to Woodrow Wilson, as well as FDR. But he brought to liberal internationalism the convictions of his religious faith, stating that, although the Ten Commandments had not been embraced universally, "we struggle constantly to achieve them, and in many ways we come closer to them each year." In a theme that permeated his private writings and public statements, he aimed no less than to convince others that the golden rule should direct international affairs. The United States must operate in an imperfect world, but Truman would not give "approval to any compromise with evil."[60]

Truman had been considering some of the particulars that he wanted to include in the Navy Day address since Potsdam, four months earlier.[61] Although the president named the Soviet Union among America's allies, he emphasized that the victorious powers must adhere with "forbearance and firmness" to the "high principles which we have enunciated" and show "a willingness to find a common ground as to the methods of applying those principles." Negotiations, according to Truman, should not violate principles but reflect policies that were appropriate for each set of circumstances. In extension of his support of universal military training, he repeated that the nation's armed forces must be fortified even in a world of atomic weaponry. Truman expressed the aim of this postwar foreign policy succinctly: "We seek to use our military strength solely to preserve the peace of the world. For we now know that this is the only sure way to make our own freedom secure. That is the basis of the foreign policy of the United States." The defense of freedom emerged as the imperative of American policy.[62]

Churchill, in particular, saw the Navy Day speech as a renewed dedication to American internationalism. In a November 7 speech to the House of Commons that anticipated several important themes of the Fulton address of March 1946, Churchill described Truman's speech as a "momentous declaration to the world"; it was "the dominant factor in the present world situation" and of "transcendant importance." He summarized the president's points as maintenance of U.S. military strength, an American determination to join with like-minded nations in opposing aggression, a pledge that tyrannies would not receive recognition from the United States, and an assurance that the United States must abandon "oldfashioned isolation" and join with other well-disposed nations to carry out these high purposes.[63]

Similar to Truman, Churchill praised the Soviet contribution in World War II, hoped the USSR would be part of the postwar peace, and expressed the gravity of atomic developments for international affairs. Churchill's remarks contained a strong dose of his inimitable hyperbole, but the main message was clear: endorsement of and encouragement for a relatively new president making an independent statement in a new postwar world.[64]

Truman Defines the Strength of Containment

Any residue of the Grand Alliance had evaporated by December 1945 at the Foreign Ministers' Conference in Moscow. Unlike Henry Wallace (FDR's vice president from 1941 through 1944), who was still urging Big Three unity, Truman was aware of the deterioration in relations and adjusted his expectations. He directed James Byrnes, his new secretary of state, to do his best in negotiations at the Council of Foreign Ministers meetings to thwart Soviet ambitions while sustaining peace. Like Truman, Byrnes did not place much trust in State Department subordinates. But Byrnes did not put much stock in the president, either, and soon developed the habit of reporting late or failing to report at all to Truman. In large part, the secretary of state believed he should have been president, having thought he had been promised the vice presidency in 1944 by Roosevelt; at the least, he assumed that he should be the architect of American foreign policy.[65]

But ego and stubbornness aside, the disagreement between Truman and Byrnes was most profound with respect to their views of America's role in the world and the Cold War. Byrnes aimed to continue a form of liberal internationalism that Truman had moved away from since becoming president. Truman believed in the goal of liberal internationalism, but he did not agree with the established approaches of Wilson and FDR. In what late 1930s U.S. ambassador to the Soviet Union Joseph Davies once referred to as Byrnes's "practical idealism," the secretary of state joined the Roosevelt policy of maintaining the status quo of the great powers through negotiations to Wilson's view of international organization. Byrnes praised

Roosevelt for concluding that there was no easy formula for dealing with the Soviets, implying that Truman's approach of strength was simplistic. He thought that Russian history was a better explanation of Kremlin actions than ideology.[66] In a combination of Wilsonianism and realist diplomacy, he was inclined to call for negotiations in the face of hostile Kremlin actions. Yet, like Truman, Byrnes hailed the UN Charter and its potential for enlarging the sphere of world peace and diminishing the chance of war. Meanwhile, however, and apart from the United Nations, the president was developing a view about the concrete, unilateral need for American strength for its own comprehensive and, in the context of Communist gains, its allies' defense.

Regardless of Soviet aggression, the American longing for peace had not waned. In his State of the Union address of 1946, Truman recognized this paradox and placed civilization's future in the United Nations. His desire for a "just and enduring peace" through the international organization and his reiteration of the twelve points of foreign policy from the October 1945 Navy Day speech once more suggested fidelity to much of interwar foreign relations and to Roosevelt's Four Freedoms. Philosophically, he agreed with FDR that primary freedoms stood as protection from concrete and perceived fears rather than as self-standing rights with inherent responsibilities. He never abandoned the belief that the wartime conferences had been the best political option and were rightly negotiated by the Americans.[67] Still, only months after the Second World War had ended, he hoped that the United Nations would develop the muscle to sustain peace. Truman frequently likened the UN to the founding and development of the United States—he was wont to say that it took eighty years, until the end of the Civil War, for America to implement correctly its Constitution. In part, he used this analogy to ask for patience with respect to the United Nations. But ideally, he wanted the UN to promote a federation for the peoples of the world, which would lead to a lasting peace.

Although Truman sounded like and was similar in some ways to Roosevelt in this speech, he accented a primary American position and did not mention the Soviet Union as a member of the peace-loving world or of a great power consortium. With regard to the origins of containment in 1946, Truman pursued what in effect was a more substantive peace based on the principled use of ideas and power. In so doing, he transformed the liberal internationalism of the twentieth century that had been crafted by Wilson and Roosevelt. Truman expressed a continual concern about preventing another world war and rejected inaction, insisting that the United States must have a pivotal international role because of its character and strength. The president invoked the use of joint force when necessary to ensure the peace and praised nations that advanced freedom and justice.[68] Practically, he saw the UN as a forum in which the peoples of the world would communicate with each other and diminish the likelihood of war.

Although there was no mention of the Soviet Union in Truman's State of the Union address of January 1946, a forceful memo written by Truman to Byrnes earlier that month revealed the president's conception of the East-West conflict and some of his earliest thought on containment.[69] Truman expressed anger over Soviet actions before, during, and after Potsdam, as well as current Kremlin designs on the Baltic states, and urged all possible vigor against the "Russian program" in Iran, where "now Russia stirs up rebellion and keeps troops on the soil of her friend and ally, Iran." Connecting Soviet conduct in Iran to larger ambitions in the Middle East, the president had not "a doubt in my mind that Russia intends an invasion of Turkey and the seizure of the Black Sea Straits to the Mediterranean. Unless Russia is faced with an iron fist and strong language another war is in the making. Only one language do they understand— 'How many divisions have you?'" Based on his understanding of Kremlin actions, geography, and U.S. policy to date, Truman concluded: "I do not think we should play compromise any longer. We should refuse to recognize Rumania and Bulgaria until they comply with our requirements; we should let our position on Iran be known and we should continue to insist on the internationalization of the Kiel Canal, the Rhine-Danube waterway and the Black Sea Straits and we should maintain complete control of Japan and the Pacific. We should rehabilitate China and create a strong central government there. We should do the same for Korea. Then we should insist on the return of our ships from Russia and force a settlement of the Lend-Lease Debt of Russia. I'm tired babying the Soviets."[70]

The political thought of containment began with Truman's recognition— first intimated in April 1945, implied elsewhere during the rest of the year and in his 1946 State of the Union address, and explicitly written in the January 1946 memo—that the Soviets could not be indulged. Ultimately, he subordinated his wish for world peace to his resolve that the Soviet Union must not be allowed to define that peace. The result was a permanent tension between the president's wish to put peace first and his commitment to meet the Soviet threat head-on. Likewise, there was a tension between his desire to trust in the United Nations and his determination to embark on a U.S.-led coalition to defend the free world. Above all, though, Truman believed that freedom, independence, and peace must be defended and that the Communists presented the primary threat to these objects. This two-part conclusion provided the practical core of the strategy of containment.

The January memo was foundational for Truman. February 1946 was a critical month, one in which the president saw the lengths, including mistreatment of American citizens, to which the Soviet Union would go to assert itself. By this time, eighty-four claimants to U.S. citizenship in Poland had been imprisoned, almost all of them for the alleged crime of being members of the underground army that fought the Nazis.[71] In addition, Truman knew about the insults to U.S. officials in Yugoslavia and Bulgaria by the Soviet-dominated governments of those countries, as well as news that American correspondents had been held incommunicado by Soviet military officials in the Manchurian city of Mukden. Faced with a State Department apparatus that largely favored accommodation and compromise with the Soviets, Truman was increasingly displeased with his secretary of state's quid pro quo approach, which he perceived—despite his long association with Byrnes— as more evidence of what he termed "shenanigans" from the diplomats in striped pants. Admiral William Leahy recorded that the president sharply disapproved "the recent attitude of appeasement toward the Soviet and said he is convinced of the necessity of our taking a strong attitude without delay." The next day, Truman told Averell Harriman that the United States had to adopt a "strong diplomatic opposition to the Soviet program of expansion."[72] This opinion did not stem from petulance with the State Department, however, but his growing discernment (before the arrival of George Kennan's Long Telegram in Washington) of the dangers of the Cold War.[73]

The Soviet Union, meanwhile, continued to solidify its hold on countries that it had occupied during World War II. Much of what was called free Europe remained devastated and beset by starvation and disrepair, which increased its vulnerability to Communist penetration. Stalin's election address of February 9, 1946, was seen as another blow and part of a broader anti-Western campaign. To justify Kremlin actions in the Second World War, Stalin contended that the conflict "arose in reality as the inevitable result of the development of the world economic and political forces on the basis of monopoly capitalism." Indeed, he attributed all war in the current stage of world development to the split of the capitalist world into two hostile camps. Capitalism failed to avert war, said Stalin, because it was against the redistribution of wealth. Presenting the next three five-year plans for the USSR, he ordered the Soviet military establishment to be ready to "deal with any eventuality," particularly from capitalism, its primary enemy. One week after Stalin's speech, news of Soviet atomic espionage became public for the first time. The situation in Iran and elsewhere in the Middle East continued to worsen during February and early March. And, over and beyond further entrenchment in Europe and the Middle East, the USSR was meddling in Manchuria, helping the Chinese Communists undercut General George Marshall's first mission to China, which had begun in December 1945.[74]

State Department official Charles Bohlen, who later would stand theoretically between future Policy Planning Staff (PPS) directors George Kennan and Paul Nitze, supported Truman's understanding of the Soviet threat in 1946. For the Communists, he explained, the existence of capitalism assured the continuing threat of world war. Bohlen treated Stalin's address as the capstone of Cold War origins, which were embedded in the wartime conferences. The speech showed that the Soviets still believed in the infallibility and correctness of Marxism-Leninism and had only muted their views during World War II.[75] Attached to the U.S. Strategic Bombing Survey at the time, Nitze concluded that Stalin's message could be interpreted as a delayed declaration of war against the United States, implying that such a war started before the declaration. He noted that Secretary of the Navy James Forrestal was concerned that no one else in Washington held the same opinion.[76] These observations—which analyzed Soviet ideology, statements, and actions as elements of a whole—echoed the president's point of view. Nitze's account also indicates the resistance that Truman encountered from many of his subordinates. More than Truman himself, Nitze and Bohlen at this point saw that the Kremlin had been engaged in the Cold War prior to the end of the Second World War, although they did not criticize America for failing to identify and respond to Soviet aggression after the battle of Stalingrad.

A Long Telegram

Stalin's election address and subsequent disdain of the World Bank and the International Monetary Fund prompted the State Department to ask

George F. Kennan, acting as the charge d'affaires in Moscow, for an evaluation of Soviet ideology and intentions, resulting in what later was famously called the Long Telegram.[77] While the Long Telegram of February 1946 crystallized the need for a coherent foreign policy with respect to the USSR, it did not—ten months into the Truman presidency—originate the political thought of containment. Kennan left unaddressed, for example, Soviet capabilities, one of containment's central concerns. Forrestal, notably, was already aware of many of the issues that were outlined by Kennan and had requested a report gauging Communist philosophy and goals in late 1945. After reading the resulting report by Professor Edward F. Willett in early January 1946, Forrestal concluded that American power was needed to respond to dialectical materialism. He agreed with Nitze that Stalin's election address was a belated declaration of war against liberal democracy, and he recorded that even Supreme Court Justice William O. Douglas had interpreted Stalin's statement as "The Declaration of World War III."[78] Kennan's conclusions, by contrast, emphasized sustaining America's "methods and conceptions" rather than its political vitality.[79] Since Forrestal had begun to circulate the Willett report inside and outside the government, Kennan's cable, in light of this report, received exceptional notice.[80] As Kennan later ruefully pointed out, the Long Telegram arrived in Washington at just the right time to galvanize action.[81]

Kennan's description of the features of the postwar Kremlin outlook was an incisive presentation of Soviet doctrine and bolstered some of the conclusions that Truman and his most trusted advisors were already making. Dean Acheson, undersecretary of state in 1946, recalled that Kennan's recommendations "were of no help" and "his historical analysis might or might not have been sound, but his predictions and warnings could not have been better."[82] Kennan elucidated the idea of capitalist encirclement expressed by Stalin earlier in the month. And he wrote of Soviet efforts to enhance their strength while reducing that of the capitalist powers, to exploit conflicts between capitalist powers, and to battle against socialism and social democracy. Although he considered these efforts to be projections only of insecurity and fear, he granted that they could damage the West. Later in the telegram, Kennan gave a keen evaluation of the policies that the Soviet Union might pursue on official and unofficial levels. He drew further attention to the strategic significance of Iran and Turkey, possible Soviet manipulation of the UN, and Kremlin aspirations in the developing world. His account of underground tactics through

Communist parties and national associations in all countries revealed that infiltration by other than military might was probable. As evidenced by Truman's ensuing words and actions, Kennan's analysis of these two levels of operations and of the Communist stance contributed significantly to the political thought of containment.

But Kennan depicted Soviet doctrine, intentions, and policy as springing from a background of traditional and instinctive Russian insecurity. He ascribed a neurotic view of world affairs to the Kremlin, arguing that Moscow stressed its dogma to avoid being seen as the latest in a long succession of cruel Russian rulers. "This is why Soviet purposes must always be solemnly clothed in trappings of Marxism," wrote Kennan, "and why no one should underrate importance of dogma in Soviet affairs."[83] Yet after alluding to the weight of doctrine in Soviet affairs, he sought to downplay its effects and never accepted it as driving Kremlin foreign policy. Kennan separated a traditional expansionistic nationalism from Communist ideology in the case of the Soviet Union and contended that the USSR acted only under the guise of Marxism. As a result, he spoke of Russia and the Soviet Union in interchangeable terms, blurring any substantive distinction between them. In following this line, he espoused a view that was the opposite of that which increasingly motivated Truman.

While he incorporated Russian history into his analysis, Truman emphasized that Communist ideology motivated Soviet aggression. Russian history was part of the Soviet reality, but the Bolshevik Revolution, by incorporating Marxist-Leninist ideology into the regime, had wrought a new national identity. In this particular, Forrestal was in agreement with Truman. Recording a conversation with Churchill shortly after the Fulton address, Forrestal said that the former prime minister "agreed with my analysis that we are dealing not only with Russia as a national entity but with the expanding power of Russia under Peter the Great plus the additional missionary force of a religion."[84] Likewise, Truman, backed by Forrestal, looked upon communism as a secular, millennial religion that informed the Kremlin worldview and caused the Soviet Union to threaten liberty and world peace.[85]

Where President Truman spoke of ungrounded Soviet suspicions that must be met with strength, Kennan laid the groundwork for interpreting Kremlin actions as based on insecurities that ought to be assuaged. The Soviet Union, he believed, could be moderated without substantive change in its form of government. Kennan implied that the Soviets possessed a reactive, although aggressive, policy that could best be cured by diplomacy. In effect, he acceded to the Marxist-Leninist and, eventually, revisionist contention that the capitalist states were encircling the USSR for imperial purposes.

Although Kennan's summary of Soviet theoretical designs was mostly accurate, his conclusion did not approach Truman's comprehensive view of their political importance. Kennan noted in the Long Telegram that "we have here a political force committed fanatically to the belief that with US there can be no permanent *modus vivendi*, that it is desirable and necessary that the internal harmony of our society be disrupted, our traditional way of life be destroyed, the international authority of our state be broken."[86] Elsewhere in the telegram, Kennan attributed Soviet intentions to an existential quality he saw pervading life in general. As a result, he believed that intervention of any type in what he designated as Moscow's sphere was futile and should be avoided.[87] While he favored educating and enhancing American society, Kennan hinted that the United States could live off its existing military capacity. Restricting his comments to Stalin's rule, he did not consider how the ideological nature of the Communist state might drive the USSR to seek worldwide dominance. In contrast to Truman, he did not see that the Soviet Union could be imperial and Communist at the same time. As a keen observer of the Soviet scene, Kennan would coin the term containment in 1947, but the debt that many in the academy believe Truman owed to Kennan existed at the practical, not the principled, level. When it came to the political thought of containment, George Kennan was not its sole, and by no means its fundamental, architect.

2

"The two giant marauders, war and tyranny"

Framing Containment

Harry Truman had much to learn about foreign policy when he became president of the United States, and he spent the second part of
1945 and early 1946 thinking about the new conditions of world politics.
In 1946, with no appropriate institutional structure and some difficulties with top advisors—in particular, Secretary of State James Byrnes and
Secretary of Commerce Henry Wallace—Truman articulated the meaning
of the Cold War and America's role in the conflict. This was remarkably
challenging, since Byrnes represented an opposing fusion of Wilson's progressive internationalism and FDR's liberal internationalism, which appealed to much of the country and Congress at the time, while Wallace
voiced a progressive critique that married aspects of Wilsonianism with
the claim that convergence with communism was positive and inevitable.
Battered in 1945 and 1946 by intraparty warfare and domestic problems,
especially in labor disputes as the U.S. economy was making the tran-
sition to peacetime, the president suggested that another struggle was
upon the country. Winston Churchill, the indefatigable British wartime
leader, most famously helped Truman explain the significance of the
war of nerves, on terms consonant with the president's remaking of liberal internationalism. Once the stage had been readied for the implementation of containment, and after having made the case for strength
and internationalism as the way to freedom and peace, Truman began
to take action, standing firm where challenged—in Venezia Guilia and
Trieste, Iran, the Turkish Straits, waterway rights to the Danube, and
Germany—pursuing universal military training, and ordering the reor-

ganization of the military. Before Byrnes spoke of the need for "patience and firmness," well before George Kennan's Long Telegram arrived in Washington, and months before the Clifford memorandum offered in-depth analysis and policy advice, Truman was already in the process of formulating and establishing perhaps the most important foreign policy of the country's history.

The Sinews of Peace

If the words of a statesman are less significant when he is out of office, the exception to this rule is Winston Churchill's speech of March 1946. The historical context for the speech indicates its importance. Against the backdrop of crises in Iran, Manchuria, and Europe, Churchill came to speak at Westminster College in Truman's home state of Missouri. "Hope you can do it. I'll introduce you," Truman handwrote on the October 1945 invitation.[1] Even though he had lost the office of prime minister, the eminent British statesman was greeted by the eight-thousand-person population of Fulton, Missouri, and another twenty thousand people who came from all over the state to see and hear him. In his introduction, Truman described Churchill as one of the outstanding men of all time and said, "I know he will have something constructive to say."[2] Although many overlooked the central message of his speech—entitled "The Sinews of Peace"—Churchill's words were immediate news.[3]

At Fulton, Churchill spoke of the developing global reach of the Cold War into Asia, as well as Europe, and the menace to Western civilization posed by the Soviet Union. Like Truman, he thought that the United States stood at the pinnacle of power and must fulfill its responsibility to lead and defend the West. And like Truman, he called for a component of military strength in the United Nations, alluding to the UN as a potential "Temple of Peace" that must be built on rock rather than on shifting sands. He also emphasized that the international organization did not preclude other special relationships from striving for freedom and peace. As explicitly as Truman, but more grippingly, he raised the call to defend freedom and the rights of individuals. Churchill designated war and tyranny as the twin dangers threatening these principles. The Allies had won the Second World War and defeated fascism and Japanese militarism, but now the Soviets were the totalitarian tyrants of the world. While others avoided publicly calling the Soviet Union a tyranny, Churchill specified the regime, its aims, and its actions as the fundamental impediment to building as well as sustaining the sinews of peace.

The Soviets, Churchill argued, desired the fruits of war and the indefinite expansion of their power and doctrine, without recourse necessarily to war. Before it was too late, the only counter to that assault was the "permanent prevention of war and the establishment of conditions of freedom and democracy as rapidly as possible in all countries." This conclusion—the establishment of the conditions of freedom and democracy—could be supported only by political and military strength. Churchill also reasoned that the United States, because of its principles and its position as the political and industrial leader of the New World, was obliged to fight this new tyranny. He hoped that Great Britain's "moral and material forces and convictions" would be joined to similar American beliefs in a "fraternal association" of the English-speaking peoples, in order to secure the victory of freedom and peace over tyranny and anarchy.[4]

Although often seen as a preeminent representative of the Old World and a practitioner of power politics, Churchill observed that previous policies of equilibrium could not counter the Communist threat, which neither recognized nor practiced moderation. In a passage that is rarely quoted today, he rejected a balance of power policy: "From what I have seen of our Russian friends and allies during the war, I am convinced that there is nothing they admire so much as strength, and there is nothing for which they have less respect than for weakness, especially military weakness. For that reason the old doctrine of a balance of power is unsound. We cannot afford, if we can help it, to work on narrow margins, offering temptations to a trial of strength."[5] Churchill conveyed that the Cold War, while a continuation of the permanent struggle between liberty and tyranny, manifested new political dimensions. Prior to Truman's strategy of containment, he focused on the combined threat of ideology and imperialism that attempted to reshape human nature and humanity in its image and warned that, if this threat prevailed, there could be no real peace because freedom would be abolished. George Kennan has been called a postwar Paul Revere; in terms of rhetoric, politics, and message, Churchill better deserves the appellation.[6]

Churchill had labored over the address and arrived early in Florida in January 1946 to use his time in America before Fulton to edit and polish the speech.[7] Even though American union strikes kept Truman from meeting with Churchill in Florida as planned, Churchill came to see the president in Washington on February 10. While no transcript exists of the conversation between Truman and Churchill, Admiral William Leahy provided an account of their hour-and-a-half meeting at the White House, "principally in regard to an address that Churchill will make on 6 [*sic*] March at Westminster College in Missouri."[8] The rest of Leahy's account disclosed that Churchill explained to Truman that he would counsel full military collaboration between Great Britain and the United States, in order to preserve peace in the world until the United Nations had the capacity to do so sometime in the "distant future."

Prior to that meeting in Washington, when they still thought they would be meeting on the presidential yacht off the coast of Florida, Truman had received from Churchill a letter expressing why the Fulton address was needed: "I have a Message to deliver to your country and to the world and I think it very likely that we shall be in full agreement about it. Under your auspices anything I say will command some attention and there is an opportunity for doing some good to this bewildered, baffled and breathless world."[9] Truman took his sponsorship seriously, having written Westminster College's president in December 1945 that "[t]his invitation was endorsed by the President of the United States who will himself introduce Mr. Churchill to the members of the College."[10] While he did not read the outline or drafts of the speech in February, Truman was briefed by Byrnes after the secretary of state and Bernard Baruch went in the president's stead to visit Churchill in Florida. In addition, Churchill showed a final copy of the speech to Truman when they traveled together by train to Fulton. Churchill wrote to Prime Minister Clement Attlee and British Foreign Minister Ernest Bevin that Truman "told me he thought it was admirable and would do nothing but good, though it would make a stir."[11]

There is and will continue to be a gap in knowledge about Truman's immediate response to Churchill's Fulton speech. The president's long-hand notes do not record his first impression. The typical view argues that Truman embraced Churchill's words only after American public opinion hardened against the Soviets. Yet the president already believed much of what Churchill would say, even before he saw the speech. He was on a parallel, though at times slower, track to Churchill's in 1945. At the beginning of 1946, before any contact with Churchill about the Fulton message's content, Truman had intensified his criticisms of the Soviet Union, as evidenced by the January memo to Byrnes and his discussions with top advisors. Beyond Truman's letter to his daughter in which he distanced himself from the Fulton address for the time being, there is no evidence that the president disagreed with Churchill's analysis or proposals—other than reservations about a "fraternal association" with the British empire; if anything, there is confirmation of his support.[12] He wanted to keep the lines of communication open with Moscow, but so did Churchill. As Churchill wrote in his March 7 letter to Attlee and Bevin, he had concluded from extended contact and conversations on the train that Truman and the rest of the "Executive forces" did not intend to abide by Soviet "treaty breaches in Persia or encroachments in Manchuria and Korea, or pressure for the Russian expansion at the expense of Turkey or in the Mediterranean." Churchill offered his belief that the "prevailing opinion in the United States" would soon support a show of strength and power as "necessary to a good settlement with Russia."[13] By settlement, however, neither Churchill nor Truman meant acceptance of the iron curtain and approval of its extension.

Although some scholars maintain that Truman separated himself from Churchill's speech in a White House press conference on March 8, 1946, it must be noted what Truman said and what he did not say.[14] What Truman did say was to deny that he knew the content of the speech in advance: "I didn't know what would be in Mr. Churchill's speech. This is a country of free speech. Mr. Churchill had a perfect right to say what he pleased." This was untrue, of course, since the president had read the text. Truman added that he was on the stage in Fulton as Churchill's host in Missouri. When asked to speak directly on the content of the speech, however, Truman said that he had no comment. He also was asked if he disavowed an Anglo-American alliance. Rather than repudiating such a premise, Truman answered, "No. I just have no comment." He remarked that Churchill was a guest in America and repeated that he had a "perfect right" to make such an address.[15] In the end, Truman said little, and none of it was a rejection of Churchill's words. The president's responses were neutral, which, under the circumstances, can be seen as a prudent course.

While on the return trip to Washington by train and air, Truman received the first reactions to the Fulton address. Churchill's words caused many to reconsider current Soviet actions and American responses. On March 6 and 7, American public opinion, including that of Congress, quietly accepted Churchill's analysis of the iron curtain but spurned the idea of a formal alliance between Great Britain and the United States. Although a small but vocal group of Democratic politicians—such as Senator Claude Pepper—attacked Churchill for destroying Big Three unity and imperiling the United Nations, most agreed with the Churchillian assessment of the Cold War.[16] The controversy of note in the domestic press and in Congress was not the general thesis but the idea of an Anglo-American alliance. Normally liberal, internationalist newspapers lambasted the concept: the *Chicago Daily News* editorialized that "all straight-thinking Americans" should reject Churchill's proposal "to safeguard and protect the British Empire"; the *Detroit News* contended that an Anglo-American alliance "would assure an armaments competition with the Russians far more likely to lead to war than to anything else"; and the *St. Louis Post-Dispatch* questioned whether Churchill's plan would not "aggravate the admittedly serious situation."[17] If Truman was waiting to see the reaction of the public, which had slowly been moving to a firm anti-Soviet position, before proceeding, then his hesitation was vindicated.

Another reason for Truman's reticence was that Churchill was no longer prime minister of Great Britain, and the president had an obligation to work with America's ally, England. Press evaluation in London was mixed. While praising the address with some reservations, the *Times* reprimanded Churchill for presenting "western democracy" and "communism" as irreconcilable opposites. Instead, the *Times* contended that each system had much to learn from the other. Referring to Moscow's "enigmatic actions," the *Daily Telegraph* deemed it premature to give Anglo-American ties "the precision which Mr. Churchill seems to desire." Since he was in the opposition, Churchill received immediate criticism and limited defense in the House of Commons. John McGovern, an Independent Labor Party member, accused Churchill of intending "to put Russia on the spot," while acting Conservative leader Anthony Eden maintained that Churchill had a sincere desire for good relations with the Soviet Union.[18] But formal reaction from Prime Minister Attlee did not come until March 11, when he told Parliament that "Her Majesty's Government had no previous knowledge of the speech" and that the British ambassador to the United States "was not called upon to approve or disapprove the speech beforehand."[19] The British government's response focused more on whether, how much, and when they knew the content of the Fulton address, rather than a clear commitment to or repudiation of its message. There was no firm answer one way or the other, and Truman did not press the British government's position.

A final reason for Truman's reserve stemmed from his domestic, partisan concerns. Most Americans still mourned the loss of Franklin Roosevelt; over time and with Churchill's help on foreign policy, the new president could deal with the death of an icon by establishing himself as an insightful and vigorous leader. But the party issue for Truman presented a more complicated and immediate challenge. As Byrnes recounted in the fall of 1945, Truman had to placate the liberal wing of the Democratic Party in order to keep the party united: "[T]here were two persons he had to have on his side, Wallace he said, first of all, because he was strong with organized labor; and second, Mrs. Roosevelt because of her influence with the negro voters."[20] In March 1946, Truman faced the fact that Senator Pepper, Secretary of Commerce Henry Wallace, and other Democrats spurned the Fulton address. Eleanor Roosevelt was worried about a detrimental effect on the United Nations. In addition to thinking that Churchill's approach would destroy the UN, Wallace emphasized that the United States should "serve as an intermediary between Britain and Russia and not as a defender of England."[21] Truman carefully and, ultimately, successfully crafted a position that neither alienated the liberal segment of his party nor rejected Churchill's Cold War analysis.

Arthur Krock of the *New York Times* referred to the Fulton address as a "trial balloon."[22] In a sense it was, although Truman had more in mind. The president was looking for help in articulating to America and the world both the meaning and the challenge of the Cold War. Because of his preeminent status, Churchill, and perhaps Churchill alone, was able to delineate the scope and meaning of the East-West conflict.[23] As a result, by mid-March, in a turnaround of public opinion, from a 30 percent disapproval rating in late 1945, 71 percent of the American public now disapproved of Soviet foreign policy and only 7 percent expressed approval; 60 percent thought that the United States was "too soft" on the Soviet Union, while only 3 percent believed that America was being "too tough."[24] The Fulton address, then, did not declare the Cold War but diagnosed its nature and recommended a necessary course of action. Given its reaction to Soviet aggression in Iran, Manchuria, and Europe, the American public was already moving steadily toward the speech's main conclusions.

Fulton Aftermath

The importance of the Fulton speech should not be underrated with respect to world politics or its impact on Joseph Stalin. But nor should the speech's importance be overrated with respect to Truman's own thinking. It deepened the president's understanding on some points, and he did incorporate its central themes into the strategy of containment, but it did not originate his reasoning. Prior to and immediately after Churchill's address, for instance, Truman moved to exert strength against the Soviet Union with respect to Iran and the rest of the Middle East. The Iranians had been subjected to Soviet pressures for a year and a half. In January 1946, Iran had protested to the United Nations that the Soviet army was occupying the northern part of its country, installing a Communist government in Azerbaijan in December 1945, and refusing to withdraw its troops. The UN answered by imposing a March 2 deadline for Soviet departure that was in keeping with the Teheran Declaration of 1943, but it also referred the matter to direct negotiations between the USSR and Iran. The Soviet Union, however, engaged in heavy troop movements in Iran past the March 2 deadline, augmented its numbers, and moved toward the capital of Teheran and toward Turkey.[25] Truman had reports that Moscow was using starvation, among other tactics, as a political weapon to subdue Iran.[26] Iran protested to the Soviet Union on March 3, to Great Britain on March 4, and to the United States on March 6. The United States made a formal protest to the United Nations on that day.

Within Iran, the Communist Tudeh Party aided the USSR by staging riots and preventing regular meetings of the Majlis, the Iranian parliament.[27] The United States made another public inquiry about Soviet troop movements on March 12. The Kremlin denounced the Fulton address at the same time that it denied its troop movements in Iran. As Truman recalled, the Soviets shifted tactics in order to divert attention from their actions in Iran, "hammering away at Winston Churchill for his Fulton, Missouri, speech and at me for sponsoring the speech."[28] In a dual expression of testing and trusting the United Nations, the president waited to see how the new international organization would react. In addition, other demonstrations of American strength were considered, and stiff diplomatic protests were registered in Moscow and at the United Nations.[29]

On March 18, the Iranian matter was scheduled again for deliberation in the UN Security Council. But before the issue was resolved there, the USSR announced in April an agreement with Iran that Soviet troops would leave in early May. In return, and after the UN had dismissed the problem officially, Iran agreed to negotiate with the Communist-imposed government in Azerbaijan and to ratify various Soviet-Iranian oil contracts.[30] American and English pressure helped force Soviet withdraw-al. On February 21, Bevin defended Iran's sovereignty in the House of Commons. In addition to public support for Iran in the United Nations, on America's part Byrnes made a nationwide radio address on February 28 calling for Soviet troop removal, which was interpreted by many as an ultimatum. After discussion with the president, U.S. Ambassador to the Soviet Union Walter Bedell Smith was apparently instrumental in per-suading the USSR to reverse course.[31] The president and his advisors were displeased that the new Iranian prime minister, Ahmad Qavam, had bar-gained with the Kremlin, but they knew that America must collaborate with non-Soviet leaders.[32] By the end of March, Soviet troops began to withdraw; by the end of May, they were gone.

Truman saw Soviet aggression in Iran as part of a pattern of Communist behavior. In contrast to previous actions by the secretary of state, Byrnes's important radio address of late February was read and approved in ad-vance by Truman, who may have seen this address as the necessary prelude to a successful speech by Churchill. Byrnes's reading copy contained the president's marginal comments and underlinings, which the secretary then emphasized. Each of these phrases or sentences echoed Truman's view, as, for example, on the prospects for peace: "[A] just and lasting peace is not the inevitable result of victory. Rather, victory has given us the op-portunity to build such a peace. And our lives depend upon whether we make the most of this opportunity." Other highlighted passages pertained to the president's conviction that Soviet intransigence must be met with "plain speaking"; that "we do intend to act" to prevent aggression; that the United States must "have some form of universal training"; and that, in line with the UN Charter, "we cannot allow aggression to be accom-plished by coercion or pressure or subterfuges such as political infiltra-tion." Finally, Truman liked the notion that "[w]e must not conduct wars of nerves to achieve strategic ends," so much that on occasion he would refer to the Cold War as a war of nerves.[33]

Truman also accepted and, then, welcomed the Republican backing of Senator Arthur Vandenberg of Michigan and soon looked to the legis-lator for bipartisan support of his foreign policy. As evidence of his com-mitment at a pivotal time in world affairs, the senator would spend 213 days in 1946, an election year for his seat, at conference tables in London, Paris, and New York. One day before Byrnes's radio address, Vandenberg indicted the USSR from the Senate floor after his return from London, where he had attended the first session of the United Nations General Assembly, and asserted that the Soviets were the impediment to the UN's mission. Often seen as a criticism of the president but, more fundamentally, directed at Byrnes, the senator's speech called for an end to American vacillation.[34] Following Vandenberg, Byrnes's radio address was popularly termed the Second Vandenberg Concerto. Byrnes's speech focused on Soviet intransigence in Iran, whereas Vandenberg's remarks criticized Kremlin activity around the world; but despite their differences, both believed in the United Nations and that UN Security Council action against the USSR was the best response.

On the day of the Fulton address, the State Department sent notes to the Kremlin requesting explanations for its actions in Manchuria and Eastern Europe as well as Iran. On March 7, the president again said that Trieste required attention. He discussed at length with War Department officials "the possibility of our making some preparations to meet a possible attack in Europe by communists."[35]

Iran emerged as the test case for the Middle East. As sketched in his January 5, 1946, memorandum and fleshed out in his memoirs, Truman concluded that there were three reasons for Moscow's belligerence in Iran: influence over Turkey if it were flanked by the Soviet Union or a Soviet puppet state; control of Iran's oil reserves; and callous disregard of wartime conference promises and of the rights of an independent nation.[36] He determined that a show of strength in defense of the overall region was necessary. On the train to Fulton, after discussion with Leahy, Truman ordered that the U.S.S. *Missouri*, carrying the body of the Turkish ambassador to the United States home, be accompanied by a naval task force. (The *Missouri* had been in the Mediterranean Sea earlier in the year as an example to the USSR of American strength.) The president decided that this contingent would remain in the Sea of Marmara for an indefinite period in order to show the Soviets the importance America attached to the region; the *Missouri* arrived in the Bosporus Strait on April 5 and stayed several weeks.[37] Operational requirements, however, prevented the task force from being assembled until August; at that time, with the new aircraft carrier *Franklin D. Roosevelt* at its center, the task force was sent to the eastern Mediterranean to help defuse the crisis in the Turkish Straits and to establish an enduring American presence in the area.[38]

Some have argued that Truman could have done more in March 1946. His actions were confined somewhat by the fact that Great Britain remained the major defender of open governments in the Middle East. The president's judgments and decisions on the region occurred almost a year before the British officially told the United States on February 21, 1947, that they no longer could guarantee the security of Greece and Turkey. Truman was also hampered by the fact that rapid postwar demobilization meant the United States lacked the military resources to fight another war, if necessary, and he did not want to resort to atomic weapons over an altercation in Iran. New circumstances called for a new structure: he believed a reorganization of the military, universal training, and an extension of the Selective Service Act were required. But until 1947 and the establishment of the Department of Defense along with the reorganization of the military, despite his best efforts, he faced disarray and infighting within and among the branches of the armed services; until 1951 and the implementation of NSC 68, he had a deficiency of conventional means and hardware to meet Cold War circumstances.[39] Truman's intention was clear, however, and he did what he thought possible at the time, given the resources at hand.

The common interpretation that this period between the second half of 1945 and early 1946 was one of American vacillation, then, is not borne out by the facts. If this interpretation is correct, the Fulton address—following Stalin's election address, the Long Telegram, and Vandenberg's and Byrnes's speeches—shifted the United States from a non-policy of uncertainty to a policy of "patience and firmness." Instead, Churchill's iron curtain message gave full voice to the move of American policy toward firmness and away from patience, and Truman—rather than those who served him—led this move almost from the moment he entered office. In February 1946, Kennan galvanized those around Truman, while Vandenberg and Byrnes stirred congressional, press, and public opinion. Churchill's words were the deciding factor; they both underscored and deepened the president's developing strategy. But it was Truman, with a world war ended only months before, who assessed the circumstances, initiated the strategy of containment, and began to educate and mobilize his country.

Henry Wallace and Opposition to Containment

In every way that mattered, Truman had already made up his mind to continue on the theoretical and practical path of containment. In summer 1946, he fully accepted the reality of the threat and conflict as articulated by Churchill rather than Kennan.[40] He sensed that freedom and American leadership must precede meaningful peace and UN wishes. In early July, he assigned Clark Clifford, his special counsel, to prepare an appraisal of American relations with the Soviet Union. Although the report would not be finalized until a later date, he asked for as much information as possible before the Paris conference in late July 1946. By early September, he concluded that Germany was a critical element in the war of nerves; he actively approved Byrnes's Stuttgart address of September 6, which called for a free, democratic, and united Germany. By the end of September, a U.S. naval task force was assigned permanently to the Mediterranean. To contain further the Kremlin's offensive purpose and policies, the United States increasingly explored the need for strength and involvement in world affairs. America could not as yet act more broadly, because it had first to restructure and mobilize an integrated military. In the meantime, Truman awaited the special report.

As he deepened his perspective and developed containment, Truman again had to contend with domestic difficulties. Many scholars assert that the president, showing hesitation and indecision, waited almost two years—from April 1945 to March 1947—to move against the Soviets.[41] But they do not account sufficiently for the depleted military resources and public opinion's gradual shift from the sense of victory in World War II to concern about the dangers of the Cold War. In addition, party affairs had been intensifying since spring 1946, precisely at a time when Truman's foreign policy was coalescing. The duties of presidential statesman outweighed those of Democratic leader, but Truman was still a partisan.

Truman's immediate concern in 1946, moreover, came from within his party rather than from the Republicans. Although there was a sizable Democratic majority in both houses of Congress, the president did not enjoy corresponding support of his opinions or policies.[42] Domestically, he was responsible for keeping together an unstable Democratic political coalition, even as he had to build consensus and bipartisanship in foreign affairs. Fault lines in the Democratic Party divided North and South, town and country, labor and agriculture, minorities and WASPs, liberals and conservatives.[43] The GOP, meanwhile, gained in popularity throughout the year, in part benefiting from organized labor's ability to manipulate and fracture large, urban portions of the Democratic Party. Within his own party, from the beginning of his presidency, Truman faced deep, intellectual divisions, especially from the Left. He was perceived by FDR stalwarts and other liberals and progressives as not much more than a competent former senator. Those on the left of the spectrum, who went on to create the Americans for Democratic Action and the Progressive Citizens for America in early 1947, believed Truman had diluted the Roosevelt domestic agenda, failed to utilize the UN properly, and exaggerated the Communist threat. Within the administration, such criticisms were embodied in Secretary of Commerce Henry Wallace.[44]

Henry Wallace, FDR's former vice president, was a progressive and a New Dealer. Truman kept him in the administration for a variety of reasons, not least because he agreed with Wallace, a fellow midwesterner, on many domestic and populist issues. Wallace also delivered a segment of liberal support to Truman, in particular those who did not view the president as a faithful adherent to Franklin Roosevelt's policies (notably, Eleanor Roosevelt, who had supported Wallace over Truman for vice president in 1944). In his fledgling administration in 1945 and with labor clashes and a congressional election year in 1946, Truman could not underestimate the importance of Wallace in his cabinet. For his part, perhaps because he had been the vice president before Truman, Wallace did not show Truman proper respect. When he criticized the president or made suggestions, he often forgot the office that Truman occupied and charted his own policies. He also went beyond the scope of economic issues, disagreeing with Truman privately and publicly about foreign affairs.

Like the rest of America, Wallace forcefully opposed fascism. His most famous statement on this subject was made in May 1942, in a speech entitled "The Price of Free World Victory." In that address, Wallace swore vengeance against Nazi Germany and promoted the creation of a new order based on Roosevelt's Four Freedoms of 1941. But he also departed from common liberal American opinion of the time, foreshadowing the revisionist view of U.S. foreign policy. Wallace disputed the idea of an American century and said that the era after World War II must be the century of the common man, devoid of privileged peoples. "International cartels that serve American greed and the German will to power must go," he said, and were to be replaced by international control, global redistribution, and "adequate control by the respective home governments." Beyond World War II and Nazi Germany, though, the stumbling block to Wallace's vision was the economic structure of the United States: "We ourselves in the United States are no more a master race than the Nazis. And we cannot perpetuate economic warfare without planting the seeds

of military warfare."[45] Viewing capitalism necessarily as economic warfare, and urging the sacrifice of the lesser interest of individuals and nations to the greater interest of the general welfare of the "people's century,"
he called on his fellow Americans to defeat not only the Nazis but also
American commercial capitalism.[46]

At the end of 1945, Wallace agreed with the president about the importance of the United Nations, including the preparation of the Bretton
Woods agreement to create a postwar liberal economic order, as the linch-
pin to peace. The secretary of commerce stressed that the welfare of all
mankind should be promoted by international organizations through
trade, economic development, and cultural cooperation. Unlike Truman,
he believed that the Soviet Union would participate willingly in this arrangement. In language that he suggested Truman include in the 1946
State of the Union address, he failed to see that the Big Three alliance already
had crumbled: "Differences of language, tradition, political institutions,
and social customs tend perhaps to make this task [of unity] more difficult
as between the Russians and ourselves; but, on the other hand, similarities
of social objectives and the complete absence of direct conflicts in national
interest make it easier."[47] Truman did not use any of Wallace's suggestions.
Since relations with the Soviet Union were strained, the president remained
quiet on the subject of collaboration with the Kremlin and instead stressed
positive accomplishments in Europe, including a loan to Great Britain.

Wallace reacted, increasingly and repeatedly, by viewing Truman's
policies as the obstruction to world peace and an abandonment of both
Roosevelt and the UN Charter. In February 1946, he "was impressed by
the vigor with which [Stalin in his election address] was taking up the various challenges which we have been making all the way from the President
on down." The next month he added that America and the USSR were in
a race to serve best the interests of mankind and that Stalin's speech was
good for "such a race in furnishing the needs of the common people without war or business crisis." Of Kremlin aggression in northern Iran, he
said that the Iranians in Azerbaijan wanted to join with the Soviet Union
because it would raise their standard of living, and he accused the British
of economic exploitation. Continuing in this vein, he depicted Churchill's
Fulton address as warlike and concluded that "what Russia feared was encirclement by the United States and England."[48] Such arguments all made
their way into academic revisionism; at the time, Wallace was seen by the
Kremlin as its ally in Truman's cabinet.[49]

As was the case with the differences between Truman and Byrnes, the dispute between Truman and Wallace must be seen in the context of the development of the president's views of the Cold War and America's purpose in foreign relations. Before his famous speech of September 12 in Madison Square Garden, Wallace limned its outlines in a letter to Truman on July 23, 1946. Drew Pearson, the noted syndicated columnist, obtained a copy of the letter in September and planned to publish it. The president viewed Wallace's twelve-page missive as a "memorandum for my use" and a "confidential document," and he asked the secretary of commerce not to release it; he added that if Pearson printed the letter on his own, its authenticity, like the columnist's reputation, would be doubted. Democratic and Republican leaders united in taking exception to Pearson's threatened action.[50] Wallace, however—in what must have been calculated timing—decided to release the letter to the press on September 17, less than a week after his Madison Square Garden speech. He hoped that the letter would reinforce his address and turn public opinion away from a growing commitment to Truman's policies of containment.

Wallace argued in the letter that the Soviet Union had a legitimate defensive purpose, and he offered one of the first American justifications for "peaceful coexistence" as a replacement for containment. "We should ascertain from a fresh point of view what Russia believes to be essential to her own security as a prerequisite to the writing of the peace and to cooperation in the construction of a world order," he wrote. "We should be prepared to judge her requirements against the background of what we ourselves and the British have insisted upon as essential to our respective security. We should be prepared, even at the expense of risking epithets of appeasement, to agree to reasonable Russian guarantees of security."[51] He decried those who engaged in the propaganda of engendering "irrational fear" of the Soviet Union and asserting that the two forms of government could not exist in the same world. On the one hand, he chastised the United States for not appreciating that it was the only nation that came out of World War II stronger than before and sympathizing with those less fortunate; on the other hand, he praised the USSR for its effort to prevent the war through collective security. In a revisionist as well as realist vein, Wallace then recommended that America adjust its postwar actions to the lessons of Allied cooperation learned during the war and to the facts of the atomic age.

The Madison Square Garden speech, which criticized the "get tough with Russia" policy as an obstruction to world peace, extended the argument in Wallace's private letter to Truman. Wallace believed that a danger of war stemmed from British or American imperialism, or renewed fascism, rather than from communism. The core of his address concerned the inevitability, indeed desirability, of convergence in which "the Russian world and the American world will gradually become more alike." Much as was the case with the critical reaction to the Fulton address, Wallace believed that the Soviets would be forced to grant more personal freedoms while America "shall become more and more absorbed with the problems of social-economic justice."[52] Until this revisionist convergence was achieved, Wallace's solution was realist: the Soviets should retain their sphere of influence in Eastern Europe, leaving the United States to operate its sphere in Latin America and, for all intents and purposes, Western Europe. Wallace saw no end to the efforts of the great powers to bring their spheres into accord with their own ideology, but he trusted that a political, equitable settlement could be achieved through diplomacy.

When considering the Madison Square Garden speech, scholars focus on whether Truman approved of the address rather than on its actual content. It is true that Truman and Wallace met before he gave the address, Wallace maintaining that he went over the speech "page by page" with the president.[53] It is also true that the president, in response to a question at a news conference only hours before Wallace gave the address, said he approved the whole speech. But Truman was led into answering the question and qualified his answer on September 14 by saying he had approved only of Wallace's right to give the speech.[54] In his longhand notes, the president explained that he and Wallace were near the end of a fifteen-minute meeting on a typically busy day when the secretary of commerce pulled out the speech. Rather than reading it carefully, Truman skimmed and, looking for a passage to praise, noted a paragraph that pleased him. It was Wallace's statement that the United States sought a world of peace and, endorsing neither empire nor totalitarianism, had no special friendship with either Great Britain or the USSR.[55] Truman expected cabinet members to endorse his policies when speaking publicly and thus assumed that the rest of the text was similar.[56]

Aside from the single passage about world affairs that appealed to him, Truman focused on the opening paragraphs of the speech, in which Wallace lambasted the Republicans and called for Democratic victory in New York in the November 1946 elections. He hoped that the speech would have a good political effect in New York, and he probably let domestic politics cloud his hurried reading of the rest of the text.[57] It should also not be overlooked that the original text was amended by Wallace during delivery: facing a crowd reportedly filled with many Communists and Communist sympathizers, Wallace dropped several sentences that criticized the Soviets and added language arguing that the danger of war was much less from communism than it was from imperialism, "whether it be of the United States or England," and fascism.[58]

When later the press covering Wallace's delivered speech described the radical audience in Madison Square Garden, it jumped on Truman's alleged endorsement. The president realized what was happening—that one of his secretaries was trying to derail his foreign policy—and quickly disavowed the speech's *content*, telling the secretary of commerce that he had overstepped the bounds of his position. Wallace, believing that he should be able to promulgate an independent foreign policy at odds with his president, said he would be quiet about foreign affairs until after the conclusion of the Council of Foreign Ministers' meeting in Paris but did not promise to restrain himself afterward. Despite midterm elections less than two months away, and aware that he would be antagonizing organized labor, Truman asked for the secretary of commerce's resignation and received it on September 20.[59]

The Clifford Memorandum

One of the first substantial formulations of President Truman's position was articulated in a report prepared and written about the same time entitled "American Relations with the Soviet Union," better known as the Clifford memorandum. Often overlooked or dismissed as overzealous anticommunism, the almost 100,000-word memorandum of September 1946 served as the theoretical basis of containment. Its thesis threaded through Truman's own words, to the administration's actions from 1947 through 1949, to presidentially approved National Security Council documents, including NSC 68.

The Long Telegram had reached the White House through the State Department, but Truman made no recorded comment about its arrival. By contrast, the president specifically asked Special Counsel Clark Clifford for a thorough assessment of the Soviet Union and for a requisite American response, giving direction to what would become the Clifford memorandum. In a July 12 meeting, Truman told Clifford and White House aide George Elsey his reasons for requesting the report: (1) now was the time to take a stand on Russia; (2) America was tired of being pushed around; (3) the Soviets were chiseling away at the free world, little by little; (4) the Paris conference would likely "bust up," because the Kremlin would want too much and America would not back down; and (5) given the probability of diplomatic failure, a thorough analysis of Soviet violations of international agreements and its aggressive actions toward the world was needed.[60] On September 24, 1946, Clifford, with much assistance from Elsey, submitted a memorandum synthesizing opinions from Secretary of State James Byrnes, Secretary of the Navy Forrestal, Admiral William Leahy and the Joint Chiefs of Staff, the Central Intelligence Group, and others such as George Kennan, who was on a speaking tour for the State Department during the summer months and would then take up residence at the National War College.

The Clifford report opened by stating that relations with the USSR were the gravest problem facing the United States. The document went on to say explicitly that the Soviet Union was running a course of aggrandizement leading to "world domination." Like Kennan, Clifford and Elsey argued that both the goal and the policies of the USSR opposed American ideals. But the emphasis on the Soviets' chief goal of domination was new and was reflected in references to Communist philosophy and Communist faith. Unlike the Long Telegram, this report set forth Communist doctrine and considered it in an examination of Soviet intentions. Kennan later accented the need to evaluate intentions, but at the time he thought that Kremlin behavior mostly stemmed from the usual ambitions of power politics, which could be contained or negotiated through ordinary means. The Clifford memorandum, however, asserted that there was an intimate connection between Soviet doctrine and intentions, resulting in a departure from mere power politics and the creation of a qualitatively different challenge. This challenge had to be met by extraordinary measures.[61]

Clifford and Elsey quoted extensively from the Long Telegram, but they diverged from it when it came to Soviet ideology. Although Clifford recalled that Elsey and he incorporated "almost every one" of Kennan's suggestions from a six-page, single-spaced commentary on their report, Clifford's memorandum differed greatly from Kennan's analysis. While Kennan maintained that the Soviets engaged in traditional power politics under the guise of Marxism, Clifford and Elsey presented the Soviet Union in 1946 as distinct from Russia and its history and argued that the Kremlin was "blinded by its adherence to Marxist doctrine."[62] This theoretical departure from Kennan reflected Elsey's input. In addition, Elsey's 1946 handwritten notes show that, while some of Kennan's points were incorporated into the memorandum, Kennan made no editorial alterations to the text itself. Instead, Kennan wrote his six-page response, which, according to Elsey, did not have much impact on the final report.[63]

The major difference between Kennan and Clifford was George Elsey, and it was significant. Kennan's limited observations were used to develop a deeper understanding of Soviet foreign policy, but the United States now scrutinized Soviet actions in terms of the USSR's ideological intentions and capabilities. According to Clifford and Elsey's report, the Soviets were striving for greater control: "The key to an understanding of current Soviet foreign policy, in summary, is the realization that Soviet leaders adhere to the Marxian theory of ultimate destruction of capitalist states by communist states, while at the same time they strive to postpone the inevitable conflict in order to strengthen and prepare the Soviet Union for its clash with the western democracies."[64] In other words, the analysis studied Communist ideology and presented Soviet imperialism as evidenced in the Kremlin's words and actions. And it took the meaning of Stalin's election address seriously, incorporated Churchill's observation that the Soviets wanted the fruits of war without war itself, and recognized that the USSR believed in the inevitability of war between democracy and communism.

Clifford and Elsey amassed considerable evidence for this report to the president. To show that the Kremlin enslaved peoples for economic exploitation, they highlighted the fact that the USSR was retaining large numbers of Germans and Japanese to work in Soviet industry. In order to bolster the need for an American policy of strength, the report juxtaposed the plight of Hungary, where Soviet troops and administration dominated, and Austria, which the Kremlin would have taken had it not been for Western opposition. The report pointed out the maturing tactics of Marxism-Leninism, such as the way the Soviets were working for a unified Germany on their terms and encouraging the French and Italian Communist parties in order to weaken their non-Communist adversaries. Reaching beyond the Western bloc, Clifford and Elsey noted that the Soviets were also interfering in the Near East and the Middle East. In

Asia, they argued, Moscow aimed to keep China, Korea, and Japan internally divided and weak "until such time as the U.S.S.R. is in a position to exert greater influence there than any other country." Clifford's report interchanged the terms "control" and "influence" as aspects of the Soviet Union's overall imperialist goal: Moscow sometimes settled for influence, but it always aimed for control.[65]

Elsey deliberately inserted these theoretical and political sections of the report (which made up the introduction and first chapter) as preamble to a consideration of Soviet violations of international agreements. As he recorded at the time, Clifford was not convinced at first of the need to consider Soviet ideology but then agreed for the sake of context. "I consider the violation of agreements to be only a symptom of the malady," wrote Elsey. "Our concern is *why* the Soviet Union violates her agreements, not *how*. This leads us into a consideration of Soviet policy, and the nature and characteristics of Soviet leadership."[66] Although Clifford's name remained in the byline on the memorandum, Elsey provided the theoretical understanding. The final Clifford report imparted a clear picture of the nature of the regimes and political actors locked in the Cold War, and Elsey should be credited with helping the president to construct the political thought of containment in a way that Kennan, who did not make such regime distinctions, cannot.

After sketching Soviet-American agreements from 1942 to fall 1946 in the second chapter, the memorandum catalogued Soviet violations of those accords in the third chapter. The acts of Kremlin aggression pertained to all the countries affected in Europe and Asia and to issues such as elections, mutual aid, and repatriation. With respect to Germany and the 1945 declaration regarding its defeat, for instance, "the Soviet government has not taken adequate steps to demilitarize industrial plants in the Soviet zone. On the contrary, some of them are still engaged in producing war materials." That the Soviets continued to prepare for war on the land of a power defeated in a world war led Clifford and Elsey to conclude that the Kremlin was less interested in the recovery of Europe than in its own expansion. The document's description of the German situation contributed to containment's political thought: it was in 1946 that Truman resolved the western half of Germany would not meet the same end as had the eastern half.[67]

Clifford and Elsey also cited Soviet intransigence in Iran. Although the Soviet ambassador in Teheran told the Iranian government on May 24,

1946, that its withdrawal from Iran was completed on May 9, the Soviet Union continued to support separatist movements. Highlighting these two cases—Germany and Iran—from a litany of other examples, the authors argued that the Soviets pursued their goal by breaking diplomatic agreements they previously, and formally, had accepted. And the Kremlin used international agreements and organizations like the United Nations as diplomatic tools for achieving strategic advantage. For this reason, Clifford and Elsey maintained, and Truman agreed, honest bargaining by the West, and the reasonable accommodation it usually sought, was not an option. On this point, the memorandum reinforced the president's growing conviction that friendly compromise was not the solution (and could only lead to greater problems) and that America must rely on its strength to enforce agreements and counter Communist actions.[68]

After a short section upholding the U.S. position on reparations and the refusal to finance Kremlin aggression, the fifth chapter considered Soviet activities affecting American security. In a main tenet of containment, the memorandum recognized that the Kremlin's foreign and defense policy was designed to prepare for war with the leading capitalist nations of the world. Clifford and Elsey noted that the Soviets' primary "enemy" had shifted from Great Britain to America. Radio Moscow and the Soviet press asserted that the United States was "the principal architect of the 'capitalist encirclement' which now 'menaces the liberty and welfare of the great Soviet masses.'" At a previous time, the Communist ideology and its attendant propaganda attacks on liberal democracy might not have posed a major threat, but in 1946 and for the foreseeable future, the Soviet Union was developing the ability to wage offensive war against the United States, as well as against other countries of importance to its national security. Clifford and Elsey further noted that the Kremlin engaged in subversion in America and around the world, including the attempt to appropriate the international labor movement. The combination of these elements—all offensive by nature—presented the free world with a formidable ideological threat that could not be ignored.[69]

The final chapter of the memorandum recommended a new and concrete U.S. policy toward the Soviet Union, concluding not only that Soviet "aggressive militaristic imperialism" jeopardized the rest of the world but also that America's primary objective was to convince the Kremlin leaders that it was in their interest to participate in a system of global cooperation.[70] A statement such as this one might seem a paradox, if containment is interpreted as a strategy to preserve a status quo through some measure of convergence. But Truman's approach to containment was different. While the free world lacked the ability to deny the previous gains of the USSR, it would refuse to allow additional aggression. Far from seeking some negotiated status quo arrangement, the United States would challenge Soviet imperialism in both principle and practice.

In the end, Clifford and Elsey advised the United States to join with Britain and other Western countries to counter the Kremlin. Strong economic support from America would bolster other nations' resistance to communism and provide for military assistance in case of attack. As a result, the ideas of recovery and alliance—already intimated by Truman in 1945 and 1946—became integral to containment in action, particularly in the Truman Doctrine, the Marshall Plan, and the North Atlantic Alliance. In anticipation of Radio Free Europe, the expansion of Voice of America, and other public information programs, the Clifford memorandum also proposed the dissemination of books, magazines, papers, movies, and radio broadcasts among the peoples in the Soviet Union. But such economic and political policies required fortification.[71] As long as the Kremlin pursued its present foreign policy, the United States had to assume that the Soviet Union pursued the twofold objective of expansion while weakening potential capitalist opponents. "The language of military power is the only language which disciples of power politics understand," noted Clifford and Elsey, as if they had read Truman's January 1946 letter to Byrnes. But this did not mean that the Soviet Union played traditional power politics. Given the ideological nature of the Soviet regime, traditional diplomacy and negotiation were naive. Truman concluded that the United States was the only nation with the will and the means to respond to the USSR and become the main deterrent in the West to Soviet gains. The president believed that America was the best regime to advance freedom in a struggle against totalitarianism.[72]

The Clifford memorandum crystallized much of the thought in the administration about U.S.-Soviet relations.[73] Truman had requested a comprehensive assessment of American relations with the Soviet Union, and the result was as seminal as the subject it evaluated was revolutionary. Just as Truman was on the cusp of subordinating his hopes for the UN's original intentions to his realization that the United States had to take the lead in world affairs, the memorandum suggested that the United Nations was a bust in current world circumstances. The Clifford memorandum confirmed for Truman that he had said the right things in his public statements and that he had done the right things in Trieste, Iran, the Turkish Straits, and elsewhere. Like Truman, the authors of the document expressed the desire for world peace, but not on the Kremlin's terms: "So long as these men adhere to these beliefs," they wrote, "it is highly dangerous to conclude that hope of international peace lies only in 'accord,' 'mutual understanding,' or 'solidarity' with the Soviet Union." Most important, the Clifford memorandum agreed with the president's opinions about the ideological component of the growing controversy. When they added that the United States' difficulties with the USSR were due primarily to the doctrine and actions of a small ruling clique, Clifford and Elsey rooted problems with the Soviet Union in Communist ideology and deeds. The current Cold War might be of indefinite duration; for fundamental change to occur, the Soviet leaders would have to reject their beliefs. Clifford and Elsey stressed that since Soviet ideology and politics were global in scope, America's purpose and course must also be international. Thus, in addition to vigor in diplomacy and economics, the United States needed to strengthen its military capabilities to form the main deterrent to Soviet attack and intimidation. In a practical sense, there was a need for a cross-governmental advisory council to the president on foreign affairs—such as that implemented through the National Security Act of 1947.[74] The 1946 Clifford memorandum preceded Truman's reorganization of the military in the following year and was a prototype for the most exhaustive Cold War report to the president, NSC 68.

Journalist Arthur Krock, who had followed Truman and his career closely since 1935, later observed that the document "charted the post-war prospect with startling prescience in which the shape and thrust of Truman's subsequent great programs—the Greek-Turk aid legislation, the Marshall Plan, the North Atlantic Alliance (including NATO), and what later became known as the 'Truman Doctrine'—were outlined."[75] While Truman clearly incorporated the Clifford memorandum's message into his political thought of containment, he chose not to publicize the report and collected all of its copies prior to circulation. "I read your report with care last night," he told Clifford, after receiving his copy. "It is valuable to me—but if it leaked it would blow the roof off the White House, it would blow the roof off the Kremlin. We'd have the most serious situation on our hands that has yet occurred in my Administration."[76] The report not only was dangerous politically—as it could have provided fodder for Truman's opposition in the 1946 midterm elections—but, more important, the public controversy generated by the memorandum would not have been conducive to the carefully chosen arguments and actions necessary for laying the groundwork for the full implementation of containment.

3

"A growing feeling of certainty in the rightness of our step"

The Truman Doctrine

Scholars have long debated to what extent communism animated Soviet behavior during the Cold War. While controversy continues, extensive materials have been released from former Eastern bloc archives supporting the conclusion that Communist ideology typically motivated the Kremlin.[1] Truman neither benefited from the academic debate nor was he privy to these materials. Instead, he drew on what he experienced and observed, and what information and analysis he received from his advisors. Some State Department officials interpreted the Soviet Union as a typical great power seeking hegemony, while others at State and within the armed service and intelligence sectors asserted the prominence of Communist ideology in Kremlin actions. As it became clear that the postwar world would be dominated by the East-West conflict rather than the United Nations, it became more common to refer to Soviet goals of territorial aggression and influence as being inspired by Communist Party totalitarianism. In 1946 and 1947, Truman received significant input—from the well-known Clifford memorandum to weekly ORE reports—to inform and support his views about the USSR.[2] In forging a new liberal internationalism to buttress his Cold War foreign policy, Truman practiced executive-legislative cooperation in a way that had been notably rejected by Woodrow Wilson in the debate over the League of Nations and employed differently by FDR to gain backing for the fledgling United Nations. It was at this point in his presidency that Truman's understanding of the war of nerves—as a total political battle with ideological, strategic, and economic elements—found its fullest expression in the Truman Doctrine of March 1947.

Summer 1946

Europe's economies remained shattered in 1946, and its peoples were defenseless against a conventional military attack. George Kennan and other specialists reported that Moscow viewed global capitalism as being in a period of crisis before its inevitable demise. To escalate that expected dissolution, the Soviets aimed to expand their reach in Germany, Trieste, and France. Red Army movements in eastern Germany in June prompted an immediate and major White House review. The USSR sought not only to speed the West's decline but also to move against nations supposedly not in the capitalist camp, such as Iran, Turkey, Japan, and Korea. The Kremlin acted both on its own and through its new satellite states. In August at the Paris Peace Conference, Bulgaria demanded part of northern Greece, and the Soviet Union suggested a Kremlin trusteeship over either Libya or Eritrea. At the Montreux Convention, also in August 1946, the Soviets tried to renegotiate control of the Turkish Straits to include Soviet air and naval bases, a month after they proposed excluding all nations except for the Black Sea powers from the Dardanelles. More directly, Communists sponsored labor strikes in Iran and Iraq in July. The next month Yugoslavia made claims on Trieste and shot down two American transport aircraft on their regular routes from Austria to Italy. And twenty-five Red Army divisions, many of them motorized, massed on the southern border of the Caucasus, geared to exert pressure on Turkey and Iran. Throughout 1946, the Communists exploited unrest in Greece. Toward the year's end, the Soviet Union tried to obtain naval bases in Norway and Iceland and succeeded in establishing one in Finland.[3]

August 1946 marked a turning point and was seen as such at the time. In addition to crises in Europe, matters came to a head in the Middle East and Central Asia, areas that Truman had studied since his youth. The Soviets issued an August 7 note on the Turkish Straits, demanding a "new regime" governing the straits by "Black Sea powers" under the joint control of the USSR and Turkey. In effect, the Soviet note picked up where the Kremlin had left off in claiming the Turkish Straits through the Molotov-Ribbentrop pact. Since fall 1945, Truman had resolved that the Soviets could not be allowed to use postwar circumstances to take the straits and dominate the region.[4] In 1946, he and his advisors believed that the Kremlin sought to coopt Turkey through this "new regime," especially since it intended to establish air and naval bases, and then seek control over Greece and the rest of the Near and Middle East. If the Soviets succeeded, they would outflank the West in the Mediterranean, as well as control the oil of the Middle East. Edwin C. Wilson, the U.S. ambassador in Ankara, warned that the fall of Turkey would open the door for Soviet expansion into the Persian Gulf and Suez area.[5]

When Truman, his various secretaries, and the Joint Chiefs met on August 15 to discuss Turkey, the president said that the straits must not fall to the Kremlin. After Army Chief of Staff Dwight D. Eisenhower questioned Truman's understanding of the consequences of his decision and the possibility of war, the president pulled from his desk a well-worn map of the eastern Mediterranean, the Middle East, and Central and South Asia and spoke for ten to fifteen minutes on the historical and strategic significance of the area. According to Secretary of the Navy James Forrestal, the president stated at the meeting that America must take a firm position and find out now, rather than five or ten years later, whether the Soviet Union was bent on world conquest. Truman implied that waiting a decade would be too late. In a note to Moscow, he said that Soviet aggression in the Turkish Straits would threaten international security and would be referred for action to the UN Security Council. Maintaining his faith in the international organization, he favored a United Nations reply over a U.S.-led response. But the president also thought that the United States must act independently and from a position of strength in order to prevent Soviet gains. He ordered a naval task force, which he had first requested in March for the region and which was now ready, to the Mediterranean. With respect to the conflict between U.S. leadership and UN primacy, Truman believed that he had struck a reasonable balance.[6]

Preparations for the Truman Doctrine

On February 21, 1947, Great Britain officially informed the United States that it no longer could fulfill its traditional responsibilities in Greece and Turkey. Truman had known that this time would come and, in September 1946, had initiated research into military aid to the two countries. He had received information about the region since becoming president and observed that the British increasingly had trouble defending the Near East, especially Greece. Through his understanding of history, he appreciated the significance of the area, in contrast to some of his advisors who singled out Europe as the chief priority. As early as April 1945, around the time of his meeting with Molotov, Truman stressed that Turkey must retain its independence in the face of Soviet demands.[7] In summer and fall 1945, the president had resolved that the Turkish Straits must not be ceded to the USSR.[8] During late 1945 and the first months of 1946, he showed his resolution with respect to Iran. During summer 1946, he again stood firm against Soviet designs in the Turkish crisis. But because the British were responsible for Greece's defense during and immediately after World War II, Truman had not had occasion to articulate and implement a policy regarding that country.

Yet Truman had come to think of Greece, Turkey, and Iran as parts of a whole, with the importance of one linked inextricably to the importance of the others. He grasped their collective historical role as the dividing line between East and West, more crucial than ever in the Cold War.[9] Iran was more settled by 1947, but the British were now withdrawing their troops from Greece, leaving it vulnerable to the Soviet Union. Meanwhile, the Kremlin continued its war of nerves on all levels against Turkey. Drawing on history and geostrategy, Truman would explain, "If Greece was lost, Turkey would become an untenable outpost in a sea of communism. Similarly, if Turkey yielded to Soviet demands, the position of Greece would be extremely endangered." The president discerned two configurations endangering Turkey and Greece that stemmed from the same source of communism: while Turkey's quandary was due to Moscow's postwar hostility, the problem for Greece began with Communist agitation dressed as nationalism during the Axis's World War II occupation of the country.[10] To counteract the Communist threat, Truman led a vigorous discussion among his top advisors about the situation in the Near East, to be followed by a speech explaining these facts to Congress and the American people and articulating an appropriate response.

Central to the creation of the Truman Doctrine in 1947 were the president's session with congressional leaders on February 27 and the cabinet meeting of March 7. The former senator realized that, constitutionally and institutionally, he needed both to involve and persuade the legislative branch. At the first meeting, Truman announced his new policy, asked Secretary of State George Marshall to summarize the recommendations for Greek-Turkish aid, and received a mixed response from the congressional leaders. After Undersecretary of State Dean Acheson then presented a more impassioned case, Senator Arthur Vandenberg responded, "Mr. President, if you will say that to the Congress and the country, I will support you and I believe that most of its members will do the same."[11] When Truman invited comments from the others, no one voiced opposition or questioned the importance of the issue.[12] With congressional backing promised, if not secured, Truman held the March 7 cabinet meeting at which he conveyed "that he was faced with a decision more serious than had ever confronted any President."[13] He did not exaggerate. Previous American presidents might have made the same decision and commitment as Truman if they had been in his place, but never before had such a choice been of such global magnitude.

Asked by Truman to outline the situation, Acheson said that the Soviets were moving to encircle Turkey and Germany through satellite nations and that Greece was key to the Communist encirclement movements in France, Italy, Hungary, and Turkey. Without U.S. intervention, collapse was imminent in Greece and Turkey, which would also affect Iran and Europe. The president recognized that the Middle East and Europe were connected, and he argued that the United States would have to be involved in European politics in peacetime, a departure from past American policy. The extraordinary circumstances of the Cold War warranted such an involvement, in Truman's mind, overriding the expected resistance from those who were still weary from World War II and focused on postwar readjustments and economic expansion at home. Politically assessing the challenge, he added that it would require "the greatest selling job ever facing a president." He emphasized that his advisors must help to win support for the policy and to deter any revival of isolationism.[14]

Truman never let up on either his efforts to gain public support or his resolve to make the most compelling case for the Truman Doctrine. Working under the direction of acting secretary of state Acheson, State Department speechwriter Joseph Jones prepared the initial drafts of a speech to Congress on the situation in Greece. Jones, in turn, was significantly influenced by a subcommittee report of SWNCC (State-War-Navy Coordinating Committee) that was organized to draft themes relating to the new policy.[15] A third draft in this process was approved by George Marshall (then in Europe) and sent to Clark Clifford on March 7. At that point, the White House took over the editing process, and Clifford, at the direct request of Truman and with the assistance of George Elsey, generated several more drafts, each of which made the speech tougher and more forceful. Elsey thought there was not sufficient time to produce such a significant speech and that the situation in Greece was "relatively abstract."

He was concerned about using the opportunity "to educate and inform the public" so that the speech would have the desired effect.[16] Clifford and Elsey's major revised draft—drawing further on their memorandum from six months earlier—was prepared on March 9, and Truman was directly involved in the drafting on March 10.[17]

Truman's calendar was cleared of planned appointments on March 11 and 12, 1947, until the time of the address, and he met frequently with Acheson.[18] At a delicate meeting with congressional leaders on March 10, the president forged ahead with a defense of his political thought about the Cold War, despite resistance on several sides from his former Hill colleagues. As Admiral Leahy recorded at the time, "He was very frank in pointing out the danger to free governments in Europe and in the world that is threatened by Communist penetration everywhere, and he said that he will be equally frank in his proposed formal address to the Congress and to the people."[19] In light of Truman's earlier statement about a "selling job," some have maintained that he exaggerated the situation in Greece and Turkey and put forth universal principles in order to persuade or scare Congress and the public into approval. But Truman was not one to say what he did not believe, and, as borne out by his attention and additions to the draft of the speech, he firmly believed in the case for the Truman Doctrine. Moreover, the Truman Doctrine address codified what the president had been learning and articulating since April 1945.[20] By March 1947, he had concluded not only that the circumstances demanded the doctrine but also that the American people were finally prepared to welcome the implementation of containment.

George Kennan, then lecturing as a foreign service officer at the National War College, expressed his dissatisfaction about American analysis of the Middle East situation while participating in State Department discussions in late February and early March. On March 6, he was shown a draft of the Truman Doctrine speech, to which he strenuously objected, not just because of its content but especially its tone.[21] Later, in his memoirs, he painted the Soviet threat as political in a narrow sense and implied that Truman blurred the differences between Greece and Turkey. Incorporating his stenographic records of National War College lectures on March 14 and March 28 into his other recollections, Kennan admitted that Greece would succumb to communism and that the United States might act in a limited way to take over the British role. But he added that the Communists, in Moscow and Eastern Europe, were ill equipped to govern Greece. The West, he argued, could then exploit Communist difficulties, even though he thought Communist rule in Greece would be successful in the long run. Regarding Turkey, Kennan made his now-famous argument that the country suffered no serious Communist penetration. As a result, he maintained that American aid should go only to Greece, which, by proximity, would bolster Turkey's stability.[22] He seemed even to diminish the strategic significance that he had accorded Turkey in the Long Telegram. Given that Kennan had joined in the dialogue at State leading up to the Truman Doctrine address on March 12, 1947, the subsequent March lectures take on a serious air. Although apprised of all American information about the situations in Greece and Turkey, and knowing that he would return to duty at the State Department in May 1947, Kennan continued his official criticism of the president and his policies.

By contrast, the president thought that the internal circumstances of Greece and Turkey, while distinct, were both subject to Communist coercion. He probably had not heard Kennan's particular realist critique, but he had contended with those in his administration and on Capitol Hill who, wittingly or unwittingly, echoed Kennan. Truman believed that free and just governments suited to the peoples of Greece and Turkey would not develop or succeed if tyranny prevailed in either or both of those countries. Concluding that the totalitarian pattern had to be broken, he stressed the wider implications of Communist pressure for the region and the world. For Kennan, no such pattern existed at the beginning of 1947, and he viewed Europe and the Middle East as discrete sectors.

In early 1947, the pace of Soviet consolidation in Eastern Europe depended on the local conditions in each country, the strength that the Communist-led wartime resistance movements retained, and the degree of direct Soviet intervention. Under the Paris peace treaties, for example, the Kremlin had promised but failed to remove its troops by February 15 from Bulgaria, Romania, and Hungary. Instead, the Communists were in control and had forced the Socialists to join them. Moscow also had engineered the January 19 elections in Poland to eliminate Stanislaw Mikolajczyk and his Polish Peasant Party. The UB, the Polish security police modeled on the NKVD, reportedly had over 100,000 agents by February 1947.[23] Because the Red Army did not occupy Greece and Turkey, Truman saw an opportunity to preserve and encourage liberty there by improving domestic conditions and preventing direct Soviet intervention to help the local

Communists. "Greece and Turkey were still free countries being challenged by Communist threats from within and without," he wrote. "These free peoples were now engaged in a valiant struggle to preserve their liberties and their independence."[24] Truman invoked strength to protect freedom and a fragile, partial world peace. In Europe, America had tried in vain to persuade the Soviets to permit freedom in Poland, Romania, and the other satellite nations. In 1945, it seemed to Truman, the United States could do nothing more for these countries without waging war at a time when a new war was inconceivable; by the time of the Truman Doctrine, Yalta diplomacy had collapsed. Acutely aware of the growing evidence of sustained Communist aggression, and continuing the thought of his previous statements and the Clifford memorandum, the president put his full weight behind the emerging American strategy.

The Truman Doctrine

The strategic policy of Greek-Turkish aid is better known as the Truman Doctrine. It signified the first formal presidential doctrine since the Monroe Doctrine of 1823 and was judged of comparable magnitude within days of Truman's March 1947 speech. For his part, the president, departing from those in the State Department who desired a narrow message, intended the speech to be a significant presidential statement. "I am fully aware of the broad implications involved if the United States extends assistance to Greece and Turkey," Truman explained in the speech, "and I shall discuss these implications with you at this time." He then succinctly defined the circumstances in Greece and Turkey and the types of actions needed. Although he did not name the Soviet Union as the main adversary—a wise diplomatic move, particularly since Marshall was going to Moscow for another meeting of the Council of Foreign Ministers—he said that totalitarianism was hindering peace and encroaching on other peoples' territories and lives. Truman saw the essence of the current world conflict as the assault of tyranny on the liberty and independence of free peoples and called for an unprecedented American involvement in foreign affairs in peacetime. For President Truman, these circumstances demanded, and his policy represented, a new dimension in American foreign policy.[25]

Truman recognized the newness but, like many at the time, misjudged the ground beneath the grand strategy. He perceived the Truman Doctrine as a break from previous U.S. foreign policy, including the origins of American foreign relations. Indeed, the Truman Doctrine was announced in the face of radically new circumstances in comparison with both the eighteenth and nineteenth centuries. But the president conflated new circumstances and policy with permanent principles. On this point and the connected matter of "isolationism," he exaggerated the extent to which America was isolationist in its earliest days and during the interwar period. With respect to the years between the world wars, he detected that some Americans invoked George Washington or Henry Clay in order to advocate noninvolvement in the world, but he did not consider the aspects of Washington or James Monroe that transcended the isolationist-interventionist debate. He remained confused, for example, about the import of Washington's Farewell Address, even while comprehending its central intent to secure the Union and consistently rating Washington as America's best president. In misinterpreting the most important document of the founding era that established the nexus between the principles of domestic and foreign policy, the president shared a flaw with many of his contemporaries, who equated the Farewell Address with isolationism and weakness.

In the congressional address, Truman stated his awareness of a new international position for the United States. In the absence of an effective United Nations, America was the one nation capable of establishing and maintaining peace. Truman's preference for a UN peace was again offset by his realization that such a peace might be a chimera. Instead, he asserted, "This is no more than a frank recognition that totalitarian regimes imposed upon free peoples, by direct or indirect aggression, undermine the foundations of international peace and hence the security of the United States." Because of Communist violations of the Yalta Conference and recent Soviet consolidation in Germany, he depicted the worldwide situation as being at a critical juncture. If America failed to aid Greece and Turkey, the gateway between the East and the West, "in this fateful hour," the effect would take on global proportions.[26]

Although some approaches (such as those advocated by Kennan, journalist Walter Lippmann, and Henry Wallace) papered over the opposing ideas and institutions of the superpowers and neglected the totalitarian tactics of communism, Truman underscored that virtually every nation was being forced to choose between alternative ways of life stemming from a fundamental difference in regimes. "One way of life is based upon the will of the majority, and is distinguished by free institutions, representative government, free elections, guarantees of individual liberty, freedom of speech and religion, and freedom from political oppression," he said. "The second way of life is based upon the will of a minority forcibly imposed upon the majority. It relies upon terror and oppression, a controlled press and radio, fixed elections, and the suppression of personal freedoms." For the president, the United States must labor to make sure the choice between these two ways of life—a choice reaching its clearest and deepest manifestation in the twentieth century—was made without coercion. The choice itself was to be made, according to Truman, in light of a universal conception of human freedom and the regime distinction between liberal democracy, which protected the rights of its citizens, and Soviet communism, which ruled by way of terror.[27]

Some critics conclude that containment was negative inherently, and others impugn Truman for standing by regimes in Greece and Turkey that were not democratic. But Truman put forth containment in order to thwart Communist tyranny and to stimulate free and just governments that protected fundamental human rights. The particular actions required to meet these goals differed according to the circumstances; the aim might be achieved by stopping or preventing Communist aggression, as in Iran, or through a combination of encouraging a regime friendly to democracy and repelling communism, as, for example, in Greece. Or prudence might dictate warding off a Communist threat and defending an already democratic regime, as the United States soon did in Western Europe. Truman's particular policies must be seen in light of his overarching purpose and understanding of the ends sought. While he did not believe that Wilsonian self-determination was an end in itself, and the United States would not and could not guarantee liberal democracy to each country in the world, America always defended the principles of liberty and upheld human rights. Truman forthrightly addressed the issue of the current forms of government in Greece and Turkey. "No government is perfect," he said. "One of the chief virtues of a democracy, however, is that its defects are always visible and under democratic processes can be pointed out and corrected." He thought that Greece and Turkey, respectively, were moving and could move in the direction of democracy but would have no chance if under Communist control.[28] The Truman Doctrine—and containment generally—could promote democracy by defending the conditions necessary for freedom.

In theory and practice, the president cast the Truman Doctrine as an approach combining political, economic, and strategic elements. "The seeds of totalitarian regimes are nurtured by misery and want," he noted (a point repeated frequently in Truman speeches), adding that the primary free nation of the world must fuel the hopes of all peoples for a better life. Truman saw an expansionistic drive in Soviet imperialism, and he believed that the Soviet Union had exploited the devastation wrought by World War II and aimed to inflict a totalitarian way of life on its ruins. So while political and economic means were preferred, a military facet had to be included; a component of strength was necessary to foster political and economic viability. With regard to its preeminent position in the world, Truman maintained that America had to accept its duty as leader, and he explained that all free peoples looked to the United States for support in maintaining their freedoms. As he later wrote, "I wanted no hedging in this speech. This was America's answer to the surge of expansion of Communist tyranny. It had to be clear of hesitation or double talk."[29] If the United States faltered in world leadership, he stressed, it endangered world peace and American welfare.

A doctrine in and of itself about the nature of American foreign policy in the Cold War, the Truman Doctrine also was a primary building block of containment and postwar liberal internationalism. Truman emphasized points that endured as themes in containment under his and successive administrations, and he defined the role of national security as part of American foreign policy in terms of both political freedom and military power. A primary objective of U.S. foreign policy, he asserted, was to create conditions in which the United States and other nations worked out "a way of life free from coercion."[30]

Truman also went beyond a Wilsonian approach to define a central theme of American leadership in its approach to the Cold War: the United States must support free peoples who were resisting attempted subjugation by armed minorities or by outside pressures, in order for these free peoples "to work out their own destinies in their own way."[31] Rather than seeking uniformity, Truman set forth in his liberal internationalism what he viewed as the indivisibility of freedom that thrived within a diversity of cultures. While the political action of the Truman Doctrine strived to strengthen the non-Soviet world by encouraging political liberty and economic prosperity, its thought challenged tyranny and concurrently promoted freedom and its many blessings. In this way, Truman made freedom the centerpiece of the most concrete step yet in the founding of postwar American foreign policy.

Debating and Defending Containment

On a practical level, Truman knew that the economic aspect of containment would have to be expanded; he had said as much in the March 12 address and had made general arguments for global economic rehabilitation since he became president, including a major speech on foreign economic policy less than one week before announcing the Truman Doctrine.[32] At the same time, he continued to grapple conceptually with the meaning of world peace with respect to containment and liberal internationalism. In his Jefferson Day dinner speech in April 1947, Truman once more revealed the tension within his own political thought about how to define and achieve peace. He began the speech by arguing that the United States bore a greater responsibility in the mid-twentieth century than in Thomas Jefferson's time because the threats to man's freedom existed in a much different world from that of the late eighteenth century, a world made smaller and more dangerous by the existence of atomic weapons.[33] As a result, Truman continued to place his longterm trust and expectations in the United Nations as a vehicle for "permanent peace" and emphasized that "the United Nations is man's hope of putting out, and keeping out, the fires of war for all time." For part of the speech, America was subordinated to the UN in a manner that, if followed, would have eroded American independence. On the one hand, the president desired a globalized peace that would override individual countries and peoples; on the other, he maintained that the United States, for itself and others, must be strong, united, free, and independent.[34]

Truman, nonetheless, proceeded to hone his conception of freedom by couching it within the context of universal human rights. He spoke of the longing for an "inalienable right" of freedom voiced by oppressed peoples and those who had lost their liberty. Stating that Americans would defend their freedom, if necessary with their lives, he also stressed that his fellow citizens recognized the right of other men and nations to share in that liberty. In short, his liberal internationalism made an argument for human rights that was true universally and autonomous of all regimes but had best been realized in a liberal democratic regime. Truman explained that in his containment there was room for freedom for all peoples. Echoing Jefferson at the time of the Monroe Doctrine and continuing the Truman Doctrine, he said, "We must make that protest [against violations of the rights of nations] effective by aiding those peoples whose freedoms are endangered by foreign pressures." In light of this commitment, Truman reiterated America's willingness to assume the burden of responsibility and leadership in the face of current world events.[35]

As Truman deepened the foundations of containment, contemporary critics of the president lambasted the Truman Doctrine. Henry Wallace immediately sent a telegram to Truman: "The mode of presentation of todays [sic] speech was tantamount to a declaration of war. We dont [sic] want war. Does the USA presume to be bigger than the UNO? We people throughout the world want that the UNO shall be given the right to give us peace."[36] By proclaiming a global conflict between East and West, Wallace said the next day on NBC radio, Truman told the Soviets that the United States was preparing for war. Wallace criticized the president for supporting undemocratic governments in Greece and Turkey and for supplying predominantly military aid. Instead of the Truman Doctrine, he urged America to reclaim its revolutionary status and "give the common man all over the world something better than communism." For Wallace, economic planning—"based on service instead of the outworn ideas of imperialism and power politics"—through the World Bank and backed by the United Nations was the only policy to pursue.[37] Yet he wanted no kind of loan to either Turkey or Greece until their governments were representative and could guarantee that the funds would be used for the welfare of the people. Wallace pressed his attack on the Truman Doctrine in the pages of the *New Republic*, of which he was now editor, and on a spring speaking tour in Europe. In both places, he expressed what would later be called the revisionist interpretation of the Cold War, viewing the USSR either as a wartime ally or a fellow great power, rather than a hostile enemy, and the United States as an instrument of militarism and global empire.

While Wallace voiced the progressive opposition, renowned journalist Walter Lippmann weighed in with a realist critique of the Truman Doctrine. On at least one point, the realist Lippmann and the revisionist Wallace were of the same mind. Lippmann thought that Truman's approach "would take us to the destruction of the U.N." Like Wallace, Lippmann believed that the Truman Doctrine entangled the United Nations in the U.S.-Soviet conflict at a time when the international organization needed the protection of its members, especially the great powers. He blamed the United States for creating problems for the UN, indeed the world, before the World War II peace treaties had been settled; and he disagreed with Truman that the impediment to those treaties was the USSR. Rather than seeing the beginnings of a countercoalition of allies against communism, he reprimanded America for imposing a plan on Greece and Turkey. "The Truman Doctrine," wrote Lippmann, "treats those who are supposed to benefit by it as dependencies of the United States, as instruments of the American policy for 'containing' Russia."[38] As a realist he favored aid to Greece and Turkey, differing from revisionism and from Kennan on Turkey, but he deplored the globalism of the "so-called Truman Doctrine" and said it promised more than it could deliver. He also echoed Kennan in maintaining that particularist policies should replace universalist doctrine. As later political scientists and historians would emphasize, Lippmann argued for a national interest that focused on what he deemed to be of vital importance.[39]

Some historians, such as biographer David McCullough, do not view Truman as universalistic or imperialistic—the interpretations of realism and revisionism, respectively—but as cautious almost to an extreme.[40] It is more accurate to argue that the president exercised prudence as opposed to universalistic impulsiveness or near passivity until pushed into action. The Truman Doctrine was a rapid (within three weeks) and comprehensive response to the message from the British and to the requests from Greece and Turkey, yet it was grounded in the president's long-established understanding of the region's history and present circumstances. And it was during preparation of the congressional address in recognition of the Truman Doctrine's requirements that the White House sent the National Security Act to Congress. At times, Truman's judgment was overshadowed by his optimistic wish for world peace, but this was not the case when it came to preparing and implementing the Truman Doctrine.

Truman built on the political thought of containment and simultaneously exhibited his desire for an unattainable peace in his news conferences of April 17 and May 13, 1947. Instead of focusing on universalism or particularism, realism or Wilsonianism, action or passivity, and issues of American empire, Truman again displayed a division in his thought: he longed for peace under the auspices of a world organization yet, at the same time, sensed that the United States alone possessed the character, regime, and capacity to lead the free-world countercoalition against Communist aggression. Meeting with the American Society of Newspaper Editors on April 17, the president explained that the Truman Doctrine had developed over a period of time following his talk with Molotov in April 1945. He also pointed out that he thought the United

States had dealt fairly with the USSR, but that the Kremlin did not honor its commitments.[41]

The tension in Truman's thought was even more evident in his May 1947 meeting with the Association of Radio News Analysts. In this news conference, the president voiced perhaps his strongest statement of intent to make the United Nations a "going concern," a phrase used frequently by UN supporters from both political parties. "All I am interested in," he said, "is the doctrine of the Republic of the United States of America to restore free government in the world, to make the United Nations work—in the same manner in which the Colonies made the Federal Government work." He championed the UN and ardently suggested he would accept, at least theoretically, a global distribution of resources in order to effectuate peace. Yet in this same May news conference, he again indicted the police state that characterized all totalitarianism.[42]

In April 1947, Eleanor Roosevelt (who was a member of the U.S. delegation to the United Nations at Truman's request and urging) wrote to the president, objecting to the Truman Doctrine on the grounds that it took over "Mr. Churchill's policies in the Near East." Truman's letter of response demonstrated that, while he held onto his hopes for the United Nations, he recognized that an "economically, ideologically and politically sound" peace in 1947 would come more from the United States than the UN. To Mrs. Roosevelt's charge that Greece and Turkey should not be helped because they were not fully democratic, he argued that "if the Greek-Turkish land bridge between the continents is one point at which our democratic forces can stop the advance of Communism that has flowed steadily through the Baltic countries, Poland, Yugoslavia, Rumania, Bulgaria, to some extent Hungary, then this is the place to do it, regardless of whether or not the terrain is good." In this regard, Truman noted the "strategic point" of sending emergency aid of $300 million to Greece and $100 million to Turkey. He told Mrs. Roosevelt that he had thought carefully before proposing the Truman Doctrine and that, "as the issues have developed here and abroad," he had "a growing feeling of certainty in the rightness of our step." To her concerns that he was forsaking liberalism in both domestic and foreign policy, the president answered that "as much as the world needs a progressive America, the American way of life cannot survive unless other peoples who want to adopt that pattern of life throughout the world can do so without fear and in the hope of success."[43]

Truman and Postwar America

Faced with a war unlike any previous one, Harry Truman laid the ground-work for peace through strength and liberal internationalism in his first months in office and throughout 1946. During 1946, against the back-drop of postwar, domestic readjustments, he also had to educate the American people and continue to persuade congressional leaders—who, especially among his fellow Democrats, focused on postwar economics at home and UN primacy abroad—that U.S. engagement in the new world struggle was a necessity. In 1945, mail to the president overwhelmingly favored treating the USSR as an ally. In 1946, while fewer writers viewed the Soviet Union as cooperative in building a postwar order, the majority did not agree that the United States must lead an internationalist foreign policy against the Kremlin. Like the members of Congress who repre-sented them, those who wrote the president favored UN rather than U.S. initiatives. Letting his assistants handle the bulk of the responses, Truman personally answered congressmen, public figures, and others he knew, at-tempting to persuade them and not apologizing for his deepening position in favor of strength. In summer 1946, for instance, he replied to author Pearl Buck's claim of Soviet friendship with a request for evidence of their kindly behavior and a defense of his firmness against Kremlin aggression. Still, his letters during this period generally expressed a hope that peace would prevail. What was becoming obvious to Truman in early 1947 was that the world peace he desired was unattainable under Cold War cir-cumstances. Stemming from his initial understanding that the USSR was expansionist and hostile, he moved to act under circumstances in which the Kremlin was the primary impediment to peace and security at the global and national levels. By 1947, the letters to Truman had changed, with most writers voicing concerns about the dangers posed by the Soviet Union.[44]

Truman did not abandon the goal of peace, however, and contin-ued to identify its prospects with an international organization. Like most Americans and members of Congress, he hoped that one day the United Nations would achieve its intended function. In implementing contain-ment, though, he subordinated a wish for peace to the components of a substantive peace: particularly, freedom and the ability to defend freedom against aggression. Long before others made the connection in this con-text, the president understood not only that domestic and international politics were related but also that the combined effect of domestic regimes and their policies was the key to what happened at the international level. Consequently, the combination of freedom and security throughout the world—established on the basis of free peoples and free nations—was the only way to construct and maintain a framework of peace.

Between 1946 and 1950, Truman reached three important conclusions that further corrected the dominating notion of liberal internationalism that had been associated with Woodrow Wilson, as well as Franklin Roosevelt. First, Truman saw that freedom must precede order so that freedom provided the first and deepest roots for peace. Although not familiar with the theoretical debates in the State Department (and later the academy), he rejected the realist preference for order above all and the Wilsonian confidence in peace through a single universal organization. Second, Truman understood that the regime of a people was decisive in both domestic and international politics; he did not echo Wilson's call for self-determination with an ancillary concern for governing principles. Here, Truman expressed his understanding of justice as a reflection of the principles of the specific regime. He always maintained that the principles that were held and practiced by liberal democracy, unlike those of Communist totalitarianism, grew from and toward concerns of justice.[45] Third, he associated security with strength, rather than FDR's negative freedom from want and fear. Truman's well-rounded definition of strength included military muscle and political order, which meant a government and people first embracing and then maintaining their liberty and justice. These realizations led to Truman's understanding of the American role in the postwar world. And because the United States, as a particular regime and as a people, upheld principles of freedom, justice, and strength, Truman believed it was capable of and obligated to thwarting communism's assault on political liberty, territorial independence, and economic prosperity.

In an undated essay that, by context, was written in early 1947, the president elaborated that peace and prosperity are best based in free governments and equal justice. He recounted the positions that he had put forth—and to which the Soviets had agreed—at Potsdam. He then pointed out the many Kremlin violations and acts of aggression: "[T]hey'd unlawfully attached part of East Prussia and Germany as far west as the Oder to Poland, and had themselves annexed Latvia, Estonia, Lithuania, and a part of East Prussia to Russia, as well as a large area in eastern Poland."

By the beginning of 1947, Truman saw the USSR as "more amenable to reason now than a year ago," but he did not mean that the Soviets had lowered their ambitions. The cause of the Soviet change was America's increasing commitment to strength in order to promote as well as sustain freedom and justice: "I told Mr. Byrnes just one year ago that we'd stand for justice and would not be bulldozed. We've pursued that policy and they've caved in just as Lewis did in the coal strike. Because they are the same sort of cattle—bullies and nothing else. We only want justice and a just peace. That we'll have and that we'll get. There is no difference in totalitarian states, call them Nazi, fascist or communist—they are all the same."[46] But the president did not believe that the challenge from communism was finished. He mildly chastised columnists, radio commentators, and what he termed the "smart boys" for failing to grasp that the American response, rather than Soviet goodwill, had improved still-tense circumstances. Unlike his critics, he thought that bullies, until they changed their attitude and reformed their behavior, had to be met with strength and certitude.

In the spring of 1947, even though he was not well liked or respected by many who were considered experts on world politics, Truman was uniquely suited to the task of articulating and implementing containment.[47] Philosophically and practically, on matters of foreign policy, Truman disagreed with his greatest Democratic models, Wilson and Roosevelt. He may have believed that he continued their general efforts in world politics, but he forged a new way of pursuing peace by promoting freedom, justice, and order at the regime and international levels; he shaped a new American liberal internationalism. Unlike FDR, his immediate predecessor, the self-taught Truman remained close to the pulse of the people and could interpret their aspirations for a peaceful world mingled with their concerns about a growing conflict with international communism. He had the utmost faith that the American people could handle the responsibilities of leading the free world, seeking peace but willing to defend freedom.

Truman's congressional experiences helped prepare him for this moment. Since he had been well liked in Congress during his Senate tenure, he could speak comfortably with his former colleagues of both parties and thus work to construct a bipartisan policy of containment and liberal internationalism. In an odd sense, he benefited from the new Republican majority in Congress and the prominence of and commitment from

Vandenberg. If the Democrats had controlled the Eightieth Congress, they might have responded to Truman as they had in the previous Congress: the United Nations—either in a Wilsonian sense or through a Rooseveltian great power approach—should be the mechanism by which to settle East-West differences. But they were not united at this time, and most still believed that Truman was a pale imitation of FDR. With a Republican Congress, the president had to rely on those who were generally as committed to the UN as the Democrats but who were first and foremost anti-Communist. Republicans such as Vandenberg in the Senate and Charles Eaton of New Jersey and Walter Judd of Minnesota in the House early on had realized, as Truman had, that the Soviet Union was the primary problem in world affairs. These political figures supported the creation of the United Nations and wanted it to work, but they believed, with Truman, that the United States was the country that had to lead the fight in the Cold War. And the president had learned the art of political timing: although he could not have convinced the country or Congress of his view in 1945 or 1946, he knew that the continued pattern of Communist aggression, his own educational efforts, and the slow but decisive turn of American opinion made containment not only a possible but also a timely strategy in 1947.[48]

4

"A noble page in world annals"

The Politics of the Marshall Plan

During World War II, Harry Truman had foreseen the need to rehabilitate a war-racked Europe, an opinion generally shared by the man who became his secretary of state, George Marshall. Attuned to domestic political difficulties, including the unprecedented commitment demanded by a large-scale program to rebuild Europe, the president delegated to Marshall—respected, nearly worshiped, by Congress and the American people—the announcement of the European Recovery Program (ERP) in June 1947. His use of Marshall, in this regard, reflected Truman's understanding not only of the primacy of the president in foreign policymaking but also of political tactics about the necessary role played by Congress, especially when it came to approval of and funding appropriations for the ERP. Although the secretary of state tended to view the ERP as a limited program with a limited, although important, purpose, Truman considered what came to be called the Marshall Plan to be the next development in the strategy of containment and postwar liberal internationalism. In the context of world events in 1947 and 1948—from Communist Party challenges throughout Europe to the Czechoslovak coup to the issue of displaced persons and Palestine—the president understood a political, economic, and strategic nexus between the Truman Doctrine and the Marshall Plan.

Truman Picks the "Wise Men"

Truman knew the importance of trusted and tried counselors, not only for the sake of executing his decisions but also to give expertise and stability to his presidency. When he became president in spring 1945, he was surrounded by Roosevelt's advisors; by the end of 1946, he had selected everyone in the cabinet. Truman was careful in his gradual replacement of cabinet advisors, in order to guarantee proper transitions and accustom the American people to him as president. Politically astute in determining when to install new people, he was able to manage the resignation of Secretary of Commerce Henry Wallace and secure George Marshall's promise to be secretary of state before encouraging James Byrnes to leave the administration.[1] How Truman formed and worked with his own team of advisors was a significant component of the development of containment.

It was no coincidence that Truman chose James Forrestal as the sole holdover from the Roosevelt administration. In 1946, Truman was impressed by Secretary of the Navy Forrestal and former director of the Army-Navy Munitions Board Ferdinand Eberstadt's proposals for reorganization of the War Department—resulting the next year in the creation of the Department of Defense and the National Security Council (NSC)—and the unification of the service branches. He specifically retained Forrestal and selected him as the first secretary of defense in July 1947.[2] Forrestal helped to lay important groundwork for European recovery, and he provided timely assistance in promoting the victory of the Christian Democrats over the Communists and their leftist allies in Italy. While he challenged the president over issues such as civilian control of atomic weapons, defense budgets, and the establishment of the state of Israel, Forrestal consistently agreed with Truman's assessment of the Cold War when it came to theory and grand strategy. Although he increasingly disagreed with him on technical questions, Truman retained Forrestal until it became clear to him that the secretary of defense was declining in mental health. Even when Truman asked for Forrestal's resignation in March 1949, he was hesitant, perhaps because he did not want to hurt Forrestal, but more likely because he did not yet have a satisfactory replacement in mind.[3]

In only one major foreign policy initiative—the Marshall Plan—did the president delegate to his advisors the announcement of a new policy. He did so for three main reasons. First, unlike at the time of the Truman Doctrine, only three months earlier, the secretary of state now believed that the USSR presented a global threat, and so Truman had someone in accord with his own strategic assessment. Second, the president thought that the policy's approval by Congress required an advocate who was perceived as immune to charges of partisanship and was friends with, among others, the prominent Republican senator Arthur Vandenberg; money for economic and political rather than strategic and political reasons, he knew, would be harder for him to extract from a reluctant Congress. Finally, Truman did so because the men in question were George Marshall and Dean Acheson. Truman thought Marshall was the "great one of the age." Acheson had demonstrated his loyalty on several memorable occasions, including his solitary presence at the train station to welcome Truman back to Washington after the loss of Congress to the GOP in the 1946 election. Although Truman retained an autonomous view of America's role in the world, containment, and the meaning of the Cold War, their influence on him concerning particular policies was often significant.

Neither Marshall nor Acheson fully saw the Soviets as a global threat until 1947. Indeed, until spring 1947, Marshall was willing to grant leniency to Stalin and thought that the Communists would respond to negotiation; he remained convinced that the Nationalists in China were little different from the Communists and made no clear anti-Communist argument for that country's future. A military man and student of history, Marshall seemed not to recognize the unique role of ideology in the Cold War.[4] As for Acheson, he maintained a largely realist attitude toward the developing East-West conflict. In late 1945, he agreed with retiring secretary of war Henry Stimson's proposal to break the Anglo-American monopoly on the atomic bomb and include the Soviets in future developments.[5] When Paul Nitze interpreted Stalin's February 1946 election address as a delayed declaration of war against the United States, Acheson told him, "Paul, you see hobgoblins under the bed. They aren't there. Forget it!"[6] The following month he thought that the American government should distance itself from Churchill's message in the Fulton address. It was Greece and Turkey—particularly, Kremlin pressure on the Turkish Straits and the possibility that the Soviets would penetrate three continents—rather than earlier events in Eastern Europe, that convinced Acheson that the USSR had to be countered by the Truman Doctrine.[7] Privately, he preferred a narrow, realist reading of containment and the Cold War, although publicly he was in strong support of and sought congressional and public backing of the president's policies.[8]

Truman consistently relied on Marshall and Acheson in 1947 and 1948, but he made them align their tactics and policy proposals with his understanding of the Cold War as a political struggle against a Communist imperial power. In this sense, it mattered who was president: if FDR had been president after World War II, Marshall and Acheson would have had more success in pushing realist policies—Marshall by temperament and instinct, and Acheson by conviction and choice. The years 1945 and 1946 witnessed the early development of the strategy of containment, and 1947 through 1949 saw containment mature under Truman, but this strategy would likely have differed fundamentally—with spheres of influence, more Soviet advances, and conciliatory negotiations on Europe's future—under Roosevelt.

Many have commented on the unlikely attachment between the unpolished Truman from the Midwest and the sophisticated Acheson of the East Coast. During the pivotal two weeks before the Truman Doctrine address, Acheson proved himself indispensable to the president, articulating the issues passionately and persuasively to members of Congress and helping Truman prepare for the speech.[9] Acheson himself remembered some of his work in promoting the Truman Doctrine as an exaggeration of threats.[10] But in 1947 and in 1948, when others thought that the president would lose the election, Acheson supported and followed Truman's interpretation of the Cold War. And in April 1945, he had believed in the president's potential and abilities when many doubted that Truman could replace Roosevelt and be an effective leader. Truman prized loyalty in his subordinates, and he believed that, with Acheson, he was getting someone who was loyal to the presidency and to him in that office. Truman knew that he wanted to elevate Acheson to secretary of state in 1949 upon Marshall's retirement; when Acheson came under severe attack in late 1949 and in 1950 for losing China to communism, the president defended his man even at the cost of contradicting his own political thought of containment.[11]

George Marshall, in contrast, was viewed by Truman in heroic proportions. The president, like many other Americans, had long admired the general: as senator (even while FDR was president), Truman often called Marshall the "greatest living American." Various reminiscences relate how the senator offered to be reactivated as a colonel in World War II in order to help "America's greatest soldier," although Marshall thought that Truman could do more good as head of the Senate Special Committee to Investigate the National Defense Program.[12] Truman's esteem for Marshall grew during the rest of the war, and they corresponded on military issues. Once president, Truman asked the general to lead a mission to China in

December 1945 to mediate a peace settlement and governmental cooperation between the Nationalist and Communist factions. After his experience with Byrnes—a former colleague who thought that he was equal to
or better than his president—Truman may have been expected to pick
a weak secretary of state. The president, however, knew that the State
Department needed someone who not only understood peace and war
but also had the administrative expertise to rebuild an agency to meet
Cold War circumstances. Displaying his own confidence, Truman sought
a person who would be respected by members of both major political
parties and by critics of the administration. In February 1947, the president handwrote in his appointment notes after a half-hour meeting with
Marshall: "The more I see and talke [*sic*] to him the more certain I am
he's the great one of the age. I am surely lucky to have his friendship and
support."[13]

In Marshall, Truman got someone who maintained nonpartisan-
ship—which the general sometimes and others often translated as bipartisanship—as his watchword and philosophy. Shortly after becoming
secretary in January 1947, for example, Marshall refused to attend the annual Jefferson Day dinner in April.[14] In a private meeting after Marshall's
swearing in as secretary, Truman expounded his foreign policy views to
the general, who, in turn, emphasized his determination not to accept any
"political office."[15]

To say that Truman nearly worshiped Marshall and saw him above the
political fray does not mean that he subordinated himself to the secretary
of state. In January 1947, Marshall did not view the Soviets as an immediate, overwhelming threat and continued to argue for postwar cooperation.
But when Marshall had realist doubts about the Truman Doctrine and
did not endorse the speech until March 11, the president acted on his
own. Truman differed from a vocal Marshall and almost everyone else in
his administration, for instance, when he championed the recognition of
Israel in 1948. With respect to the Cold War, the secretary of state soon
changed his mind as a consequence of the Moscow conference in spring
1947, where he experienced Stalin's obstructiveness and Molotov's deceit,
and his close relations with Vandenberg and Forrestal probably fortified
the development in his opinions. Marshall's memoranda to the president
from Moscow in March and April 1947 reveal a man who aimed to dis-
charge Truman's command to stand firm against the USSR, although the
secretary of state was frustrated when the White House radioed him to

"give the Russians hell." As he remembered, "At that time, my facilities
for giving them hell—and I am a soldier and know something about the
ability to give hell—was 1-1/3 divisions over the entire United States.
This is quite a proposition when you deal with somebody with over 260
[divisions] and you have 1-1/3."[16] What Marshall brought back to the
president was a firsthand observation about Soviet ideology, policy, and
intransigence. "General Marshall felt that Stalin was obviously waiting
for Europe, harassed and torn by the war and in virtual ruins, to collapse
and fall into the Communist orbit," recorded State Department Soviet
expert Charles Bohlen, conveying Marshall's conviction that recovery was
needed for Europe to stand against Moscow.[17]

The Moscow conference, and what he learned on his trip to the Soviet
Union, reshaped the context of Marshall's contribution to the plan that
would bear his name. The secretary of state returned from Moscow with
handwritten notes of what he wanted to say to the American people. The
radio address that developed out of those notes—which was endorsed by
Truman—was a pivotal moment for Marshall. Perhaps the most famous
line from the speech expressed his concern about the need for a quicker
economic recovery of Europe: "The patient is sinking while the doctors
deliberate. So I believe that action cannot await compromise through exhaustion." The chief impediment to any agreement concerning Europe's
recovery, he said, was the Soviet positions regarding Germany and Austria:
for the former, the USSR wanted not only centralized control of the government and its economy but also excessive reparations from its produc-
tion output; for the latter, the Kremlin demanded "such a large portion"
of the Austrian economy that its survival "as an independent self-supporting
state would be dubious." In advancing such criticisms, Marshall reprimanded the Soviet Union for violating the Potsdam agreements, rewriting
the Yalta accords, and prompting an economic decline that would lead to
the "inevitable emergence of dictatorship and strife." While he stated that
the United States must try to understand the point of view of those with
whom it differed, he also rejected "compromise on great principles in order to achieve agreement for agreement's sake." He then praised the assistance of Republican Senator Arthur Vandenberg and Democratic Senator
Tom Connally in helping to formulate a "unity of purpose" in American
foreign policy and the Truman Doctrine.[18] The change in Marshall's position (and the difference between him and Byrnes) was clear. Although he
believed that economic conditions and problems preceded and undergird-

ed governmental arrangements—and his chief worry remained more economic than political or military—the secretary of state was now a strong public supporter of the Truman Doctrine.

The Marshall Plan

In the weeks preceding the announcement of the Marshall Plan, the tensions in Truman's general theory of international politics—especially between American independent action and UN leadership—were ever present. In a special conference with the Association of Radio News Analysts on May 13, 1947, he said that repeated Soviet violations of agreements proved that the Kremlin understood only the language of strength. (Truman also noted that he spoke that language and would speak it to the Soviets.) At the same time, he wanted peace more than anything in the world so that all could work together for a "proper distribution of the things that we need today."[19] At the signing of Congress's passage of Greek and Turkish aid on May 22, 1947, the president persisted in equating American and UN goals, saying, "the United States is helping to further aims and purposes identical with those of the United Nations." He pledged American support of the UN as a part of the Truman Doctrine.[20] By June 5, however, when the secretary of state gave his address at Harvard announcing the European Recovery Program, Truman termed the Greek-Turkish aid program a twofold effort to restore the two countries' economies and "to help those nations which want to preserve their freedoms and to set up a bulwark against totalitarian aggression."[21] At least implicitly, if not outright, the president increasingly set aside the United Nations as the primary vehicle for freedom and peace and presented the United States as the fulcrum of a countercoalition against Communist tyranny.

Events in Europe provided the context for the American response and stiffened its resolve. While Europe suffered another harsh winter and further economic despair, the Communist parties in France and Italy were making new advances. Indeed, throughout 1947 and into 1948, it was unclear if France and Italy could prevent Communist takeovers; although ejected from the two countries' cabinets in May 1947, Communists did not concede defeat. In France, for example, under the guise of a purge of alleged wartime collaborators, anti-Communists were removed from the armed forces, administrative system, courts, schools, and universities. Infiltrated by Communists, various political parties, coalition governments, and mass media in both countries sabotaged political, economic, and military recovery. Between 1945 and 1951, when special courts under Communist influence ceased operating in France and Italy, a minimum of 320,000 Frenchmen were killed or purged, or otherwise disappeared. Of the estimated 112,000 killed in that number, many were subject to summary executions. At least 360,000, meanwhile, were killed in Italy, where similar infiltration occurred. In Eastern Europe, the Soviet coup in Hungary on May 30, 1947, which ousted Premier Ferenc Nagy, indicated the worsening situation not only there but throughout Europe.[22] American aid to Hungary, which had been intended to encourage resistance to communism and foster economic recovery, was terminated.

The Marshall Plan denoted the second major step in containment's political thought and implementation. Some have argued that it grew out of Undersecretary of State Dean Acheson's Delta Council speech in Cleveland, Mississippi, on May 8, 1947.[23] What Acheson said, however, reinforced containment as the president had formally promulgated it on March 12 and specifically extended the president's official remarks on foreign economic policy delivered at Baylor University on March 6, 1947. The Baylor address was billed in advance as a major new statement and was covered as such by the press. In describing the indivisible connection between politics and economics, Truman argued that in a world of doubt and flux "the decisive factor will be the type of leadership that the United States gives the world," adding, "We are the giant of the economic world. Whether we like it or not, the future pattern of economic relations depends upon us."[24] In his memoir, the president paired this address with his Truman Doctrine speech less than a week later as the twin bases for American Cold War policy. As he explained at Baylor, political freedom and economic freedom are related, but political freedom precedes economic freedom. Apart from revealing Truman's general understanding of the relationship between politics and economics, this address shows that Truman was thinking and speaking about what would become the ERP. The president was probably not more explicit at the time of the Baylor University remarks because he did not want to deflect attention from his upcoming message to Congress and the specific crises in Greece and Turkey.[25]

Acheson could be more explicit in the Delta speech two months later. The president had been invited to speak but was unable to attend and sent the undersecretary as his substitute. They had talked over the content of the speech, and Truman approved its final contents.[26] It is not surprising, then, that Acheson presented the tentative plan for European recovery as an extension of Truman's policy announcement of March. Most of the speech pertained to economic specifics, appropriate to the topic of his remarks and to his position as undersecretary. But even in a somewhat dry economic talk, Acheson was building on the president's emerging containment, stressing that free peoples "seeking to preserve their independence and democratic institutions and human freedoms against totalitarian pressures, either internal or external" would receive top priority in American aid. Then he quoted from the Truman Doctrine speech regarding the nature of totalitarian regimes and their undermining of peace and, thus, U.S. security.[27]

Marshall's June 5, 1947, commencement address at Harvard University—also approved by Truman—followed within a month. Billions of dollars, much more than the millions of the Truman Doctrine, were involved in the program. Because the president and the secretary of state were concerned that the scope of the program would divide members of Congress, wanted no advance debate to mar the chances of its passage, and sought an early European commitment to the ERP without adverse publicity, secrecy surrounded the announcement of the Marshall Plan.[28] It is clear from the speech that Marshall now grasped the strategic challenge confronting the United States, and he championed Truman's emphasis on the interplay of politics and economics in free and healthy governments.[29] For almost a year, Marshall, as a tireless tactician, would supplement the president's efforts to obtain congressional approval of the European Recovery Program: he not only worked intensively with Vandenberg to secure the votes of representatives and senators but also lobbied trade-related interest groups.[30]

Despite his contributions to the Harvard speech, George Kennan rejected Truman's sense of the Marshall Plan. Within days of Marshall's address, he contended that the Communists in France and Italy did not threaten those countries; rather, he said, in what quickly became a realist refrain, the real source of the problem was the lack of food and raw materials and the need for economic rehabilitation.[31] From a utilitarian perspective, Kennan argued later in 1947 that stability in international relations must rest on a "natural balance of national and regional forces" and that the "chief beauty" of the Marshall Plan was removing "some of the burden of 'bi-polarity'" from American shoulders.[32] By the end of the year, he was pessimistic about the ERP's future and angry at both the Europeans and Congress—the former for clutching at American dollars rather than accepting responsibility for their own economic recovery, and the latter for dissipating the psychological benefit of the Marshall Plan in Europe through their months of debate. Kennan defined politics in terms of efficiency, as well as the balance of power. He recanted any support he might have given containment, on the grounds that the U.S. government lacked "the ability to 'operate' politically at all, in the foreign field" and that, "even if Congress passes the aid bill, its administration will be cumbersome, inflexible and unpolitical."[33]

In the coming months, despite having called for massive aid for Western Europe, Walter Lippmann also would doubt the Marshall Plan's possibilities. His criticism echoed that of Kennan, because he thought that the State Department—including Marshall, Undersecretary of State Robert Lovett, Bohlen, and Kennan—was suffering from "a real case of schizophrenia": "When they study the realities they come to one set of conclusions; when they construct their political ideas they come to an opposite set." According to Lippmann, a paranoid view of the USSR most likely would prevail in framing the Marshall Plan, which would defeat what he saw as the necessarily narrow economic rehabilitation of Europe apart from a Cold War setting. He believed that the Soviets had been put on the defensive in 1947 by American military power in the eastern Mediterranean, rather than by the announcement of the Marshall Plan. His solution was for both the United States and the USSR to leave Europe.[34]

Like Lippmann, but for more progressive reasons, Henry Wallace favored the European Recovery Program if it were removed from the Cold War conflict. In a campaign manifesto of 1948, Wallace argued that "unused American capital" should underwrite well-planned relief programs. He said that he had supported the humanitarian aspects of the Marshall Plan, and the plan itself, "until it became apparent that it was to be administered altogether outside the U.N., in the spirit of the Truman Doctrine." Wallace thus rejected the Marshall Plan for being an "instrument of cold war against Russia," and called for the program to be brought under UN control as quickly as possible. And he thought that the ERP should be exclusively economic. Sensitive to charges that he was aiding the Communists, he maintained that his position was "not necessarily" either Communist or pro-Russian.[35]

While mostly commending the Marshall Plan in a June 1947 letter to Secretary Marshall, former secretary of state James Byrnes fused the Lippmann and Wallace criticisms of the Truman Doctrine. Like Wallace and Lippmann, as well as Kennan, Byrnes thought that the Truman Doctrine and attendant American foreign policy were "only leading us to World War III." He misconstrued Marshall's speech as a plan for the economic federation of Europe, and he proposed a political federation of Europe followed by a "democratic federation" of the whole world, preferably with Russia included. Similar to other critics of Truman, Byrnes divorced the Marshall Plan from the Truman Doctrine; he viewed the Marshall Plan as a corrective to the Truman Doctrine and as a step toward what he called "democratic Federal World Government."[36]

The Marshall *Plan* must be understood as it was presented, however, in light of the Truman *Doctrine*. To be sure, the ERP addressed the economic devastation that defined the early postwar period of the Cold War. But as Truman later explained, "the world now realizes that without the Marshall Plan it would have been difficult for western Europe to remain free from the tyranny of communism."[37] Marshall connected the idea of recovery to containment. At Harvard, he said of the plan precisely what critics overlook: "Its purpose should be the revival of a working economy in the world so as to permit the emergence of political and social conditions in which free institutions can exist. . . . Furthermore, governments, political parties, or groups which seek to perpetuate human misery in order to profit therefrom politically or otherwise will encounter the opposition of the United States."[38] According to the Truman Doctrine, as elaborated here by Marshall, free nations require a concomitant infrastructure of free institutions in order to prosper.

Some have argued that the Marshall Plan constituted a New Deal for Western Europe. In terms of being a massive national response to an immediate and continuing economic crisis, this is correct. But in the Marshall Plan, the American government was not only investing outside its borders in an economically devastated Western Europe but also acting within the extraordinary—and ongoing—circumstances of the Cold War. There were always clear objectives, in terms of goals and time, to the program. Priming the pump through the ERP meant using every possible opportunity for aid, but concentrating it at points where it would cause immediate recovery, with the final aim of establishing a self-sufficient European economy. And as Truman had stressed at Baylor University, the

European Recovery Program would not be simply a series of government programs: "Freedom has flourished where power has been dispersed. It has languished where power has been too highly centralized."[39] If government had to be involved in emergency circumstances, he also expected the private sector to participate in recovery and growth for the political as well as economic health of Europe and the world. The Truman Doctrine granted political, economic, and military assistance for sustenance; now the Marshall Plan offered economic and political aid for recovery. Both intended to deter the advance of totalitarianism, as well as to promote liberal democracy and economic growth. Although they differed in practice according to the particular conditions they addressed, they were united in the political thought of containment.

Aftermath and Developments in Europe

The United States offered the Marshall Plan to all of Europe. After Poland, Hungary, and Czechoslovakia expressed interest in June 1947, Stalin rejected the ERP and prevented his satellite countries from participating in the program. Indeed, the Soviets saw the Marshall Plan as "directed toward the establishment of a West European bloc as an instrument of American policy."[40] Stalin personally ordered the Czechoslovak delegation to withdraw "immediately" from the first Marshall Plan talks held in Paris in July.[41] The Kremlin also intensified its hold on Eastern Europe by exploiting the conditions in each country. The Red Army controlled the countries it still occupied, as well as the political trials during the second half of 1947 that were particularly ruthless in the former allies of Nazi Germany, notably Hungary, Romania, and Bulgaria. The communization process in Hungary, which began at least as early as November 1945, when the Communists chipped away at the coalition government elected at that time, built on Soviet occupation of the country and the ouster of Nagy. In rigged elections held in August 1947, the Communists claimed 22 percent nationally, purged left-wing anti-Communists, and eventually took over the government, much as they did in Bulgaria and Romania. In the case of Romania, Iuliu Maniu and other opposition leaders against communism were arrested in July, and the National Peasant Party was dissolved by the Communist-dominated national assembly. (Later Maniu was tried, convicted, and sentenced to life in prison, where he died in 1952.) The Agrarian Union Party in Bulgaria was eliminated similarly, and its leader, Nikola Petkov, was arrested in June for planning a coup against the Communists; in September, Petkov was hanged in Sofia. Violent purges by the Communists continued until December, when a Communist government was secured and Soviet troops were able to leave Bulgaria.[42]

In fall 1947, the Kremlin also formally set up the Communist Information Bureau—better known as the Cominform—with the stated purpose of expanding international communism according to the conditions in each country. Many scholars have argued that this enterprise was defensive and short-lived on the part of the Soviets, created in reaction to the Marshall Plan. Archival evidence from Hungary, however, shows that the Kremlin had set Cominform plans in motion as early as March 1946, but delayed implementation until late 1947 so as to maintain Communist popularity during the 1946 elections in France, Czechoslovakia, and Romania, as well as Moscow's "neutral position" in the European peace settlement talks.[43] And the British government recently revealed that it intercepted Moscow's instructions to the European Communist parties from mid-1943 through 1945, during which the Department of International Information (OMI)—the successor organization to the Communist International (often called the Comintern)—pursued a highly developed national-front strategy for the liberated countries throughout Europe.[44] Further, the Cominform included the French and Italian Communist parties as part of its manifesto, and both parties were seen as likely advancing the cause of communization in the forthcoming 1948 elections. Although the Kremlin had technically disbanded the Comintern in 1943 and publicly sworn off world revolution, the Cominform sought to validate the ideological and physical expansionism of Soviet foreign policy.[45] It spearheaded a Moscow peace movement against the West that took shape and intensified over the next few years.[46]

The Cominform reflected the renewed emphasis on ideology and Soviet patriotism embodied in Zhdanovschina—a policy named after Politburo member Andrei Zhdanov—which exterminated and otherwise removed Communists at odds with Stalin's policies. Zhdanov asserted that Marxism-Leninism had a messianic destiny and the right to teach others the new human morality of communism by any means. He highlighted the Communist conception of the two-camp theory of the world, an imperialist and "antidemocratic" one dominated by the United States and a "democratic" one of peace and socialism led by the USSR. Zhdanovschina, theoretically, and the Cominform, institutionally, became integral to the

Soviet propaganda effort that strived to undermine Europe. In addition, they targeted the strongest link within the free-world countercoalition, the U.S.-British relationship, by depicting the Marshall Plan as a direct threat to British independence.[47]

Knowledgeable contemporary critics minimized the danger to Europe from the Soviets in summer and fall 1947. Lippmann, for one, argued in November 1947 that the Soviets already had lost the Cold War to superior American power, although, "of course, like the Germans and the Japanese after they knew they were beaten, they continued to fight on."[48] By contrast, Truman saw a direct and indirect threat. In September, he explained that the French and Italians were in dire straits, worse than in 1946, because of their shortage of food and fuel, and that the Communists sought to exploit this predicament. Focusing on the "exceedingly grave" situation in Italy, he told a group of editors of business and trade papers in September 1947, "Should anything happen that Italy would go and the Jugoslavs should move in, France would go, and we have the Iron Curtain at the Atlantic Ocean. There would be nothing for us to do then but move out completely and prepare for war. That we don't want to do."[49] As he had said the previous day to congressional leaders, given the losses in Eastern Europe, it was imperative that France and Italy survive the critical winter of 1947–48 as free and independent nations.

Truman formally affixed the Marshall Plan to containment in a December 1947 message to Congress, and he publicly conveyed the magnitude of the program in his November speech before Congress's special session to consider passage of interim aid (especially to Austria, France, Italy, and China) and the ERP. He emphasized that the economic strength of the United States, which was able to help other countries in their recovery from World War II, came from America's free institutions. Truman also stressed the significance of unalienable rights and of liberal democracy, and he argued that they must be protected for the nation to remain strong. "Our moral strength, resulting from our faith in human rights," he noted, "is the inspiration of free men everywhere." American strength, he continued, was not due to chance but to the "wise decisions and bold actions taken by free and courageous men" throughout its history. And although he spoke of that strength "with humility," adding that the American people were still learning that great responsibility came with great power, he argued that the United States had a responsibility to build a world community of free, strong, and independent nations.[50] When Congress approved the European Recovery Program, Truman concluded, it "will have written a noble page in world annals."[51]

After Congress passed the interim aid act and as it debated the ERP in December, Truman urged that America complete its duty toward Europe's recovery from the devastation of World War II.[52] He carefully distinguished real recovery from a relief program that, to him, would be insufficient and improper in the long term. And again Truman united the Marshall Plan with the overarching thought of containment: "It will also determine in large part whether the free nations of the world can look forward to a peaceful and prosperous future as independent states, or whether they must live in poverty and fear of selfish totalitarian aggression." European recovery, he asserted, was essential to maintaining the civilization at the root of the American way of life, the civilization that Communist imperialism sought to destroy. He spoke of the necessity of shoring up the nations of Europe internally and externally against totalitarian pressures, and, praising all the free and democratic nations of Europe, he termed them a bulwark for the principles of freedom, justice, and the dignity of the individual. Within the parameters of the UN's principles yet relying on American leadership, and reflecting his desire for world peace, he said the Marshall Plan was called for out of both wisdom and necessity.[53]

Palestine

The Truman Doctrine and the Marshall Plan can, of course, be seen in a humanitarian light. What we now call human rights, the president placed in the context of his political and, even, theological understanding of world events and liberal internationalism. Truman, often depicted as unsentimental, felt keenly the displacement, enslavement, and death of various peoples by tyranny, whether Nazi or Communist. From the early postwar period into 1948 when the problem was at its worst, he frequently commented in private meetings about the starvation of people throughout Europe and sometimes saw the Soviets aggravating the grim food situation. And he deplored the displacement of hundreds of thousands of Europeans in the wake of World War II and communism's spread. Truman was more successful in promoting larger immigration numbers to the United States, especially of Jews and Asians, later in his presidency; nevertheless, he tried to liberalize immigration in 1945 through 1947 (in the face of much congressional hostility), particularly as a way of addressing the problem of displaced persons. He wanted the same for those who sought to stay in their native countries or, when that was not possible, make homes in new countries. Apart from the ERP's stated intentions, the president hoped that the program directly and indirectly would ameliorate a postwar problem that he viewed as a calamity.

In this regard, a homeland for the Jews, who made up 20 percent of the displaced persons, was vital to Truman. Much has been speculated—ranging from domestic politics to preemption of Soviet influence in the Middle East—about his motivations for promoting a Jewish homeland and, in May 1948, recognizing the new state of Israel. To be sure, the president aimed to prevent a Kremlin foothold in the region, as evidenced by the Truman Doctrine. And it was hoped that the new Jewish state would introduce democracy to the Middle East. On the home front, Truman never forgot that Jews were a core constituency in the Democratic Party and could deliver New York State in a presidential election. But beyond Cold War strategic concerns and various domestic interests, Truman had long been sympathetic to the plight of the Jewish people. His study of history and the Bible informed his opinions of the Jews and the region of the Middle East, while his lifelong friendship with businessman Eddie Jacobson—which, apart from their army service in World War I and owning a store together from 1919 into 1922, included many poker games with other Jewish friends—and his working relationships with advisors Max Lowenthal, David Niles, and others during his senatorial and presidential years reinforced his religious tolerance.[54] He believed firmly in the Balfour Declaration of 1917, in which the British had promised support to the Jews for a national homeland in Palestine. In the 1930s, he handled many requests to facilitate Jewish emigration from Germany and, in 1939, charged that a shift in British policy toward Palestine undermined Balfour's promise to the Jews and added "to the long list of surrender to the axis powers."[55] Along with many other members of Congress in March 1942, Senator Truman signed a declaration of support for the Balfour Declaration on the occasion of its twenty-fifth anniversary and, in April 1943, openly recognized that the Nazis sought to slaughter the Jews, which was another reason to support a Jewish homeland: "Today—not tomorrow—we must do all that is humanly possible to provide a haven and place of safety for all those who can be grasped from the hands of the Nazi butchers. Free lands must be opened to them."[56]

Although the Holocaust had caused the displacement as well as deaths of millions of Jews, Truman identified a legitimate Jewish right to Palestine that preceded the horrors of the Second World War and the Balfour Declaration. He would cite, among other biblical passages, 1 Deuteronomy 8 as his evidence—"Behold, I have given up the land before you; go in and take possession of the land which the Lord hath sworn unto your fathers, to Abraham, to Isaac, and to Jacob"—and believed that historical, moral, and religious rights met in their defense of a Jewish state.[57] Special Counsel Clark Clifford stressed that Truman was a student of the Old Testament, especially its commitment to a homeland for the Jewish people, and would make references to Isaiah and other prophets to make his case. Truman's reading of the Bible and ancient history led him to take up Palestine as the proper homeland, "even when others who were sympathetic to the plight of the Jews were talking of sending them to places like Brazil."[58] It is striking that one of Truman's favorite psalms was 137: "By the rivers of Babylon, there we sat down, yea, we wept, when we remembered Zion."[59]

The aims of immigration to Palestine and recognition of a new Jewish state became intertwined for Truman. He dealt with the compound issue from almost the beginning of his presidency, including after the debate of partition versus trusteeship for Palestine became a thorny test for the fledgling United Nations. Building on the foundation of the Balfour Declaration, President Truman first backed partition of Palestine and then, on May 14, 1948, within minutes of its declaration of independence, had the United States confer de facto recognition on the state of Israel. Within a week of Israel's first elections in late January 1949 to establish its government and having been informed officially of the results, the United States extended de jure recognition.[60] Before, during, and after these developments, Truman advocated a home, as well as general, liberalized international immigration, for the Jews, and did so in the face of significant opposition from the Arab world.

In this way, he advanced a strategy in which immigration to Palestine—morally important in and of itself—became the wedge to achieve the end goal of a Jewish state; and he acted, at the time without expectation that Israel could be established as early as May 1948. Truman was at odds with many of his advisors and the leadership of the British government, who thought that the president's Palestine policy was ill conceived, had deteriorated to the point of failure in summer 1946, and should be handed over to the State Department and the UN. But Truman refused. His October

1946 Yom Kippur statement—issued on the eve of the holiest Jewish holiday—
was disapprovingly viewed as a two-step endorsement of immediately increased immigration followed by the "creation of a viable Jewish state."
His polite but firm message later that month to the king of Saudi Arabia
reiterated his belief that at least 100,000 Jewish survivors of the Holocaust
should receive immediate entry to Palestine—to find shelter and to "contribute their talents and energies to the upbuilding of the Jewish National
Home"—and that the U.S. government remained committed to a Jewish
state in Palestine.[61]

Truman persevered in spite of resistance from most of the State Department,
the secretary of defense, and other top advisors in his administration.
With respect to the State Department, Truman had thought that Marshall
would "set them right but he has had too much to do and the 3rd & 4th
levels over there are the same striped pants conspirators." He blamed them
in March 1948 for having "balled up the Palestine situation" by promoting trusteeship rather than partition for Palestine.[62] In this context, the
president came the closest he ever did to criticizing Marshall. On the same
day that he expressed his frustration with lower-level State Department
personnel, he also wrote, "I spend the day trying to right what has happened. No luck. Marshall makes a statement. Doesn't help me a mite."[63]
No help was forthcoming. Two days before the president's recognition of
the state of Israel in May 1948, the secretary of state intensified his objections to Truman in a tense Oval Office meeting. Marshall went as far as to
say that, if he voted in the next election, he would vote against the president if Truman recognized the Jewish state.[64] Clifford was the only key
advisor who consistently advocated the president's position on Palestine.
Truman relied on him to manage the opposition from Marshall, Forrestal,
and others, so that he could concentrate on the larger international picture. Between them, Clifford and Undersecretary of State Robert Lovett
(who sided with Marshall) placated the secretary of state, and Truman
conferred recognition of the state of Israel without causing a public breach
with Marshall.

Truman was under intense pressure domestically and internationally. At home, he refused to take sides with not only pro-Arab and other
leery State Department professionals but also with Zionist interest groups;
abroad, he withstood the Arabs, British, and Zionists. He believed that
Jews deserved equality, not preferential treatment, in setting up their state
and government.[65] "I surely wish God Almighty would give the Children

of Israel an Isaiah, the Christians a St. Paul, and the Sons of Ishmael a peep at the Golden Rule," he told Niles, an FDR holdover and long-time White House liaison to northeastern Jewish liberals, in May 1947.[66] Late in February 1948, he explained his disappointment with the fighting among the parties involved to his friend, Jacobson: "The Jews are so emotional, and the Arabs are so difficult to talk with that it is almost impossible to get anything done. The British, of course, have been exceedingly noncooperative in arriving at a conclusion. The Zionists, of course, have expected a big stick approach on our part, and naturally have been disappointed when we can't do that."[67] Still, a visit from Jacobson in mid-March prompted Truman to meet secretly with Zionist leader Chaim Weizmann five days later and promise recognition of a new Jewish state even if the United Nations abandoned partition for a trusteeship. Although Truman voiced doubt at the time about the possibility of a desirable outcome, he vowed to continue his support for the partition of Palestine and recognition of a homeland for the Jews. In doing so, he acted independently, avoided the extremes, and steadily pursued what he saw as his moral commitment to the Jewish people. Two months later the new state was born, and Truman met openly with Weizmann, the first president of Israel, at the White House in late May.

The Czechoslovak Coup and American Strength

While drawn, as always, by his desire for perpetual peace, Truman consistently reaffirmed the thought and action of containment. His words and deeds were propelled, in large part, by mounting evidence of Communist aggression. In the spring of 1948, this evidence crystallized in a Communist coup in Czechoslovakia.[68] The Soviets had begun the communization of Czechoslovakia in 1944 through Red Army occupation. After the May 1946 elections, they had followed up by infiltrating the government and eliminating political opposition. These moves gained them a parliamentary majority and control of the cabinet and, therefore, the key ministries. The Communist minister of the interior transformed the police into an arm of the party. But by November 1947, the anti-Communists in Czechoslovakia had rejuvenated themselves, giving the United States and the rest of Europe hope that this country might shake off Communist domination. Despite Czechoslovak President Eduard Benes's forced cooperation with the Soviets (and the Nazis before them), Czechoslovakia previously had closer ties with the West than any other central European nation. Before the elections scheduled for spring 1948, the Democrats and Socialists resigned from the government with the belief that they could force the issue their way. After the deputy foreign minister of the USSR, Valerian Zorin, appeared in Prague, however, the physically and politically weakened Benes agreed that a Communist should head the next government. After the Communists staged street demonstrations, searched the headquarters of non-Communist parties, arrested hostile politicians, and organized Soviet "action committees" to take over the ministries, factories, newspapers, radio stations, and combat organizations, the Social Democrats once again offered to collaborate with the Communists rather than join the anti-Communist elements.[69] Under pressure from the Czechoslovak Communist leader, Benes swore in a new cabinet of Communists on February 27. Zorin only then returned to Moscow.[70]

From the beginning, Truman thought that the collapse of Czechoslovakia fortified Communists in Finland, Greece, and Italy and could provide a springboard for Communist infiltration of other parts of Europe. The president's sense of urgency after the coup was not merely rhetorical. For at least six months, despite objections from members of his cabinet, he had maintained that political and economic strength needed more military backing.[71] The democracies of Western Europe gradually had come to the same conclusion. Believing that inaction invited defeat, Truman endorsed the Brussels pact, ordered the buildup of American military strength and training, and planted the theoretical seeds for NATO. It was in light of the Czechoslovak coup that Congress not only approved the president's request to fund the Marshall Plan but also dramatically increased military appropriations and reinstated the Selective Service program.[72] Some critics (dismissing Zorin's presence in Czechoslovakia during the coup, for instance) downplayed the importance of events in Czechoslovakia and referred to the American response to the coup as commencing the March "war scare." Kennan disparaged the whole year as such and claimed that Western hysteria was "a sublimated fear—fear of our own inadequacy."[73] Wallace, for his part, argued that Greek and Turkish aid and the ERP forced the Kremlin to react defensively, if not inevitably, in Czechoslovakia. The president, however, saw Soviet aggression and concluded that the Cold War was worsening.

In a special message to Congress on March 17, 1948, Truman listed instances of Soviet belligerency, stressing that the USSR and its agents had destroyed the independence and democratic character of much of

Eastern and Central Europe, and he traced Communist attempts to undermine the recovery program they had been invited to join. He argued that "measures for economic rehabilitation alone are not enough. The free nations of Europe realize that economic recovery, if it is to succeed, must be afforded some measure of protection against internal and external aggression." Since Poland had been lost during the Second World War and Czechoslovakia was now gone, he continued, Germany had become the pivotal battleground. Because of this development, and in order to protect the free nations of Europe, he reiterated that Western forces would remain in Germany until a real peace was secured in Europe. He explained his actions as a strengthening of the forces for freedom, justice, and peace, as represented by the United Nations and the free world. Even though Truman referred to the UN, he went on to recognize that all "the free men and women of the world" must face the Communist threat to their liberty. While never abandoning his hope for peace of a permanent nature under the United Nations, he now realized that "free peoples"—those peoples that collectively came to be called the "Western alliance"—superseded the international organization, a conclusion that informed all of his liberal internationalism along with containment. Within the context of the Cold War, the president advanced a practical approach that relied on American initiative: "We have learned that we must earn the peace we seek just as we earned victory in the war, not by wishful thinking but by realistic effort."

Although he welcomed genuine cooperation from the Soviets, Truman stated that America should not confuse such cooperation with the evident fact of totalitarianism's threat to the free world. This threat, he said, was of global proportions not only because of the reach of the Soviet army but also because of the Kremlin's form of diplomacy and tactics of subversion. Unlike his contemporary critics, Truman also condemned the Soviet Union's totalitarian ideology, which, through force, terror, or subversion, coopted and radicalized power. This ideological component set the USSR fundamentally apart from and against democratic civilization. Under these circumstances, the United States had a responsibility to exercise its power to defend democracy and freedom in the world. Rather than seeking a mere balance of power, America aimed to strengthen and expand freedom as a good in and of itself and as a lever against totalitarianism.[74]

On the same day, March 17, 1948, in a St. Patrick's Day address in New York City, Truman imparted one of his most profound intellectualizations of the Cold War. Defining the great issue confronting the world as that of tyranny's challenge to freedom, he described communism as just the latest manifestation of tyranny under a new disguise—that of totalitarian ideology. Because this new ideology broke all the old rules of hegemony, Truman declared that Communist tyranny was a threat to the deepest underpinnings of the West. "Communism masquerades as a doctrine of progress. It is nothing of the kind. It is, on the contrary, a movement of reaction. It denies that man is master of his fate, and consequently denies man's right to govern himself," he said. "And even worse, communism denies the very existence of God. Religion is persecuted because it stands for freedom under God. This threat to our liberty and to our faith must be faced by each one of us." Complementing his Jefferson Day speech of 1947, which emphasized freedom as an unalienable right, the president in this address presented communism as the negation of freedom. Where freedom liberated man and celebrated his rational faculty of thought, tyranny bound man to his material being and subjugated him to so-called inevitable forces of history, which were determined by a despot. Truman looked on communism's assault on democracy as nothing less than a modern version of the timeless struggle between tyrannical and free government.[75]

With such principles at stake, Truman would not tolerate conciliation. (Indeed, he consistently expressed distaste with the lower levels at the State Department who advocated a soft position.)[76] To carry out its duty as the principal protector of the free world, the United States had to maintain its military, economic, and moral strength. But even this first and most important step, according to Truman, was insufficient by itself for the task at hand. In anticipation of a fuller alliance with other democracies, he argued for coupling American strength with the strength of all free men "who believe as we do in liberty and justice and the dignity of man."[77] He sketched the worldwide imperative for democracies to work together using economic and military power to defend peace through strength, all within the context of freedom. In the end, he realized that the United Nations could not ensure this kind of peace and, reluctantly, that this hard-won peace came with no guarantee of permanence. At times in late 1947 and more steadily in 1948, he shifted in his liberal internationalism from a call for an idealistic "permanent peace" to enforcing a plan that might achieve a lasting peace. With the West's growing confrontation with Soviet communism, Truman concluded that his containment strategy was the only way to achieve a durable and acceptable peace.

5

"Bonds far greater than those of mere ideology"

Kennan's Sources
of Soviet Conduct

It is no coincidence that scholars have written more about George F. Kennan—and his version of containment—than about any other advisor in the Truman administration. Adept in foreign languages, Kennan was respected for his intellect and prose throughout his career. A foreign service officer of the State Department who had postings in Geneva, Hamburg, Tallinin, Riga, Prague, Berlin, Lisbon, London, and Moscow, he worked his way up through the ranks from vice consul in 1927 (when he was twenty-three years old) to acting as charge d'affaires between two U.S. ambassadors to the Soviet Union in 1946. During those nearly two decades abroad, he spent only one year stationed in Washington, D.C. In mid-1946, in part because of the impact of the Long Telegram written that February, he was assigned to lecture at the National War College in Washington and returned to the United States. At the request of Secretary of State George Marshall, Kennan became the first director of the Policy Planning Staff (PPS) of the State Department in April 1947. At odds with most of Truman's containment—even as he indisputably contributed to America's Cold War foreign policy—and clashing increasingly with new secretary of state Dean Acheson, Kennan left the PPS position at the end of 1949 and was briefly a counselor at the State Department in 1950. Later that year, at the invitation of famed physicist Robert Oppenheimer, he joined the Institute for Advanced Study at Princeton University. His association with Princeton lasted for the rest of his career, except for brief stints as U.S. ambassador to the USSR for part of 1952 and to Yugoslavia for two years under President Kennedy. In the prominent way that he straddled the governmental and academic realms, Kennan is a unique figure.

While there exists some debate over his precise meaning, there is an academic consensus that Kennan expounded the theoretical approach of realism and largely crafted the policy of containment. Although he often said that Reinhold Niebuhr was "the father of us all" among realists, Kennan shaped the realist perspective of the Cold War. He considered diplomacy the most important tool, if not the end, of Cold War politics, and he endorsed the concept of spheres of influence in order to achieve a stable balance of power in world affairs. He rejected the notions of internationalism as defined by both Wilson and Truman and found Franklin Roosevelt to offer only a slight improvement over either of them. If his realist approach prevailed, he thought, war would not be inevitable between the two superpowers. As with other realists and revisionists, Kennan's concern for world security grew to be dominated by the atomic, and then the nuclear, threat. By late 1949, he was troubled that the world would destroy itself by the weapons of mass destruction it had produced, and, more and more, he objected to what he viewed as perversions of his theory of containment.[1]

Diplomacy, History, and Hegemony

Kennan's disagreement with Truman's containment in the contemporaneous period of 1946 to 1951 was rooted in his definition of diplomacy and its supremacy over politics. "The stuff of diplomacy is the entire fabric of our foreign relations with other countries," said Kennan in fall 1945, "and it embraces every phrase of national power and every phase of national dealing so I think you have to include these other things in it." "These other things" referred to psychological, economic, and political elements, which he ranked in that order. He also allotted a necessary but subordinate role to grand strategy, which he said was composed of political, economic, and moral strength and was separate from "military strength alone."[2] Kennan described diplomacy in 1948 as "the methodology by which the other weapons [of foreign policy] are used" and which could make a "great difference in the end result." He regretted that few appreciated the centrality of diplomacy; in a theme that he would develop throughout his writings, he noted the dilemma that "[t]he diplomacy of a democracy can never be as effective as that of an authoritarian state" and that, as a seeming consequence, the quality of current foreign service personnel in the United States was poor.[3] Indeed, because of democratic politics' dependence on popular opinion, Kennan often criticized it as an impediment to professional diplomacy and the establishment and maintenance of a global balance of power.

Of course, Kennan did see difficulties with communism and, broadly, totalitarianism. As a diplomat, he, along with the rest of the American embassy staff, was detained incommunicado by the Nazis for five months in wartime Berlin, and he was declared persona non grata by the Soviets—ending his brief tenure as U.S. ambassador to the USSR in 1952—for comparing living in Moscow to being interned under the Nazis. In 1940, he wrote that war against the Nazis was worthwhile, as long as the mistakes of Versailles were not repeated.[4] He criticized Roosevelt, as well as the president's civilian and military advisors, for siding too much with the Soviet Union at the expense of other World War II allies, arguing that they misread Stalin's personality and misjudged his willingness to cooperate in a postwar world order. Kennan was skeptical of the USSR during the Second World War and in the early postwar period, and he rejected "the more hypocritical aspects of left-wing thought on Russian relations" in 1946.[5] But realist moral equivalence and a corresponding professional rigor prevented him from making regime distinctions and, as a result, from seeing the fundamental essence of the Cold War as Truman understood it. While he warned America and the West in 1944 against expecting postwar collaboration from the Soviet Union, he misunderstood the grounds on which the Kremlin would think and act: "People at home would find Soviet words and actions easier to understand if they would bear in mind the character of Russian aims in Eastern and Central Europe. Russian efforts in this area are directed to only one goal: power. The form this power takes, the methods by which it is achieved: these are secondary questions. It is a matter of indifference to Moscow whether a given area is 'communistic' or not. All things being equal, Moscow might prefer to see it communized, although even that is debatable. But the main thing is that it should be amenable to Moscow influence, and if possible to Moscow authority." Because he viewed politics primarily in terms of power, Kennan minimized the role of ideology in the East-West conflict. He carried his 1944 analysis—which he described in his memoir as "broader, more balanced, and more specific than the so-called X-Article"—into his post–World War II writings about the Soviet Union and recommendations for an American response.[6]

Kennan wrote that his experience with the Nazis between 1939 and 1941 and his study of historian Edward Gibbon gave him the "feeling that one must not be too frightened of those who aspire to world domination," especially since no one people were great enough to establish global hegemony.[7] In the immediate background for the X article of July 1947, Kennan grappled with the role of ideology in elucidating Soviet intentions after World War II. He depicted the Soviet leaders as "first and foremost international Marxists of the sternest Leninist school" in October 1946 but, at the same time, rendered ideology as "the figleaf of Soviet respectability."[8] This suggestion—the instrumental use of ideology—was fleshed out by Kennan in January 1947 on at least two occasions and became a consistent theme of his work. In a Council on Foreign Relations discussion that foreshadowed the X article, he maintained that "ideology" (his deliberate quotes), Russian traditions and national habits of thought, and the internal circumstances of Soviet power underlay the Soviet Union's behavior. According to Kennan, although the Kremlin used Marxist-Leninist doctrine, Communist theory did "not provide the mainspring of Soviet action. That mainspring is something deeper," which appeared to be the deep-seated habits of thought and method of looking at the world, "which is anchored in the experience of centuries."[9] As he elaborated in late January in remarks to the American Press Institute, ideology played a definite part in "Soviet psychology," but it was characteristic of Soviet psychology to seek full political control first and to envisage the introduction of socialism as a consequence, rather than the primary goal, of the establishment of a form of political power that was acceptable to Communist minds.[10]

Since world hegemony was impossible in Kennan's interpretation of history, so, too, was Communist hegemony after World War II. As a result, he called for a measured American foreign policy that avoided the extremes of "the hysterical sort of anti-communism which, it seems to me, is gaining currency in our country" and Henry Wallace's personal approach, which relied on a "glad hand and a winning smile." In positing these conflicting extreme positions, Kennan laid the foundation for his later presentation of containment. He argued in January 1947 that the Kremlin had never been a menace to the United States, "except as we have been a menace to ourselves," and that, instead of a "get-tough policy," he preferred that "we should take a dignified and self-assured position in the world. As long as we show that our purposes are decent and that we have the courage to follow them through, the Russians will never challenge us."[11] Also in early 1947, he employed a simile to explain his nascent form of containment: "The shape of Soviet power is like that of a tree which has been bent in its infancy and twisted into a certain pattern. It *can* be caused to grow back into another form; but not by any sudden or violent application of force." He concluded that the desired effect could be produced "only by the exertion of steady pressure over a period of years in the right direction." But "another form" in the "right direction" did not mean the collapse or democratic transformation of the Soviet Union. In fact, he implied that this "steady pressure over a period of years" could provide time for the international Communist movement to "bite back" the USSR and for the United States to accept "certain elements [found in the theory of Soviet communism] which I think are probably really the ideas of the future."[12] Thus, although he rejected Wallace's diplomatic style, Kennan accepted the historical inevitability of progressive social doctrine. A realist and a fatalist, he previewed his theory of limited containment as a means to ride out and check, if possible, active expressions of Soviet power, while awaiting the future convergence of socialism and democracy.

Containment, Kennan, and the X Article

While there is a debate as to the beginning of the Cold War in the postwar era, most scholars point to the July 1947 publication of "The Sources of Soviet Conduct" in *Foreign Affairs* as the first, if not definitive, articulation of the American strategy of containment. Its publication came four months after the Truman Doctrine address calling for Greek-Turkish aid and one month after Marshall's Harvard speech announcing the idea of the European Recovery Program. Since the article was a classified government paper that then became public—and since "X," its author, turned out to be George Kennan—it has long been considered a statement of Truman administration policy.[13] As a result and because he was an expert on Russia and the Soviet Union and left a wide, long paper trail in government, Kennan has been recognized as a major figure in the development of postwar American foreign policy. Walter Lippmann stands out as the first and, in some senses, most important writer in a lengthy line of realists and revisionists who have criticized the article as the intellectual justification for what they termed the policies of exaggeration being pursued by Truman. The result is that the X article has been considered the blueprint for containment. As such, it must be analyzed and placed in the overall context of the Truman administration's Cold War strategy.

Paul Nitze, Clark Clifford, George Elsey, and other presidential advisors commented that there was nothing in the article that was new to the Truman administration and that it left more of an impression with the public than within the executive branch. (In particular, the article probably had the most effect not on the public at large but on the academic establishment and other professional policymakers who read *Foreign Affairs*.)[14] The X article combined Kennan's political theory with a practical analysis of the Cold War, and most in the administration could agree with the latter. With proposals for counterforce measures and vigilance against Soviet expansionism, as well as the conclusions of the article regarding the God-given responsibility of the United States to meet the Kremlin's challenge, the article struck many officials as familiar and harmonious with the president's developing strategy.[15] Yet these points, however widely accepted, were not central to the primary argument of the article. Kennan later abandoned practical positions on the use of counterforce and pressuring a breakup of the USSR, for instance, causing some to refer to an early Kennan and a late Kennan. But in terms of the ideas informing those positions, he did not change: the X article presented Kennan's articulation of the nature of the Soviet regime and of the Cold War and represented his version of containment.[16]

As in all his writings, Kennan emphasized the psychological over the political realm in the X article. Despite the title "The Sources of Soviet Conduct," he depreciated the most basic source of Soviet conduct: communism.[17] He started with the "political personality of Soviet power" as the product of ideology and circumstances. At first, Kennan seemed to have recognized ideology as a calculus for Soviet thought and action; but he immediately specified that one must measure the interaction of ideology and circumstances through "psychological analysis" and assign the relative weight appropriate to each of them. According to Kennan, circumstances, rather than ideology, determined Kremlin behavior. Although he conceded that the Russian revolutionaries sincerely adopted Marxist theory, he did not think that they believed in or were motivated by communism.[18] To the psychological explanation he deemed preeminent, he added the realist conception of power and its manifestation in human nature as "these revolutionaries found in Marxist theory a highly convenient ratio-nalization for their own instinctive desires. It afforded pseudo-scientific justification for their impatience, for their categoric denial of all value in the Tsarist system, for their yearning for power and revenge and for their inclination to cut corners in their pursuit of it."[19] Lenin, Kennan believed, impatiently followed his instinctive desire for power and used Marxism to gain that power. As he had only intimated in the Long Telegram, Kennan now explicitly wrote that the Soviets employed ideology as a justification for their behavior.

Kennan argued that the Communists established a dictatorship out of necessity, due to their minority status, the foreign intervention after World War I, and the ongoing Russian civil war through 1919. He at-tributed their behavior to insecurity arising out of Russian culture and nationality. While he thought that Lenin kept this insecurity in check, Kennan said that Stalin and his successors could not be as successful because "[t]heir sense of insecurity was too great" and their "particular brand of fanaticism, unmodified by any of the Anglo-Saxon traditions of compromise, was too fierce and too jealous to envisage any permanent sharing of power."[20] In the end, Kennan interpreted all governing as the exercise of power; dictatorship simply signified that fewer persons held the power. He explored neither the nature of tyranny and liberty nor whether Communist behavior, apart from factors of history and culture, stemmed from its ideology.

Nevertheless, Kennan maintained that the Kremlin used "the word" of the Communist Party and dogma to create an external enemy. After capi-talism had been eradicated within the Russian empire, the Soviets were forced to "justify the retention of the dictatorship by stressing the menace of capitalism abroad." He viewed this phenomenon as one of necessity, not of deliberate choice, and for Kennan, beliefs that did not accord with necessity were psychological. There was a parallel between "the word" of the Soviet leaders and their ideology, but it came from a psychological disposition to fanaticism that was embedded in the oriental mind.[21] Here Kennan interchanged totalitarian ideology with terms associated with re-ligious faith, not to distinguish between ideology and religion but seem-ingly to suggest that the two were similar, if not identical, figments of rationalization: "But we have seen that the Kremlin is under no ideologi-cal compulsion to accomplish its purposes in a hurry. Like the Church, it is dealing in ideological concepts which are of long-term validity, and it can afford to be patient." Through another melding of psychology and ephemeral religion, the psyche became so important to Kennan that the idea of an implacable, hostile foe was "canonized in Soviet philosophy" and "anchored in the Soviet structure of thought by bonds far greater than those of mere ideology."[22] The USSR saw an enemy in the West, yet Kennan depicted this not as a result of communism but as derivative from political necessity, an irrational psyche, and national characteristics.

Kennan's interpretation of the Soviet Union as psychologically disturbed but nonimperialistic became characteristic of postwar realpolitik.[23] By this reasoning, diplomacy treated the Soviet Union as a patient to be cured. Kennan maintained that the Soviets knew the rules of power and could engage in international politics like any other state, but he wanted to handle them as an insecure state instead of as a global imperial power. Insecurity could be assuaged and the personality problem tempered by patience and discipline, if only professionals such as Kennan were allowed to prescribe the correct medicine. His method is ironic, given that he construed the United Nations and most other American efforts as idealistic placebos that would not effect change.

In the X article and most of his other works, Kennan maintained that power was the Soviets' goal. He initially presented this power as relative, however, rather than absolute. He argued, for example, that part of the despotism of the Kremlin flowed from the fact that Stalin had not consolidated his power. He then briefly offered a rationalization for totalitarianism and once again elevated psychological speculation over political reality. Thus, it seemed plausible, according to Kennan, to alter the "political personality of Soviet power" by waiting out the consolidation of the Kremlin's power and appealing to Soviet prestige. In clear form, he laid out his contention that Russian behavior should determine the American response, instead of America weighing the sum of Communist ideology and action. Kennan painted the Kremlin leaders as consummate realists with their main concern "to make sure that [the USSR] has filled every nook and cranny available to it in the basin of world power."[24] While they will not cede their aim, he added, they will be patient; he even complimented the Soviet Union for accepting philosophically the barriers put up by the West.

Within this context, Kennan put forth the concept that prompted almost everyone to associate the X article with America's Cold War strategy: a "long-term, patient but firm and vigilant containment of Russian expansive tendencies."[25] But aside from the word "containment," nothing was new in the phrasing. U.S. Ambassador to the Soviet Union Averell Harriman had talked about the necessity of firmness with the Soviet Union in late 1944 and in 1945; in April 1945, Truman picked up this language and used it as the base for an incipient containment. And after Harriman and Truman had invoked firmness, Secretary of State James Byrnes was given the credit for the policy of patience and firmness in 1946. In 1947, at the time of the X article, Truman's policy could already be seen as one of firmness more than patience.[26] Kennan used familiar words in order to call on the American leadership to prove that it did not cling to the false religions of insecurity and sentimentality.[27] Indeed, Kennan presented the United States as the adversary in the Cold War and as becoming the more unstable actor in international relations, if his advice were not heeded. Although he sketched the moderation he thought would evolve in communism, he also suggested that order and control were required to improve liberal democracy.[28]

For Kennan, the Russians were a national expression of the irrational passions found in all human nature. "The fact of the matter is," he said in March 1947 at the National War College, "that there is a little bit of the totalitarian buried somewhere, way down deep, in each and every one of us. It is only the cheerful light of confidence and security which keeps this evil genius down at the usual helpless and invisible depth."[29] The Soviets lacked confidence and security, according to Kennan, but Americans could exercise reason, moderation, and patience in their foreign affairs. And this was not because of cultural or political institutions particular to American liberal democracy but the extent to which trained experts were able to guide U.S. foreign policy. Indeed, this advice was the central message of the X article: a patient, professional policy on the part of the United States, maintained Kennan, would permit time—perhaps ten to fifteen years, according to the X article—for the impatient and insecure leaders of the USSR to mellow and loosen their grip on the Russian people. On the one hand, he thought that this change was feasible and might result in the breakup of the Soviet Union; on the other hand, Russian impatience was encouraged by the fanaticism in the "Russian or oriental mind" and rooted in human nature. Only fortune and circumstance—and the careful administration of foreign policy managers—would prevent the United States from stimulating the immoderation of the oriental mind.

Lippmann's Criticism and Kennan's Reaction

Walter Lippmann's famous analysis of the X article is a realist criticism of aspects of Truman's containment, just as it is a criticism of Kennan. Like Nitze, Clifford, Elsey, and other Truman administration advisors, Lippmann did not delve beneath a superficial reading of Kennan's article. Nevertheless, the well-known journalist believed that Kennan was repeating the mistakes of Wilsonianism, and in the process committing the United States to an unbounded, unnecessary expansion of its foreign policy. In a series of articles that was republished in a 1947 book, *The Cold War* (which popularized the phrase), Lippmann urged Kennan and the Truman administration to curtail their exuberance and eschew the role of ideology in constructing foreign policy toward the USSR.[30] Lippmann analyzed the X article and found it wanting in light of the excesses he perceived in the Truman Doctrine and its applications in American policies toward Europe and the Near East; he contrasted the Truman Doctrine with what he saw as the pragmatic Marshall line prevailing in China, which refused to align the United States with a particular faction and avoided unnecessary entanglements. He maintained that the X article and the president flirted with a risky diplomatic policy—containment—which invited war when the United States should be dealing with geostrategic realities. As a result, he urged the Truman administration to return to balance of power politics in order to achieve an equilibrium with the Soviet Union. And in doing so, Lippmann provided the first serious critique of Truman's containment, one that most realists, including Kennan himself, largely have accepted.[31]

Equating the X article with official Truman administration policy, Lippmann linked Kennan's words with key sources of American foreign policy in the early postwar era. Overall, he deplored what he saw as containment's inefficiency and unpredictable outcome. He deemed the Truman Doctrine and the X article's presentation of containment to be both expansive and reactive in nature. Consequently, he found fault with Kennan's hypothesis that the containment described in the X article would induce the mellowing of the Soviet Union in ten to fifteen years. According to Lippmann, this policy would cede the strategic initiative both politically and geographically to the Kremlin, and the United States and its allies would be forced to react at the points of the Soviets' choosing and timing. He viewed this aspect of the X article and the Truman Doctrine to be passively expansive: passive, because Moscow "would define the is-sues, would make the challenges, would select the ground where conflict was to be waged, and would choose the weapons"; and expansive, because America would apply such public statements to the whole world.[32]

Lippmann provided a realist counterweight to the X article and, by association, the Truman Doctrine. First, he argued (as did Kennan) that ideology did not drive the Cold War conflict. He did not see a threat from the West European Communist parties' allegiance to Moscow, and he thought that the threat from the Kremlin stemmed from the power of the Red Army rather than the ideology of Marx. There was no connection between the objective of the latter and the force of the former. Second, Lippmann elevated the Marshall Plan and separated it from its growth out of the Truman Doctrine. He believed that, in reality, there was no Marshall Plan for Europe, since "the essence of [Marshall's] proposal was that only a European plan for Europe could save Europe, or provide a basis on which the American people could prudently and fairly be asked to help Europe save itself." He added that the application of the Marshall line, in partnership with the United Nations, would encourage self-reliance rather than dependence on the United States and settle troublesome situations from Germany to China.[33]

The longterm solution, argued Lippmann, was to return to balance of power politics. He lambasted America for getting involved in what he viewed as peripheral disagreements in China, Iran, Turkey, Greece, and Eastern Europe. Contradicting Truman's foreign policy, Lippmann warned that the United States "must not deceive ourselves by supposing that we stand at the head of a worldwide coalition of democratic states in our conflict with the USSR." He stressed that America had weakened its standing with its natural allies of the Atlantic community, leading them to believe that they were a geographic battlefield between the Soviet Union and the United States. Instead, he proposed a realist approach focused on the geography of the matter: "The aim of the leading democratic states of Europe and probably also of the Americas is at best to hold the balance of power between Russia and America, and thus to become mediators of the conflict." Lippmann wanted to encourage European independence and discourage the vulnerabilities of neutrality, but he thought that de-velopment precluded American leadership and West European strength. The United States, for its part, would be served best by using its military power to bring about a settlement with the Soviets and redressing the balance of power that was upset by World War II. In the end, Lippmann speculated that the containment described in the X article, especially its diplomatic measures, would frustrate the Americans long before it affected the Russians.[34]

In April 1948, while in the hospital, Kennan wrote a ten-page personal letter to Lippmann responding to *The Cold War*. Kennan agreed with Lippmann that a reasonable goal would be to come to a settlement and hold the Soviets to what they already had obtained by dint of their military advance in World War II. But since he thought that the Soviets would negotiate only when it was to their advantage, he disagreed with Lippmann and argued that such a settlement depended on a carrot being offered to the Kremlin. To that end, in a realist way similar to Lippmann's, Kennan argued that the United States should not interfere with the Soviet regime. But he departed from Lippmann in maintaining that Soviet violence derived from an internal structural problem rather than an external military force. If the Kremlin ceased to threaten the United States, he said, the Soviets should be allowed to develop their tradition according to their wishes. As an incentive, the United States should even help the USSR in its economic development. Although he reached it by different means, Kennan's foremost concern, like Lippmann's, was stabilization of relations between the two great powers.[35]

In *The Cold War*, Lippmann had contended that the current American disposition of troops and involvement in Europe prevented both a balance of power and a peace treaty. Kennan, while accepting credit for the containment policy that he thought had been followed for well over a year, strenuously objected to the focus on its military content. He said that there were only "isolated spots" in Japan, Germany, Austria, Trieste, and possibly Italy "where the accent of containment rested on the military element." Kennan then told Lippmann that the existence of troops in Europe and Japan "was the result of previous commitments which originally had nothing to do with the containment policy." In short, Kennan by 1948 was already distancing himself from the military component of containment, saying it was the result of troop dispositions at the end of World War II. Instead, he emphasized to Lippmann that he too believed containment should be aligned with the Marshall Plan rather than with the Truman Doctrine.[36] Kennan's larger concern, however, differed from Lippmann's interpretation. While Lippmann stressed geostrategy and saw the Red Army (with the attendant brewing conflict between Soviet and American troops) as the chief threat to Europe, Kennan thought that the Soviets' main goal was a political attack with local Communists as their spearhead. The challenge was to remove the "shadow" cast by Soviet armed strength, as well as by American forces, "for in Europe today what things *seem* is more important than what things *are*, and the Europeans are obsessed with the fear of invasion." Kennan thought that Lippmann was confusing a shadow with reality, yet he agreed that perceptions were most important. Overall, then, he concurred with Lippmann about the centrality of the Marshall Plan, because he thought the problems of Europe were primarily political and economic.[37]

As Kennan explained in his memoirs, the X article originally was a response to a request from Secretary of the Navy James Forrestal for commentary on a report by a third party.[38] Citing the character of the paper to defend himself from some of Lippmann's criticisms, Kennan said that he must have omitted Eastern Europe and other points about Russian history because Forrestal had not asked for that information. According to Kennan, the article had not set out to present a complete strategy, and he largely agreed with Lippmann.[39] He later noted that the article only seemed to advocate counterforce at each point of Soviet encroachment; in actuality, it proposed an asymmetrical response.[40]

Although he popularized the term "containment" in his 1947 *Foreign Affairs* article, Kennan did not conceive containment as formulated by the Truman administration. In retrospect, at least, he maintained that he wanted to dispel the thought that war with the Kremlin was inevitable; in the process, he underestimated the depth of the covert side of the Cold War by the Soviets and the possibility of a hot war within the Cold War. Kennan himself stressed that he did not author the idea of containment as it developed under Truman, but he accepted praise for what he regarded as a different and superior containment based on diplomacy, economic rehabilitation of Western Europe, and negotiation with the Soviets. This message is the core of Kennan's government, public, and private writings from 1946 through 1951, as well as the central teaching of postwar realism; he maintained and honed this position in his memoirs and later writings.

Compared with other chapters in his memoir, the one on the X article is filled with the most rationalizations. Kennan did not write the chapter in 1947, and it is where he most distanced himself from actual containment policy. Realist and postrevisionist scholars present Kennan as the original author of containment who was shunted aside by the Truman administration, but Kennan proved himself more radical than his academic students on this point. Kennan again described himself as the victim, misunderstood and ignored by the president, parties, and public. He redefined the X article, arguing that one of its primary intentions was to convince the "despairing liberals" and the "hotheaded right-wingers" that war was neither inevitable nor the suitable answer; it aimed to create a middle ground of political resistance, which, if followed, would have left America in better shape than the containment pursued by Truman and his followers. "This was simply to cease at that point making fatuous unilateral concessions to the Kremlin," he wrote, "to do what we could to inspire and support resistance elsewhere to its efforts to expand the area of its dominant political influence, and to wait for the internal weaknesses of Soviet power, combined with the frustration in the external field, to moderate Soviet ambitions and behavior."[41] Both then and later, Kennan offered his containment—and not Truman's—as the pure form. He believed that the X article was wrongly attached to the combination of the Truman Doctrine and the Marshall Plan and lamented that the essay helped to create an "indestructible" myth and a confusing history about the origins of containment.[42]

As such, Kennan said, containment did not fail; only its follow-up did not occur. Looking back, he applied his realist analysis to the situation in 1947, but without the context of the founding and development of the Soviet regime. "When I used the term 'Soviet power' in the X-Article," he explained, "I had in view, of course, the system of power organized, demonstrated, and inspired by Joseph Stalin."[43] For all that he viewed Russian history as the determinant of Kremlin action, Kennan only noted general circumstances and did not address the implications of the most significant event in modern Russian history: the Bolshevik Revolution. All he needed to explain Soviet behavior in 1947 was the power drive that animated Stalin. But even this drive was not as important to Kennan as the forces of the historical process itself. In this view, it did not matter what a person thought or a regime did, because, in the end, history would not only settle the course of events but would also pass judgment. Kennan's supposed clarification of the X article would not have resonated with Truman or Nitze, Clifford, and Elsey: many of the functional aspects of containment outlined in *Foreign Affairs* were already under way.

Kennan as Architect?

Truman's containment, according to many accounts, was the perversion of Kennan's theoretical line of containment—rather than the other way around. The Truman Doctrine moved away from Kennan's established position, whereas the Marshall Plan rectified this deviation. Truman and the United States tried to stray again in the North Atlantic Treaty but were stayed until the formation of NATO. It was in 1948 and 1949 that Kennan openly rejected Truman's containment as it was shaping the North Atlantic pact, and he left the Policy Planning Staff at the end of 1949 (initially as a sabbatical leave, which became permanent).[44] He soon condemned what he viewed as the misguided militarization of NATO before and during the Korean War. Kennan's famous, oft-repeated passage from his memoirs—that he intended only the political containment of a political threat—was not a retroactive rationalization but an admission that his view of containment was never the containment of President Truman.[45]

At the end of his first memoir, Kennan quoted himself in August 1950: "Only the diplomatic historian, working from the leisure and detachment of a later day, will be able to unravel this incredible tangle and to reveal the true aspect of the various factors and issues involved."[46] He added in 1955, in describing the successes of the PPS under Marshall, "[W]e were permitted to operate as we were supposed to operate; and there has remained from this, in the Dept's deepest files, a literary legacy which I hope will some day be published."[47] In the summer of 1950, Kennan charged that neither the president nor Congress, the press, or the public understood U.S. foreign policy. Someone of his position, he said, could contribute little more unless he first became a historian and then educated the public. Except for his brief stints as ambassador to the USSR and to Yugoslavia, Kennan followed his own counsel.

In 1978, two scholars took Kennan's words about diplomatic historians to heart and compiled *Containment: Documents on American Policy and Strategy, 1945–1950*, a volume of PPS and other papers, many of which were written by Kennan and previously were unpublished. Historians John Lewis Gaddis and Thomas Etzold present the documents, which they see as the underpinnings to containment, largely as a defense of the development of Kennan's position. This argument was spelled out by Gaddis four years later in *Strategies of Containment*, a narrative political history that incorporated passages from government documents to support Kennan's view of containment.[48] *Containment* emerges as a companion volume of documents to Kennan's first memoir and a documentary predecessor to *Strategies of Containment*. The central argument of *Containment* is that Kennan conceived containment, that the Truman administration never understood it properly, and that Truman's containment departed from Kennan's original intentions. Not only does Kennan's containment argument become clear in these pages, but so does the union between Kennan's political thought and that of postrevisionism. And all this despite that Kennan's Policy Planning Staff writings—as is the case with such papers—were never signed and probably were rarely, if ever, seen by the president.[49]

In May 1947, under the directorship of Kennan, the Policy Planning Staff presented its first paper, PPS 1, entitled "Policy with Respect to American Aid to Western Europe." Largely authored by Kennan, PPS 1 declared as discrete the Communist threat and the economic despair facing Europe at that time.[50] In a separation that he maintained throughout his career, Kennan wrote, "The Policy Planning Staff does not see communist activities as the root of the difficulties of western Europe. It believes that the present crisis results in large part from the disruptive effect of the war on the economic, political, and social structure of Europe and from a profound exhaustion of physical plant and of spiritual vigor. This situation has been aggravated and rendered far more difficult of remedy by the division of the continent into east and west." He added that the American effort should aim "to combat not communism, but the economic maladjustment which makes European society vulnerable to exploitation by any and all totalitarian movements and which Russian communism is now exploiting." While Kennan identified correctly the need for economic rehabilitation, he did not consider Communist advances a possible cause of Europe's problems. In his memoirs, for example, Kennan noted delightedly that a passage from PPS 1 appeared almost verbatim in Marshall's Harvard University speech and showed that the PPS paper exerted much influence in drafting the Marshall Plan.[51] The passage in question pertained to the necessity of the Europeans first requesting assistance and then helping to organize their recovery, a point that was not new to Marshall or others, such as Chip Bohlen and Will Clayton. Kennan did provide some words for the Harvard address, but he departed from the thought behind the

Marshall Plan and from Truman's containment when he argued that economic recovery alone would deter the Soviet Union.

In PPS 1, Kennan put on paper his criticism of the Truman Doctrine. Continuing to accent psychological over political factors, he defined the future Economic Recovery Program as psychological and then economic aid, but nowhere did he place the idea of the Marshall Plan in a complete political context. He concluded, instead, that the Truman Doctrine left two damaging impressions. Once more revealing his preference for limited involvement even in the extraordinary circumstances of the Cold War, he said that the Truman Doctrine demonstrated that the U.S. approach to world problems was to react suspiciously to Communist pressure, and reiterated his complaint that the American economic concern for other countries was a byproduct of that touchy reaction. Then he criticized the Truman Doctrine as a "blank check" of economic and military aid to any area in the world where the Communists showed signs of being successful.[52] Anyone as steeped in history as Kennan knew what he implied by the term "blank check"—a suggestion that the onus for future instability or war would lie more with the Americans than with the Soviets. With his penchant for economic, sociological, and psychological factors, Kennan disagreed fundamentally with Truman's understanding of the primary political and ideological characteristics of the Cold War.

Gaddis and Etzold present PPS 1 as the enunciation of the containment originally pursued by the Truman administration. For them, PPS 1 established three principles that guided subsequent U.S. foreign policy: a psychological malaise stemming from the dislocations of war and reconstruction, not the danger of Soviet military attack or international communism, constituted the chief threat to the European balance of power; America could solve this problem most effectively through economic, not military, assistance; and such aid could be provided most efficiently through a program run largely by the Europeans themselves.[53]

The third point was characteristic of the ERP, but the first two came from Kennan rather than Truman. In his speeches from the end of the war and into 1947, Truman articulated the devastation, cruel winters, and hunger afflicting Europe, but he did not perceive these harsh realities as psychological malaise. Additionally, aside from Acheson, no top official invoked the balance of power in the realist sense that Kennan did. In 1946, and culminating in the March 1947 address to Congress, Truman pointed to communism as the foremost hazard to Europe and the Middle

East, if not the world. Through the Greek-Turkish aid program, he conveyed that American aid, including military assistance, would take whatever form was most suited to particular circumstances.[54]

Kennan and Europe

PPS 4 of July 23, 1947, can be considered another step in the articulation of Kennan's containment. According to Gaddis and Etzold, the more-than-forty-page document gave as "complete an expression as exists from the period of why Washington officials considered European stability a vital national interest."[55] In fact, PPS 4 was a preliminary report from Kennan and not a definitive statement or even a complete expression of American foreign policy toward Europe. Although the paper was dated a month after Marshall's Harvard address and therefore considered how the plan might work, PPS 4 emphasized the limitations of American resources and insisted that the ERP should not be viewed as a precedent for U.S. policy in other parts of the world. Entitled "Certain Aspects of the European Recovery Program from the United States Standpoint," the report offered Kennan's notions on economic containment and stability, rather than Truman's thought on political containment of tyranny and on peace based on freedom, independence, and strength. The paper was never published in the *Foreign Relations of the United States*—the official compilation of government documents—and did not go beyond the introductory stage.[56]

The first section of PPS 4 looked for the source of American interest in Europe. While Kennan asserted that U.S. interest lay in the cultural European heritage of civil liberties and governmental restraint in exercising power, he did not begin with this point.[57] He rightly spent time elaborating the current situation that inhibited European recovery, but he misconstrued the circumstances. Starting with the dismal picture in Europe, Kennan focused almost exclusively on psychological despair. He paired the "physical and psychic" exhaustion of the European people and emphasized the feelings of disillusionment, insecurity, and apathy occasioned by postwar hostilities, particularly "the tendency toward the division of the continent between east and west." In opposition to Churchill's iron curtain speech of the prior year, to all of Truman's addresses in 1947, and even to aspects of his own Long Telegram, Kennan rooted the beginning of the Cold War in psychological depression and insecurity. He referred to a tendency toward division but did not believe that the Kremlin strived to divide and conquer Europe; he never pointed to the USSR as having caused the division of Europe.[58]

PPS 4 catalogued six problems facing Europe after the Second World War, including the destruction and depreciation of physical plant and equipment, the depletion of financial reserves, social and economic dislocation worsened by the breakdown of prewar institutional patterns, and a prolonged delay in adjusting the German economy to peacetime purposes. Writing two years after the war's end, Kennan constructed an internal, self-caused crisis in Europe. Making his nascent argument about the key industrial and population centers of the world, he alluded to "other lesser" factors faced by the principal centers on the continent—one of the "lesser" factors in 1947 being the Kremlin. Kennan noted, for instance, that the "common apprehensions over the possibility of 'communist control'" would be of little concern if the principles of law, justice, and restraint in the exercise of political power were lost in the meantime. During the expanding Cold War, he believed that these principles were threatened more by psychological despair than by Communist aggression.[59]

PPS 4 also demonstrated Kennan's limited definition of the principles that help to compose a civil society. Truman worried about the integrity of society and the dignity of the individual, but he was also concerned about the American regime and the principles on which it was based. For him, the Kremlin's ideology and the tyrants who sought to overpower Europe—both the ones of World War II and those of the Cold War—threatened liberal democracy. After what had happened to Europe, and in the midst of what was occurring at the time, Truman recognized that the Europeans had not brought all their problems upon themselves. For Kennan, by contrast, the Europeans were their own undoing, and he feared the possibility of the renunciation by the Europeans of the "values of individual responsibility and political restraint which has become traditional to their continent." Kennan saw man as a creature motivated more by passion than reason, and, without considering a deeper context, his concern fixed on the negative freedom associated with the modern rule of law. As a result, he believed that commonly held traditions—instead of fundamental principles of right, justice, and virtue—were the source of individual responsibility and political restraint. And the loss of tradition was a matter of *internal* decline rather than *external* threat. Truman understood the importance of tradition but was convinced that, ultimately, the

Cold War was a battle of ideas that went beyond common traditions. The problem was less that European traditions were weakening and more that the principles behind the traditions were being challenged by a philosophy inimical to freedom. Kennan, for his part, did not think that the Soviet Union, through ideology or advantageous circumstances, pressured the Europeans or was trying to impose its ideological worldview—and thus its traditions—on the West. For him, the difficulty had less to do with ideas than with the rupture caused by the Second World War, which had given European man the opportunity to revert to his natural, less civilized state. European man jumped at the chance, according to Kennan, and the result was the moral decline of Europe and the danger of its total implosion.[60]

In the end, Kennan offered a variation on realpolitik, with the two great powers, the United States and the Soviet Union, as counterweights.[61] He therefore predicated the success of Europe on a two-fold belief that the insecure Kremlin, on the one hand, did not want more territory or influence and would settle for a buffer zone of security and that, on the other hand, a self-sufficient United States would not involve itself greatly in Europe—which is to say that both the Soviet Union and the United States would moderate their ways. Kennan recognized that if this premise were invalidated, America and the rest of the world "would suffer a cultural and spiritual loss incalculable in its long-term effects." PPS 4 concluded by invoking the primary importance of restoring hope in Europe—the "sort of Europe now in jeopardy"—in order to revive confidence and security in the world at large.[62]

In his memoirs, Kennan presented PPS 4 as a careful and more detailed study of the problem he had written about hastily two months earlier in PPS 2. He described PPS 4 as an "official rationale" for those at the operational and at the highest levels of government, and he explained that PPS 4 was helpful in the formulation of the European Recovery Program. But he believed that what he saw as the paper's lesson of regionalism would be forgotten. According to Kennan, "The congenital American aversion to regional approaches, and the yearning for universal ones, were too strong to be entirely overcome even by the success of the Marshall Plan—on the contrary, they were only stimulated by it."[63] In Kennan's containment, the Marshall Plan proved the superiority of particularism over universalism; it was a regional recovery program and an exception to Truman's transregional containment. As Kennan understood it, the ERP was the essence of limited, nonideological containment that he had posited against Truman's containment. As he confided in his memoirs, "It is my hope that [PPS 4] may some day be published in full, because I think it gives the most succinct and yet comprehensive picture of the official rationale of what our government attempted to do in this connection."[64] But Kennan's more thoughtful paper, despite his later comments (and the efforts of Gaddis and Etzold), departed from Truman's containment—and thus the official policy of the U.S. government.

Kennan Looks at the World

Kennan commented in his memoir that the X article did not put forth his comprehensive view and suggested that PPS 13 of November 1947 was a clearer explanation of his view of containment.[65] It was in PPS 13, entitled "Resume of World Situation," that Kennan argued that the Soviet Union was a defensive power (as in its "purely defensive move" during the Czechoslovak coup), which the United States incorrectly viewed as offensive. He saw the American interpretation of Soviet behavior in Czechoslovakia as lamentably leading to NATO and the militarization of the Cold War and recalled that "this development [in Czechoslovakia] represented a defensive reaction—and one foreseen by ourselves—to the success of the Marshall Plan initiative. This, however, was understood neither by American opinion nor by people throughout our governmental bureaucracy. The result was that the Communist crackdown in Czechoslovakia, when it came, was received generally as a new Communist success—the evidence, in fact, of the inadequacy of the methods of containment employed up to that time."[66] Since Kennan believed that the Soviets behaved defensively (and understandably), he wanted his narrow interpretation of the Marshall Plan to prevail. But this view did not correspond to either the threat assessments or policy intentions of the Truman administration. Kennan, by contrast, indicated that the United States, rather than the Soviet Union and its Communist ideology, caused the militarization of the Cold War.

At the beginning of PPS 13, Kennan summarized world trends, especially from the Soviet perspective. He argued that the Kremlin did not want war with the West in the foreseeable future, but he did not consider—to use Churchill's phrase—whether the Soviets still worked for the fruits of war. Conflating "Soviet" and "Russian" (as in the Long Telegram, the

X article, and elsewhere), Kennan did not evaluate the tactical flexibility of Communist ideology, but spoke narrowly of the temporary halt of Russian expansion in Western Europe largely because of American aid and the temporary presence of American troops in territories of former enemies. He accented the economic character of the Marshall Plan and again stated that economic aid alone would thwart the political aspirations of communism. Submitting his view that the Soviet Union was acting in the historical context of the Russian effort to extend domination over all, or as much as possible, of the Eurasian land mass, he deduced that the USSR was merely taking advantage of the power vacuums in Europe and Asia after the defeats of Germany and Japan. Although he identified the expansionism of the Kremlin and accepted the Soviets' natural inclination to fill the power vacuums, he did not perceive a totalitarian goal behind the actions.[67]

In PPS 13, Kennan attributed Soviet behavior to what he labeled a wave of radicalism that must follow any great military-political upheaval, which, in turn, would be succeeded by a receding wave of antiextremism. In a realist sense, Kennan agreed with the progressive idea that it was the diplomat's duty to help America effectively ride the inevitable waves of the forces of fate and history—a perspective that illuminates his focus on psychology and appearances. Because of these unavoidable and powerful waves, Kennan championed exploiting the Western psychological advantage of confidence over Russian insecurity. In an isolationist fashion later refined by academic revisionism, Kennan sketched a future Europe in which a Soviet sphere and a West European sphere independent of the United States balanced each other. His version of the ERP went beyond an economic policy and became the incubator for a revamped balance of power in Europe.[68]

Kennan admitted that, for a time, the Kremlin permitted Czechoslovakia the appearances of freedom in order to serve as bait for other nations. But he misconstrued the intentions of the Kremlin—the standard that he wanted to make preeminent—as "purely defensive." He focused on Moscow's fear that a crackdown in Czechoslovakia might inspire more underground anticommunism in the Soviet satellite region. In other words, although he recommended bolstering the local forces of resistance opposing communism in Western Europe, especially in France and Italy, he accepted the Soviet bloc as a sphere of influence due a great power. "All in all," he wrote, "our policy must be directed toward restoring a balance of power in Europe and Asia." Kennan did believe that the East Europeans would rebel one day from the Russians. But he suggested that their longing for a "higher cultural level"—rather than a more practical desire to be free from Communist threats and repression—would lead them to challenge their Soviet masters.[69]

In brief sections on Germany, the Middle East, and the Far East, PPS 13 advocated realist stability through a balance of powers and order, especially in the latter two chaotic regions. For Germany, the most critical state in the European arena of the Cold War, Kennan argued that, while the Russians would consider a genuinely democratic nation as a breeding ground for anti-Communist resistance, they would accede to a united and neutral state. Although Kennan advanced a united neutral Germany, he knew that this outcome (as with a united democratic Germany) was unlikely, and he maintained that the American solution should be "to make the best of a divided Germany" and convince the West Europeans to do their part so the United States would not have to "continue to bear the lion's share of the responsibility for handling it." This would involve enlightening the French, Belgians, Dutch, Danish, and others to the "necessities of the German situation." In addition to the curious omission of Great Britain and his own further effort to create continental and Soviet spheres independent of Britain, Kennan prescribed a rather imprudent solution: not only were the countries enumerated by him still digging out from Nazism and the economic and political disarray caused by the world war, but they also were trying to withstand the threats and pressure from the Soviets. In this context, the carrots of concession associated with realpolitik, not to mention the notion of Kennanesque "enlightenment" of the West Europeans, were maladroit, if not dangerous.[70]

All of this fed into Kennan's conclusions that the current American anxiety about the USSR rested on an incorrect appraisal of Soviet intentions. Because he thought that the most grievous threat stemmed from the possibility of a hot war, particularly between the two superpowers, he omitted in PPS 13 and his other writings the possibility that the Kremlin was waging a global cold war.[71] As John Lewis Gaddis later summarized, containment for Kennan involved no indiscriminate projection of commitments around the world; it was a means-based policy "precise in its identification of American interests, specific in its assessment of threats to those interests, frugal in its calculation of means required to ward off those threats, vague only in its public presentation."[72] Gaddis emphasized that the Truman administration's vagueness corrupted the original intent of the policy over time and sacrificed containment to idealistic rhetoric. And he persisted in maintaining that Kennan's containment had been the accepted approach of the administration, notably reflected in the Marshall Plan.[73]

Kennan kept his outlook on behavior and psychology as measures of the Cold War but refined the presentation of his containment in 1948. Faced with the successful beginnings of Truman's containment, Kennan lambasted the universalism and idealism he detected in the principles of the president and the American public. In PPS 23, "Review of Current Trends: U.S. Foreign Policy," of February 24, 1948, he rendered his next examination of the world situation and promulgated his concept of particularism versus universalism; central to this sketch, he perceived and criticized the universalistic tradition in America, which he associated with legalism and moralism in later writings. With a scrutiny of events and attitudes in Great Britain, Germany, and the rest of Western Europe; the Soviet Union and Eastern Europe; the Middle East, the Far East, and the Mediterranean, PPS 23 undergirds all of Kennan's general thought on international politics, including his political thought of containment. Gaddis and Etzold, as well, viewed the paper as pivotal; they introduced this paper as Kennan's organizing principle, and thus faulted Truman for deviating from Kennan's containment as expressed by PPS 23.[74] For Gaddis and other scholars of postrevisionism, PPS 23 built on PPS 13 by elucidating a particularized or realist foreign policy, which pinpoints only vital interests and abides by limited resources, that should guide America in foreign affairs.[75]

In the first and most theoretical extract from PPS 23, Kennan coined new terms for idealism and realism: universalism and particularism. Because he believed in no invariable qualities except for power and order, he began in a way that ruled out thinking and acting according to universal principles of freedom and justice. Instead, Kennan identified a confused duality of universalism and particularism in American foreign policy, especially evident in 1948. Leaving the president and Congress out of the equation, he rooted this duality—and the dual practice in the workings of American engagement in the world—in the U.S. government and the State Department, terms he interchanged. The idealist or universalist, according to Kennan, solved international problems through a universalistic pattern of rules and procedures applicable to all countries—or at least to all countries prepared to join the world plan—in an identical way. Although experts at State were torn between the two practices, Kennan believed that the American public, and Truman by association, favored universalism. He argued that, in order to simplify the complexities of different peoples, U.S. citizens embraced the legalism, moralism, and vagaries of international organizations.[76]

Kennan displayed a degree of impatience, if not scorn, for the American people (and for liberal democracy) by saying that many of them found the "national peculiarities and diverging political philosophies" to be "confusing and irritating." He also worried that this universalistic mentality eliminated what he regarded as political solutions achieved through diplomatic professionalism. He offered this analysis because he thought that ordinary people were incapable of understanding "the world as it is." Accusing Americans of a "strong vein of escapism," he showed a preference for a return to traditional diplomacy able to handle "involved political choices" that Americans considered sordid. The best possibility, given his low view of man, was for professional diplomats to organize power to bring order.[77]

Outlining his particularized approach in PPS 23, Kennan praised skepticism of "any scheme for compressing international affairs into legalistic concepts." In accord with the realist school of thought, he declared that people's "thirst for power" could be assuaged or controlled only by counterforce. Alliances could be helpful, insofar as they based themselves in a community of interests and outlook, "which is to be found only among limited groups of governments, and not upon the abstract formalism of universal international law or international organization." Kennan felt more comfortable with the old tradition and endurance of European governments.[78] After decimating the abstraction of "peace," Kennan depicted men and their polities as capable of acting merely according to their base interests—that is, the urge toward power. For these reasons, he dismissed the theory of national sovereignty, which he said had abetted foreign aggression, under the guise of autonomy, in other nations. Although he perceived the danger that universal undertakings through an international organization could circumscribe American action at critical times, he did not put this problem in terms of the United States' continued ability to defend its own sovereign independence.[79]

Ultimately, in PPS 23, Kennan wanted American measures only on behalf of the country's "own defense and for the defense of concepts of international relations which might be of vital importance to world stability as a whole." Big powers, more than small states, should have sway in world affairs, because they possessed more power. But for Kennan, such a result did not raise questions of justice; instead, he focused on the stability of "the world as it is," even if it were made up of stable tyrannies and well-ordered despotisms. Attempting to pilot the dual policy of the U.S. government toward seemingly permanent realism, he reiterated his support for the regional or particularized approach over the functional or universalistic concept. Kennan desired a morally neutral statesman, who made no distinctions among regimes, to practice diplomacy in bringing about an orderly world that enlightened people would deem truly at peace. And again he advocated an elite corps who would make the policies and justify them to the public. Indeed, Kennan recommended keeping from Americans the knowledge that the State Department had turned from the universalistic to the particularized policy, because many people could not deal with any abrupt changes assailing the "symbol of our belief in the possibility of a peaceful world."[80]

Hoping to avoid the pitfalls of world government, Kennan propounded a network of regional arrangements that would lead outward in ever-widening circles to an organized global order. To correct the tendency toward universalism, he relied on custom and tradition, guided by the wisdom of expert diplomats. "For a truly stable world order can proceed, within our lifetime, only from the older, mellower and more advanced nations of the world—nations for which the concept of order, as opposed to power, has value and meaning," Kennan argued. "If these nations do not have the strength to seize and hold real leadership in world affairs today, through that combination of political greatness and wise restraint which goes only with a ripe and settled civilization, then, as Plato once remarked: ' . . . cities will never have rest from their evils,—no, nor the human race, as I believe.'"[81] International order demanded the coincidence of diplomacy and power, just as the city formulated in the *Republic* required the coincidence of philosophy and power.[82] But the end was not the ordered harmony of soul that Socrates propounded; rather, the realist strived for an imposed, artificial international order. As a diplomatist-king, Kennan implied that unless diplomats ruled, or those that ruled turned to diplomats, there would be no peace in the world. Plato understood the impossibility of philosopher-kings; Kennan's world was equally unlikely.[83]

6

The Beginning of
the Atlantic Alliance

Some would say that the United States in 1947 and 1948 had done as much as (or more than) it should have in the Truman Doctrine and the Marshall Plan, but Harry Truman did not think so. He believed that primarily political and economic aid were insufficient under the unprecedented circumstances of the Cold War; a strategic military component, he reasoned, was needed as part of containment. So Truman endorsed what he saw as an unprecedented yet proportionate response: the Atlantic Alliance, a collective defense arrangement that protected its member states from attack without the sacrifice of national sovereignty. This original contribution to postwar liberal internationalism rejected the primacy of both collective security and the international organization as required, for different reasons, by Woodrow Wilson's progressive internationalism and Franklin Roosevelt's version of liberal internationalism. The president supported programs, notably the Brussels Treaty in March 1948, that demonstrated the West Europeans' resolve to deter Soviet aggression. Only in such a context, and after publicly promoting the idea and securing congressional approval in the Vandenberg Resolution of June 1948, did he commit the United States to the North Atlantic Treaty in 1948 and 1949. With continued Communist pressure on Western Europe in the mid- to late 1940s, especially the Czechoslovak coup in February 1948, Truman saw a world made dangerous by the Soviet Union. He hoped that the Atlantic Alliance would defend its members against Soviet belligerence and possible invasion. For NATO's contribution to containment overall, he had greater hopes.[1] The combination of political, economic, and strategic elements, he said, should eventually enable the free world "to carry the ideological war to the Soviet sphere itself."[2]

"At the Water's Edge"

Events in Europe and the Middle East in the spring of 1948 seemed to confirm Truman's political thought. On April 3, the president signed the Marshall Plan—enacted by Congress as the Foreign Assistance Act of 1948—in time to influence elections later that month in Italy. It was clear to him, though, that political and economic support required the addition of a coherent military program. Truman had already learned, for instance, that the Communist guerrilla assault on the people of Greece necessitated more military aid and, consequently, in November 1947, had proposed transferring funds from the economic to the military program in Greece.[3] But he also knew that if such programs were implemented haphazardly, measures would be only makeshift. There was no policy in place, for example, to help Norway, which was concerned that the Soviets would demand a treaty similar to the one with Czechoslovakia. The president repeatedly illuminated his point by contrasting relief and recovery. Some of his domestic programs veered toward short-term relief. The foreign policy programs associated with containment, however, were intended to bring about a more complete recovery; relief implied a temporary respite, whereas recovery meant a thorough rebuilding. In the context of postwar Europe, recovery meant not only healing the devastations of war but also restoring human rights, stimulating democratic institutions, and defending freedom. Just as Truman's overall foreign policy stemmed from axioms of independence and freedom, rather than self-determination or stability, so did his containment policies.

The situation in Germany again marked the tensions of the war of nerves in spring 1948. While a half dozen American, British, and French divisions remained in the western half of Germany, estimates of 175 to 200 Soviet divisions or their satellites occupied the eastern side of the country. As well, reports circulated that a "people's police" was training some fifty thousand Germans in the East, recruited from cadres of the former "free" German committee, the Communist party, and graduates of the antifascist schools. At the same time, large numbers of refugees from eastern Germany and Czechoslovakia were permitted to push into the western zones of Germany. (Members of the "free" German committee and other Communist-trained prisoners of war also returned to western Germany to try to infiltrate industry and government.) Although it did not succeed, economic pressure was applied to eject the Allies from Berlin and the rest of the western zones of Germany.[4]

The Czechoslovak coup, Soviet demands on Finland, continued Communist problems in Greece, and new Soviet constraints on western portions of Berlin and Germany prompted five West European nations to sign the Brussels Treaty in March 1948. This treaty gave some political teeth to the essentially powerless Western Union of Great Britain, France, Holland, Belgium, and Luxembourg. Despite its structure as a regional mutual defense pact, the Brussels Treaty lacked military muscle, and the countries involved, especially Britain, had been asking the Truman administration for an assurance of American strength. Truman and his top advisors had supported the initiative since before its March inception, precisely because it committed the West Europeans to their own defense prior to the United States helping them militarily in what probably would be a long-term formal arrangement. Knowing that Senate approval was required for America to join an alliance (which the country, historically, had avoided), that some might interpret the terms of the new treaty as an infringement on the congressional power to declare war, and that future congressional funding would be needed, the president turned to Republican Senator Arthur Vandenberg of Michigan, the majority party leader on foreign policy, for help.[5]

By a vote of sixty-four to six, the Vandenberg Resolution passed the Senate on June 11, 1948, to enable the United States to pursue what became the North Atlantic Alliance. Vandenberg and other Republicans who favored American involvement in foreign affairs merged with Truman and many of his fellow Democrats to support the idea of peace through strength. As a result, the political thought and action of containment reflected a strong sense of bipartisanship, rather than a distinctively Democratic or Republican theme.

While they conveyed their partisan differences in speeches, letters, and memoirs, Truman and Vandenberg respected and worked with each other when it came to America's policies in the Cold War. Although Truman would have preferred a Democratically controlled Eightieth Congress and Vandenberg would have liked a Republican as president, each searched for the highest common ground in foreign affairs so that bipartisan unity would begin "at the water's edge"—in the senator's memorable phrasing.[6] In doing so, they found what was permanent and rejected a mere consensus or synthesis of diverging opinions. As Vandenberg wrote Churchill in 1949, "Our job is *not* finished until we have stabilized a *free world of free men*."[7] The men who framed containment agreed about a threat to universal liberty and justice from an ideologically expansive USSR. They believed that the United States was the only people and government with the philosophy, means, and will to lead a countercoalition against Soviet totalitarianism.

The Election of 1948

If it were not enough to deal with Czechoslovakia, Germany, and a Republican Senate, 1948 was also an election year. In April, Truman wrote in longhand of the grave situations around the world, including Greece, Turkey, Palestine, and another "half dozen with Russia which no one knew anything about—and which could not be broadcast." He pointed out that "[n]ever in our history have we been faced with such conditions—and a presidential campaign year. The campaign must go on, but remember the safety of the world and ourselves are inextricably tied together." We might think that his tactics would resemble his bipartisan foreign policy. On the campaign trail, he said as much: "It has been the policy of the United States under this administration to keep foreign policy out of politics; that is, politics within the United States. It is necessary for us as a nation to go to the water's edge with a solid front." At various times, he remarked that, since there was great accord between Democrats and Republicans in foreign policy, he would not have to talk much about the subject during his whistlestop trip across America. His comments echoed Vandenberg's formulation that bipartisan collaboration would result in a nonpartisan, foreign policy unity "at the water's edge." But as he privately noted, to honor his God-given responsibility in world politics, "we must have complete cooperation from the waters [*sic*] edge—at home it is not so important."[8] In a short passage, he alluded to what became a masterful, and sometimes mean-spirited, political campaign. Although reference to foreign policy was infrequent in comparison with domestic concerns, it was tactically deployed. While Special Counsel Clifford, as is widely recognized, was important to Truman's winning strategy, the president himself was the key to it.

Truman waged a deliberate strategy in which he aimed to distinguish himself from his main opponents: the Republicans and the Progressives. In so doing, he worked to appear as a liberal acceptable to a plurality (as it turned out) or majority (he hoped) of his fellow citizens. The easier and smaller of the two targets was Henry Wallace and his Progressive Party. While the president did not want to alienate Democrats who supported Wallace, he knew that there was a percentage of apathetic Democrats whom he needed to ignite in his favor. His challenge was to add to the firm core of support for the Democrats—which Truman sensed was there, even though polls only hinted at it—by drawing from both otherwise stay-at-home voters and Progressives.[9] He first argued against the concept of a third party, attempting to eliminate the Progressive Party as an option for undecided and unexcited Democrats; then he honed his points to woo the Democrats who thought that the Progressives represented true liberalism. Not only did he bluntly state that the Communists were guiding the third party, which meant that Wallace and his supporters undercut liberal ideals, but he also said that voting for the Progressives would weaken the Democratic Party, strengthen the "Republican forces of reaction" and their party, and injure American liberalism.[10]

Before and during his courtship of Progressives and torpid Democrats, Truman launched his dominant assault on Republican candidate Thomas Dewey and his party. On numerous occasions, he hit this larger and harder target with charges that the Republicans were rapacious, self-indulgent, responsible for the Great Depression, and "dominated by the forces of reaction." He would praise the unity of bipartisan foreign policy based on shared, basic principles in one section of a speech and argue that the "Republican Party either corrupts its liberals or it expels them" in another part of the same address.[11] Truman inverted his argument against the Progressives and applied it to the Republicans, but to the same end: Dewey and his party would destroy liberalism and lead the country in the wrong direction. By conceding harmony with the Republican Party on what most voters supported, especially containment and the nobility of the United Nations, the president was free to accuse Republicans of illiberalism on the home front. He did so knowing that Americans, if they thought much about such terms in 1948, would call themselves forward-looking—a stock Truman phrase—or liberal rather than reactionary and, wittingly or unwittingly, helpful to Communists. On the whistlestop tour, he reiterated, for example, that the Communist Party achieved its maximum strength in the United States in 1932 under Herbert Hoover, thrived on misery, and supported the Progressives in order to assure a Republican victory. "Communists count on a reactionary Republican administration to make all the mistakes that ignorance and greed can inspire," said Truman, in a typical statement. "And they expect that a Republican administration will reduce the American people to another Hoover depression that will undermine the Marshall plan and pave the way for world revolution. That's what they want. That's what the Communists want."[12] Reaching a crescendo in late October, he argued that a Democratic vote was a vote to fight communism and that U.S. foreign policy would be safer in the Democrats' hands.

Despite Truman's partisanship and his often fierce tactics, his 1948 campaign should not be viewed as an abandonment of his political beliefs. It is commonly argued that Harry Truman ran left in the 1948 election in order to steal votes from Wallace. On domestic issues, however, the president did not have to try to sound more progressive, because his political opinions and legislative agenda proved his liberalism. He never changed his foreign policy or domestic positions in order to beat his Progressive and Dixiecrat opponents. With respect to foreign policy, he articulated his principles toward the Cold War and containment similarly to his noncampaign—or "nonpolitical," in his words—speeches and writings. Although his domestic campaign attacks on the GOP became increasingly strident, his understanding of foreign policy remained focused on the need for the United States to stand firm, be strong, and remain vigilant. On many matters, however, he became distracted by the 1948 election and was as partisan as any American politician has been on any campaign trail. This partisanship sometimes became excessive and immoderate, including his comparisons of Dewey to Hitler and his implications toward the end of the campaign that the Republicans abetted the Communists because the GOP aimed to defeat him.[13] If he had used the same restrained yet uplifting tone in his final radio remarks on election eve throughout the campaign, we can only speculate as to the effect on the outcome.[14] Clearly, however, Truman thought that making U.S. security—supposedly a moot area of agreement with regard to the Republicans—into the critical issue of distinction between the two major parties would provide him with a wedge. His rhetoric and his tactics were one and succeeded in terms of winning the election, but he temporarily sacrificed the unity of American purpose that was vital to his Cold War strategy of containment and his liberal internationalism.

As part of his whistlestops, Truman was making public arguments to lay the foundation for the Atlantic Alliance and setting forth a three-part program in foreign policy: making the United Nations the vehicle for international law and world order; ensuring the political and economic imperatives for the ERP; and asserting the need for peace through military strength, beginning in the United States. Stumping on June 11, he made his "I like old Joe" comment, which stands as a Truman irregularity that some historians and political scientists dwell on disproportionately to explain the dichotomy within his thought.[15] Looking at his remarks on June 11 and 12 overall, however, especially in a commencement address at Berkeley, Truman continued to contrast Communist tyranny and peace with freedom and justice.

Clark Clifford noted that Truman rarely used the term "cold war." In the Berkeley speech, the president explained that the United States was not waging a "cold war" but found itself in a "twilight period, between war so dearly won and a peace that still eludes our grasp." Truman did not want the United States and the free world to be seen as equivalent in any way to the Soviet Union, an aggressive and subversive regime. As such, he hoped to make "cold war," a relatively new term, illegitimate. "The cleavage that exists is not between the Soviet Union and the United States," he stated with regard to communism and the Cold War. "It is between the Soviet Union and the rest of the world." Truman thought that the goal of the Kremlin—through indirect aggression in Eastern Europe, extreme pressure in the Middle East, and intervention in the internal affairs of other nations by means of Communist parties directed from Moscow—was to expand the realm of Communist tyranny. The United States sought to provide for the recovery of Europe and, in general, the defense of free peoples, but Truman knew that there was nothing to negotiate "when one nation habitually uses coercion and open aggression in international affairs."[16]

In his campaign against Truman for president in 1948, Henry Wallace returned to Madison Square Garden to promote a progressive American foreign policy that would exclude the Atlantic Alliance. On May 11, Radio Moscow made public an exchange from the week before between U.S. Ambassador to the Soviet Union Walter Bedell Smith and Soviet Foreign Minister Vyacheslav Molotov. Smith had stated that Wallace's opinion in foreign policy would never be the Truman administration's position and ended with rather routine diplomatic language: "As far as the United States is concerned, the door is always open for a full discussion and the composing of our differences"; Radio Moscow reported that the Kremlin was willing to meet with the U.S. government for "a discussion and settlement of the differences existing between them."[17] President Truman immediately issued a press release that the "statement by Ambassador Smith represented no new departure in American policy. It was a reiteration of the American position as it has been repeatedly expressed both publicly and privately."[18] Wallace, who had been working on an open letter to Stalin since April (after dropping the notion of a visit to Moscow), decided to read his message publicly that evening at a rally already scheduled for Madison Square Garden. His reading of the letter was aired nationwide on radio, and the complete text was published in the *New York Times*. "I present my thoughts on the steps necessary to achieve the Century of Peace," said Wallace. Neither country should maintain foreign bases or "terrorize the citizens of member states of the UN by massing land forces, establishing air bases, or making naval demonstrations," he continued. "Neither the USA nor the USSR should use financial pressure, economic pressure or the pressure of secret agents to obtain political results in other countries."[19] What he said was a criticism of Soviet actions, but also of existing Truman policies. Stalin—probably to undermine the Brussels Treaty and influence debate about the Vandenberg Resolution in the Senate Foreign Relations Committee—said on May 17 that "Mr. Wallace's program could serve as a good and fruitful basis" for an agreement between the United States and the USSR. The episode came to a close with a statement from Secretary of State George Marshall, although in speeches Wallace continued to offer to meet with Stalin if it would "advance the cause of peace."[20]

As a rule and in his campaign, Wallace held his own country accountable for the problems between East and West. He faulted the United States, generally, and Truman, implicitly, for failing to get along with the USSR and for appealing to American "Russia-haters," rather than understanding the Soviet Union's problems and helping the Soviets to understand American problems. Wallace blamed U.S. policy for causing the Kremlin to protect its borders with "friendly" governments, and he argued that Soviet methods were carried over from the absolutism of Czarist Russia and in response to the United States' and Western Europe's practice of similar methods. Because he thought that the West had wrought the Cold War, Wallace believed that U.S. conciliation and East-West convergence would resolve the conflict. "American capitalism must become progressive," he argued, and the "Communists must attain a sufficient feeling of security in Russia so that they are willing to grant democratic civil liberties." Wallace foresaw these changes happening at a slow pace, but he thought that without them there would be a perpetuation of two worlds and of war.[21]

The Berlin Airlift

If Truman needed verification that NATO was the appropriate measure to fortify political and economic growth, he got it with the Berlin blockade, which began officially on June 24, 1948, but had been brewing since March, when the Soviet Union imposed restrictions on highway and rail traffic into West Berlin.[22] Scholars typically offer several reasons for the Soviet action in western Berlin, including the Vandenberg Resolution itself, U.S. support for an expanded Western Union as a prelude to the North Atlantic Alliance, and American circulation of the new deutsche mark in western Berlin and western Germany. In terms of the intersection between profound and proximate causes, though, the blockade followed from the Kremlin's late 1947 realization that the ongoing presence of the Western Allies in Berlin prevented the consolidation of eastern Germany as a Communist state and hinted at the creation of a democratic state in western Germany.[23] Significantly, Truman saw Berlin as the heart of the struggle over Germany and, in a larger sense, over Europe, and he understood that "Berlin had become a symbol of America's—and the West's—dedication to the cause of freedom." He described the blockade as part of a Soviet plan to test the will and capacity of the West to resist; he did not want to start a war, but he refused to abandon the city.[24] Although he differentiated their tactics, Truman likened the latest Kremlin maneuver to its earlier probing in Greece and Turkey and considered both moves to have originated from the same Communist ideology.

At first, Truman was almost alone in thinking that an airlift would work as an effective response to the Soviets and as a mechanism to convey food, fuel, and medicine to the besieged in West Berlin. The majority of his advisors concluded that the West should give up its position. Four days into the crisis, however, when the topic was raised at a White House meeting, Truman interrupted to say that there was "no discussion on that point, we were going to stay period." When more opposition was aired, he added "that we were in Berlin by terms of an agreement and that the

Russians had no right to get us out by either direct or indirect pressure."[25] The president also had to push for support of the airlift—even after it had begun—and was frustrated with the defeatist attitude of those around him, especially his military advisors. In July, he privately wrote that he had "to listen to a rehash of what I know already and reiterate my 'Stay in Berlin' decision. I don't pass the buck, nor do I alibi out of any decision I make."[26] Even General Lucius Clay, who had initiated the airlift, doubted that it would work and wanted more direct military action.[27] Nevertheless, Truman pursued the policy that, in hindsight, seems the prudent course: he avoided withdrawal from Berlin (which would have translated into capitulation to the Soviets), on the one hand, and he avoided either sending a convoy of tanks and trucks into the western sector or directly striking the Communists, on the other (either of which would have risked starting a hot war). While it was not superior in terms of land strength and most likely could not have sustained a military convoy if blocked or attacked, the United States could and did outperform the USSR technologically and tactically in the air during the Berlin crisis. The Soviets lifted the blockade on May 12, 1949, although the airlift continued until September 30 to build up stocks in order to deter further threats. In the end, the airlift delivered 2,325,809 tons of supplies in 277,804 flights. Truman had selected the appropriate display of strength, which demonstrated to the Kremlin the West's resolve over time to stand by West Berlin and, by extension, West Germany and Western Europe.[28]

During and after the Berlin crisis, Truman saw the necessity of the Atlantic Alliance, but he also knew that American strength must precede the rebuilding of a free Europe; he had already asked for a buildup of U.S. ground capabilities and again for the enactment of universal military training (UMT) in spring 1948. The question remains, however, as to why the president did not spend more on defense if he had pledged himself to containment. Even a sympathetic biographer like Alonzo Hamby takes Truman to task in 1948 for locking "himself into a rigid and dangerous budgetary formula that tolerated a growing disparity between escalating commitments and military capabilities."[29] Part of the answer lies, as Hamby and others indicate, in Truman's belief in balanced budgets and in his judgment that he could not get more defense spending out of Congress. When the Second World War ended unexpectedly in the Pacific, demobilization followed rapidly. Truman thought that he could not stop the process, given public and congressional opinion. For fiscal year 1948, the House of Representatives trimmed his military budget proposal, and it took Senator Vandenberg to persuade the Senate to keep cuts to a minimum. Perhaps as important to Truman was that financing the war debt and solving the job shortage for returning soldiers had given rise to inflation, which had been a problem since the end of World War II. Although lower in 1948 than in previous years, inflation had not been tamed, and it dominated domestic economic questions posed to the president at news conferences. As a fiscal conservative in certain respects, Truman aimed to avoid deficit-fed inflation and had to be convinced that any government expenditure was necessary.[30] When satisfied, he gave his unqualified support. He targeted billions of dollars for the Marshall Plan beginning in 1948, for example, and lobbied Congress for approval of the funding. Because he believed that unrestrained military spending would result in lasting budget deficits, the president—perhaps thinking back to his time as chairman of the Truman Committee—looked for ways to spend his defense dollars effectively. In 1948, he again called for a draft and UMT. Truman reasoned that more manpower would help the United States be prepared for and fight the Cold War, especially in the wake of the Czechoslovak coup and growing tensions in Germany, but he refused to spend the United States into a situation that the Soviets could exploit.[31] Intelligence reports, meanwhile, stressed the Soviet Union's economic weaknesses and unreliable allies and projected that mid-1950 would be the earliest time by which the Kremlin would develop an atomic bomb. Given America's current atomic monopoly, the Truman Doctrine, the ERP, and the promise of the North Atlantic pact, Truman thought that the 1948 defensive capabilities were adequate.

In the years 1947 through 1949, around $13 billion was spent each year on national security, excluding veterans' benefits. While this amount was a significant reduction from World War II levels, it accounted for about one-third of the government's annual expenditures. In each of these years it was the largest single item in the budget, and Truman did not want it to rise above a third of all spending. Although he consistently asked for UMT and was denied it, he took some satisfaction in the fact that the armed forces were four times larger in the postwar era, despite demobilization, than they had been before the war.[32] Besides, in his evaluation of current and future defense spending, he had discovered that the military establishment was inflating its needs out of interservice rivalry. His disdain for waste and dishonesty was as strong as when he headed the

Truman Committee. He was somewhat justified in this view, because Forrestal had to submit combined and coordinated military budgets under the National Security Act but was unable to control the vying service secretaries.[33]

Truman searched for ways to use defense dollars most efficiently. Part of his attraction to NATO seems to have been fiscal, although American economic commitments to it quickly disabused him of that idea. By late 1949, with further developments in the Eastern bloc and in China and with amendments to the National Security Act that strengthened the hand of the secretary of defense, he reevaluated his view of military spending. It is speculative to say what global difference larger defense budgets would have made in 1947 through mid-1949.[34] More military strength on the part of the United States in this critical period might have slowed the Communist solidification of Eastern Europe and more quickly impeded the Kremlin's efforts in Western Europe and the Middle East. But since the Soviets had acquired early and wide intelligence about atomic weaponry through espionage, they likely would not have stopped their pursuit of the bomb if faced with larger American capabilities.

In this context usually comes the charge that Truman contemplated a "peace mission" to Moscow in October 1948 by Chief Justice Fred Vinson in order to prove his progressive credentials to disgruntled Democrats who had left their party and sided with Wallace. For a briefly considered notion on the part of the president, the Vinson mission receives significant attention from scholars. Yet, like the "I like old Joe" comment, it was an anomaly. While Truman understood that the settlement of Germany's future was critical to all of Europe, indeed the world, he knew that a divided Germany would fundamentally alter Europe. He believed that NATO was imperative, but that it would change, perhaps forever, both Europe and America. When Truman evaluated the proposals for an independent democratic West Germany and NATO, he perceived them as necessary but unprecedented. These exceptional steps responded to Soviet ideology and actions. Unconventional times, reasoned Truman, called for unconventional measures. Only in light of these circumstances was the president willing to think of sending Vinson to Moscow or even calling Stalin himself. But upon reflection and after speaking with Marshall, who objected strenuously, Truman thought better of it and rejected the idea.[35]

The North Atlantic Treaty Becomes a Reality

The gestation of the North Atlantic Treaty ran from July 1948 to the signing ceremony by the foreign ministers of the member countries in Washington, D.C., on April 4, 1949.[36] Senate ratification, and Truman's signature on the treaty ratification, followed in late July. In explaining the passage of months, some scholars argue that action could not be justified quickly because the Soviets were relatively quiet in winter 1948–1949, in comparison to 1945 through 1948. Others contend that the U.S. election delayed progress on NATO. But the most salient reasons were logistical: the State Department team of Secretary George Marshall and Undersecretary Robert Lovett was replaced by Dean Acheson and James Webb in January 1949, and there was a different majority in Congress from that which passed the Truman Doctrine and the Marshall Plan. Acheson, who had been so essential in 1947 while working with Marshall, had been in private life for over a year and was unaware of the negotiation nuances of 1948. As secretary of state, he displayed a sharp, sometimes sardonic, personality, which exerted a sometimes detrimental influence, different from when he had been undersecretary. His undersecretary, Webb, immersed himself in detail work and provided little help on broad policy matters. On the Senate side, Democrat Tom Connally had replaced Vandenberg as chairman of the Foreign Relations Committee, although the latter was an important minority figure. Connally defended the Atlantic Alliance but, not surprisingly, insisted on a revision that guaranteed Congress's primacy in committing the United States to war. Acheson had mostly civil working relationships with the two senators, but Lovett had gotten on well with Vandenberg.[37] Despite Truman's leadership, the process to convince the Senate to ratify a unique treaty—which pledged the United States to the defense of other nations for the foreseeable future—was lengthened by the personnel and personalities involved.

During the 1948 campaign, Truman had talked about the United Nations and the goal of "permanent peace." In his January 1949 State of the Union and inaugural addresses, he returned, significantly, to speaking of an "enduring" rather than a "permanent" peace. While the State of the Union speech pertained more to proposed domestic policies of the Fair Deal than to foreign policy, the inaugural address once again set forth the principles of containment, calling for freedom and eventual peace through strength. The president placed freedom first as an idea and indisputable right, followed by greater liberty for all in practice, and resulting in justice, harmony, and peace. He also spoke of the new period in world affairs in which the United States found itself standing against the "current human oppressors" and called for the equality and liberty of all peoples under God and law. In a litany that expounded the unbridgeable differences between Communist tyranny and democratic liberty, he labeled communism a false philosophy that denied both human rights and free government: "Communism is based on the belief that man is so weak and inadequate that he is unable to govern himself, and therefore requires the rule of strong masters. Democracy is based on the conviction that man has the moral and intellectual capacity, as well as the inalienable right, to govern himself with reason and justice," said Truman. "Communism subjects the individual to arrest without lawful cause, punishment without trial, and forced labor as the chattel of the state. It decrees what information he shall receive, what art he shall produce, what leaders he shall follow, and what thoughts he shall think. Democracy maintains that government is established for the benefit of the individual, and is charged with the responsibility of protecting the rights of the individual and his freedom in the exercise of those abilities of his."[38] Truman reiterated the importance of accruing strength at home and in the North Atlantic Treaty in order to protect and further freedom and peace abroad. He also pointed out that peace meant nothing—or, conversely, could be construed as anything—if it could not be grounded in man's natural right to freedom and upheld by regimes dedicated to human liberty.

While not discounting its psychological boost to Western Europe and the free world, President Truman regarded the North Atlantic Treaty primarily as one more step in the evolution of American foreign policy, assisting the UN charter, the Truman Doctrine, and the Marshall Plan in containing Soviet imperialism and Communist tyranny.[39] Because he knew the problems of Europe were more than economic, he sought to create an integrated defense mechanism that would mitigate the fears of the people and prevent the gains of aggression and worked to include all nations that were essential to Atlantic security. In harmony with this understanding, the preamble of the North Atlantic Treaty defended freedom in a positive sense. Its participants "determined to safeguard the freedom, common heritage, and civilization of their peoples, founded on the principles of democracy, individual liberty, and the rule of law." As a practical political document, it not only contracted to maintain collective defense and preserve peace and security, but it also promised to strengthen free institutions and enhance understanding of those institutions. Its members sought effective self-help and mutual aid in order to sustain the capacity, individually and collectively, to defy armed attack.[40]

At the signing ceremony of the Atlantic Alliance charter in April 1949, Truman made three distinctions, each of which underlined his understanding of liberal internationalism. First, he contrasted the compulsive sameness of tyranny and the heterogeneity of freedom. Second, in light of his direct experience in two world wars, Truman constructed a spectrum with freedom as the mean and tyranny and anarchy as the excesses, making freedom the virtue between the two contrasting vices. Third, he contrasted war and peace, coupling the former with slavery and the latter with freedom and rejecting dialectical materialism, while upholding the ability of man to determine his fate. (Invoking the Truman Doctrine, he returned to this theme of the chasm between slavery and freedom in his speeches throughout 1949.) The date of the pact's signing, April 4, 1949, exemplified these differences, for on the same day the Communists purged three hundred of their own in Bulgaria. One month later, in May, the North Atlantic Treaty became tied with the birth of an independent Federal Republic of Germany at the same time that the Berlin airlift convinced the Soviets to lift the blockade on the western part of that city. The police state method preferred by the Kremlin imposed uniform beliefs and the rule of force, while, as Truman put it, "We believe it is possible for nations to achieve unity on the great principles of human freedom and justice, and at the same time to permit, in other respects, the greatest diversity of which the human mind is capable."[41]

As candid as he was in public, Truman was more so in a confidential discussion with the NATO foreign ministers on April 3, 1949. He made it clear that, in his mind, the North Atlantic Treaty embodied the West's resolve to fight Communist ideology in a strategic organization, without any intention of military dominance. Because "our best estimate is that we have several years in which we can count on a breathing spell" with respect to Soviet acquisition of atomic weapons, the president thought that the Atlantic Alliance could safely rely for the time on conventional forces for its defense. But NATO, by itself, was insufficient. Once more, he showed the political, economic, and military pieces of containment as interdependent and the overall strategy as anything but passive. Only through democratic economic development, which would prevent communism from taking hold in the West and undermine it the East, could the Cold War be won. Foreshadowing both NSC 68's message and the birth of Radio Free Europe in 1950, as well as the ongoing efforts of Voice of America, he told the NATO foreign ministers, "We should appreciate that Soviet nationalism is dynamic; it must expand, and the only way to defeat it eventually is not merely to contain it but to carry the ideological war to the Soviet sphere itself."[42]

The president articulated another essential aspect of his political thought in July 1949, at the same time as the Senate ratified the North Atlantic Treaty and shortly before the alliance became operative in August. While still hewing to his expectations for an international organization, he presented an almost Tocquevillian argument for a voluntary and loose agreement among democratic nations on international matters. Truman not only repudiated the idea of making human beings "pawns in the game of power politics" but also expressed his great optimism for the cause of freedom. In the battle for men's minds, he said, the democratic faith would always be more appealing, more dynamic, and stronger than any totalitarianism. As the idea of freedom had prevailed against the absolute monarchies of old, so, too, Truman believed, would it succeed against "the new and more terrible dictatorships of the 20th century." After Senate ratification of the North Atlantic Treaty, the president immediately took the step of asking Congress for approval of a $1.4 billion military assistance program for, among others, the NATO countries, Greece, Turkey, and the Philippines.[43]

As a statesman, Truman had concluded—and wanted others to understand—that the war of communism against democracy could not be settled by wishing for peace, in large part because Kremlin imperialism pursued its goals through an ideological strategy and amoral tactics. This belief did not diminish Truman's hope for peace, but it did lead him to put freedom first. As he told reporters in October 1949:

> Someone was in to see me just recently, and he asked why we didn't go ahead and make peace. "Why don't you get to the Russians and fix this thing up?" he said. I said, "All right, we will give them Berlin, we will give them Germany, we will give them Korea, we will give them Japan, we will give them East Asia. Then they will settle. Is that what you want?" "Oh no, that isn't what we want at all," he said. "That's what they want."[44]

Truman summarized at the end of the year, "Much as we prize peace and friendship, we prize freedom more." For Truman, freedom required the security of free men and free governments, not just a stability that acquiesced to the permanent division of Europe or a status quo that validated tyranny. The president's understanding of "the great principles of human freedom and justice"—with freedom as the virtue between tyranny and anarchy, and the polar opposite of slavery—was the backbone of his American liberal internationalism.[45] Practically, Truman considered the North Atlantic pact both a political and a military instrument to ensure that free peoples would determine their own future. Together in containment, the Truman Doctrine, the Marshall Plan, and NATO aimed to overcome tyranny and further the cause of human freedom.

The Critics Reject NATO

Contemporary critics of Truman and NATO argued that political psychology and a neutral balance of power—instead of considerations of Soviet intent and power—obviated the need for the alliance and worried that NATO would provoke the Soviet Union. In early 1949, Kennan wrote that there was no military threat to Western Europe and that the North Atlantic pact addressed the wrong problem. Extending his interpretation of 1948 as a yearlong needless war scare, he perceived a "sublimated fear" in Western Europe, which stemmed from a fear of inadequacy, and he held that NATO should be considered "pure psychological warfare" rather than a military alliance. In terms of balancing, he described as "embarrassing" the tendency "to jam [the alliance], so to speak, as close as possible to the Soviet borders."[46] Some modern scholars contend that by 1949 containment had largely achieved its primary objective, the restoration of a stable balance of power in Europe, and, following Kennan, criticize the "militarization" of NATO in 1950 as a threat to this status quo.[47]

By the end of 1949, Kennan had developed this analysis into a sophisticated critique. Concerning the military level of the Cold War, he commented, "I would rather wait thirty years for a defeat of the Kremlin brought about by the tortuous and exasperatingly slow devices of diplomacy than to see us submit to the test of arms a difference so little susceptible to any clear and happy settlement by those means." A military mindset masked a deeper problem: he thought that the rejection of his position would lead to the West internalizing the worst of the Soviet method of operation and becoming inured to its own weaknesses. In the end, according to Kennan, method was more important than principle: "I am saying that the real distinction between a liberal democracy and a totalitarian dictatorship lies only in the matter of method, not in the matter of aim, and that if the communists can induce us to make their methods our own, then we have lost, whether or not they have won; for that distinction of method is really all that we have to fight for." NATO, to Kennan, was symptomatic of the American tendency to regard the Cold War as an end in itself. He believed that the United States had perhaps already ignored the "internal enemy who is all around us and within us."[48]

Like future revisionists, Wallace meanwhile denounced the United States in March 1949 for replacing the United Nations with NATO and for pushing a "war alliance" in response to what he viewed as Stalin's willingness to discuss areas of disagreement. Since the pact gave "the United States Army military bases up to the very borders of the Soviet Union," he said, could anyone believe that, "as [the Soviets] stare across their borders at our jet bombers and our cannon, calm visions of peace will be born in their minds?"[49] Before the Senate Foreign Relations Committee later that spring, Wallace branded the North Atlantic pact the product of an alliance between "certain elements in the Catholic Church," "British imperial interests," and "our own big-business interests"; and in May 1949, he again attacked the formation of the Atlantic Alliance and said that he had been vindicated in his prediction that the Truman Doctrine "would cause us to bleed from every pore."[50]

In a somewhat fusionist manner, Lippmann agreed with Kennan and Wallace that the scope of the pact violated the balance of power, geographically and psychologically. He preferred a "little NATO," if any, which was limited "to nations not in immediate contact with the Soviet orbit." Objecting strenuously to any notion of the eventual inclusion of West Germany, he believed that the Atlantic Alliance would not only exhaust Western Europe and strain the United States but also "probably throw western Europe into political convulsions." Along with realism and anticipating revisionism, Lippmann thought that, since the Soviets did not appear to have the will to engage in a general war, local defenses against them were largely unnecessary; he maintained that the overall power of the United States could be increased within a reasonably short time after the outbreak of a war.[51]

George Kennan's formal criticism of NATO, however, demands elaboration, for when he disavowed the Atlantic Alliance in PPS 37 of August 1948—only two months after congressional passage of the Vandenberg Resolution—it marked the first time that Kennan's Policy Planning Staff disagreed with the rest of the State Department. And this despite that, at the end of the paper, Kennan called PPS 37 his "personal view."[52] All parties involved understood that the settlement of Germany was crucial to the future of Europe. For Truman, the disposition of Germany turned on the need to defend Europe from Soviet aggression. By this time, Kennan was convinced that the USSR would not use its military strength against the West, that economic measures were sufficient for recovery, and that the creation of a German state as part of a Western political and strategic alliance was unjustified, aggressive, and militaristic. Because of the intimate relationship between Germany and the defense of Europe, Kennan's advocacy of a unified, independent Germany required his opposition to a Western military alliance.[53]

Kennan began his analysis in PPS 37 with the premise that one day all American and Soviet forces would have to leave central Europe. The division that existed in Germany (and thus in Europe) was caused by the zonal boundaries started by the United States and imitated by the Soviet Union. As a solution, Kennan sought a great power compromise among the four occupying powers, and he proposed the withdrawal of occupying forces from the "major portion" of Germany, with some Allied forces retained on the periphery in a garrison status. He expected that such a military periphery, perhaps in the Rhineland and Silesia, would not interfere with the management of civil affairs in Germany. Since he saw no theoretical justification for any "treaty of peace" between the Germans and the Allies and felt "that it complicate[d] unnecessarily the real issues of German settlement," he left it up to the four powers, as the custodians of German sovereignty, to decide how much sovereignty Germany should receive, and when.[54]

As he had distanced himself from the Vandenberg Resolution, so Kennan also impugned the Western Union, which, already fortified by the Brussels pact, was in the process of being superseded by the Atlantic Alliance and London Conference developments (among the United States, Great Britain, France, and the Benelux countries to debate creation of a democratic West Germany) from March to June 1948. He did not believe that the Kremlin hardened the line of division in Europe through its aggression and infiltration—he ignored the recent imposition of the Berlin blockade by the Soviets, for example—and maintained that the West's decisions closed the door on the withdrawal of Soviet troops.[55] Kennan thought the division of Europe could be avoided (despite that it already had occurred) and the Berlin situation solved through the withdrawal of American and Soviet troops. (He concluded that the United States should withdraw its military forces in 1948.) For the United States, he put this move in terms of appearances "without loss of prestige." There was no way, of course, that he could ensure that the eastern half of Germany would become free or that the western half would remain free. The greatest advantage, he said, would be the savings in size, expense, and scope of American responsibilities in Germany and Europe. In broaching a compromise—a federated Western Europe that embraced a partitioned Germany—he omitted the cost, perhaps irredeemable, in leaving Western Europe undefended and the Soviet control of Eastern Europe unchallenged.[56]

Kennan finessed the disadvantages of his own plan for settlement, which he condensed into a concern about a viable German state. Pointing out that the "Germans, from all accounts, [were] confused, embittered, self-pitying and unregenerate," he admitted the possibility that a new Germany might cooperate with Moscow or succumb to the Communists and remarked that his settlement would work if Germany were the only great state in central Europe. Withal, he accented the psychological insecurities of the Soviets and French (who feared such a German state). In short, Kennan wanted to bypass the circumstances of the Cold War and build a new Germany in a political vacuum. He was willing to take chances on the "political evolution" of the German people, without recognizing that the Kremlin would challenge the establishment of a free, democratic, and strong nation in the heart of Europe. In truth, he did not expect them to evolve by themselves, and he looked on the unification of Europe as a check on resurgent German aggression.[57]

Kennan understood the central interests of both America and Europe in vastly different terms from Truman. Kennan rightly saw that "the development of life in Europe cannot await the composure of east-west differences" and that the circumstances of Germany needed special attention. But while he prided himself on his ability to decipher vital from peripheral interests in PPS 37, he did not consider that countering the Communist threat was a vital interest, because he did not believe, as did Truman, that communism strived to prevent (as it already had prohibited in Eastern

Europe) that very "development of life." Kennan, in effect, did not view the Cold War as the primary conflict of the international politics of his day and, instead, referred to the tragic differences between East and West. As a result, he criticized what he viewed as the incipient militarization of the London Program—which proposed the creation of a West German state that would be clearly a part of the West and, by implication, a potential member of any Western strategic alliance—because it provided no basis for negotiations with the Russians.[58] As he recollected in his memoirs, "Once, again, as is so often the case in American diplomacy, what was conceived as an instrument became, little by little, an end in itself. What was supposed to have been the servant of policy became its determinant instead."[59] Kennan did not aim for a containment, as Truman did, that encompassed political, economic, and strategic elements over time. Nor did he consider the freedom of as much of Germany as possible crucial to that containment. Instead, Kennan preferred the combination of economic and diplomatic policies, under the expertise of professionals like himself, that assigned little weight to military strength and, in its place, sought a nonideological, negotiated compromise with the USSR.

At the conclusion of two months of the Washington Security Talks in September 1948, the United States affirmed the rationale for a North Atlantic security pact and moved to include West Germany in the reach of such an organization. Representatives from the United Kingdom, Canada, Belgium, Luxembourg, France, and the Netherlands also signed on to a collective defense association and abjured the possibility of "peaceful coexistence" with the Kremlin. With his "Plan A," which was a form of PPS 37, rejected, Kennan issued PPS 43 and, in a slightly less contentious manner than in PPS 37, again repudiated the Atlantic Alliance in late November 1948.[60] Entitled "Considerations Affecting the Conclusion of a North Atlantic Security Pact," PPS 43 further reflected Kennan's growing divergence from American foreign policy.[61] (Gaddis and Etzold described PPS 43 as part of Kennan's containment—like PPS 37 and other Kennan papers, PPS 43 was neither read nor signed for approval by the president—and chided the acceptance of the "Washington paper" by the administration and the North Atlantic defense community, "[d]espite the misgivings of Kennan and the Policy Planning Staff.")[62]

In PPS 43, Kennan focused on the psychological factors involved in European politics, conceding that the Atlantic Alliance would confer a "general sense of security" on the area and could deter outside aggressive forces, but downplaying its significance because it would "not appreciably modify the nature or danger of Soviet policies." Instead of responding to Kremlin actions with military strength, the West, Kennan proposed, should respond on the level that he deemed adequate and legitimate: diplomacy. Although he noted that the "prestige engagement of the Russians and the western powers" in Berlin could lead to military danger (without mentioning an existing military threat), he sought to prevent a containment reinforced by a united and collective defense. The Cold War for the Soviets, according to Kennan, was at the level of prestige and influence. He chastised the West for failing to grasp that the basic Russian intent was the psychological conquest of Europe by political means and that, as in Berlin, "military force play[ed] a major role only as means of intimidation." Or as he had asserted in the past on the same topic, "I personally believe that armed force is a poor weapon with which to meet a political assault."[63] Kennan believed that it was not only wrong but also dangerous for the West to introduce a military element into its (meaning Truman's) containment. He therefore planted the seeds for the later realist contention that the USSR aimed only for a share of influence commensurate with the other superpower's rather than for military dominance.

Kennan argued that the heightened sense of Western security engendered unpredictability, inviting, as it did, a West European and an American preoccupation with military affairs. Nevertheless, he went on to speculate that such a preoccupation might need to be encouraged as an imaginary cure-all to stiffen the self-confidence of the masses in the face of Soviet pressures. Here, Kennan spoke to fellow policy professionals: "We have to deal with [that preoccupation] as a reality; and to a certain extent we have to indulge it, for to neglect it would be to encourage panic and uncertainty in western Europe and to play into the hands of the communists. But in doing so, we should have clearly in mind that the need for military alliances and rearmament on the part of the western Europeans is primarily a *subjective* one, arising in their own minds as a result of their failure to understand correctly their own position." Ultimately, Kennan believed that military strength was not required to augment containment, but that a psychosis on the part of the West—a psychosis of fear and insecurity—required its maintenance by foreign policy elites.[64]

If the Atlantic Alliance had to exist, Kennan maintained, it should be limited, literally, to include only those nations "whose homeland or insular territories are washed by the waters of the North Atlantic, or which form part of a close union of states which meets this description."[65] He did not want all of the Marshall Plan countries to join, because he thought that would harden the line of division in Europe. (Later, Kennan made a formalistic argument to exclude Italy from NATO because it was not in the Brussels pact.) Nor did he see any reason to involve Greece and Turkey, two of the first postwar battlegrounds of the Cold War. He failed to consider that his roster of and main criterion for membership left large areas of the ERP unprotected.

For Kennan, the danger in the North Atlantic pact, in addition to its militaristic tendencies, was its bent toward universalism. Although the Soviets already had globalized the Cold War, he envisaged a North Atlantic Alliance with a psychologically strengthened sense of security but unable either to defend itself or to broaden its scope and reach to meet the world threat perceived by Truman.[66] In his memoir, Kennan remembered PPS 43 as a personal paper for Marshall, intended to voice his view of the "entire NATO project." After paraphrasing portions of the paper in order to bolster his contention that the United States had become preoccupied with military affairs, he pointed out that, looking back, the thought behind it was "the desirability of avoiding anything that could appear to the Soviet leaders as an aggressive encirclement of their country."[67] (In a similar vein, Gaddis commended PPS 43 for warning of a system of anti-Russian alliances that would encircle the globe and alienate the Soviets from negotiations.)[68]

In the end, Kennan said that the United States never should have talked about the North Atlantic Alliance in the first place; once it had, it should have confined it to a guarantee of the Brussels Treaty and a military assistance program designed to give its members "whatever was necessary to bolster their internal morale (which was, after all, the heart of the matter)."[69] The result was, at best, a narrowly confined security pact among a few nations based on certain geographical criteria, set apart from both the Truman Doctrine and the Marshall Plan. Kennan never understood NATO to be—indeed sought to prevent it from becoming—what President Truman intended, namely, a crucial element of a political, economic, and strategic view of containment.

7

"Peace with freedom and justice cannot be bought cheaply"

The Purpose and Structure of National Security

In the mid-1940s, the dominant method for gathering and interpreting data, as well as developing policy, was the age-old memorandum process, often based on months of research that culminated in one lengthy report. From a process angle, let alone that of national security, it was inadequate. Harry Truman knew that U.S. national security, a constant imperative, needed an institutional framework with built-in continuity and stability to address new Cold War circumstances. In 1947, Truman's establishment of the National Security Council (NSC) marked the start of America's national security arrangements after the Second World War. In subsequent years, the NSC corroborated the political thought of containment and suggested policy implementation, most famously in NSC 68 of 1950. While incorporating input from the Long Telegram and George Kennan's other observations in Policy Planning Staff (PPS) papers and NSC drafts, the final NSC reports extended the meaning of the Clifford memorandum and hewed to the president's position, supporting the nucleus of Truman's political thought and action about both containment and liberal internationalism in 1946, the Truman Doctrine and the Marshall Plan in 1947, and, eventually, NATO.

Thus, one of Truman's early lessons in developing the strategic thought of containment was that the United States could not fight the Cold War indefinitely through ad hoc policies. By 1947, the president knew that he needed more than the Truman Doctrine or the Marshall Plan: he needed a governmental network to support his decisionmaking and then to implement and sustain the resulting policies. In order to combat the Communist threat and to defend the free world, Truman not only had to craft the strategy but also to create the institutions of containment. NATO became an institution (as later would Radio Free Europe [RFE] and Radio Liberty [RL], for example), as much as it was the embodiment of policy ideas. Truman's management skills and administrative acumen, then, were also a part of his Cold War statesmanship.[1] And in a way that could never have been the case under either Woodrow Wilson or Franklin Roosevelt, the institutionalization of national security became a new, unique component of Truman's liberal internationalism.

The Meaning of National Security

The institutions that gave the president the best and most coordinated military, intelligence, and diplomatic input were created under the National Security Act (NSA) of 1947. Truman described the need for the Central Intelligence Agency (CIA) in a comment that as easily could have been applied to the National Security Council: "Only two people around the White House really knew what was going on in the military affairs department [in April 1945], and they were Admial [*sic*] Leahy and Admiral Brown. I would talk to them every morning and try to get all the information I could." Recalling that it took a disproportionate amount of his time to read all the reports from various sources, Truman said, "And finally one morning I had a conversation with Admiral Leahy, and suggested to him that there should be a Central Intelligence Agency, for the benefit of the whole government as well as for the benefit of the President, so he could be informed." For Truman, such institutions became essential to making prudent decisions.[2] In the American context, they were radically new.

In the president's view, the security of the United States and the free world was at stake in the Cold War. This security had political, military, economic, and diplomatic facets. Truman defined security in a comprehensive way and looked for institutions and policies that would guarantee the freedom of America and its allies. His critics, especially modern Cold War analysts, have merged his definition of security with his administrative style of government, arguing that the president overreacted and erected an unbounded national security state in order to meet an exaggerated threat. They make more sophisticated Henry Wallace's 1948 condemnation of the National Security Act as a "completely authoritarian setup."[3] Truman, however, philosophically and temperamentally, resisted any entity that would override the prerogative of elected representatives and undermine executive responsibility. While he believed that the NSC, CIA, and other new bodies were Cold War necessities, he also perceived them as legitimate under the authority of the executive branch and within the context of the American constitutional structure. As president, Truman welcomed recommendations about policy formulation regarding containment, but he was the one who determined that path of containment; he issued broad directions and aims and did not attempt to author every procedure for each set of circumstances. He knew—indeed, expected—that his advisors would often disagree with each other and hash out policy options. In short, he let others focus on the trees while he focused on the forest: the overarching plans and the main components involved in fighting the Cold War. This approach enabled him to gather useful details and advice from his subordinates while he prudently judged what was necessary to implement his strategy of containment. Truman viewed the various advisory councils, the highest of which was the NSC, as important, but as the famous sign read on the president's desk: "The buck stops here."

The National Security Act of 1947 derived from the broad concept of national security that Truman put forth in his idea of containment. It recognized the need for as comprehensive as possible protection of the United States, a point that is underappreciated or absent in later academic Cold War analyses. Because they are driven by the balance of power and scarce economic means in policy, realists and postrevisionists contract American defense. Although they accept a defensive national security for communism, revisionists and corporatists rule out a complete American defense. By contrast, the NSC was to advise the president "with respect to the integration of domestic, foreign, and military policies relating to the national security so as to enable the military services and the other departments and agencies of the government to cooperate more effectively in matters involving national security." When pertaining specifically to military matters, it was intended to "assess and appraise the objectives, commitments, and risks of the United States in relation to our actual and potential military power, for the purpose of making recommendations to the President in connection therewith."[4]

Far from the militarily dominated structure identified by Kennan after he left government, the National Security Council gave to the president evaluations and policy proposals that were narrow or general, according to the circumstances, and that combined domestic, foreign, and military concerns. In fact, the popular realist and revisionist criticism of the NSC pertains to what never was: the council could have ended up emphasizing the military, but language to this effect in the legislation was changed by Congress. The president decided the worth of the NSC and its papers; the military served without determining the objectives of national security. Even after Paul Nitze replaced Kennan as director of the Policy Planning Staff, the State Department was intrinsic to the council's process, at least in part because Secretary George Marshall had set up the PPS several months before the NSA's passage and, effectively, weighted State's presence in the NSC.

Truman and His Council

At first, Truman did not attend the NSC group meetings. Not knowing how the National Security Council would evolve, the president deliberately remained detached from it in its early months because he wanted to emphasize its advisory status and to see how effectively it and the rest of the new defense arrangements worked—the NSC was, after all, the latest untested weapon in the Cold War.[5] While conscious that he was setting precedents on several levels, Truman was also aware that some had favored the council because they did not think he was equipped to be president. Others wanted to push the executive branch in the direction of the British cabinet government model. In a confidential memorandum in February 1947, Marshall baldly stated that the NSC "by statute would dissipate the constitutional responsibility of the President for the conduct of foreign affairs" and that "the Secretary of State would become the automaton of the Council."[6] Even after changes in the legislation removed the NSC's proposed statutory powers and responsibilities, Truman refused to be seen as a lackey. As the president put it in fall 1947, the NSC was "*his* council and . . . he expected everyone to work harmoniously without any manifestations of prima-donna qualities."[7] Despite new and needed institutions, he believed that the primary foreign policy relationship would remain that of the president and his secretary of state. When Truman did begin to attend some of the NSC meetings, he used the council as a sounding board about possible courses of action. He wanted the council to be seen in its proper perspective: process would support, not drive, substance.

Historians and political scientists who dwell on Truman's initial absence from the NSC overlook his heavy presidential schedule. It should not be forgotten that while administration and congressional debate was taking place over the National Security Act, the president was pressing for the Truman Doctrine. And when the NSA was enacted, Truman was busy promoting congressional approval of the Marshall Plan. In June 1948, he made his decision that the United States would stay in Berlin; he then presided over NSC meetings from July to September 1948 to organize specifics of the airlift. Then, after deciding that America would defend South Korea in 1950, he regularly attended NSC meetings for recommendations about coordinating military, diplomatic, and intelligence policies. In April 1949, Truman said that NSC and CIA reports had "proved to be one of the best means available to the President for obtaining coordinated advice as a basis of reaching decisions."[8] The president considered the new national security institutions to be an effective tool in his Cold War arsenal, enabling him to reach the best policies based on the most information and with input from the keenest minds across his administration.

Originally, the members of the National Security Council were the president; the secretaries of state, defense, army, navy, and air force; and the chairman of the National Security Resources Board. (Amendments to the National Security Act in 1949 eliminated the three service secretaries and added the vice president.) The first NSC executive secretary, Admiral Sidney Souers, was careful to make sure that Truman endorsed the coverage of a question or issue by the council before a paper became an official part of the NSC process. Aside from his stated duties, Souers developed close relationships with Truman, Clark Clifford, James Forrestal, and others, which helped him assist the president by smoothing occasional testiness among advisors. "You can depend on this guy," Truman wrote of Souers in 1954. "He was one of my greatest assets."[9] The formal channel at the National Security Council passed memos and draft papers, especially from the PPS and the secretary of defense, to the full council for discussion and amendment. Then Souers submitted two copies of a particular paper to the president for his consideration. After signing his approval or disapproval, Truman would keep one copy and return the other to Souers, who would then inform the NSC of the president's decision.

Merely because a paper was written in the NSC process did not mean it became national security policy. The president neither saw nor endorsed many papers that flowed from various sources within the NSC, and many papers he did see had changed considerably before they reached his desk. Likewise, Truman received informal policy advice, which we sometimes do not know to what degree he accepted or rejected, and for which we rarely have a paper chain. In the end, Truman's signature shows what NSC material he formally endorsed.[10]

The president infused the NSC with his political thought about foreign affairs, especially regarding containment. His definition of national security as a combination of domestic strength (through democracy, prosperity, and defense) and international peace (through strength and freedom)— which was prefigured in 1946 and advanced in 1947 and 1948—came to the fore in 1949. After identifying the need for strength to support moral leadership, Truman said in mid-1947, about a month before he approved the National Security Act, "Weakness on our part would stir fear among the small or weakened nations that we were giving up our world leadership. It would seem to them that we lacked the will to fulfill our pledge to aid free and independent nations to maintain their freedoms, or our commitments to aid in restoring war-torn economies. In such an atmosphere of uncertainty, these nations might not be able to resist the encroachments of totalitarian pressures. We must not let friendly nations go by default."[11] Because the United States was the leader of the free world, Truman believed, American strength must come first. With diligence over several years, he educated the people and Congress about the need for this strength. Then he worked to build up the strength of America's allies and forge the Western countercoalition against Communist tyranny. By 1949, he explained to his fellow citizens and the world, "Peace with freedom and justice cannot be bought cheaply." Jettisoning the "false security" of isolationism and positing the inseparability of a defendable peace that springs from freedom, Truman added, "We have learned that the defense of the United States and the defense of other freedom-loving nations are indivisible. We have learned that we can serve our country best by joining in the common defense of the rights of all mankind."[12] From today's vantage and in its chief respects, the NSC was, at the same time, a precursor to and an outgrowth of the thought behind NATO. In the context of Truman's liberal internationalism, the council was a logical move in 1947 and beyond to undergird the political thought and action of containment, for the security of the United States and for the continuing independence of other free nations.

The NSC encouraged, if not obliged, the president to define more fully his conception of peace for America and the world. The documents that he approved spelled out the peace-through-strength theme behind his containment. From the latter part of 1947 through the fall of 1950, NSC papers that attracted Truman's attention depicted global peace, if it could occur, as a composite of free individuals and peoples who lived in liberty according to justice and a concomitant order. The National Security Council documents signed by the president also extended, as they reinforced, Truman's words and deeds in the building blocks of containment. In his broader political theory regarding man and the world, Truman did not abandon his expressed wishes for a parliament of man or a kind of universal brotherhood.[13] But in the political thought and action of containment that was supported in a strategic direction by the NSC, he endeavored to bolster independent regimes that acknowledged and defended, or had the potential of securing, the equality and freedom of citizens.

Truman believed that man lived best in a liberal democracy but that this system of government had to be chosen freely. This choice would not be wholly free or not be made at all, unless the regime under which the individual lived both protected private rights and permitted political freedoms. Under the best circumstances, he thought, a good regime would nourish the rights and institutions inherent in liberal democracy; under promising circumstances, he expected, an improving regime would encourage similar rights and institutions. But he knew that the peoples within states controlled by tyranny would not be able to choose freedom for themselves. At its strategic summit, Truman believed that peace through strength should be grounded in liberty and inform national security. In the context of the Cold War, the strength within national security was applied to maintain the best circumstances in the liberal democracies, boost the promising circumstances elsewhere in the non-Soviet world, and alter the worst depredations within Communist countries.

The "War Scare"

While 1946 and 1947 were fraught with Communist aggression and postwar readjustments, 1948 shaped up as the most challenging year yet. According to most contemporary and later critics of Truman, 1948 was a year of exaggerated threats and a "war scare," either created or exacerbated by the president in particular and the United States in general. Kennan and Wallace are perhaps the most famous among those who charged that

America fabricated a war scare. Truman was not without an opinion on the chance of war. Everyone had one. Along with continuous Soviet pressures on Western Europe and specific constraints on Germany, the Czechoslovak coup and the final consolidation of Communist power in Hungary gave additional verification of Kremlin designs. Concerns about war reached their height in March and April, in the aftermath of the Czechoslovak coup, during the actions in Berlin that led to the blockade, and before the results of elections in Western Europe, especially in Italy.[14] Pelted by evidence of the accelerating Cold War, Truman thought that a hot war would be probable if the United States failed to maintain and act from a position of strength and permitted the Soviet Union to exploit weaknesses. As he wrote in an April 1948 draft of a speech, "We are a peaceful nation. But we must be prepared for trouble if it comes. Twice in a generation brave allies have kept the barbarian from our borders. It can't happen that way again." This comment typified the president's Cold War reasoning: there might be occasions, such as the early months in 1948, when America seemed closer to war than at other times, but the threat would be present as long as the East-West conflict endured.[15]

It is fair to say, in light of ongoing events, that the president perceived an extra urgency in March 1948. Responding to Eleanor Roosevelt's worry that the Soviets and Americans were headed toward a third world war and her recommendation that they should sit down to negotiate, he agreed that "[i]t is the most serious situation we have faced since 1939. I shall face it with everything I have." In conveying this resolve, Truman did not talk about war's inevitability or appeasement but wrote that "[o]ur European Recovery Program and the proper strengthening of our Military setup is the only hope we now have for peace in the World." Such measures were necessary, he told her, because "Russia has not kept faith with us."[16] Earlier, in March 1948, he wrote his daughter that the United States might have to fight for peace and previewed his remark to Eleanor Roosevelt—that the United States was facing a situation similar to that of Great Britain and France in 1938 and 1939. While repeating his long-held opinion that totalitarian states were alike (whether they were ruled by Stalin, Hitler, Franco, Louis XIV, Napoleon, Charles I, or Cromwell—Truman's usual list of tyrants), he distinguished the Soviet Union as being "a Frankenstein dictatorship worse than any of the others, Hitler included."[17]

Despite these private sentiments, Truman did not agitate publicly for war—or even its possibility—but, instead, did everything in his power to minimize the chances of a hot war. At the end of March, for example, in response to the Soviets with respect to Germany, he "decided against calling in congressional leaders because (1) it would become immediately known, and (2) it would add unnecessarily to the creation of a war hysteria."[18] It had become clear to him that the war of nerves would last a long time. By managing the East-West conflict well and thoroughly, the president thought he was diminishing the chances of a third world war. For Truman believed that if he maintained a consistent strategy of peace through strength and freedom, he would check Communist tyranny in the short term and defeat it in the long term. He also had faith and was optimistic about the future of man and democracy. In handwritten notes for a May 1948 speech to honor the founder of Girard College, Truman made three points: he wished he were eighteen again, a great age lay ahead, and students should not listen to pessimists.[19]

The Yugoslav split with the Kremlin in June 1948 further validated Truman's thought and American action, especially with respect to the Berlin blockade. Marshal Josef Tito's parting with the Soviet bloc did not signal the rise of independent nationalism but a distinction without a real difference. Milovan Djilas, who knew both parties well, saw the breach as a split in personalities between two Communists, Stalin and Tito.[20] Even more deeply, though, the personality difference revealed a disagreement about the application of Communist tactics. Stalin wanted communism to be centrally directed from Moscow, while Tito was throwing his military weight around in Albania and attempting to form a Communist Balkan federation with Albania and Bulgaria. Apart from Tito's ambitions, Stalin thought that if Yugoslav troops entered Albania "the reactionaries in England and America would be able to use it and step forward as defenders of Albanian independence."[21] The split reflected a breakdown of Soviet, not Communist, control that could be exploited by the West. If Yugoslavia had not conformed to communism, Stalin would not have permitted the country's isolation.[22] Around this time, Moscow began to develop bilateral arrangements, under its command, with each of the satellites, depending on the situation in each country.

The fact that the Titoists were Communist and possessed an army on the continent second in strength only to the USSR's helped them establish a degree of Communist autonomy within the East bloc. The Red Army had not occupied Yugoslavia in the way it had other East European countries during and after World War II, leaving Tito more maneuverability than any other satellite.[23] Moscow ejected Yugoslavia from the Cominform on June 28, although Tito gave the Soviets active support in the Belgrade conference and elsewhere. In fact, the split enabled Yugoslavia to pose as a primary leader of the nonaligned and neutralist bloc, which typically sided with communism, over the next several decades.[24]

The American response showed again President Truman's independence of mind. Initially, he may have looked with some skepticism upon the split, given the recent memory of Tito's aggression in Trieste and the shooting down of two U.S. army transport planes by the Yugoslav air force in August 1946. In late September 1947, Truman wrote Bess about tense political and economic conditions in Western Europe: "Yesterday was one of the most hectic of days, as I told you. I'm not sure what has been my worst day. But here is a situation fraught with terrible consequences. Suppose, for instance, that Italy should fold up and that Tito then would march into the Po Valley. All the Mediterranean coast of France then is open to Russian occupation and the iron curtain comes to Bordeaux, Calais, Antwerp, and The Hague. We withdraw from Greece and Turkey and *prepare for war.* It just must not happen." After confiding in her his frustrations about obtaining sufficient Marshall Plan and emergency aid for Western Europe, he added, "I shouldn't write you this stuff but you should know what I've been facing since Potsdam."[25] For Truman, the Soviets had been the problem since the beginning of his presidency, and Tito had been loyal to the Communist agenda. Truman seems to have concluded that if Yugoslavia had been able to rival the Soviet Union's military strength, Tito would have emulated Stalin in other ways and perhaps attempted to take the leadership of international communism. Whatever his opinion about Titoism, however, he knew that the Kremlin remained the primary threat. "We are in the midst of grave and trying times," he wrote Churchill in July 1948, shortly after the split and in the midst of the Berlin crisis. "'Communism'—so-called, is our next great problem [after Nazism and fascism]. I hope we solve it without the 'blood and tears' the other two cost."[26] The president authorized limited economic relations between the United States and Yugoslavia in February 1949, in NSC 18/2, not because he thought that Tito had been reborn as a nationalist in the conventional sense but in order to put pressure on Soviet control of Eastern Europe.

Whereas Truman interpreted Titoism as the effort of a Communist leader to break away from Moscow's control, not its ideology, realists combined this interpretation with that of nationalism. Eventually, realists and postrevisionists weighed nationalism more heavily than communism in analyzing the phenomenon of Titoism. In December 1949, the president approved NSC 58/2, which outlined U.S. policy toward the Soviet satellite states in Eastern Europe. This document supported the elimination of Soviet power from the satellite states, even if this goal meant temporary cooperation with "schismatic communist regimes." (NSC 58/2 originated as NSC 58, a Policy Planning Staff draft, with some modifications in its conclusions. According to Gaddis, NSC 58 and NSC 58/2 aimed to bring about fragmentation within international communism and were part of Kennan's containment strategy.)[27] Policies in 1949—ranging from Voice of America broadcasts and human rights campaigns in the United Nations to covert action and economic pressures—preceded NSC 58/2.[28] The president apparently saw NSC 58/2 as a logical extension of such measures, all of which aimed to eradicate Soviet power from Eastern Europe.

After Soviet efforts to oust Tito in late 1948 failed, Stalin's response to Titoism was to prevent its spread: during 1949, he purged party leaders, especially in Poland, Hungary, and Bulgaria, who were suspected of Titoism, nationalism, or other insubordination to Moscow.[29] While Kennan thought that encouraging Titoism—along with restoring a balance of power in Europe and Asia and trying to alter the Soviet concept of international relations over time—was the key to containment, Truman believed that promoting Titoism was a peripheral element of a larger strategy that recognized the deficiencies of realpolitik in the modern age, as well as its inherent incompatibility with democracy. Although he supported immediate corrections in Soviet behavior, Truman's larger objective was the fortification and expansion of the free world, and this required the eventual defeat of Soviet communism.

The NSC 20 Series

The longest-standing and most famous NSC analysis of containment and the Cold War is NSC 68, yet the document did not generate spontaneously in spring 1950. Many scholars have attempted to explain NSC 68's development as a lineal descendant of the Long Telegram and of another NSC report also authored by Kennan. For the revisionists, Daniel Yergin has depicted NSC 68's debt to the Long Telegram by way of NSC 20, lumping together the papers of the NSC 20 series to show that Kennan's political thought undergirded the 1950 document. Yergin summarizes NSC 68 as a government paper meant to rationalize the need for the hydrogen bomb and an expanded military establishment. (Given that Truman resolved to proceed with the H-bomb because of emerging Soviet capabilities in atomic weaponry, Yergin's portrayal is misleading; the president asked for a draft of a general study on the nature and future of U.S.-Soviet relations directly *after* the hydrogen bomb decision.) He condemns the document for concluding that a necessary connection exists between a domestic government and its foreign affairs.[30] John Lewis Gaddis, too, has made this argument, for postrevisionists. In *Containment: Documents on American Policy and Strategy, 1945–1950,* Gaddis and his coeditor, Thomas Etzold, reprint NSC 20/1 of August 18, 1948, and NSC 20/4 of November 23, 1948, the initial and final papers of the series that became NSC 20 as approved by Truman. As a result, Gaddis and Etzold correctly present NSC 20 (NSC 20/4 as approved by Truman) as the definitive statement of American policy toward the USSR prior to NSC 68, but assert that NSC 20/4 reached in modified form the conclusions of NSC 20/1 "without elaborating much of the reasoning which went into that predecessor document."[31] The effect is to connect the two NSC 20 documents and blur the dissimilarities between them, thus preserving the intent of Kennan's original "document" and thereby stamping NSC 68 as the ultimate break with Kennanesque containment.[32]

But in actuality, the reasoning and judgments of NSC 20/1 and NSC 20/4 differed—and therefore tell a different story about the development of NSC 68 and containment policy. While useful to parse as an example of Kennan's theory, NSC 20/1 served as a Policy Planning Staff first draft that was fundamentally changed and rewritten. NSC 20/4—a new document in political thought and, to a significant extent, in political action—was the final product shown to the president and signed by him.

Kennan's draft text of NSC 20/1 outlined his conception of containment.[33] Notably, it separated the Soviet Union's conduct from international communism, and it emphasized that the Titoist form of nationalism might be a source of behavior modification for the USSR. As he had elsewhere, Kennan propounded nationalism as a splintering force within Soviet totalitarianism, rather than considering whether Tito's Yugoslavia was an autonomous pocket of communism in one country. He also did not consider substantively the nationalities of other peoples except in their fragmentizing tendencies. Although NSC 20/1 sought a retraction of Soviet power, it concentrated on Kremlin intentions rather than, as Truman's containment did, on a fusion of ideology and capabilities.

NSC 20/2—entitled "Factors Affecting the Nature of the U.S. Defense Arrangements in the Light of Soviet Policies"—originated as PPS 33, a paper that Kennan thought would help answer Forrestal's original request to the National Security Council.[34] Although Kennan asked Admiral Souers to submit PPS 33 to the council for consideration in August, he objected strongly when the NSC staff combined NSC 20/1 and NSC 20/2 into one statement. "If it is really desired that a paper be written which would attempt to set forth the bases of U.S. foreign policy from the standpoint of national security," said Kennan, "I should prefer to sit down . . . and draft another paper on the subject."[35] But the two papers were combined, and various offices from the State Department, including the Bureau of Near Eastern Affairs and the Office of European Affairs, as well as Paul Nitze, then working at the Treasury Department, all commented positively on the NSC 20 draft paper. Members of the Policy Planning Staff, however, expressed concern to Kennan in October that the draft did not "bring out clearly your idea that the basic Soviet objective and the most dangerous threat is political rather than military domination" and overstated Soviet potential capabilities.[36] Kennan, for his part, was already tussling with the NSC staff over their proposed revisions.[37]

In terms of containment's theoretical and policy formulation in the Truman administration, NSC 20/4 erected a bridge between the Clifford memorandum (not NSC 20/1) and NSC 68.[38] NSC 20/4 drew some of its points from the shortened version of NSC 20/1 (published in *Foreign Relations of the United States* as a brief catalogue of general objectives, peacetime aims, and wartime aims with respect to Russia), but, unlike either form of NSC 20/1, NSC 20/4 differentiated "Russian" from "Soviet," as evinced by apposing the titles of the two papers: "U.S. Objectives with Respect to Russia" and "U.S. Objectives with Respect to the USSR to Counter Soviet Threats to U.S. Security." Upon inspection of the two documents, it becomes clear that the NSC comprehension of the Soviet threat and of a requisite action had changed since the NSC 20/1 draft written by Kennan.[39]

Communist ideology and Soviet behavior, according to NSC 20/4, demonstrated that the ultimate objective of the Kremlin leaders was world domination. Similar to the Clifford report, NSC 20/4 identified the gravest threat to U.S. security as stemming from the hostile designs and formidable power of the USSR and from the nature of the Soviet system. Endorsing the previous actions of containment, NSC 20/4 commented that without vigorous American measures to stiffen the resistance of Western Europe and Mediterranean countries to Communist pressures from 1946 to the present, "most of western Europe would today have been politically captured by the communist movement." While reiterating concerns about Communist infiltration and subversion advanced not only by Kennan but also by others in government, NSC 20/4 did not assume that future Soviet subversion and aggression, given its ideological source, would decrease voluntarily. And, although the document expressed hope that the United States could provide an enduring political framework for world affairs, it put forth many of the ideas associated with peace through strength, NATO, and the rest of Truman's containment.[40]

Also in contrast to Kennan and NSC 20/1, NSC 20/4 made plain that the USSR would not be satisfied until it had accomplished its immediate goal—the political conquest of Western Europe—and its long-range aim of spreading communism around the world. Rather than using the realist terminology of the Soviet "sphere of influence" in Europe, NSC 20/4 identified the Soviet "orbit" without granting the Kremlin a natural area of domination. It discussed the increase of Soviet capabilities under present and future circumstances, including a possible hot war. Leaving ambiguous the question of whether the United States would act only during such a war, the document proposed: "If the United States were to exploit the potentialities of psychological warfare and subversive activity within the Soviet orbit, the USSR would be faced with increased disaffection, discontent, and underground opposition within the area under Soviet control." In additional rejections of realism and of isolationism, NSC 20/4 warned against Soviet political warfare exploiting American vacillation, appeasement, or isolation in foreign policy. It stood firmly by the suggestion that in a post-Soviet world, the regime or regimes existing on Russian territory could not possess sufficient military power to wage an aggressive war and could not impose any arrangement resembling the current iron curtain.[41] On this last point, it concurred with Kennan's policy position of NSC 20/1 but rejected his political theory.

As a forerunner of NSC 68, the document discussed the ways in which the United States and the free world could offset and set back Soviet capabilities and gains. Like the Clifford memorandum before it and what would follow in 1950, NSC 20/4 departed from Kennan's accent on intentions and evaluated Kremlin capabilities in light of Marxist-Leninist ideology. Although it repeated the NSC 20/1 objective of moderating Soviet behavior, NSC 20/4 began by formulating a guide to measures that would counter the Kremlin threat and ended by calling for the actual reduction of Soviet power and influence under current circumstances or in a hot war started by the Kremlin. In addition, with respect to the modification of Soviet behavior, NSC 20/4 intended to achieve this change by working among the Russian peoples to revive "the national life of groups evidencing the ability and determination to achieve and maintain national independence." This understanding of behavior modification would accord with the Voice of America and Radio Free Europe–Radio Liberty under Truman's containment. In NSC 20/1, Kennan described behavior modification of the Kremlin leaders in a top-down approach and advised waiting for such an evolution while negotiating a political settlement with those in power at the time. NSC 20/4 encouraged active resistance by and sought independence for all those held under Communist rule.[42]

In the realm of policy, Truman's containment endeavored to reduce the USSR's power and influence to the point at which it did not constitute a threat to peace, at minimum achieving a relinquishment of its external empire in Eastern Europe. Viewing Soviet power and influence as discrete factors united in the service of communism, NSC 20/4 deepened the understanding of the Clifford memorandum and reflected Truman's growing convictions. As with prior reports approved by the president, NSC 20/4 proposed disseminating information among the peoples within the Soviet Union and helping the world comprehend "the true nature of the USSR and the Soviet-directed world communist party." In support of containment, its summary of U.S. objectives mixed domestic and global enterprises: building military preparedness, protecting internal security, maximizing economic potential, strengthening non-Soviet nations, straining the Soviet power structure and Moscow's relationships with the satellite countries, and supplying full information to the American public.[43]

Approximately half of NSC 20/4 articulated an understanding about U.S. foreign policy, the Cold War, and the nature of the Cold War opponents' regimes, which was absent from Kennan's NSC 20/1 and which was carried over from NSC 20/3 (the draft of the combined NSC 20/1 and NSC 20/2 after being significantly reworked by the NSC staff). Although many of the recommendations of the two documents corresponded, NSC 20/4 went over theoretical ground that had been missing or misconstrued in NSC 20/1. Critically, NSC 20/4 did not accept the degree of continuity between czarism and communism that Kennan had deduced but, rather, agreed with Truman's fundamental distinction between the American and Soviet regimes. Whereas the Kennan paper was dominated by the aims and methods of the Russians, NSC 20/4 emphasized the ideology and behavior of the Soviets that imperiled the whole of American security: "The gravest threat to the security of the United States within the foreseeable future stems from the hostile designs and formidable power of the USSR, and from the nature of the Soviet system."[44] This statement augmented the Clifford memorandum, deepened Forrestal's NSC 20, departed from NSC 20/1, and, from the perspective of hindsight, adumbrated NSC 68.

As for November 23, 1948, the date of submission for NSC 20/4, it indicates an additional measure of the document's distance from Kennan. Nitze remembered Kennan as the mastermind of NSC 20/4, but the facts do not bear out this recollection.[45] At the time of the later document and during the writing process of its antecedent, NSC 20/3, Kennan was immersed in two other papers. On the same day on which NSC 20/4 was passed to Truman, Kennan submitted to his superiors PPS 39/1, "United States Policy toward China," and PPS 43, "Considerations Affecting the Conclusion of a North Atlantic Security pact."[46] The paper on China was not intended as an official expression of the State Department position regarding China, but Kennan felt that it was worth his time to preserve in writing his displeasure with the DOD reaction to an earlier NSC draft he had sent them on the same subject.[47] His commitment to PPS 43 shows how he separated himself from NSC 20/4. While NSC 20/4 implied an endorsement of the North Atlantic pact, Kennan's PPS 43 grudgingly accepted the concept of NATO as a psychological and economic effort to dispel the "subjective" West European fears about a Soviet attack.[48] A full three months after the North Atlantic Treaty had become operative, Kennan still fought it. In terms of timing and political thought, Kennan did not affiliate himself with NSC 20/4, which President Truman signed on November 24, 1948.

NSC 7 and NSC 10/2

Aside from the Clifford memorandum and the president's own words and actions, NSC 20/4 grew out of NSC 7 of March 1948.[49] Its title—"The Position of the United States with Respect to Soviet-Directed World Communism"—suggests a kinship to NSC 20/4, not NSC 20/1. Indeed,

NSC 7 helps to track the thread from the Clifford memorandum to Truman's developing containment (NCS 7 echoes the political understanding of Truman's two speeches of March 17, 1948), to NSC 20/4, to NSC 68.[50] Although NSC 7 was never finalized as a document, its central political evaluations were folded into the presidentially approved NSC 20/4, and it contributed to the strategic line of Truman's containment more substantively than did NSC 20/1.[51] As such, it is an initial study that requires examination.

NSC 7 was prepared by the National Security Council staff, in consultation with representatives from the army, navy, air force, State Department, National Security Resources Board, and CIA. (In this respect, NSC 7 was written in a way similar to NSC 68 in 1950.)[52] In keeping with Truman's containment, NSC 7 stated that the ultimate objective of Soviet-directed world communism was the "domination of the world." It proffered a more sophisticated analysis of the power vacuum after World War II than Kennan had, one that comprehended a Trumanesque juxtaposition of two opposing regimes: "The Soviet Union is the source of power from which international communism chiefly derives its capability to threaten the existence of free nations. The United States is the only source of power capable of mobilizing successful opposition to the communist goal of world conquest." Like Truman, NSC 7 did not deny but differentiated power, attaching its exercise to the character and precepts of the regime responsible for the action. NSC 7 cogently expressed the circumstances of the Cold War, a term used explicitly in the paper. And because the national security of the United States was at stake, American withdrawal from the struggle would be the equivalent of "eventual national suicide."[53]

NSC 7 supported Truman's containment by arguing that Soviet-directed world communism presented the non-Soviet world "with something new in history." It identified a worldwide fifth column with an organized, total, and subversive technique of Communist strategy. Emphasizing this subversive stratum of communism (including legal and illegal political and economic measures), NSC 7 extended not only a point raised by Churchill in the Fulton speech but also an important aspect of the Clifford memorandum: the USSR—guided by Communist dogma—rejected coexistence and amity in the long run and might resort to war to gain its ends; but the Soviet Union preferred the fruits of war and had avoided major conflict so far, "since time is required to build up its strength and concurrently to weaken and divide its opponents." Consequently, the advantage of time was on the Kremlin's side as long as the USSR "can continue to increase its relative power by the present process of indirect aggression and internal subversion."[54] On this issue, NSC 7's writers dissented from the popular argument voiced by Kennan, Walter Lippmann, and others, which contended that time—even without comprehensive action by the West—was more of a boon for the United States than for the Soviet Union.

For the first time in more than an inchoate way, NSC 7 expounded the view that the United States should understand and present itself as the leader of an international countercoalition against the Communist tyranny of the USSR. In its words, the document urged the "organization of a world-wide counter-offensive against Soviet-directed world communism." First, as Truman had said, this task required the strengthening of American military potential. Second, as articulated by the president in the same order of priorities, this undertaking necessitated the mobilization and strengthening of the potential of the non-Soviet world. Not only was this two-step strategy viewed as pivotal to gaining the initiative against the Soviets and shoring up the will of anti-Communists globally, it also would be the most effective in deterring Kremlin aggression and proving the U.S. determination "to thwart the communist design of world conquest."[55]

NSC 7 should be viewed against the backdrop of the NSC 4 series of late 1947 and as contributing to the debate that led to NSC 10/2 of June 1948. "Special operations" to help organize and assist resistance movements in Europe and "morale operations" for propaganda purposes had been successful secret intelligence activities of the Office of Strategic Services—the predecessor to the CIA—during World War II. In 1946, government officials saw a growing need to prepare during peacetime for the "psychological warfare" measures that would be needed in wartime or warlike situations; in 1947, Director of Central Intelligence Rear Admiral Roscoe Hillenkoetter, Forrestal, Souers, presidential advisor Averell Harriman, and others urged that the United States focus on peacetime "psychological operations," including overt and covert propaganda, as well as domestic and international information programs. The heads of the military services concluded at a War Council meeting in November 1947 that peacetime psychological warfare should be carried out only in the foreign field and under State Department responsibility, and that a "black" covert program should also be operated by the State Department, with advice from and in consultation with the director of Central Intelligence and a military representative. The National Security Council considered these proposals (with Secretary of State Marshall distancing himself from the proposed program) and separated overt foreign information activities from "psychological warfare" and covert action: the former became NSC 4 (which led to NSC 43, establishing State Department responsibility for foreign information programs), and the latter was designated NSC 4-A and later became NSC 10/2, dealing with covert action.[56]

NSC 7 stated outright that the defeat of the forces of Soviet-directed world communism was vital to American security. (In a concurring report, the Joint Chiefs of Staff endorsed this point.) Certainly, Truman's containment as a whole implied this objective, but not so candidly. In addition, NSC 7 included among its conclusions the need to "[d]evelop, and at the appropriate time carry out, a coordinated program to support underground resistance movements in countries behind the iron curtain, including the USSR," and to elevate the importance of the "present anticommunist foreign information program," including the intensification of Voice of America and future plans for RFE–RL.[57] NSC 4-A (later NSC 10/2) was part of the effort to achieve the first goal, while NSC 43 was central to the second goal.

In December 1947, the National Security Council (in NSC 4-A), "taking cognizance of the vicious psychological efforts of the USSR," instructed the director of Central Intelligence (DCI) to "initiate and conduct . . . covert psychological operations designed to counteract Soviet and Soviet-inspired activities which constitute a threat to world peace and security or are designed to discredit and defeat the United States."[58] Soon thereafter, the State Department, which asserted no new program was needed but worried about pressures from the armed services and the Joint Chiefs (in light of NSC 7) to begin such operations, proposed a program of its own (designed by George Kennan and the PPS) that would have complete authority for covert operations and would be under the State Department rather than the CIA.[59] Therein occurred an intense jurisdictional battle between the State Department and the CIA over control of such activities that was settled (for the immediate period) by NCS 10/2.

Approved by Truman on June 18, 1948, NSC 10/2 set up the Office of Special Projects, soon called the Office of Policy Coordination (OPC), which served as the center for American psychological warfare and covert activities for the next six years. The OPC was created within the CIA "to plan and conduct covert operations," yet it operated "independently of other components of the Central Intelligence Agency" and reported directly to the DCI with a chief "nominated by the Secretary of State, acceptable to the Director of Central Intelligence and approved by the National Security Council." The DCI was also responsible for ensuring, through designated representatives of the secretaries of state and defense, that covert operations were "planned and conducted in manner consistent with US foreign and military policies and with overt activities." Disagreements between the director of Central Intelligence and the state and defense representatives would be referred to the NSC "for decision."[60]

In endorsing covert political action in May 1948, the Policy Planning Staff recommended liberation committees (led by political refugees from Eastern Europe), support of indigenous anti-Communist elements in threatened countries of the "Free World," and preventive direct action in free countries.[61] These ideas were integral to the future activities of the OPC—some of which were successful, especially the National Committee for Free Europe (which sponsored Radio Free Europe)—but were not unique to Kennan and the PPS. Declassified documents suggest an intense interest in and knowledge of these activities beginning in fall 1947.[62] The revisions to NSC 10, when it was still in the draft process, incorporated the PPS view to the extent that the operations advisory committee consisted of representatives of the secretaries of state and defense and that the NSC would resolve disagreements between the DCI and the state and defense representatives. But Kennan did not prevail on the bureaucratic control issue and grew irritated during 1948 and 1949 with the military mind-set he encountered at Defense and on the NSC staff.[63] He even urged withdrawing his proposal and abandoning the idea of political warfare when it became obvious that the program would not be controlled by the State Department, but then accepted the proposal as "the best arrangement we can get at this time."[64] As he put it in 1975 testimony about NSC 10/2 and the OPC, "It ended up with the establishment within CIA of a branch, an office for activities of this nature, and one which employed a great many people. It did not work out at all the way I had conceived it or others of my associates in the Department of State. We had thought that this would be a facility which could be used when and if an occasion arose when it might be needed. There might be years when we wouldn't have to do anything like this."[65]

National Security as Domestic Security

More and more frequently in 1948, but throughout his presidency, Truman was accused of being soft on communism. This charge was aimed at him on several levels, particularly in 1948, in the context of domestic security. This reproach is somewhat ironic, in that he wrote in June 1945 of the trouble posed by the "Crazy American Communist. There is only one in a million of our population but they are loyal to Stalin and not to the American President." His opinion was clear: "I'd like to send them to Russia. Uncle Joe would promptly send them to Siberia or a concentration camp I'm sure. But I can't do that and wouldn't if I could."[66]

In late 1945, Truman was apprised of the Igor Gouzenko case, which brought proof that the Soviets had infiltrated the Manhattan Project through a spy ring in Canada. While he did not know the extent of the damage, he understood that the U.S. atomic monopoly in the Cold War would be vital but temporary. In 1945 and 1946, he, Attorney General Tom Clark, and others were deluged by memoranda from Federal Bureau of Investigation Director J. Edgar Hoover detailing allegations by Elizabeth Bentley, a former courier for Communist agents, of widespread Soviet espionage in the United States. At the time, there was no corroboration for her claims, and the government did not pursue them officially.[67] By September 1946, the Clifford memorandum suggested that the United States needed to protect itself from Communist espionage. Truman recognized the problem but thought in March 1947 that by issuing Executive Order 9835, which established the Federal Employee Loyalty Program, and relying on the combined efforts of the FBI and the Civil Service Commission to enforce it, he had settled the matter. In so doing, he was torn between wanting to stop domestic communism, to preserve civil liberties, and to prevent Hoover (with whom Truman shared a mutual dislike) from overstepping his duties of internal security. "Let's be sure that we hold the FBI down," he said to Clark Clifford in May 1947. "If we leave them to their own devices and give them what they want, they will become an American Gestapo."[68] Since the balance of funding between the FBI and the Civil Service Commission to administer the loyalty program had shifted in the former's favor, against Truman's proposal to Congress (and after intense lobbying from Hoover), the president was disquieted about the enactment of his executive order.

The resulting loyalty program may have been tainted in Truman's eyes, but he publicly defended it and the FBI as effective tools to find and root out Communist infiltration. Privately, he continued to conclude that the loyalty program, as implemented, violated individual civil liberties. The largest public test of the Communist infiltration of government came with the Alger Hiss affair. By the end of the two trials, Truman was convinced of Hiss's guilt, but he disapproved of what he saw as the political stratagem that accompanied the legal proceedings. In retrospect, he stated that the general approach of the Communists, Senator Joseph McCarthy, and the House Committee on Un-American Activities (HUAC) "cannot be squared with the Bill of Rights" and argued, if "the government cannot produce witnesses in court, then it cannot prosecute. And if a man cannot be prosecuted in the courts, then he should not be persecuted by a Senate or House committee."[69] Apart from his disgust at a politicized process, he may not have been vocal about Hiss (especially after the conviction) out of loyalty to Secretary of State Acheson, who left himself politically vulnerable when he made his famous January 1950 statement: "I should like to make it clear to you that whatever the outcome of any appeal which Mr. Hiss or his lawyers may take in this case I do not intend to turn my back on Alger Hiss."[70] Although Acheson described Truman's support of him concerning Hiss, we do not have the president's final word on the subject, and there is no mention of Hiss in Truman's memoirs. (He also did not address Communist infiltration under Franklin Roosevelt, which was deep, broad, and at high levels, or consider what it might have meant for his own presidency in its early months.) He may have wanted to forget the Hiss case and not dwell on its implications, particularly for the negotiating atmosphere of the Yalta Conference (where Hiss was a personal advisor to Roosevelt), the birth and infancy of the United Nations (where Hiss presided as secretary-general over the United Nations Conference on International Organization in San Francisco, which resulted in the UN Charter), and his executive responsibility for government security.[71] Yalta was a legacy from FDR that could not be disavowed publicly, but Truman had trusted in the UN as a vehicle for democratic peace and could not accept that America's national security had been compromised.

On three occasions between August 5 and September 2, 1948, about two years before the advent of what came to be termed McCarthyism, the president used the phrase "red herring" to describe the search for Communist agents in the federal government. His words should be seen in the context of late summer 1948, before Hiss's legal future had been resolved. Truman's statements have been distorted by most political scientists and historians to mean that he assumed the charges against Hiss were fabricated. In fact, the president thought that the House Committee on Un-American Activities hearings served "no useful purpose," as no information had been revealed that was not already known by the FBI and presented to a federal grand jury. He believed that the HUAC hearings were a "red herring," in that they enabled Truman's opponents to divert attention from themselves and "from doing what they ought to do" in Congress.[72] But he defended the success of the loyalty program and attendant legal process in August 1948: "All the things that have been presented to these [congressional] committees have been FBI files and have been presented to the grand jury long before that. And the only two people who were in the Government employ who have been accused of disloyalty—which hasn't been proven on them by any means—have been placed on indefinite leave, before the committee ever started any hearings."[73] In short, he deplored what he saw as HUAC's partisanship in examining the serious, though in his view small, problem of Communist espionage in the federal government at the time. Later, he maintained that of the 378 people who were dismissed or denied employment through mid-1952 under the workings of the loyalty program boards, not one was a top advisor.[74]

Not only did Truman detest HUAC's political maneuvers in 1948, but he also believed that the committee made it more difficult than it should have been to prosecute Communist spies. In a memorandum to his attorney general, on the same day that Hiss was indicted by a grand jury for perjury, the president accused the committee of having "dried up sources of information which would have been accessible in the prosecution of spies and communists" and asked for FBI confirmation of this charge. He offered perhaps the definitive meaning of "red herring," arguing that HUAC's "meddling efforts were in fact a 'red herring' to detract attention not only from the shortcomings of the 80th Congress but also contributed to the escape of certain communists who should have been indicted."[75]

In 1996, the publication of the Venona files revealed the extent of Soviet espionage—including that of Hiss—in the United States. Because of a flaw that was common in their encipherment, these files were decrypted and deciphered from portions of more than twenty-nine hundred Soviet telegrams intercepted between 1940 and 1948. American and allied services then deciphered the original texts and puzzled over their meanings for almost four decades. In the 1940s and 1950s, the full data that had been processed at the time were kept from prosecutors in internal-security cases by the army and the FBI, in an attempt to prevent Moscow from learning that its codes had been broken. Not known immediately to the United States, it seems that Communist agents William W. Weisband and Kim Philby conveyed the flaw in the Soviet encipherment system to the Kremlin in the late 1940s.[76] In terms of protecting intelligence sources, the army's and FBI's tactical decisions were understandable, yet they undercut the effectiveness of the government's prosecution of spies.

In a 1998 book on secrecy in government, the late senator Daniel Patrick Moynihan concluded that Truman was "never told" about the Venona files. Likewise, the Commission on Protecting and Reducing Government Secrecy, of which Moynihan was chairman, found that "[w]hat seems increasingly clear is that the entire VENONA project was kept secret from Harry S [*sic*] Truman and his Attorney General, Tom Clark."[77] While it appears that the president never saw the raw Venona data (which would not have been unusual), General Omar Bradley—who became the first chairman of the Joint Chiefs of Staff in August 1949 and who had an open, respectful relationship with Truman—took "the responsibility of advising the President or anyone else in authority if the contents of any of this material so demanded."[78] We do not know, then, what Venona evidence that had been processed fully was given to Truman in 1948; but we may presume that, in late 1949 and after, Bradley probably conveyed pertinent available details from the Venona record to the president. If Truman knew little or nothing in 1948 about the contents of the Venona files, his skepticism about what he viewed as yet-unproved charges of espionage and his reliance on the American legal system make sense. Without the information that is now available on Soviet espionage in the United States, Truman's instinctive anticommunism is that much more striking.

8

"To assure the integrity and vitality of our free society"

The Culmination of
Truman's Containment

On January 31, 1950, Harry Truman decided that the United States had to pursue the development of the hydrogen bomb. That same day, independent of the H-bomb decision, the president also requested a broad-based report on the continuing world crisis. Drafted in February and March 1950 by new director of the Policy Planning Staff Paul Nitze (who had replaced George Kennan) and a nine-member team of State and Defense Department officials, NSC 68 was submitted to the president in April. It cited and quoted NSC 20/4, not NSC 20/1, as its institutional touchstone. Long dismissed as a crude propaganda effort—scholars have typically quoted Acheson's comments that NSC 68's purpose "was to so bludgeon the mass mind of 'top government' that not only could the President make a decision but that the decision could be carried out" and that "[i]f we made our points clearer than truth, we did not differ from most other educators and could hardly do otherwise"—NSC 68 was a sophisticated analysis of the situation.[1] Truman's political thought and action of containment, as well as his understanding of internationalism, resonated in the document. In some places, Nitze and his cowriters carried the president's thought to a natural conclusion beyond his actions. More than a justification for the buildup of conventional and nuclear forces, NSC 68 was a permanent record of containment's political thought (especially its defense of freedom) and a justification for Truman's liberal internationalism (especially the centrality of the democratic regime).

The Hydrogen Bomb Decision

In January 1949, the Kremlin organized the Council of Mutual Economic Assistance (Comecon), which would help tighten its hold on Eastern Europe throughout the year. On October 7, 1949, the USSR created the German Democratic Republic. At the beginning of October, Mao Zedong had proclaimed the establishment of the People's Republic of China (PRC), the "New China," although outside of Beijing much of the rest of the country was still gripped by war. Coupled with the Soviet move back into Manchuria, Mao's announcement was considered at the time to be evidence of totalitarian collaboration and an advance of worldwide communism; the Kremlin immediately recognized the PRC, and the new Soviet ambassador presented his credentials and met twice formally with Mao in the second half of October. By the end of the year, the Communists declared formal victory in China and the Nationalists fled to Formosa. Mao left Beijing for a nine-week trip to the Soviet Union, which included the celebration of Stalin's seventieth birthday; he had promised back in April that China would side with the Soviet Union in the event of a third world war.[2]

While China was falling to the Communists, the Soviets successfully exploded an atom bomb in September 1949. The Truman administration had not expected such a development until mid-1950 at the earliest. Based on intelligence estimates, President Truman had hoped that Soviet acquisition of the A-bomb would be several more years in the future. On February 3, 1950, Klaus Fuchs confessed the extent of his espionage during his involvement with the Manhattan Project, publicly revealing to the free world the extent of the atomic threat from the USSR. Within two weeks, on February 14, 1950, the Soviet Union signed its Treaty of Friendship, Alliance, and Mutual Assistance with the PRC, shortly after walking out of the UN Security Council in protest over its refusal to grant a seat to the Chinese Communists. Truman, Nitze, and others reasoned that the United States now faced a confident and aggressive Communist tyranny armed with weapons of mass destruction. An atomic capability—seen in the A-bomb and a future hydrogen bomb—in the hands of the Soviet Union added an element of terror in its conduct of foreign affairs. In addition to the levels of Communist diplomacy and the strength of the Red Army and its satellites, the subversive stratum of Moscow's foreign policy now included the nuclear threat, as well as propaganda, indirect aggression, and infiltration.[3]

That the Soviet detonation of the atom bomb and the consolidation of Communist rule on the Chinese mainland occurred almost simultaneously had a major effect on the Truman administration, particularly on the commander in chief. In November 1949, the president created a special committee of the National Security Council, whose membership included the secretaries of state and defense and Atomic Energy Commission Chairman David Lilienthal, to debate and then present to him the advantages and disadvantages of building the H-bomb, or Super, as it was also known. While Secretary of State Dean Acheson favored development of the hydrogen bomb for strategic reasons, Secretary of Defense Louis Johnson, though he agreed, tried to gain political concessions from Acheson for his acceptance of the new weapon. Lilienthal, meanwhile, agonized about the ethics of making such a decision, let alone researching and developing the H-bomb.

With his mind focused on the Cold War, Truman cut through the disagreements. At a meeting with the special committee on January 31, 1950, which lasted less than ten minutes, he inquired whether the Soviets could build a hydrogen bomb. When told that the Soviets probably were pursuing their own H-bomb, the president ordered that the United States do the same.[4] Truman decided that since America did not know for sure whether the Kremlin had begun its own pursuit of the hydrogen bomb, the leader of the free world must expand its program in nuclear weapons as a defensive measure.[5] As he said in May 1950, "But I am here to tell you that discovery [of the atom bomb] in the long run is going to be more important for the peace of the world than for its destruction." Reflecting his study of world history, Truman pointed out that the worst casualties ever known had occurred not in the First and Second World Wars but when the short sword was the main weapon of attack, in ancient times and in hand-to-hand combat in the Middle Ages.[6] The president defined the two components of U.S. military strength in the Cold War: keeping the conventional capacity modernized and trained universally and, now, maintaining a similarly updated nuclear edge over the Communists. While the Truman Doctrine, the Marshall Plan, and the Atlantic Alliance provided the pillars to containment atop the base of the president's political thought, the infrastructure of Truman's containment required new attention.

The existence of nuclear weapons was part of that infrastructure. But it did not describe the nature of America's strength or that of the war of nerves. In the political thought of containment, the president believed that the Communists employed three levels in their totalitarian strategy. Only the middle level, that of soldier and diplomat in war and peace, resembled the foreign policy of a free state. But even this layer was distorted by the Kremlin's bottom and overlying tiers. Underneath their demonstrations of diplomacy and military power, the Soviets depended on the dictates of Communist revolution; superimposed on the other two layers, they followed a strategy of terror, in which they sought to use the threat of atomic weapons to force accommodation. As a result, Truman thought that the postwar concern about nuclear weapons derived from a Cold War caused by Communist tyranny. Paul Nitze, Truman's Policy Planning Staff director as of February 1, 1950, agreed.[7] Kennan, by contrast, had tried during his tenure as PPS director to invert the relationship between totalitarianism and nuclear terror. The East-West conflict, he claimed, was a derivative of the atomic problem, and thus dealing with the Communists could be seen only in light of the threat of global destruction. In 1949 and 1950, Kennan's final government writings developed this position and revealed his paralysis concerning military strength.[8] Combined with his PPS and other papers from 1946 through 1948, these writings make clear that by 1949 Kennan had separated himself from Truman's containment.

The Context for NSC 68

Although it was not addressed in NSC 68, China must have been in the minds of Nitze and his coauthors. Indeed, NSC 68 offered the president a way to include China in the administration's commitment to fight world communism. It is fair to say that Truman was ambivalent about how to oppose China as a Communist state, given its size and its support by the USSR. It is also fair to say that his unwillingness or, as he saw it, inability to do more in late 1949 about China stemmed in part from his lack of familiarity with and knowledge of Asia and in part from his conviction that Chiang Kai-shek and the Nationalists were little better than Mao and his Communists.[9] In this sense, the charge that the president, along with Acheson, "lost" China is true. Yet Truman's disdain of tyranny was consistent. China was omitted from containment in 1949, but it was not left out of Truman's general political thought. Although in November 1945 he wrote that the United States should not interfere in China's internal affairs, in January 1946 he told Byrnes that "[w]e should rehabilitate China and create a strong central government there."[10] By mid-November 1949, he said that America would settle matters in China, "and not as a Communist State," while showing an uncharacteristic patience that was absent in his attitude toward the USSR: "Of course, it may take a long time. We are in too big a hurry. All we can do is set the spark that may bring it about."[11] He did not want to legitimate the Chinese regime, however, as he wrote in 1951 to William Douglas, who had suggested recognition of the PRC: "As long as I am President, if I can prevent it, that cut throat organization will never be recognized by us as the Government of China and I am sorry that a Justice of the Supreme Court has been willing to champion the interest of a bunch of murderers by a public statement."[12] The message of NSC 68 and the Korean War eliminated any residual uncertainty in Truman's opinion about the PRC, but he thought that the best way to change China over time was first to defeat the primary force of communism, the Soviet Union.

Truman signed NSC 68—which had been delivered to him six months earlier—on September 30, 1950, but the reasons for his delay did not stem from his disagreement with the thrust of the document or its conclusions. He clearly agreed with its political philosophy, since his own speeches had paved the way for NSC 68's argument. The president received the paper on April 7 before it was circulated officially to the National Security Council, and on April 12, in a letter that ordered the report referred to the NSC, Truman wrote, "I am particularly anxious that the Council give me a clear indication of the programs which are envisaged in the report, including estimates of the probable costs of such programs."[13]

Various scholars point to this statement to suggest that the president was mostly concerned about economics; some historians see this statement as equivocation.[14] The more likely explanation is that the president, having already asked for the NSC 68 report, wanted to figure out how to implement the policies recommended by the document. Indeed, an ad hoc committee for the rest of the NSC 68 series was formed by Truman for this purpose. The documents produced by that committee—NSC 68/1, which became NSC 68/2, and NSC 68/3, which became NSC 68/4—concentrated on the economic and force-structural requirements to implement the policy framework of NSC 68. Although brief reports, their research took up most of the rest of the year, augmenting for Truman the first paper in the series.[15] Likewise, the start of the Korean War on June 24 became tied with NSC 68 but was not the direct catalyst for the president's signature on the document. At an NSC meeting in July, Truman was more focused on developments in Korea that could tempt the Soviets to make other moves, possibly in the Persian Gulf or Black Sea Straits, in order to obtain and protect access to adequate oil reserves for war against the West.[16] Korea, even though a hot war, was one of many strategic concerns in what the president saw as a global Cold War. The original NSC 68 remained the definitive statement of containment's political thought and policy goals by reinforcing Truman's strategy of containment and extending the argument about strength he had been making from almost the start of his presidency.

Although he did not write any of NSC 68, Dean Acheson argued for building "situations of strength" in February 1950, and stressed in late March that "the Soviet Union has one purpose and that is world domination."[17] Even with Acheson's support throughout the development of the document, Truman felt keenly the departures of Special Counsel Clark Clifford from the White House and Executive Secretary Sidney Souers from the National Security Council, both in early 1950. James Lay, who replaced Souers as NSC executive secretary, brought a different administrative style and considered himself more a servant of the council than an assistant to the president.[18] At the same time, Acheson and Secretary of Defense Louis Johnson, who was already at odds with much of the administration's policies and personnel, were feuding. The president trusted Acheson and doubted Johnson, especially since the latter had endorsed NSC 68 only because he could not suppress the report and, in so doing, had further alienated himself from almost everyone in government. As a partial solution, Truman announced the appointment of Averell Harriman on June 15, 1950, as the special assistant to the president.[19] Not only did he expect Harriman to soothe matters between Acheson and Johnson, but he also relied on him as, in Souers's words, "the President's man to follow up and assure implementation" of the NSC process.[20] Truman needed the evidence from the NSC 68 follow-on papers to prove that the United States possessed the will and the wherewithal to implement Nitze's military recommendations. Acheson and Harriman were crucial in helping the president process the rest of the NSC 68 series and convert the primary document into American policy.

The Analysis of NSC 68

NSC 68 was almost seventy pages long and divided into nine sections and a conclusion. Often described as narrowly rhetorical or hyperbolic, the first six parts of NSC 68 gave a political, at times philosophical, evaluation of liberal democratic thought and Communist ideology.[21] Arguably, the document rebutted the insecurity thesis first advanced by Kennan in the Long Telegram and which matured in his other writings.[22] In its first section, NSC 68 described the USSR as a tyranny with an unprecedented drive: "The Soviet Union, unlike previous aspirants to hegemony, is animated by a new fanatic faith, antithetical to our own, and seeks to impose its absolute authority over the rest of the world." As with the Clifford report, this document accentuated Truman's definition of the USSR as a Communist empire. Distinguishing the various tactics employed by the Kremlin, the authors sketched the violent and nonviolent means at Moscow's disposal, as well as the possible use of atomic weapons. Rather than following a defensive policy grounded in insecurity, they said, the USSR operated according to a goal—limitless domination. NSC 68 recapitulated Truman's view that the Soviets acted ideologically and with unwarranted suspicion at the same time.[23]

In the second and third parts of the analysis, the authors juxtaposed the fundamental purpose of the United States with the fundamental design of the Kremlin. They agreed with Kennan that America and the Soviet Union had become superpowers, but, unlike Kennan, they did not view the two regimes as equivalent and, as a consequence, equated neither their natures nor their deeds. When it came to the United States, the document (as did Truman) went to the primary sources of America's principles. Citing the Declaration of Independence, the Constitution, and the Bill of Rights, NSC 68 argued that the essential purpose of the United States was "to assure the integrity and vitality of our free society, which is founded upon the dignity and worth of the individual." As a free society, it honored the fundamental rights of life, liberty, and the pursuit of happiness. Because of this dedication, and by upholding the ends of a good society, the United States considered itself to be a good regime. The Kremlin's design, on the other hand, was to retain and solidify absolute power and extend it to the non-Soviet world. Whereas liberal democracy upheld the freedom of the individual, according to NSC 68, Communist tyranny enslaved the individual. Communism played on fear by creating fear, thus stripping man of his complete being and dignity. In order to achieve total power, the USSR needed to subvert or destroy the integrity and vitality of the individual and of the free society, especially the United States, which, as the principal center of power and chief defender of freedom in the world, was the bulwark of opposition to Soviet expansion.[24]

Following Truman, Nitze and his cowriters argued that the principles of freedom and tyranny were fighting each other in the war of nerves. Harry Truman believed—and NSC 68 asserted—that the Soviet Union embodied evil in the world. So the president reasoned that the United States entered the struggle of the Cold War not to gain power but to defend the freedom of man and the integrity of free regimes. "We are a people who not only cherish freedom and defend it, if need be with our lives," said Truman, "but we also recognize the right of other men and other nations to share it."[25] The Kremlin design assailed not only liberal democracy but also the essence of liberty by denying the truth of inherent equal rights. And NSC 68 concluded that the society imposed by the Kremlin's totalitarian dictatorship destroyed man's freedom to the point that the individual participated in the degradation of his own dignity. The overarching theme of the document was that free society must reject communism as an alternative way of life, because tyranny denied human dignity, equality, and freedom.[26]

After presenting the diametrical opposition of the regimes, NSC 68 considered the underlying conflict in the realm of political ideas. Again reflecting Truman, the fourth section of the document pitted the idea of freedom under a government of laws against the idea of slavery under the Kremlin's despotism. While the free society valued the openness of freedom, democratic freedom rested on the individual exercising his rights with proper discipline. NSC 68 deemed liberty an absolute right not because it was rooted in man's passions but because it was grounded in man's natural capacity to reason. A free society welcomed diversity, and Nitze and his coauthors were confident that free men would choose the best wares in the marketplace of ideas and then "grow to a fuller and better realization of their powers in exercising their choice." While communism did not allow intellectual free trade in its empire and attempted to delimit it elsewhere through subversion, NSC 68 heralded freedom as "the most contagious idea in history, more contagious than the idea of submission to authority."[27]

In explicating the nature of the conflict, the document also stressed the "polarization of power" in the Cold War. The crisis and accompanying power struggle did not stem from realpolitik: the idea of freedom is "peculiarly and intolerably subversive of the idea of slavery," and "[t]he implacable purpose of the slave state to eliminate the challenge of freedom has placed the two great powers at opposite poles." NSC 68 viewed the Soviet Union as both expansionist and autarkic, making the Kremlin offensive by nature, unlike the United States. "The antipathy of slavery to freedom," wrote the authors, "explains the iron curtain, the isolation, the autarchy of the society whose end is absolute power." Kennan perceived this combination as defensive insecurity, but NSC 68 argued that the blend of domestic insularity and overall aggression was the product of Marxism-Leninism. And given the absolute power of the Communist state, the individual existed only to serve the ends of the system. As a result, according to the document, freedom was anathema to the Marxist-Leninist society. The Kremlin design, NSC 68 concluded, aimed to impose a monolith to extinguish that very freedom and, if possible, bring about a new, false philosophy of the absolute state.[28]

Nitze and his coauthors also refused to Europeanize the Cold War, in contrast to Acheson and others in the administration. With Truman, the Clifford memorandum, and NSC 20/4, NSC 68 detailed the struggle of communism against freedom as the gravest problem in American foreign relations: "The assault on free institutions is world-wide now, and in the context of the present polarization of power a defeat of free institutions anywhere is a defeat everywhere." While most of the academy later dismissed such words as a simplistic zero-sum view of the world, Truman, with support from NSC 68, posited the totalitarian nature of a Soviet regime that sought to demolish fundamental rights and the organizational bases of liberal democracy. The document's writers explained, for example, that the material loss of Czechoslovakia was compounded by the elimination of the freedom of its political and social institutions. Because of the indivisibility of freedom, all free society was thus mortally challenged by the Soviet system. The polarization of global power existed, with the forces for both chaos and tyranny pressuring free governments around the world. With Soviet gains arrayed against the inadequate defenses of the United States and the free world, NSC 68 used Truman's spectrum of anarchy and tyranny to argue for a concerted political, economic, and military defense of freedom.[29]

The document next outlined the objectives and means necessary to meet Communist imperialism, highlighting one long-term objective and one immediate objective, both of which supported Truman's approach. NSC 68's fixed goal was to maintain a strong free world—politically, morally, economically, and militarily—and to frustrate the Kremlin design and effect its internal change. Specifically regarding the USSR, U.S. policy should aim to affirm the moral and material strength of the free world and to bring the Soviets to acknowledge this strength. The culmination of that goal, as NSC 68 stated, must be to "foster a fundamental change in the nature of the Soviet system, a change toward which the frustration of the design is the first and perhaps the most important step." Although he never achieved it, Truman let this objective stand in the document. In the short run, American foreign policy should create a situation to induce the USSR to accommodate itself peaceably to the non-Soviet world. Such change within the Soviet Union would grant to the "Russian peoples" a new chance to work out their own destiny. In the event of war (which the document's authors considered a real possibility but not an inevitability), America not only would win but hoped to see the Soviet Union reconstituted according to less-hostile principles.[30]

By virtue of its character, NSC 68 argued, free society was based on liberal regime principles and renounced compulsion and unnecessary force as the means to its end. The society imposed by the Kremlin was also defined by its regime principles, which thrived on any means—especially force, compulsion, and imposition of will—to gain its end of world domination. As a result, "the Kremlin is able to select whatever means are expedient in seeking to carry out its fundamental design." Following Truman and formerly approved NSC reports, NSC 68 stated that the United States must heighten the articulation of its principles and develop its military and economic strength to defend them. Also in accord with the president's thought, the United States had the responsibility for global leadership. More decisively than Truman, the authors called for justice and order through means consistent with the principles of freedom and liberal democracy but detached from international organizations. Key to it all, though, was NSC 68's extension of the president's view: the judgment that the Cold War was a worldwide battle between freedom and slavery. As Nitze and his coauthors wrote, "The idea of slavery can only be overcome by the timely and persistent demonstration of the superiority of the idea of freedom." Unless the fundamental conflict against communism was vanquished in the realm of principles and ideas, military victory would be inadequate.[31]

In the fifth section, NSC 68 dealt with Soviet intentions and capabilities. The Soviet Union was inescapably militant because "it possesses and is possessed by a world-wide revolutionary movement, because it is the inheritor of Russian imperialism and because it is a totalitarian dictatorship." Distinct from Kennan's dilution of ideology as a justification for actions already taken, NSC 68 posited that Communist doctrine "is not a limiting factor; rather it dictates the employment of violence, subversion and deceit, and rejects moral considerations." The USSR's primary obstacle to world domination, and thus its target, was the United States. According to their ideology, the Communists made no distinction between military aggression and measures short of such belligerence.[32] NSC 68 therefore concluded that the only consideration that limited the Kremlin's means in pursuit of its policies—whether infiltration, intimidation, aggression, or war—was expedience.

Soviet intentions and capabilities were linked fundamentally by Communist ideology, which informed and motivated the Kremlin's intentions and was the goal of its capabilities. In the Long Telegram, Kennan referred to all Russian actions as garbed in the trappings of Marxism-Leninism.[33] But NSC 68 did not concur that communism was a pretense. Nitze made this point in February, which would reverberate in NSC 68: "It should be stressed, however, that Soviet actions make clear that Moscow's faith in the inevitable disintegration of capitalism is not a passive faith in automatic historical evolution. Instead it is a messianic faith that not only spurs the USSR to assist the transformation of the Marxist blueprint into a reality, but also gives the Soviet leaders a sense of confidence that in whatever particular course they follow they are riding the waves of the future."[34] If Soviet aims had been nebulous before and during World War II, the claims of Stalin's election address and the postwar actions of Kremlin aggression demonstrated to Nitze that the USSR believed in world Communist domination.

In his memoirs, Kennan protested that containment should be concerned only with Russian intentions, because the United States could not withstand Soviet capabilities. The result was that containment was often debated as intentions versus capabilities.[35] But the Truman administration saw intentions and capabilities as interlaced. The president looked at what the Soviets believed, what they aimed to do as a result of that belief, and how much of that desire they could achieve. Had he gauged capabilities with no reference to ideology and intentions, Truman would have given way to the Soviets in Berlin rather than arranging the airlift. Kennan prized settlements as a constant worthy end, but NSC 68 contested that the Soviet Union geared its economy toward a war-making capacity to support its drive for world domination. In this sense, the document was the first to expound fully that communism was offensive by definition and that no distinction between totalitarian offense and totalitarian defense existed.

In evaluating Soviet intentions and capabilities, NSC 68 also explored the Kremlin's liabilities. Although the document ranged over economic and military weaknesses, the primary defect identified by NSC 68 concerned Soviet political and psychological capabilities. Indeed, the Kremlin's greatest vulnerability was the basic nature of its relationship with the Soviet peoples. More deeply than Kennan, NSC 68 maintained that it was the iron curtain around the East bloc—not to mention the various forces of suppression within it—that held together the Soviet monolith. Realism postulated a possible splintering, accenting the ethnic fights that ensue from nationalism. But NSC 68 saw the strength of particular peoples stemming from man's intrinsic inclination for freedom and looked to the independence of nationalities as a natural, potent, and positive threat to communism.[36] In the internal and external empires of the Soviet Union, the "Soviet ideas and practices run counter to the best and potentially the strongest instincts of men, and deny their most fundamental aspirations." The implication was that a Communist dictatorship based on power politics and repression was illegitimate and would crumble eventually from the peoples' moral pressure from within and from the free world's combined strength from without.[37]

In the sixth section, NSC 68 contrasted U.S. intentions and capabilities with those of the Soviet Union. In order to promote a world environment in which the American system survived and flourished, the development of a healthy international community and the containment of the Soviet system were both required. In Truman's eyes, a thriving global community, especially with respect to economic prosperity, was a self-standing goal of liberal internationalism and a component of containment. If the Soviets decided to join that community, he said, they must abandon their design. Nitze and his coauthors gave a basic definition of containment, more limited than Truman's, but it supported the president's political thought and action. Within the Cold War, containment sought to block the further expansion of Soviet power, expose the falsities of Communist ideology, induce retraction of the Kremlin's control and influence, and foster the seeds of destruction within the Soviet system, with the minimum goal of making the USSR conform to generally accepted international standards.

NSC 68 nevertheless left open the possibility of negotiations with the Soviet Union. In fact, it noted that the current diplomatic freeze tended "to inhibit our initiative and deprives us of opportunities for maintaining a moral ascendency in our struggle with the Soviet system." For agreements to take place, though, the issues had to be negotiable. NSC 68 emphasized, among other examples, that world communism waged a campaign of propaganda against liberal democracy and capitalism, notably the United States. Because the Soviets were creating overwhelming military force to back up their disinformation, infiltration, and intimidation, the United States—unless it betrayed its ultimate purpose—could negotiate only from strength and with the capabilities necessary to defend its principles.[38]

But strength did not translate flatly into military might. The last sections of NSC 68, usually quoted for their military and atomic proposals, suggested what was seen as the best practicable course of action for America and the free world. Truman's commitment to peace through strength was upheld in a program for rapid buildup of the political, economic, and military strength of a free society. In strategic terms, this buildup constituted a firm policy "to check and to roll back the Kremlin drive for world domination" and protect America's fundamental purpose, while in geopolitical terms it meant that free countries must combine their political, economic, and military elements to form a coalition of strength.[39] Truman understood this strength as an affirmation of liberal democracy's tenets—the ultimate objective, after all, was the preservation of a free and democratic way of life. Particularly in the seventh section of the document, NSC 68 shared Truman's belief—in turn, in keeping with the tradition of American political thought—that a free people must defend its freedom. As NSC 68's authors wrote, "No people in history have preserved their freedom who thought that by not being strong enough to protect themselves they might prove inoffensive to their enemies." This quote carried both political and strategic connotations, comprehending World War II's lessons about fighting tyrants. Those lessons were timeless, now applying to communism. America's fundamental purpose, according to NSC 68, was more likely to be defeated from a lack of will than by asserting a robust will against a Communist threat.[40]

In the end, NSC 68's authors noted that freedom will not always and everywhere triumph. But they had concluded from the study of Communist doctrine and experience that the victory of communism over freedom meant a total defeat. The risks of the Cold War were "of a new order of magnitude, commensurate with the total struggle in which we are engaged," and must be met accordingly. Just as had the Truman Doctrine, ERP, and NATO, NSC 68 called for a positive program. At minimum, its writers wanted to create a situation in the free world to which the Kremlin would be compelled to adjust. Ultimately, they understood that "[t]he only sure victory lies in the frustration of the Kremlin design by the steady development of the moral and material strength of the free world and its projection into the Soviet world in such a way as to bring about an internal change in the Soviet system."[41] Rather than coexisting with the USSR, the free world's combined strength was intended to change the Soviet system. The seeds of this argument can be found in Truman's political thought, and the president also put the moral and material strength of the West on the line in Korea. NSC 68 went further, holding out the goal of the abolition of Communist tyranny, which, directed as it was by Moscow, meant the defeat of the Soviet Union.

Throughout his memoirs, Kennan protested that the instruments of containment became the simultaneous determinants and ends of Truman's policies. The Marshall Plan, which Truman believed would have foundered by itself, was the exception for Kennan. From Truman's point of view, however, the various instruments of containment were all pillars of the same edifice. Before the ERP, the Truman Doctrine provided political, military, and economic aid; as the Marshall Plan tried to take root, NATO furnished the necessary political and military support. Truman's policy of containment reached its fullest and clearest articulation in NSC 68. Its conclusions anchored American foreign policy, and they pointed to a comprehension of the nature of the Cold War and of the regimes at battle in that war.[42] In large part, the document grew out of the president's liberal internationalism and strengthened his political thought and action by aiming for its fulfillment. In achieving that goal, NSC 68 embodied the culmination of the founding of American foreign policy after World War II and was the definitive statement of the United States' decision to expose and act against Communist tyranny.

The Culmination of Kennan's Containment

George Kennan's *American Diplomacy: 1900–1950*, based on lectures given at the University of Chicago in 1951, completes the Kennan of the

Truman era. While the argument of NSC 68 remained classified until the 1970s, Kennan's book launched his public and ex post facto defense of his containment. In doing so, it dispelled the now-popular notion of two distinct Kennans and revealed the Kennan of the 1940s and the mature Kennan as analogous.[43] While NSC 68 and *American Diplomacy* both went beyond the specifics of containment and delved into general political thought and an understanding of human nature, the main difference lay in that the former set forth and fulfilled Truman's containment, whereas the latter culminated Kennan's containment and rejected the president's approach.

In his preface, Kennan explained that the bulk of the lectures covered the period from 1900 through World War II, and so for the book he added "two articles on Russian-American relations which can be taken as reflecting the application of that same intellectual approach to problems of the present day."[44] For Kennan, the situations may have varied from the turn of the century through 1950, but the application of his approach remained constant: he indicted moralism and legalism as sentimental and unrealistic, and he invoked a philosophy and policy of realism in foreign affairs. The psychological Kennan was present, too. The intellectual approach of Kennan in this volume, then, undergirded his political thought and suggested a course of action concerning containment.

Kennan began *American Diplomacy* by compartmentalizing politics such that the politics of external relations required a separate political theory and foundation from domestic politics. Although Truman separated foreign and domestic affairs on occasions of excessive partisanship, he believed that constant principles animated all politics. At home and abroad, Truman always understood himself to be responsible to democratic principles, enshrined in the American constitutional system, which were universally true. Kennan, in contrast, referred to republican governance and democracy, but worried about the popularization of world affairs and preferred that professional elites handle foreign policy and international politics. Rather than evaluating the circumstances of the Cold War and the battle of two worldviews, as had Truman, Kennan concentrated on the general concepts, common assumptions, and popular feelings of the United States in order to illuminate the extent to which American diplomacy was at fault for the Cold War.[45]

Security was a mental more than concrete substance, according to Kennan, and *American Diplomacy* aimed to shape such perceptions. America's culpability in the Cold War, he thought, and a central reason for the conflict's cause, lay in a misperception of its security. Before 1940, he contended, the United States overestimated its security; after World War II, it exaggerated its insecurity. While acknowledging that some of the change in attitude was "objectively real," he attributed it more to fear and an excessive sense of insecurity. For Kennan, appearances either filtered or outweighed reality. Consequently, American concepts, assumptions, and feelings caused problems in international politics. In the case of the Cold War, Kennan sketched a generation "surrounded by a world part of which seems to be actually committed to our destruction and another part to have lost confidence either in ourselves or in itself, or in both."[46] In Kennan's containment, extreme insecurity on the part of the Americans caused their equally extreme response in policy, leaving the USSR, by implication, no course but to react in kind. To solve the problem, Kennan wanted to recalibrate the concepts, assumptions, and feelings of the United States, including its State Department elites, who should hold the most sway in foreign affairs.[47]

The theoretical orientation of *American Diplomacy* was steeped in realism. In an overview, Kennan maintained that the founding generation of the late 1700s adopted realpolitik and aimed for a balance of power to protect the national interest. He admonished later generations for believing that American wisdom and virtue restrained the United States from involvement in the differences of the Old World. (Kennan credited only the British fleet and English continental diplomacy for American security before 1898.) Although he appreciated the insights of geostrategists such as Brooks Adams and A. T. Mahan, he thought realism remedied their deficiencies by introducing the psychology of human nature and applying it to historical phenomena. He catalogued the psychological and political reactions of fear, ambition, insecurity, jealousy, and boredom as the "prime movers of events."[48] Expanding the implications of his government writings, he subordinated the faculty of reason rooted in man to such desires and suggested that reason is but another human passion. Politics belong in the realm of appetites and reaction, said Kennan, stemming from man's natural inclination toward power through pride and avarice. He felt that it was up to enlightened leaders like him to stimulate the lesser passions and diminish those of pride and glory, except in a select few.

The structure and thrust of Kennan's book provided the prototype for the New Left. In order to arrive at the Cold War, Kennan evaluated American policies from 1898 and the Spanish-American War to the Open Door in China to overall involvement in the Orient to World War I and through World War II.[49] As revisionists would in the next decade, he contended that the many arguments for acquisition of the Philippines in 1898 covered up the real motivation: expansionist leaders "simply liked the smell of empire and felt an urge to range themselves among the colonial powers of the time."[50] Stamping the United States as a colonial power and praising the opponents of expansion, he indicated the inconsistency of empire with the social compact of liberal democracy. Unlike the New Left, however, Kennan thought that America had diverged from its realist roots and that men of insight could return the country to realpolitik.

Orthodox cold warriors, from Winston Churchill to Robert Conquest, have traced the roots of the Cold War to the year 1917 and the Bolshevik Revolution. In *American Diplomacy*, Kennan also returned to 1917, but for a different purpose. He posited the beginnings and origins of the Western diplomatic predicament of the twentieth century in World War I: since the United States and others failed to preserve the more moderate Germany of 1913, they helped to promote the First World War. Kennan extended this line to the cause of the next world war, writing that, from 1914 to 1920, World War II was extensively predetermined by the sickness and impatience of Germany, the weakness of Eastern Europe, and the phenomenon of Bolshevism.[51] He believed that America should have supported pre–World War I Germany and suggested that Bolshevik Russia should have been accommodated. These U.S. failures, according to Kennan, led to Nazi Germany and Stalinist Russia. He reprimanded the United States for making the world wars into moralistic crusades, which, in the case of the Second World War, incited the Cold War.

During World War II, the Allies needed the Soviet Union in order to defeat Nazi Germany. Kennan said that America and the West should not have been surprised when the Kremlin took its spoils after the war, and he added that the United States should have done more at the time to win respect and liking from the USSR. In a subtle determinism, he excused Soviet behavior on the grounds that it was due to "the political personality of the Bolshevik leadership" and to the animosity found in deep psychological roots of specifically Russian phenomena.[52] He did not think that America could have altered the Soviet "political personality" before 1920, yet he reproached the West for not realizing that the Kremlin, in the midst of the Second World War, had evolved to the point of being receptive to diplomacy. On the one hand, he implied in his government writings and elsewhere in *American Diplomacy* that Stalin was a power politician, a paranoiac, and a great threat to peaceful relations. On the other hand, he claimed that the Soviet Union supposedly was most pliant to diplomacy at the height of Stalin's power.

In the X article, Kennan condemned the false religion of sentimentality. In his 1951 book, he gave it a name: legalism-moralism. *American Diplomacy* blamed the United States for the worst diplomatic failures and violence of the twentieth century, citing its immature historical evolution and its dependence on public opinion, legalism, and moralism. Kennan combined these factors in assessing the American response to Communist aggression at the end of and in the wake of World War II. He disapproved the Rooseveltian approach to the USSR, and he foresaw a time when the United States could handle a realist diplomacy of detachment, once men like Kennan were in charge. Assigning a confusion to the American public that was fanned by ambitious politicians, he depicted a mistaken understanding that permeated society: "This failure stemmed from our general ignorance of the historical processes of our age and particularly from our lack of attention to the power realities involved in given situations."[53] He exhorted the United States to discard its blinders and to accept the "power realities" practiced by all states, whether tyrannical or democratic. Accenting psychology, he speculated that the use of coercion and force was most difficult for liberal democracy, because the passions of public opinion fanned ambivalent feelings about employing force. Kennan, in *American Diplomacy*, told his audience that they must be willing to abandon the charade of international law and of reliance on the public's whims. Regarding World War I, realism meant early action in 1913 to uphold Berlin for the overall goal of moderation and stability in world affairs. With respect to World War II, Kennan translated realism into American action before the Nazi declaration of war for the same end. If they adopted a realist attitude, he contended, people would realize that the "stupidity or bad faith" of others did not cause the Cold War. In the war of nerves, however, the realist did not account for the ideological component of Kremlin aggression; instead, he attempted to reshape the "mental outlook" of his country to conform with realpolitik.[54]

American Diplomacy advanced the particulars of Kennan's containment by reprinting "The Sources of Soviet Conduct" (the X article of July 1947) and "America and the Russian Future," from *Foreign Affairs* of spring 1951.[55] Publicly, Kennan stood by the previously anonymous X article and augmented it with his first postgovernmental writing of note. To provide the conditions for his containment, though, he examined diplomacy in the modern world and found it wanting. He longed for the days of the State Department in the 1920s, when he entered the diplomatic corps. Kennan lauded the old men who, like similar professionals once found in other countries, had exercised diplomacy in a civilized manner, with quality and dignity and without regard for nationality or citizenship. He extolled them—as opposed to later U.S. diplomats—for having come closest to embodying the national interest and genius of America. This statement is curious, since Kennan ascribed nothing particularly American to these diplomats, save the universal and commendable qualities of integrity, moderation, modesty, and generosity. He thought these traits and others—delicacy of character, loyalty in personal relations, and kindliness toward the weak—were now rare. Because most people had become universalist, legalistic, and nationalistic, he implied that good diplomatic officers were representatives of the past.

Although he wanted to resurrect his view of early-twentieth-century American diplomacy, Kennan deemed that this practice itself was inferior to the realpolitik of the classical balance of power. He referred to the previous generation of State Department personnel as the intellectual fathers of his age. They understood their own circumstances, according to Kennan, but incompletely perceived the larger historical situation. As their heirs, Kennan thought, he and others formed a new generation able to perceive not only the gap between "challenge" and "response" that existed in the 1920s but also the wider and more dangerous breach that had developed by 1950.[56] Since the public mind, especially in Congress and the media, resisted professionalism in foreign policy, he searched elsewhere for his solution. Adumbrating his memoir position, Kennan called for scholars to educate others in "the question of concept" and usher in the "principle of professionalism."[57] He thereby concluded that the intellectual would have the best opportunity to eradicate the legalistic-moralistic approach and to inculcate realism in tomorrow's diplomats, politicians, and students of international relations. As realism's stamina in the academy attests, Kennan's insight was useful in disseminating his school of thought.

Kennan's political thought of containment, while wrapped up in the American diplomacy of the twentieth century, grew out of the eighteenth century. In turn, this diplomacy inhered in the movement of history.

"History has shown that the will and capacity of individual peoples to contribute to their world environment is constantly changing," he stated. "It is only logical that the organizational forms (and what else are such things as borders and governments?) should change with them." The insecurity of regimes and territory was a constant for Kennan. He joined the expected reaction of man's appetites and reason to the certain evolution—sometimes degeneration—of man's regime. Given such precariousness, he argued, the United States must employ diplomacy, "in the most old-fashioned sense of the term," in order to control the evolution of regimes.[58] He believed that only professionals, like himself, could sustain a modicum of stability through the balancing of great powers.

Kennan looked forward to the reign of realism in world politics that would transcend individuals and their governments. He argued that truth was a poor competitor in the marketplace of ideas, not because it reflected what was transcendent or because it might exact a demanding and virtuous life, but because truth—"complicated, unsatisfying, full of dilemmas, always vulnerable to misinterpretation and abuse"—was too difficult for most to understand.[59] He aimed, rather, to educate the few who could apprehend the complicated truth of realism and train the rest to accept their leadership. Then, these few could determine and pursue the national interest and precipitate an era of order. Gone were the "legalistic" standards of the regime and the "moralistic" defense of liberty in the face of tyranny; such principled distinctions would no longer be characteristic of politics. Statesmanship and prudence, the art of applying principles to politics, were replaced by diplomacy and professionalism, the skill of implementing realpolitik in history.

Kennan consistently maintained that he authored containment in its perfect form and that Truman sullied its purity through excess and moralism. He wrote that he did not advocate containment as the military response to a military threat, "but the political containment of a political threat," and that he disliked other definitions: "I am afraid that there has been a general misinterpretation of the term 'containment,' as I first used it. It was never meant as exclusively, or even primarily, a military concept. What was meant was simply that there was a large area of maneuvre for ourselves between the alternatives of 'war with Russia' and a despairing abandonment of the peoples of Europe and Asia, and intelligently addressed, wherever possible, to opposing a further expansion of communist influence, then there was a reasonable possibility that the immediate postwar period, with all its bitter problems, might be survived without disaster."[60] Kennan stated that his assessment of Soviet intentions in the Long Telegram pertained only to the period during which Stalin controlled the Kremlin, and that containment overall "was a doctrine that lost much of its rationale with the death of Stalin and with the development of the Soviet-Chinese conflict."[61]

Contrary to Kennan's indictment, however, Truman's approach *was* the political containment of a political threat. It placed the roots of the global menace of the 1940s in the Bolshevik Revolution of 1917. Since politics, economics, and strategy were interconnected, the president sought out a fully political response. As he explained, "Our foreign policy was mistakenly called by some a policy of containment. This is not true. Our purpose was much broader. We were working for a united, free, and prosperous world."[62] In his liberal internationalism, Truman never abandoned his certainty that global peace could prevail. But while he sometimes seemed to desire an unattainable human peace, he recognized that freedom was both the end and the chief component of the defense against tyranny. Practically, a totality of strength in the Truman Doctrine, the Marshall Plan, and NATO would bring peace through the promotion of freedom. Through his words, actions, and documents like NSC 68, the president defined this understanding of freedom not only for his presidential successors but for the Western alliance as a whole. Kennan never accepted the totality of strength argument of containment, nor did he see its roots in the defense of liberty.

Thus, although he coined the term, George Kennan neither conceived nor directed containment. Harry Truman, working not from foreign policy textbooks or State Department manuals but from his knowledge, experience, and convictions—and his conclusions about tyranny's assault on freedom—did that. Aspects of the Long Telegram and the X article contributed to but did not steer Truman's unfolding liberal internationalism and containment strategy. As for other Kennan government writings, they may have served as important input for ideas and policy, but many were discarded and never, except perhaps in hindsight, formed an alternative Kennan doctrine.

9

"We must put on the armor of God"

History, Faith, and Peace
in Truman's Thought

A t the beginning of the last year of his presidency, during the height of the
Korean War, Truman summarized his abhorrence of human rights
violations and compared dealing with Communist governments to "an
honest man trying to deal with a numbers racket king or the head of a
dope ring." He indicted the Soviets for breaking every agreement made at
the three main wartime conferences; castigated them for raping Poland,
Romania, Czechoslovakia, Hungary, and the Baltic states; and chastised
them for sending citizens who believed in self-government to slave labor
camps. He also mourned the some three million prisoners of war who were
"still held at slave labor contrary to cease fire terms" and the thousands
of children who had been kidnapped in every country occupied by the
Soviet Union and never heard from again. He rededicated the free world
to stopping Communist aggression—both Soviet and Chinese—through
all available means.[1]

Truman's longhand notes of May 1952—written in the imperative
form to the Communists, which makes them that much more striking—
returned to the same theme. He was particularly troubled by the Soviet
kidnapping and deportation of thousands of young people from Germany,
Greece, and Korea, assuming that they must have been murdered. He
went on to wonder if the one million German prisoners had been killed
by the Soviets, as they had shot the Poles at Katyn—"How many South
Korean and Allied prisoners have you shot without cause. You claim you

199

hold only 12,000 prisoners"—and what had happened to the thousands of civilians and soldiers who had been taken from South Korea. Again, Truman accused the Communists of lacking any morals or honor and threatened them with destruction.[2] He did not say how he would destroy them, although previously he had mentioned "all out war."

In his longhand notes, Truman often vented his frustrations about Communist dishonesty and, even more, its destruction and ruination of innumerable lives. The language was harsh, yet, in his view, the circumstances warranted it. If asked about it, he might well have said that he was expressing Christian righteous anger. He supported the use of appropriate force, as he had shown on many occasions during World War II and the Cold War, but within the context of hoping for a peace that might arise from the transformation of the Communist world. Truman wanted to challenge the Communists and make them change their thought, as well as their behavior: "Read Confucius on morals to them. Read Buddha's code to them. Read the Declaration of Independence to them. Read the French declaration, Liberty & Fraternity. Read the Bill of Rights to them. Read the 5th, 6th & 7th Chapters of St. Matthew to them. Read St. John's prophecy on Anti Christ and have your own interpreter do it." Then he concluded, "You've enough real truth here to last you a month. Be sure the world press is briefed on every meeting where you follow these instructions."[3]

Truman's primary conclusions about man, politics, and human nature were drawn from his observations of life, to be sure, but more fundamentally from his comprehension of history and religion. In order to appreciate Truman, his presidency, and how he understood America during the pivotal moment of U.S. foreign policy in the twentieth century, it is important to realize how these deeper themes—his historical sense and his religious faith—shaped the man.

Truman on Man and History

Regarding the low points of World War II, not surprisingly, Truman's views about man were pessimistic. Consider this appraisal of the human race that he offered in describing the devastation of Berlin in July 1945: "The most sorrowful part of the situation is the deluded Hitlerian populace. Of course the Russians have kidnaped the able bodied and I suppose have made involuntary workmen of them. They have also looted every house left standing and have sent the loot to Russia. But Hitler did the same thing to them. It is the Golden Rule in reverse—and it is not an uplifting sight. What a pity that the human animal is not able to put his moral thinking into practice!" His observations of the many displaced persons prompted him to think "of Carthage, Baalbek, Jerusalem, Rome, Atlantis, Peking, Babylon, Nineveh; Scipio, Rameses II, Titus, Herman, Sherman, Jenghis Khan, Alexander, Darius the Great. But Hitler only destroyed Stalingrad—and Berlin. I hope for some sort of peace—but I fear that machines are ahead of morals by some centuries and when morals catch up perhaps there'll be no reason for any of it. I hope not. But we are only termites on a planet and maybe when we bore too deeply into the planet there'll [be] a reckoning—who knows?"[4] Yet in May 1945, he wrote that "the human animal can't be trusted for anything good except en masse" and that "[t]he combined thought and action of the whole people of any race, creed or nationality will always point in the Right Direction."[5] These interpretations, recorded within a two-month span, seem to contradict each other. What is consistent, though, is Truman's belief that those, alone or collectively, who refuse to live by a higher law will invert the golden rule, err, and bring ruin upon themselves and their country. Doing unto others as you would have them do unto yourself was understood by "all moralists," Truman noted in May 1945. But man, unassisted by some sense of the transcendent, will always get into trouble.

The impression that machines had outpaced morals was one that Truman returned to on occasion. He had a bifurcated view of technological progress, which was tied to his perception of human nature. While he expressed concern that new technology would enable man to wreak greater havoc, he was also excited at advances that enlarged human opportunity.[6] In addressing the development of total war and weapons of mass destruction, Truman turned to old-fashioned methods to solve the dilemma: "Man will have to learn how to save himself from destruction, and one nation by itself cannot abolish wars. Good courageous leaders and statesmen will be needed more than ever."[7] Man's flawed nature could not be overcome or corrected by technological progress, but it could be moderated by the development of good character.

Over the long term, Truman's faith in man and his positive attributes prevailed. From the late 1940s on, even during difficult times in the Cold War, he repeatedly said that he wished he could be young again and experience fully the great age that he believed was ahead. His expectation that technology could serve a good end was attached to his hope for world peace. Truman wrote at the start of the last year of his presidency, "1952 is here and so am I—gloomy as can be. But we must look to the program of world peace, and keep on looking." He longed to have the same energy that he had at the age of seventeen "to learn and to know world history."[8] In the study and application of history's lessons, he found examples that could be emulated, which would elevate man and promote the common good. Truman adduced many bad and good examples in history, but he believed that it was important to study both with an eye to recognizing and fighting the former and embracing and living the latter. Applying this message to the war of nerves, he said that the course of prudence and hope would enable America and the West to prevail over world communism.[9]

Truman thought it was most important to know the actors, rather than what was acted on or the trends, in history and politics. "So study men, not historians," he wrote in 1950. "You don't even have to go that far to learn that real history consists of the life and actions of great men who occupied the stage at the time. Historians' editorializing is in the same class as the modern irresponsible columnist."[10] This statement contained not only Truman's contempt for modern historiography and opinion journalism but also his preference for what is often called the great-man theory of history—that the most significant movements of history are caused by the decisions of individual actors on the world scene. He held this view of history from the first time he was exposed to the subject. Around the time Truman was ten years old, his mother gave him a series of books, *The Lives of Great Men and Famous Women*, edited by Charles Francis Horne. He read these volumes many times, retained them in his personal library, and eventually asked that they be housed at the Truman Library.[11] With other books that he read frequently and repeatedly, such as the Bible, Plutarch's *Lives*, Marcus Aurelius's *Meditations*, Edward Gibbons's *The Decline and Fall of the Roman Empire*, the works of Shakespeare (especially *Hamlet*, *Julius Caesar*, and *Macbeth*), Sir Edward Shepherd Creasy's *Fifteen Decisive Battles of the World*, and Abbott's biographies of famous historical figures—a popular set of the late nineteenth and early twentieth centuries—he formed at a young age the conclusion that studying the lives of great men, and imitating the finest in them, was essential, particularly for those who aimed to be public servants.

In his postpresidential years, in discussing what made a good candidate for office, Truman said that an honorable man with broad experience in government was best, but that some level of chance was involved "whether you appoint or elect him to high position. Experience shows many make good and a great many don't. That's the difficulty. It's the human animal all over again, and you do the best you can in trying to find the right man."[12] History provided him with success stories and suggestions, as well as disappointments and choices to reject. Although he did not conclude that it was easy, he thought that great men could be good men, if they sought virtue and the common good over glory and ambition.[13]

In July 1953, Truman wrote a memorandum in which he fleshed out his reasoning. Providing a litany of "all sorts of men and women who have made history," he recommended the study of the lives of "the truly great men" who "have made sacrifices for the betterment of the world and their individual countries and communities." As the recently retired leader of the free world, he might have been expected to value the role of statesmen above all others, but he found that "[t]he moralists and philosophers left the world a much greater heritage than did most of the rulers and conquerors." The two categories, however, were not mutually exclusive. According to Truman, the best rulers were also moral, such as Marcus Aurelius, Antoninus Pius, and Justinian. At some length, he then considered "three great men in government" that he long had admired: Cincinnatus, Cato the Younger, and George Washington. Some might say that such a trio showed a simplistic use of history. To Truman, however, these men were exemplars for all times: they not only ruled well and honestly but also tempered their ambition and governed for the good of their people rather than themselves. On the second point, he was struck especially by the characters of Cincinnatus and Washington, the latter of whom "could have been king, president for life if he'd been ambitious for power" but "knew when and how to quit public office and lay down the immense power he wielded with the people." Although the first American president had been a statesman who had "won the war to create this United States, presided over the Constitutional Convention, and set the country on the right road to greatness," Truman esteemed him as much or more because he "returned to his farm and became a model citizen of his country."[14]

Although his interpretation of history might seem outmoded and limited to various historians and political scientists, Truman's thoughts about history were both serious and essential to his worldview.[15] He frequently said that there was nothing new in human nature and that history offered timeless insights; he did not believe that history ran in predictable cycles, was deterministic, or was necessarily progressive. In February 1939, for example, while he condemned Hitler, he hoped that the world was not "at the end of another enlightened age, as the Greeks were in 300 B.C. and as the Romans were 600 years later."[16] When called on to make decisions as president, he typically read in the evenings "something in history which might help me form an opinion as to the course I had to take."[17] Human nature remained the same, according to Truman, and this meant that, throughout the course of one's life, each individual could freely choose to act well or badly; each person had the capacity for both self-improvement and self-destruction. As a result, how peoples arranged themselves or were forced to be arranged was crucial, because the structures of government either encouraged or discouraged the freedom necessary for individuals to govern themselves and make choices in accord with what was morally right. For Truman, the partnership of freedom and justice within a liberal democracy was the best practicable environment for defending as well as encouraging good character and conduct at the individual and state levels.

This view seems incompatible with the Truman, brimming with unbridled optimism, who carried in his wallet a copy of Lord Tennyson's "Locksley Hall" and drew inspiration from the lines:

> For I dipt into the future, far as human eye could see,
> Saw the Vision of the world, and all the wonder that would be
> Saw the heavens fill with commerce, argosies of magic sails,
> Pilots of the purple twilight, dropping down with costly bales;
> Heard the heavens fill with shouting, and there rain'd a ghastly dew
> From the nations' airy navies grappling in the central blue;
> Far along the world-wide whisper of the south-wind rushing warm,
> With the standards of the peoples plunging thro' the thunderstorm;
> Till the war-drum throbb'd no longer, and the battle-flags were furl'd.
> In the Parliament of man, the Federation of the world.
> There the common sense of most shall hold a fretful realm in awe,
> And the kindly earth shall slumber, lapt in universal law.

The practical president who championed freedom and liberal democracy appears at odds with the man who hoped for the end of political and economic strife and a reign of perpetual peace. In his political thought, he still exhibited the tension between a permanent peace obtained through a globalized order and a peace composed of strength, freedom, justice, and order that was voiced by American liberal internationalism and practiced by like-minded regimes. To understand Truman, it is still necessary to evaluate his views of history, human nature, and experience in light of his religious faith. In so doing, we see how Truman reconciled the seeming contradiction within himself.

Truman and Religion

Political scientists and historians have generally ignored Harry Truman's faith and its influence on his politics, or they have characterized his religion as crude and simplistic.[18] Even his best biographers have given faith a restricted role in Truman's thought and action. Neither Robert Ferrell nor David McCullough discusses Truman's religion at length. Ferrell describes Truman's Baptist faith as part of a rural upbringing and credits Truman with considerable open-mindedness toward other creeds.[19] McCullough, meanwhile, makes a reference to Truman's emphasis on acting out rather than talking about religion.[20] Like Ferrell and McCullough, Alonzo Hamby states that Truman left the formal practices of religion to his wife. Hamby is the only major biographer who speaks of a "larger religious sense" in Truman, but his treatment is nonetheless limited. Although Hamby refers to Truman's reliance on the Bible and prayer for guidance, he considers Truman's Baptist religion only an aspect of traditional midwestern values and his selection of that denomination in keeping with his democratic attitude. Hamby does a good job of dissecting Truman's liberalism; ultimately, he believes Truman's religion was part of, and subordinate to, his politics.[21] Since biographers who know their subject well think that religion was incidental to Truman, the conclusion seems to be that matters of faith are not central to understanding the man.

Yet religion was important to Truman and his worldview. Upon inspection, what emerges is a man of deep, if simple, faith, who depended only a little on formal religion but prayed daily. And Truman did not change when he became president. He carried his faith into his approach to and practice of statecraft, arguing that an ethical code was necessary to politics properly understood. Reflected in private writings, public speeches, and other official documents, his religious convictions also informed his Cold War statesmanship.[22]

Truman chose the Baptist religion in part for the reason given by Hamby: he was comfortable with the democratic bearing of Baptists. Yet Truman did not select his religion because of his politics. In fact, his politics seemed to have derived from his faith perhaps more than from his parents. He joined the Baptist church at the age of eighteen and was baptized shortly thereafter, in 1903. Although his family background was mostly Baptist, he chose that denomination deliberately, after exposure to Presbyterian Sunday school as a child, interaction with members of the main Christian and Mormon churches, and many readings of the Bible. He believed that his Baptist sect gave "the common man the shortest and most direct approach to God."[23] Around the same time, his interest in politics was minimal, even though his father was a partisan Democrat. Through his father's friend, he served as a page at the 1900 Democratic national convention in Kansas City, where he saw and heard William Jennings Bryan from afar. Truman paid attention to the 1912 thirty-eighth ballot Democratic nomination of Woodrow Wilson, but he did not seem to develop strong ties to the party until his participation in Missouri state politics in the 1920s.[24] Even then, as he appealed to independent Democrats, he at times sided with Republicans who supported the Pendergast political machine.

Truman biographers are partially correct about Truman's outlook on religion. He did not have much use for any religion that he considered a sensationalized kind. In the early months of their formal courtship, he explained his view to Bess in a February 1911 letter: "I am by religion like everything else. I think there is more in acting than in talking." McCullough quotes only these lines from the letter, but the context of the two sentences is critical. Truman was describing to Bess a revival meeting that he had heard about, where the antics of those present (especially the jumping, dancing woman who had a lizard on her dress rather than "religion" in her heart) amused him; he was also unimpressed by the preacher, who had "exhorted and ranted and done everything else they usually do when they try to get something started as they call it." He went on to tell Bess that, while religion had its place at regular assemblies and on Sunday, the preacher's meeting was "mostly excitement and when the excitement wears off people are as they always were."[25] This last observation underscores the consistent view of human nature held by Truman. He maintained that mankind could be good and achieve good, particularly when helped by government, but that individuals made their choices primarily because of their character rather than their religion. In his opinion, character was created by a moral code (of which Christianity embodied the best) that was revealed in action.

The letter was written by a man who had reached his late twenties and had formed his convictions on the question, and sent to the woman he knew he wanted to spend his life with (and had known since childhood).[26] Truman observed to Bess that a person's religious enthusiasm in words could be hypocritical. He described a neighbor "who could pray louder and talk more fervently in meetin' than anyone I ever heard." Yet, he added, "[w]e finally found that he beat his wife and did everything else that's 'ornery.'" To Truman, then, the fact that he danced and played cards, against the dictates of his religion, was not significant, as long as he was of sound character and deeds. He explained that the *good* (Truman's emphasis) church members were glad to hear his descriptions of such activities and that he was "a member but not a strenuous one."[27] The precepts of his denomination mattered less to Truman than what he viewed as the essential message of Christianity embedded in the golden rule.

About six weeks later, Truman returned to the subject of religion in another letter to Bess, who had changed her denomination from Presbyterian to Episcopalian. He apologized for perhaps offending Bess's "religious principles," since the couple had enjoyed a musical program during Lent. He wrote that he liked his first service at an Episcopal church in her company, but that he would remain a "Lightfoot Baptist" for the time being, and that he would not ask her to dinner again until after Easter Sunday. There is a self-deprecatory and humorous yet repentant tone to the letter. But although Truman wanted to be assured that he had not offended Bess, he reiterated that religious form did not matter to him. As in the previous letter, he characterized himself as "not very strong as a Baptist," especially when it came to dancing and cards. In the midst of his somewhat lighthearted explanation to Bess, though, he offered a more fundamental interpretation of religion: "Anyhow I don't think any church on earth will take you to heaven if you're not real anyway. I believe in people living what they believe and talking afterwards, don't you?"[28] As he had spurned sensationalism in religion, he gently questioned the need for formal structure in religion. Even though the woman he was seeking to marry was more devout, Truman did not reserve his opinion.

Truman's ideas about religion remained constant to the end of his life. When they were courting, he told Bess that he eschewed hypocrites; in his postpresidential years in the 1950s and 1960s, he wrote that all his family "disliked a hypocrite." He used the same story once told by his grandfather to make his point in 1911 to Bess and in the late 1950s and 1960s to a broad American audience.[29] He was, in short, leery of showiness in religion, in and of itself and because it could be hypocritical. Echoing what he wrote Bess in 1911, Truman noted privately in the 1940s that "I've always believed that religion is something to live by and not to talk about." After speculating that God was not interested in pomp and circumstance, he added, "Religious stuffed shirts are just as bad or worse than political ones in my opinion."[30] His religious views, on this point, informed and correlated with his political outlook: in both cases, excessive form could lead to or hide hypocrisy and might result in a sensationalism that masked man's nature and purpose. In his twenties and in his sixties, he insisted that people know right from wrong and practice what they preached.[31]

Harry Truman was ecumenical, and remained so over the course of his life. While fighting in World War I, he wrote to Bess in 1918 that "all churches, even the Roman Catholic can do a man a lot of good. I had a Presbyterian bringing up, a Baptist education, and Episcopal leanings, so I reckon I ought to get to heaven somehow, don't you think so?"[32] Writing in 1936 to his wife, he summarized his distinction of faith from religion: "It was a pleasure to hear of Margaret going to the Baptist Sunday school. She ought to go to one every Sunday—I mean *a* Sunday school. If a child is instilled with good morals and taught the value of the precepts laid down in Exodus 20 and Matthew 5, 6, and 7, there is not much to worry about in after years. It makes no difference what brand is on the Sunday school."[33] In longhand notes from 1952, Truman reflected both his ecumenism as well as his religious personalism: "If Jesus Christ were to return he'd be on the side of the persecuted all around the world. . . . He'd no more recognize his teachings in St. Peter's or Canterbury Cathedrals than he would in Riverside or Trinity Churches in New York or the First Baptist or Foundry Methodist Churches in Washington. . . . He taught that every man is the creation of a merciful God, that men are sinners and that he had come into the world to teach sinners how to approach His Father—and the way was not through Caiaphas the High Priest or Augustus the roman Emperor. The way is direct and straight. Any man can tell the Almighty and Most Merciful God his troubles and directly ask for guidance. *He will get it.*"[34]

To Truman, all Christians, even every revealed religion, could agree on the meaning as well as the value of the biblical precepts of the Ten Commandments and the Sermon on the Mount. In his later years, he recounted what his grandfather had told him: that all Christians "wanted to arrive at the same place but they had to fight about it to see who had the inside track with the Almighty." His grandfather concluded that "none of them had any special 'in' with God Almighty because He would make His own decision about who had been good or bad on this planet." Truman adopted this opinion and its attendant ecumenism from a man "who belonged to no church, but he supported many of them."[35] Shortly after becoming president, he wrote in his longhand notes, "A lot of the world's troubles have been caused by the interpretation of the Gospels and the controversies between sects and creeds. It is all so silly and comes of the prima donna complex again." God, he wrote, never played favorites.[36]

Faith, Freedom, and the Cold War

NSC 68 (primarily and theoretically) and Korea (secondarily and practically) confirmed what Truman already believed: in the end, the war of nerves would be won or lost on moral grounds. But he could not turn to the United Nations for moral authority, since the Soviet design and actions had subverted the international organization's original intent. Instead, the president endeavored to take the moral high ground in the Cold War by developing a two-pronged political strategy involving the mass media and the world's major religions that also coupled the governmental and private sectors.

In this project, Truman focused first on the dissemination of public information. On April 20, 1950—within two to three weeks of reading NSC 68—he launched in a speech to the American Society of Newspaper Editors what he called the Campaign of Truth. Central to the undertaking was an expansion of the Voice of America (VOA) beyond what the president had requested in preceding years. As he stated in announcing the campaign, the Cold War "is a struggle, above all else, for the minds of men." Truman went on to argue that the propaganda used by the "forces of imperialistic communism" could be overcome by the "plain, simple, unvarnished truth." On the home front, he urged the press to enlist in the campaign by informing the American people "well and completely." "If you misinform them," he said, "their decisions will be bad; our country will suffer and the world will suffer." On a global scale, an enlarged VOA would join with the private efforts of international businessmen, labor unions, newspapers and magazines, radio, motion pictures, and others in communicating information in simple form to people of varied backgrounds and cultures. Truman emphasized that the truth must reach people around the world or "we will lose the battle for men's minds by pure default."[37] Assistant Secretary of State for Public Affairs Edward Barrett, who came up with the actual "Campaign of Truth" phrase, testified before an executive session of the Senate Foreign Relations Committee in July 1950 that it derived from the "inevitable conclusion" of NSC 68 "that the world situation was deteriorating and deteriorating rapidly. On the basis of that the President, on the advice of numerous people, reached the conclusion that we needed to step up [overseas propaganda] activities."[38] William Benton, a Democratic senator from Connecticut who had once held Barrett's position, sponsored a Senate resolution for "a Marshall Plan in the field of ideas," in recognition "that the central issue of our time is intellectual and spiritual, and that the heart of the present conflict is a struggle for the minds and loyalties of mankind."[39] After the Korean War began, Truman submitted an appropriation request in July for $89 million to implement the campaign; after the House of Representatives reduced the amount by over $20 million, he pressed in August for his original allocation.[40]

Truman saw the dangers of what came to be known technically as disinformation and misinformation. He had seen the inroads made by Soviet propaganda in Western Europe, particularly in 1947 through 1949, and he believed that American will and policies had defeated the USSR's efforts to sway elections and upset the Marshall Plan. The Voice of America, Radio Free Europe, and, in the following year, Radio Liberation (soon Radio Liberty) became part of the institutional fabric of containment, as well as integral to the political clash between East and West.[41] The president thought that he had learned correctly from recent history, and he went on to the next step of his strategy in the partnership between the public and private sectors: the moral suasion and power of faith. As leader of the strongest power of the free world, he intended to harness and coordinate the world's religions in an effort to stop the Communists and what he viewed as their elemental godlessness.

In 1946 and 1947, Truman attempted this component of containment with mixed results. On the day after Churchill's Fulton address, he urged Protestants, Roman Catholics, and Jews to spur a "moral and spiritual awakening" in the aftermath of the Second World War and to deploy the full power of freedom in meeting the threats of "new conflicts, new terror, and new destruction."[42] In May 1946, he reappointed Myron Taylor as his personal representative to Pope Pius XII, this time with the added rank of ambassador, marking the Vatican City's first full diplomatic recognition by the United States. He reasoned that the Roman Catholic Church was his strongest religious ally in the moral battle against international communism, but numerous objections, particularly from Protestants, led the president to retract the proposal of an ambassador to, and formal recognition of, the Vatican. Nevertheless, Truman sent Taylor on special missions to the pontiff for the next several years and, in 1947, involved him in embarking on a global endeavor. "Had Myron Taylor in too," he wrote to Bess. "Looks as if he and I may get the morals of the world on our side. We are talking to the Archbishop of Canterbury, the bishop at the head of the Lutheran Church, the Metropolitan of the Greek Church at Istanbul, and the Pope. I may send him to see the top Buddhist and the Grand Lama of Tibet. If I can mobilize the people who believe in a moral world against the Bolshevik materialists, who believe as Henry Wallace does—'that the end justifies the means'—we can win this fight." Truman then added that "[t]reaties, agreements, or a moral code mean nothing to Communists. So we've got to organize the people who do believe in honor and the Golden Rule to win the world back to peace and Christianity."[43] The Catholic Church expressed interest, but the other faiths rejected the idea and, perhaps, the implied ecumenism. Although the president's efforts came to naught, he maintained that a world crusade of religions against communism would be unbeatable over time. He also continued to argue that recognition of the Vatican was past due, in and of itself and as part of a Cold War strategy.

Upon the foundations of practical containment, strengthened theoretically by NSC 68, and faced with recent Communist gains, Truman resurrected the idea of an international religious campaign in 1951. At minimum, he hoped that the major religions would agree to an international conference; at maximum, he looked for the defeat of communism through a concerted religious effort, which would place before the peoples of the world the superiority and strength of what he called truth and freedom. The president laid the groundwork to renew his proposal for a crusade by the world's religions during the course of 1950, especially after reading NSC 68 in April. Joining politics and faith, he set forth his argument for the union of strength and freedom as the precursor to genuine peace in May 1950 at Gonzaga University in Washington: "In the face of aggressive tyranny, the economic, political, and military strength of free men is a necessity. But we are not increasing our strength just for strength's sake. We must be strong if we are to expand freedom. We must be strong if free men are to be able to satisfy their moral obligations. It is the moral and religious beliefs of mankind which alone give our strength meaning and purpose."[44] Truman considered the speech a significant address at a critical time to an important audience; because he believed Catholic participation was crucial to a global campaign against communism, he deliberately chose to speak at a Catholic school.[45] Taylor had resigned as of January 18, 1950, and Truman wanted to replace him with an ambassador. With this speech, the president hoped to further both goals.

Truman led up to his conclusion at Gonzaga University by establishing a connection between America's meaning and purpose at home and abroad. He described how a good society existed when men followed "the will of the Lord" based on the fundamental belief "that all men are equal before God." From this understanding, he said, flowed the securing of individual rights and equal opportunity for all citizens. Just as this belief in equality had enabled America to build a great nation of liberty, Truman added, so too could it serve as the foundation of world peace. The president held that equality before God, recognized in good government, would undergird a brotherhood of man—much in the sense that Pius XII sketched in their Christmas 1949 exchange of messages—around the world.[46] Truman believed that peace would follow, not from world government but from the understanding of equality, morality and religion, strength, and freedom. Not surprisingly, he identified impediments to such an outcome: "The greatest obstacle to peace is a modern tyranny led by a small group who have abandoned their faith in God. These tyrants have forsaken ethical and moral beliefs. They believe that only force makes right. They are aggressively seeking to expand the area of their domination." But he did not claim that ridding the world of tyranny would bring eternal peace. As a Christian, he saw the "barriers of ignorance and poverty" and the "barriers of tyranny"; as a Christian statesman, however, he concentrated his attention on the worst offender.[47]

Shortly after the Korean War began, Truman expounded on his belief that a revival of religion and a rededication of the United States to the "unchanging truths" of the Christian religion were needed to defeat communism. He contrasted America's freedom of religion to the suppression of freedom and a concomitant denial of human rights by communism behind the "impenetrable iron curtain." To the president of the Baptist World Alliance in his home state of Missouri, Truman forthrightly disclosed these views in July 1950: "To succeed in our quest for righteousness we must, in St. Paul's luminous phrase, put on the armor of God." At the time, various religious leaders and journals of the Truman era—notably, the *Christian Century*—consistently criticized what they viewed as the president's simplistic religious exhortations on complex issues.[48] But Truman believed, as he explained in the letter, that problems—including the threat from international communism—could be best solved if free men were to use their intelligence, courage, and faith and to seek solutions in the spirit of the Sermon on the Mount.[49] He invoked a consistent theme of his life and presidency: that all, especially but not only Christians, could understand, accept, and act on the message of Jesus' Beatitudes and golden rule. And by emphasizing the spirit of the Sermon on the Mount, he left open the possibility that many could join in the fight against communism. Nevertheless, Truman made clear that he judged religious faith to be the key to a successful battle against communism.

In preparing the American people and the world for what was, essentially, a religious Campaign of Truth in 1951, President Truman closed 1950 with an accent on the theme of comprehensive strength. He placed the fighting in Korea in the context of "the struggle between freedom and Communist slavery" in order to remind his audience that, in respect to defense, "we need the combined resources and the common determination of the free world to meet the military threat of communism." While not playing down the military aspect of the Cold War, the president focused again on the moral and spiritual dangers of the ideology: "Communism attacks our main basic values, our belief in God, our belief in the dignity of man and the value of human life, our belief in justice and freedom. It attacks the institutions that are based on these values. It attacks our churches, our guarantees of civil liberty, our courts, our democratic form of government. Communism claims that all these things are merely tools of self-interest and greed—that they are weapons used by one class to oppress another."[50] Truman wanted the American people to understand, as fully and deeply as they could, the whole of the Cold War. He strived to educate his fellow citizens about the war of nerves, and he urged that future citizens (he spoke these words at a conference on children) be educated morally and mentally in order to build the character necessary to continue the struggle in defense of freedom and justice.

It is unclear whether Truman had a specific date in mind for the announcement of a new international religious campaign against communism in 1951, but he worked toward that end during the early part of the year. In large measure, he did so by bolstering the commitment of religious believers to faith, freedom, and peace. In February 1951, Truman used the dedication of a chapel commemorating four chaplains (Protestant, Catholic, and Jewish) who forfeited their lives on a torpedoed, sinking ship during World War II so that four other men could survive, to stress that the unity of the United States, as with these four men, was also unity under God. "It is a unity in freedom," he remarked, "for the service of God is perfect freedom." Truman repeated his stated 1950 goal for peace through freedom and brotherhood—quoting the famous passage from St. John: "Greater love hath no man than this, that a man lay down his life for his friends." Using the story of heroism at hand, he argued that the United States could not lead the forces of freedom from behind. He compared the chaplains' sacrifice with that of those who fought in the American Revolution, and he contrasted both of them with the summer soldiers and sunshine patriots rebuked by Thomas Paine. While drawing an additional parallel to the Americans dying in Korea "to save us from the terrible slaughter and destruction which another world war would surely bring," the president upheld the American model of religious diversity and political unity as an example to the world.[51]

In April 1951, between the third anniversary of the Marshall Plan's enactment and the second anniversary of the signing of the North Atlantic Treaty, Truman developed further his argument that faith was integral to any meaningful shift—let alone victory—in the Cold War battle. Speaking at the New York Avenue Presbyterian Church in Washington, D.C., he reiterated that the American republic was founded on the same principles of the moral law taught by the great religions. He contended that faith should set moral standards for both domestic and international conduct and that "[w]e should judge our achievements, as a nation, in the scales of right and wrong." Quick to emphasize that freedom was the most important principle of American civilization, he distinguished freedom—based on moral principles—from an unmoored freedom, which degenerated rapidly into selfishness and license in individuals and anarchy in society. The president then returned to familiar themes of preceding years: he tied the application of moral standards to American efforts in the world and the buildup of the country's defenses; he stressed that international communism was opposed to the tenets, including the right to worship God, which Americans lived by and cherished; and he concluded that religious faith gave the United States the ability to answer the false beliefs of communism.[52] This cumulative argument was, for Truman, the basis for the American understanding of the war of nerves. He saw the United States as the primary free power of the world and believed that that was a sufficient justification for world leadership. Yet he thought that the obligation to lead stemmed from America's moral underpinnings.

Truman did not presume to say that this moral obligation was easy to execute or, even, to ascertain; he admitted that the task was full of uncertainties and sacrifices. But he maintained (as he frequently had done before) that while the United States had shirked its obligations in the past, "God has created us and brought us to our present position of power and strength for some great purpose." This purpose, he believed, related to cooperating with other nations in helping to create and maintain peace in the world and to defending "the spiritual values—the moral code—against the vast forces of evil that seek to destroy them."[53]

To the Washington Pilgrimage of American Churchmen in September 1951, Truman made explicit the renewed call for a religious Campaign of Truth. By this point, he believed that he had done all he could to encourage the cooperation of the world's major religions in such a movement. It was time not only to present his case definitively to the public but also to entreat, perhaps shame, his prospective crusaders. To the domestic audience, he linked the American founding and the country's religious heritage and commented that "at this time of international peril and uncertainty we should look back to these beginnings and rededicate ourselves to those ideals." Reminding his listeners of the difficulties faced by the people of Israel, he urged American believers to live up to their religious and political heritage, since, like the chosen people, they were held to higher standards and would be judged more harshly if they failed in their responsibilities. All but calling his fellow Christians hypocritical, he drew extensively on Jesus' condemnation of those "who were superficially and publicly good" yet refused to act on their words. In place of self-interest and noninvolvement, he preached that believers should be guided by the principle of charity, not in the sense of condoning the actions of one's enemies or liking one's foe but in the biblical sense of loving one's fellow man.[54]

For the international audience, Truman suggested the link between America's future and that of the world: "Today, our problem is not just to preserve our religious heritage in our own lives and our own country. Our problem is a greater one. It is to preserve a world civilization in which man's belief in God can survive. Only in such a world can our own Nation follow its basic traditions, and realize the promise of a better life for all our citizens." The president argued that the "whole human enterprise is in danger" from Communist expansion, which employed the "weapons of deceit and subversion as well as military might." The enemy at the root of either totalitarian expansionism or nuclear devastation in war was communism, which, in attempting to master life, might eradicate mere life. Truman hoped that all men of goodwill would realize that acknowledging God as "the ruler of us all" and asking Him for the strength and wisdom to carry out His will would be the first step in preserving civilization throughout the world.[55]

Once again, the president called for a religious campaign—now an international crusade—against communism. He requested that all men who believed in God set aside their differences during the current crisis in human affairs and come together "in a common affirmation of faith." Truman insisted, as he often had in the past, that all creeds could agree on the teachings of the Ten Commandments and the Sermon on the Mount. And he expected that Christians, at least, would support the affirmation, testifying "to the strength of our common faith and our confidence in its ultimate victory over the forces of Satan that oppose it." He regretted that "the great religious leaders of the world" were not joined yet in such a declaration of faith, but he was especially distressed that the main Christian churches would not agree to a statement "of their faith that Christ is their Master and Redeemer and the source of their strength against the hosts of irreligion and danger in the world."[56] The president ended his forthright remarks with a prayer to unite the churches and the free world.

Despite the resistance to a common affirmation of faith, Truman did not abandon his conviction that spiritual strength must inform and augment political strength and that it would be most effective in an organized movement. Less than a month after calling for the international religious crusade, he turned again to the Roman Catholic Church. Secretary of State Dean Acheson hoped that he had convinced the president to delay indefinitely an appointment of a U.S. ambassador to the Vatican. In Acheson's view, recognizing the Vatican would start a religious controversy when the need for national unity against the USSR was great.[57] Truman, however, still wanted official recognition, for political, diplomatic, and strategic reasons that he thought he had explained well over the space of several years. He nominated General Mark Clark as ambassador on October 20, 1951, since, aside from recognition being overdue, the Vatican was "vigorously engaged in the struggle against communism" and "[d]irect diplomatic relations will assist in coordinating the effort to combat the Communist menace."[58] The president's nomination met with fierce objections from Protestants generally and from U.S. senators, especially southern Democrats, who were ostensibly unimpressed by Clark's World War II record. Substantial amounts of White House mail, at one point, ran six and a half to one against sending an ambassador to the Vatican.[59] Although Truman remained committed to the nomination, Clark asked to have his name withdrawn from consideration in January 1952. With no support and no nominee, the president reluctantly abandoned recognition of the Vatican and, effectively, the religious Campaign of Truth.

It frustrated Truman that the world's religions rejected his reasoning that faith was the most powerful weapon in the Cold War. And he was irked that Protestant denominations would not grant the Catholic Church a unique religious and political role in combating communism. Shortly after Clark's withdrawal as nominee, the president described privately his conversation with the head bishop of the Episcopal Church, who was objecting particularly to the idea of a representative to Vatican City and a papal nuncio from the Vatican in Washington, D.C. Truman replied that his concern was not protocol but "to organize the moral forces against the the [*sic*] immoral forces. I told him that Stalin and his crowd had no intellectual honesty and no moral code, that they had broken 30 or 40 treaties they'd made with us and the free world and that all I wanted to do was to organize Exodus XX, Matthew V, VI, & VII to save morals in the world." Apparently, the bishop disparaged the Catholic Church as another version of totalitarianism and a menace to free religion. "What a travesty," wrote Truman. "If a Baptist can see what's toward—why not a high hat Church of England Bishop?"[60] In the president's containment strategy, the Catholic Church was always the fulcrum of a global religious movement for faith and freedom and against communism, but it was also always the main impediment in Protestant eyes.[61]

The "great purpose" of the United States, according to Truman, was to defend "the spiritual values—the moral code—against the vast forces of evil that seek to destroy them."[62] While admittedly establishing a broad agenda, the president had fleshed out how to achieve such a purpose through containment, now including the widespread dissemination of accurate information and the previously untapped reserves of religious faith. Truman sought to combine moral and religious, political, military, economic, and rhetorical means in a grand strategy. In order to face the extraordinary circumstances of the Cold War, he started with what many others refused to acknowledge: that the war of nerves began and ended with a clash of moral and political worldviews manifested in opposing regime types. Harry Truman supplied what was missing from the narrow, negative version of containment that was preferred by his realist critics; in so doing, he created and implemented a different strategy entirely.

Faith, Freedom, and Peace

Truman always wanted to be remembered as a man of peace, especially in his efforts as president of the United States. Peace, in fact, remained his deepest wish and preeminent political goal. Harboring few illusions, however, about the city of man—when looking at the world around him or the historical examples he had studied—he put his trust and hope for peace in the Bible. Consistently, he argued that if man read or heard and lived by the truths of Exodus, the prophets, and the Gospel of Matthew, the people of the world would be at peace and truly free. The Prince of Peace, he maintained, would make peace viable when man chose well and received His grace. In the end, the president envisioned a supernatural peace, rather than a temporal permanent peace. He said that peace would occur if these criteria held, and he believed in the possibility. But he did not expect such a peace without divine intervention.

From the first day of his presidency, Truman invoked the Almighty and believed that America had been called to a responsibility, which had been dodged after World War I, to foster peace in the world. He often explained that this duty now extended from U.S. participation in the United Nations to combating the onslaught of worldwide communism. Indeed, the president suggested that many of the problems of the interwar period that caused the Second World War and the Cold War could have been averted or diminished by American leadership. In numerous speeches, he said that God meant for the United States to be a beacon of liberty and hold out the same right for others. But only in the context of freedom, he believed, could man exercise the free will necessary to the formation of peace and happiness. As he concluded in his 1949 inaugural address: "But I say to all men, what we have achieved in liberty, we will surpass in greater liberty. Steadfast in our faith in the Almighty, we will advance toward a world where man's freedom is secure. To that end we will devote our strength, our resources, and our firmness of resolve. With God's help, the future of mankind will be assured in a world of justice, harmony, and peace."[63] The problem was that the free world faced a foe that denied that "human freedom is born of the belief that man is created equal in the image of God and therefore capable of governing himself."[64] The framework of freedom in which peace could be established, as well as the tenuousness of the extant peace in the free world, must be protected.

In a postpresidential collection of reflections and articles, *Mr. Citizen*, Truman spelled out the political theory of peace that stemmed from his faith. Writing to Bess and then as president, he had touched on the same themes, but, as an elder statesman, he had the public opportunity to speak at greater length about them. In one week, he addressed twelve hundred students at a Baptist college, spoke to sixty-five hundred young people at the annual Catholic Youth Conference, and dedicated a plaque at the Jewish Chapel at the University of Missouri. Excerpting from his subsequent remarks to a Methodist congregation in Dallas, Truman "preached"—his word—about the moral code that the Bible conferred.

When he was young, Truman began, he preferred the Bible "as it should be," in the King James form rather than the Revised Version. When sworn in as president, however, he selected the Vulgate or Latin translation of the Bible. "And as you know," he wrote, "I had them turn to the twentieth chapter of Exodus."[65] This chapter in the second book of the Old Testament provided the cornerstone to Truman's thought. For Truman, "the fundamental basis of all government" was found in the Bible, starting with the laws given to Moses on Mount Sinai. Moses, he noted, was familiar with the Babylonian lawgiver Hammurabi, who established the first code for government; in Moses, Truman perceived revelation and reason joining to assure a peace of justice and harmony. He then added (Truman noted the specific biblical passages throughout his remarks) the sixth chapter of Deuteronomy, the fourth book of the Pentateuch.[66] The primary purpose of man, he pointed out, was revealed there: "[A]nd thou shalt love the Lord thy God with all thine heart, and with all thy soul, and with all thy might." Throughout his career in political and private service, Truman pointed out that Deuteronomy's fifth chapter was a reiteration of the Decalogue, leading, significantly, to the statement of the great commandment in the sixth chapter.

Truman then turned to the prophets to illustrate his understanding of peace. Concentrating on Isaiah, Micah, and Joel, he argued that, major and minor prophets alike, "[t]hey were all trying to get the people to understand that they were on this earth for a purpose, and that in order to accomplish that purpose they must follow a code of morals." Of Isaiah, the great prophet who presaged the Gospel of St. Matthew, Truman quoted the verse where Isaiah explained that God would judge among the nations and rebuke many people, and they would beat their swords into plowshares and spears into pruning hooks. But then he quoted the prophet Joel, who seems to make the opposite point. Truman noted that in Joel 3:10, the prophet proclaimed, "Beat your ploughshares into swords and your pruning hooks into spears. Let the weak say: I am strong." Truman maintained that the passages were not contradictory: "Which one do you want? It depends on what the condition is." Joel, Truman explained, was trying to teach the people that they had to protect their regime if they "expected ever to have a free government."[67] Different circumstances demanded different actions, and the prudent leader—Isaiah, Joel, or even Harry Truman—must determine whether the time demands plowshares or swords.

If the Decalogue laid the cornerstone of peace, the prophets contributed to the structure of the building, and the Sermon on the Mount completed the edifice. Maintaining that they could never be read too much, Truman turned to chapters five through seven of the Gospel of Matthew. In presidential speeches and press conferences, he often referred to living by the golden rule, doing unto others as you would have them do unto yourself, found in Matthew 7—he believed that the golden rule was the touchstone for everyone—and often recommended all of Matthew 5–7 for its guidance in life. In one of his earliest foreign policy speeches as president, Truman argued that the golden rule should direct international affairs.[68] As he wrote in 1952, "Confusius [*sic*], Buddah [*sic*], Moses, our own Jesus Christ, Mohomet [*sic*], all preached—'Do as you'd be done by.' Treat others as you'd be treated. So did all the other great teachers and philosophers."[69] Now, in his comments to the Methodists, he emphasized the fifth chapter of Matthew and the Beatitudes and quoted: "Blessed are the peacemakers, for they shall be called the children of God." Here, he believed, was the universal wish of all people of goodwill: "That is exactly what we all want to be. We want to be peacemakers. Not just individually, but *internationally*."[70] Harry Truman thought that he was called to advance God's peace, particularly around the world in his presidential foreign policy. "I am here this morning to try to get you to understand that I believe what these things say," he concluded, "and I try to act like it."[71] To Jews, he emphasized that the unabridged law was in the Ten Commandments and the Hebrew Bible; to Christians, he accented that Christ as Messiah fulfilled the law of the Old Testament. To all of goodwill, he offered a high common ground touched by the transcendent. "Oh, Almighty and Everlasting God," began Truman's daily prayer, which he said from his high school days until his death. "Creator of heaven and earth and the universe: Help me to be, to think, to act what is right, because it is right: Make me truthful, honest and honorable in all things: Make me intellectually honest for the sake of right and honor and without thought of reward to me. Give me the ability to be charitable, forgiving and patient with my fellow men—Help me to understand their motives and their shortcomings—even as thou understandest mine: Amen."[72]

In the end, the peace Truman desired was the peace of the Bible. Not that he expected this peace to come easily, or any time soon; only God could effect the peace that Truman longed for. In the meantime, for the individual, it meant constant humility and the seeking of grace. And for nations, it required a dedication to justice and the rule of law, based on a moral code and standards of right and wrong. These things, through education and habituation, shaped men and citizens by forming their character. Over the course of history, Truman's readings had convinced him, human nature had not changed much. Man still had "to be guided in the proper direction under a moral code, and then there must be some machinery to make him live within that moral code. A man cannot have character unless he lives within a fundamental system of morals that creates character."[73]

The Cold War modified, and further moderated, Truman's optimism about the possibilities of global peace. On the one hand, he rejected the idealism of those who ignored reality—he may have preferred plowshares, but he knew that now was a time to turn those plowshares into swords and not the other way around. Truman also rejected, on the other hand, that narrow realism which failed to recognize the moral challenge of communism. The Cold War, for all of its complications and confusions, was for Truman a battle between the "world of morals" and the "world of no morals," and only the combined strength of the West—military, political, economic, and moral—could defeat the immorality of communism and bring international peace. [74] In the end, this conflict made the peace he envisioned all the more distant, and perhaps unattainable. It also made Truman think hard about what could be achieved, and what had to be done to achieve it. Freedom, justice, and order emerged in his writings and speeches as the principles that created the circumstances under which a real and durable peace might be possible. And of those principles, Truman reasoned, freedom had to take root first—and had to be defended first. Peace was the fruit of liberty, he concluded, not its precondition.

The lesson of peace—that it is sometimes necessary to learn and make war—was difficult for Truman and a generation of Americans who had fought one war to make the world safe for democracy and another, recently, to rid it of Nazism. They had hoped, and many had believed, that the second had accomplished what the first had failed to achieve. Instead, they found themselves in a different kind of war, a war of nerves, which was even more terrifying and more threatening to liberal democracy and the cause of free government. In this circumstance, with fortitude and prudence, Harry Truman reminded his time of the centrality and universality of human freedom and, like the prophet Joel, that peace requires not only freedom but also the strength and willpower to defend it.

Conclusion

Harry Truman's Cold War was a conflict between good and evil, between freedom and tyranny, between liberal democracy and totalitarianism, between capitalism and communism. In his liberal internationalism—which both was informed by and undergirded the strategy of containment—he was generically American, not specifically Wilsonian, as he aimed to articulate and project America's basic principles of freedom and equality, assist those who also lived under such principles to maintain and defend them, and aid those under totalitarianism to realize them in the future.

Truman based his understanding of politics, and hence of liberal internationalism, on regime distinctions. In his Truman Doctrine speech, he described the war of nerves as a choice between stark alternatives: "One way of life is based upon the will of the majority, and is distinguished by free institutions, representative government, free elections, guarantees of individual liberty, freedom of speech and religion, and freedom from political oppression." By contrast, "the second way of life is based upon the will of a minority forcibly imposed upon the majority" and relies on terror and oppression and negating free will and choice.[1] In grounding his conception of the universal reality about freedom in the nature of regimes, Truman rejected the moral equivalence of democratic and Communist regimes.

Truman did not intend for his strategy to preserve the status quo. But he did not believe that Wilsonian self-determination was an end in itself, either. He put forth containment in order to thwart future Soviet gains and to stimulate free and just governments that protected fundamental human rights. Truman's immediate goal was to enable free peoples "to work out their own destinies in their own way," and in the long run to promote democracy by defending and advancing the conditions necessary for freedom.[2] To that end, the president included political, economic, and military elements in his Cold War strategy, while making freedom the centerpiece of postwar American liberal internationalism. Woodrow

Wilson had put justice first in his progressive internationalism, and Franklin Roosevelt had placed order first in his version of liberal internationalism. For Truman, justice and order lacked meaning, or could be easily distorted, unless they were rooted in the principles of ethical and political freedom.

Truman directed a strategy to fight the Cold War at the theoretical and practical levels. The initial theoretical articulation of this strategy—moral, political, strategic, and economic—was his own. In Truman's mind, the prudent use of strength in order to defend and maintain freedom where it existed and to enkindle freedom where it was denied would lead to peace. When he became president in April 1945, Truman talked in a tough manner to Molotov, and the Potsdam conference of summer 1945 strengthened his resolve to impede aggressors from gaining further territory and erecting obstacles to peace and freedom. "Unless Russia is faced with an iron fist and strong language another war is in the making," he was writing by early January 1946.[3] It was the existence of a dangerous and organized Communist tyranny in the form of the Soviet Union that made the strategy necessary.

The president viewed freedom—which tyranny threatened and aimed to eliminate—as the necessary precondition for all ethical action. With freedom, man could be fully a social being and join with others in forming communities and governments based on consent and the rule of law. Truman's faith helped him see the political centrality of freedom, the danger from totalitarianism, and the necessity of strength. His religious beliefs underlay his political understanding that peace (like justice and order) is meaningless if it is not grounded in freedom—as in free peoples, free institutions, and free countries. The ideas Truman expressed over the course of his presidency—from his private writings and public statements to the Clifford memorandum of September 1946 to NSC 68 of 1950—defined the theoretical underpinnings of containment.

NSC 68 was crucial because it confirmed and elaborated Truman's interpretation that the Cold War was a clash of two opposing worldviews. It rejected realism's endorsement of coexistence and the moral equivalence of regimes, suggesting that the free minds, democratic institutions, and market capitalism of liberal democracy eventually would prevail over the suppression, totalitarian rule, and command economy of communism. This victory would only come, however, if the Kremlin design were frustrated through "the steady development of the moral and material strength of the free world and its projection into the Soviet world in such a way as to bring about an internal change in the Soviet system."[4] The president consistently advocated that the Cold War strategy of the United States and the free world be broadly political and combine moral, diplomatic, military, and economic means.

On the practical level, Truman spent the first year and a half of his presidency educating and marshaling public opinion, while he observed Soviet transgressions and aggression and refined his view about the USSR. He stood firm on Trieste in 1945 through 1947; he invited Winston Churchill to give the Fulton address of March 1946, relying on him to articulate and underscore the stakes of the Cold War to the American public as only Churchill could; and he led the United States and the United Nations in pressuring the Soviets to withdraw from northern Iran in 1946. During this same period, the iron curtain extended its reach, enclosing those areas the Red Army had liberated and occupied in the final months of the Second World War. The president realized that a coherent strategy was needed in order to prevent additional encroachment by the Soviets, as well as to continue and build on successful American policy. Thus, when circumstances permitted in 1947, he embarked on the prudently ambitious program of containment, including—in an institutional sense—the Truman Doctrine, the Marshall Plan, NATO, the expansion of Voice of America, the Department of Defense, and the National Security Council. Theoretical containment reinforced practical containment: despite the final loss of Czechoslovakia in 1948, a Soviet military buildup, and the Berlin blockade, the United States and the free world appeared to be holding their own in what was becoming, seemingly, an international stalemate.

The Soviet explosion of an atomic bomb and the fall of China to communism in late 1949, followed by the start of the Korean War in June 1950, challenged the perceived status quo. Meanwhile, the Soviet anti-American propaganda drive of 1950 was making the Kremlin's 1948 campaign against the Marshall Plan look mild. The main components of containment had not stopped the momentum of international communism. Combined with the USSR's tangible successes in Eastern Europe and Asia, as well as the formal economic arrangement of the East bloc into Comecon in 1949, the West justifiably could wonder about the strains on the Truman Doctrine and the limited parameters of NATO. In the latter part of 1949 and the first half of 1950, the Soviet Union had seized the initiative not only from a military and territorial point of view but also in terms of political propaganda. In response, Truman added the hydrogen bomb decision, NSC 68, the Campaign of Truth, and, soon, the growth of Radio Free Europe–Radio Liberty to the strategy of containment.

Not having a Congress controlled by his party in the pivotal years of 1947 and 1948, Truman practiced bipartisanship in order to achieve his theoretical and practical goals. As FDR had succeeded in building a bipartisan consensus behind plans for the United Nations, so Truman's inclination was to work across party lines with those who agreed with him about the nature of the Cold War conflict and the primary role that America should have in leading the free world. The operational difference between Truman and Wilson is again apparent, since Wilson rebuffed both bipartisanship and executive-legislative cooperation in his efforts to restrict public debate over the League of Nations. Since Truman had been a senator himself, he already knew well—and was friends with—those across the aisle whom he needed to forge a successful foreign policy. A combination of bipartisanship and executive-legislative cooperation between 1947 and 1950 brought about some of the greatest policies and institutions of containment—the Truman Doctrine, the Marshall Plan, and NATO among them—and was rooted in the liberal democratic position that the war of nerves was caused by the ideology and conduct of the Soviet Union, which had to be fought by the ideas and actions of the United States and its allies.

Public opinion came to support this understanding of the Cold War during the mid-1940s. While Americans were still wont to see the Soviets as allies into 1946, they changed their minds after Joseph Stalin's election address, Winston Churchill's iron curtain speech, and Truman's show of strength with respect to Kremlin aggression in northern Iran.[5] In this respect, there was a great degree of coincidence between presidential statesmanship, executive-legislative cooperation, bipartisanship, and public opinion. Indeed, when we refer to the golden age of bipartisanship in Cold War foreign policy, we really mean the meeting on common ground of several key players: president, public, and congressional leaders. To be sure, there were debates—serious ones—about how and to what extent America should involve itself in the postwar world, but a majority thoughtfully and deliberately accepted Truman's approach that America had to take the lead, both in terms of leading the free world and combating the Communists on all fronts: politically and diplomatically, strategically and militarily, economically, and morally and spiritually.[6]

Truman's weak point was, arguably, Asia. While putting in place the architecture to fight and even win the Cold War, he carried the battle best to Europe and the Middle East. In the Korean War, Truman accepted the premise that a victory would be a return to the status quo of the immediate postwar division—itself a major concession to the Communists. The man who promised that West Berlin would be kept part of the West did not take advantage of circumstances in Korea that might have turned the Cold War in Asia to the free world's favor. When it came to China, Truman assented to his future secretary of state George Marshall's assessment that the Nationalists were little different from the Communists. The man who had perceived the potential for a democratic future in Turkey and elsewhere did not see a similar potential in China, although he ordered the Seventh Fleet into the Taiwan Strait in June 1950 at the start of the Korean War. Had he not done so, the Chinese Communists likely would have seized the island of Taiwan and accomplished their plans for eliminating any hope of a free China. Truman was less familiar with Asia on the whole than with either Europe or the Middle East, and perhaps he was hampered as a result. As well, he believed in the late 1940s and early 1950s that the United States had to concentrate its energies on fighting the primary threat from the Soviet Union. In doing so, he still applied his containment policy to Asia, but inconsistently and with uneven results.

Truman left office an unpopular president.[7] In addition to the scandals that had surrounded various members of his administration, he was accused by the Republicans of losing China to communism and miring the United States in a stagnating war in Korea. Dwight Eisenhower, his successor, was admired as an experienced, capable leader who was right for the times of the 1950s. His Cold War policies overall were a continuation of Truman's containment, since they protected Western Europe and refused the Communists further gains. But they were not the policies of "rollback" or liberation that are associated with the rhetoric of Eisenhower's secretary of state, John Foster Dulles. Indeed, one could argue that there was more liberation and rollback to Truman's containment, in the form of the Truman Doctrine, Marshall Plan, the expansion of the VOA and creation of the "freedom radios" (RFE-RL), the psychological and spiritual warfare of the late 1940s and early 1950s, and NSC 68. Truman and Eisenhower handed down a legacy of generally strong responses to the Soviet Union, a resolve that the Communists must not take more than what they had already in terms of peoples and territory, and, on Truman's part, a strategy to frustrate and transform the Kremlin's design in the long run. With American superiority in nuclear weapons, NATO, and developments in satellite reconnaissance in the Eisenhower administration, many could believe that the United States was engaged in a protracted yet winnable struggle against the USSR. Although the Eisenhower administration laid the groundwork for a shift in U.S. strategy and an emphasis on summitry, negotiations, and relative compromise with the Kremlin, Americans had settled in for a long fight and accepted the conflict as defined by the first Cold War president, Harry Truman.

Perhaps the greatest statesman of the twentieth century, Winston Churchill, once told Truman that he had held him in "low regard" when they met at Potsdam in 1945 and "loathed your taking the place of Franklin Roosevelt." When he heard these words in January 1952, Truman was hosting Churchill, four months after his return to the British premiership, on the presidential yacht *Williamsburg*. Truman was not happy with such comments, and, according to an eyewitness account, his trademark grin vanished. "I misjudged you badly," Churchill continued after a long pause. "Since that time, you, more than any other man, have saved Western Civilization. When the British could no longer hold out in Greece, you, and you alone, sir, made the decision that saved that ancient land from Communists. You acted in similar fashion with regard to Azerbaijan when the Soviets tried to take over Iran. Then there was your resolute stand on Trieste, and your Marshall Plan which rescued Western Europe wallowing in the shallows and easy prey to Joseph Stalin's malevolent intentions. Then you established the North Atlantic Treaty Alliance and collective security for those nations against the military machinations of the Soviet Union. Then there was your audacious Berlin Airlift. And, of course, there was Korea."[8] Although the prime minister had played a key part in the birth of containment, he knew that his—and England's—time had passed. Churchill considered Truman to be the only person, by dint of both character and circumstances, who understood the meaning of the Cold War and had the capacity to lead the free world in opposing the Soviet Union's design and actions; and he commended the president for having the foresight to conceive and the will to implement the strategy of containment. Truman's grin returned after hearing Churchill's judgment, and he must have hoped that history would agree with Churchill's settled opinion rather than his initial impression.[9]

Mainstream scholarship may be coming around to Churchill's assessment. More information is continually becoming available from Soviet and other former East bloc archives, along with the publication of such U.S. intelligence successes as the Venona files (which now show us, for instance, the extent of Soviet espionage in the United States in the 1940s). At every turn, Truman's containment seems more reasonable and less re-actionary. John Lewis Gaddis—the preeminent postrevisionist, as well as dean of Cold War historians—has modified his position to allow for the weight of ideology in shaping the conflict. His 1997 book, suggestively entitled *We Now Know: Rethinking Cold War History*, has been commend-ed for its insights, though it should also be recognized for its hindsight. Despite his inclusion of ideology in this and other work, Gaddis has con-tinued to define containment as a mechanism "to keep the peace while preserving the balance of power" and to argue that "its chief instrument was the Marshall Plan." Although considering Truman more frequently in *We Now Know* compared to his previous books, Gaddis has still portrayed Kennan as the most important architect of containment. As for the role of ideas in the war of nerves, it turns out that they animated the Soviets more than the Americans, and that the Kremlin—while generally au-thoritarian—was never specifically totalitarian.[10]

In his beautifully written and well-received *Surprise, Security, and the American Experience* of 2004, Gaddis again depicted George Kennan as the great strategist of containment and elevated him to the status of Franklin Roosevelt's heir, able to craft the best policy to pursue once it was clear that FDR's hopes for cooperation with the USSR had failed in 1946 and 1947. In this characterization (initially put forth by Kennan, Walter Lippmann, and others in the 1940s), the excesses of the Truman Doctrine were repaired by the Marshall Plan, in which "Kennan and the other architects of the Marshall Plan maneuvered Stalin into building the wall that contained him in 1947." Gaddis throughout explores Kennan's famous notion of assiduously avoiding "something worse" in policy, warn-ing that the United States in the war on terrorism risks becoming the "something worse" that the Soviet Union was during the Cold War.[11]

To his credit, Gaddis has raised the larger, central question about containment's transferability, as he puts it, to the strategy to fight the war on terrorism. Unfortunately, he transposes Kennan's, not Truman's, con-tainment to our time, and he persists in presenting Kennan's version as the primary, legitimate strategy. Gaddis condenses the main objectives of containment into "avoiding the extremes of war and appeasement while waiting for the Soviet Union to change itself."[12] As we have seen, however, there were indications in the mid- to late 1940s that pressure—both direct and indirect—needed to be placed on the Kremlin, rather than just waiting for it to change itself, and Truman, like others who had learned the lessons of the world wars and interwar period, believed that world war and tyranny, on the one hand, and appeasement, on the other, were the extremes to be avoided.

Gaddis offers three limitations on the transferability of Kennan's containment, two of which show the limitations of Kennan's containment, and five principles of Kennan's containment that he finds applicable today, almost all of which are not original to Kennan. Regarding limitations, Gaddis writes that Kennan's containment "required that the adversary to be contained share one's own sense of risk." It is true that the radical Islamic terrorists of today do not share America's sense of risk. But if the United States had followed Kennan's realist containment during the Cold War, the Soviet Union would have had much latitude to redefine risk and thus act more expansively. Of limitations, Gaddis also echoes his theme of *Surprise, Security, and the American Experience* that the United States has made its hegemony appear worse than the terrorist alternative through ill-chosen and clumsy intensification of its unilateralism. Gaddis contends that if the United States continues this course, "the basis for American power will indeed have shifted from invitation to imposition, a very different context from the one in which containment arose during the Cold War."[13]

The principles of Kennan's containment that Gaddis deems transferable to the war on terrorism are generally good advice, but they are not unique to Kennan. They include the propositions that deadly alternatives should be avoided, enemies should be encouraged to defeat themselves, history is more useful than theory in anticipating what is to come, and containment must not destroy what it was attempting to defend.[14] From the beginning of his presidency, Truman clearly wanted to avoid choosing direct military conflict with the Soviet Union or acquiescing to Communist ideology. He thought that part of encouraging the Kremlin to defeat itself was to put both direct and indirect pressure on the USSR. He always drew on the lessons of history and was skeptical of theory. And Truman had faith that the principles and institutions of American democracy would stand against the temptation to abuse power in order to fight totalitarianism. In fact, it was Kennan whose fatalism and growing fear of nuclear annihilation led him to consider conciliation to, and convergence with, communism. He was the one who let his realist theory supersede his impressive knowledge of history. And Kennan was the one who rarely had faith in American democracy and was convinced that, deep down, we all have a bit of the totalitarian in us.

But even an improved academic interpretation still finds it hard to acknowledge the full import of Truman's understanding of the conflict. Nor does it comprehend his strategy of containment as he understood it at the time. Theoretically as well as practically, Truman could have followed Wilson's progressive internationalism or embraced Roosevelt's liberal pragmatism. If this had been the case, he could have agreed with Kennan's definition of the East-West struggle and goals of containment. Or if there had been no Cold War and the postwar situation had resembled what Franklin Roosevelt was expecting, Truman very well could have picked Wilson, FDR, or a fusion of them. He could have used Wilsonian rhetoric and sought Wilsonian goals, while relying on Rooseveltian spheres of influence to defray the costs of maintaining U.S. power. He would not have reorganized the government and created new departments related to national security, nor would he have significantly increased defense spending from prewar levels. He would have endorsed collective security and the United Nations and never contemplated collective defense and a regional organization such as NATO. But through his politics, faith, and study of history—as well as his understanding of the serious and total nature of the Cold War—Truman grasped the meaning of the war of nerves, and he not only remade liberal internationalism but also constructed a corresponding grand strategy of containment.

We are accustomed today to critiquing American actions as either unilateral or multilateral. Much recent debate, especially in the United States and Europe, has centered on which is superior and, even, more moral; this debate misses what it means to deliberate at the level of grand strategy. Truman, however, did not view the tools of unilateralism and multilateralism as part of an either/or proposition. Depending on the circumstances, the United States under Truman led or acted by itself (unilateral) or acted in concert with others (multilateral) through bilateral ties, as well as regional and international organizations. Not only did Truman use both unilateralism and multilateralism, but he also regarded these and other tools as tactics to further containment through U.S. leadership, rather than as principles to define either his general approach to liberal internationalism or his grand strategy of containment.

With over five decades of hindsight—after Sputnik, the Cuban Missile Crisis, Vietnam, the fall of the Berlin Wall, the collapse of the Soviet Union, and an estimated 100 million deaths at the hands of Communist dictators since the birth of the USSR in 1917—we now can understand what Truman perceived at the time to be the truth about communism and what he called Communist tyranny. That timely perception and his willingness to act on it—all of which might seem obvious in retrospect—was the essence of Truman's statesmanship.

Notes

Introduction

1. "The President's Farewell Address to the American People," January 15, 1953, in Harry S. Truman, *Public Papers of the Presidents of the United States: Harry S. Truman—Containing the Public Messages, Speeches, and Statements of the President, April 12, 1945, to January 20, 1953* (Washington, D.C.: U.S. Government Printing Office, 1961–1966) (hereafter, Truman, *Public Papers*), vol. 8, 1197–1202. For more on the context and implications of Truman's farewell address, see Richard S. Kirkendall, ed., *Harry's Farewell: Interpreting and Teaching the Truman Presidency* (Columbia: University of Missouri Press, 2004).

2. [George F. Kennan] X, "The Sources of Soviet Conduct," *Foreign Affairs* 25, no. 4 (July 1947): 575.

3. A useful comparative study of Wilson and Truman that sees Truman amending Wilsonianism is found in Anne R. Pierce, *Woodrow Wilson and Harry Truman: Mission and Power in American Foreign Policy* (Westport, Conn.: Praeger, 2003).

4. For more on the differences between Wilson's and Roosevelt's operational styles (and a different conclusion about Truman), see Charles A. Kupchan, *The End of the American Era: U.S. Foreign Policy and the Geopolitics of the Twenty-First Century* (New York: Alfred A. Knopf, 2002), 181–200.

5. Roosevelt, Winston Churchill, and others were known to use the term "war of nerves" during World War II, especially to condemn the Nazis' use of ideology, propaganda, and other means in their arsenal of totalitarian weapons. Truman applied this meaning to the Soviets in the Cold War, in part to capture how the Kremlin was an unconventional power causing an unconventional war.

6. For a typical portrayal of Truman's universalism and vagueness, see Norman A. Graebner, *Cold War Diplomacy: American Foreign Policy, 1945–1960* (Princeton, N.J.: D. Van Nostrand, 1962), 40–43. For a portrayal of the important role of declaratory policy, see Louis J. Halle, *The Cold War as History* (New York: Harper Torchbooks, 1975; originally published 1967), and Hans J. Morgenthau, "Essay," 79–102, in Lloyd C. Gardner, Arthur Schlesinger Jr., and Hans J. Morgenthau, *The Origins of the Cold War* (Waltham, Mass.: Ginn, 1970). Other classic realist analyses of the Truman era are George F. Kennan, *American Diplomacy, 1900–1950* (New York: New American Library, 1951; Chicago: University of Chicago, 1951); Walter Lippmann, *The Cold War: A Study in U.S. Foreign Policy* (New York: Harper and Brothers, 1947); Arthur M. Schlesinger Jr., "Origins of the Cold War," *Foreign Affairs* 46 (October 1967): 22–52; Arthur M. Schlesinger Jr., *The Vital Center: The Politics of Freedom* (Cambridge:

Riverside Press, 1949); and Hans J. Morgenthau, *In Defense of the National Interest: A Critical Examination of American Foreign Policy* (New York: Alfred A. Knopf, 1951).

7. On capitalism and economic imperialism, see Robert James Maddox, *The New Left and the Origins of the Cold War* (Princeton, N.J.: Princeton University Press, 1973). For the revisionist view of the Soviet Union, see, for example, Lloyd C. Gardner, "Essay," 3–40, in Gardner, Schlesinger, and Morgenthau, *The Origins of the Cold War;* for a 1980s explication of this view, including a defense of Wallace, see Thomas G. Paterson, *Meeting the Communist Threat: Truman to Reagan* (New York: Oxford University Press, 1988), xi, 15–17, 53. For classic revisionism on the Truman era, see William Appleman Williams, *The Tragedy of American Diplomacy,* rev. ed. (New York: Delta, 1962); Gar Alperovitz, *Atomic Diplomacy: Hiroshima and Potsdam* (New York: Vintage Books, 1967); Thomas G. Paterson, ed., *Cold War Critics: Alternatives to American Foreign Policy in the Truman Years* (Chicago: Quadrangle Books, 1971); Athan G. Theoharis, *Seeds of Repression: Harry S. Truman and the Origins of McCarthyism* (Chicago: Quadrangle Books, 1971); and David Horowitz, *The Free World Colossus: A Critique of American Foreign Policy in the Cold War* (New York: Hill and Wang, 1965). For a recent revisionist account using old sources and newer archival materials, see Arnold A. Offner, *Another Such Victory: President Truman and the Cold War, 1945–1953* (Stanford, Calif.: Stanford University Press, 2002). For a provocative and often compelling analysis of the staying power of revisionism, even in light of Soviet archival evidence to the contrary, see John Earl Haynes and Harvey Klehr, *In Denial: Historians, Communism and Espionage* (San Francisco: Encounter Books, 2003).

8. For a summary of these points, see John Lewis Gaddis, *The United States and the Origins of the Cold War, 1941–1947* (New York: Columbia University Press, 1972), 353–61. Also concerning the Truman period, see John Lewis Gaddis, *Strategies of Containment: A Critical Appraisal of Postwar American National Security Policy* (Oxford: Oxford University Press, 1982); John Lewis Gaddis, *Russia, the Soviet Union, and the United States: An Interpretive History* (New York: Alfred A. Knopf, 1978); and John Lewis Gaddis, "The Emerging Post-Revisionist Synthesis on the Origins of the Cold War," *Diplomatic History* 7 (Summer 1983): 171–90. Other postrevisionists have focused on the Soviet side of the Cold War or regional aspects of the Cold War. As examples, see Vojtech Mastny, *Russia's Road to the Cold War: Diplomacy, Warfare, and the Politics of Communism, 1941–1945* (New York: Columbia University Press, 1979), and Bruce Robellet Kuniholm, *The Origins of the Cold War in the Near East: Great Power Conflict and Diplomacy in Iran, Turkey, and Greece* (Princeton, N.J.: Princeton University Press, 1994, with epilogue; originally published 1980).

9. For a summary of this approach, see Michael J. Hogan, "Corporatism," in Michael J. Hogan and Thomas G. Paterson, eds., *Explaining the History of American Foreign Relations* (Cambridge: Cambridge University Press, 1991), 226–36; also see Thomas J. McCormick, "Drift or Mastery? A Corporatist Synthesis for American Diplomatic History," *Reviews in American History* 10 (December 1982): 318–30. On the Truman years, Hogan is considered a prominent scholar of corporatism; see Michael J. Hogan, *The Marshall Plan: America, Britain, and the Reconstruction of Western*

Europe, 1947–1952 (Cambridge: Cambridge University Press, 1987), and Michael J. Hogan, *A Cross of Iron: Harry S. Truman and the Origins of the National Security State, 1945–1954* (Cambridge: Cambridge University Press, 1998). Although Hogan does not consider Melvyn Leffler to be a fellow corporatist, Leffler is typically presented as such; see Melvyn P. Leffler, *A Preponderance of Power: National Security, the Truman Administration, and the Cold War* (Stanford: Stanford University Press, 1992), and Melvyn P. Leffler, "The American Conception of National Security and the Beginnings of the Cold War, 1945–1948," *American Historical Review* 89 (April 1984): 346–81.

10. Lippmann did not care for Truman, and the sentiment was mutual. Truman criticized Lippmann, Arthur Krock, and the Alsop brothers for being "ivory tower" columnists, and he wrote angry letters that he never sent to Lippmann and Krock. See Franklin D. Mitchell, *Harry S. Truman and the News Media: Contentious Relations, Belated Respect* (Columbia: University of Missouri Press, 1998), 120 and 120 n. 21.

11. It is pertinent to note what Truman wrote of his words and speeches and placed as the foreword to each volume of his *Public Papers*: "[T]he importance of this series lies in the extraordinary character of the President of the United States." According to Truman, "A President's written and spoken words can command national and international attention if he has within him the power to attract and hold that attention. It is partly through the use of this power that leadership arises, events are molded, and administrations take their shape," and "[i]t is this power, quite as much as powers written into the Constitution, that gives to the papers of Presidents their peculiar and revealing importance."

1. The Beginnings of Truman's Internationalism

1. Truman, "Woodrow Wilson—Too Smart to Be President?" in Harry S. Truman, *Where the Buck Stops: The Personal and Private Writings of Harry S. Truman*, ed. Margaret Truman (New York: Warner Books, 1989), 345. Truman wrote, "Even my father and I decided that Bryan was right and Wilson was the right man." Also see pages 341–42, for Truman's description of how all Missourians hoped that Clark would be nominated and elected and how they were stunned when Wilson was nominated. This book, edited by Margaret Truman, is drawn from a couple of thousand pages left by Truman, either in his hand or dictated to his secretaries, wife, and daughter. Historian Alonzo Hamby has argued that Harry Truman liked Wilson from the start; see Alonzo Hamby, *Man of the People: A Life of Harry S. Truman* (New York: Oxford University Press, 1995), 40.

2. In a display of courage, Truman said: "I've been very badly frightened several times in my life and the morning of July 11, 1918 when I took over that Battery was one of those times. I was most anxious to make good in my new rank of Captain and I was rather doubtful of my ability to handle that obstreperous battery." See Autobiographical Sketch, Biographical File, Box 298, President's Secretary's Files (hereafter, PSF), Harry S. Truman Papers (hereafter, HSTP), Harry S. Truman Library (hereafter, HSTL).

3. Truman to Bess, January 21, 1919, in Harry S. Truman, *Dear Bess: The Letters*

from Harry to Bess Truman, 1910–1959, ed. Robert H. Ferrell (New York: W.W. Norton, 1983), 293. Truman and Bess were married later that year, less than two months after he returned from World War I.

4. Memorandum, July 1954; Memorandum, July 8, 1953; and Truman to Michael J. Kirwan, August 13, 1962—all in Harry S. Truman, *Off the Record: The Private Papers of Harry S. Truman,* ed. Robert H. Ferrell (New York: Harper and Row, 1980), 307, 294, 403–4. On the last, Truman added, "I, in all probability, would have moved Andrew Jackson into that row and made six of them but I didn't have anything to do with making it up."

5. "Address before the League to Enforce Peace," First Commitment to the Idea of a League of Nations, May 27, 1916, in Woodrow Wilson, *The Public Papers of Woodrow Wilson,* vol. 2: *The New Democracy: Presidential Messages, Addresses, and Other Papers (1913–1917),* ed. Ray Stannard Baker and William E. Dodd, auth. ed. (New York: Harper and Brothers, 1926), 184–88.

6. "Address to the United States Senate," Essential Terms of Peace in Europe, January 22, 1917, in Wilson, *Public Papers,* vol. 2: *New Democracy,* 407–14.

7. "Address Delivered at a Joint Session of the Two Houses of Congress," Declaration of War against Germany, April 2, 1917, in Woodrow Wilson, *The Public Papers of Woodrow Wilson,* vol. 3: *War and Peace: Presidential Messages, Addresses, and Public Papers (1917–1924),* ed. Ray Stannard Baker and William E. Dodd, auth. ed. (New York: Harper and Brothers, 1927), 6–15.

8. "Address Delivered at a Joint Session of the Two Houses of Congress," the Fourteen Points Speech, January 8, 1918, in Wilson, *Public Papers,* vol. 3: *War and Peace,* 155–62.

9. "Address before the Third Plenary Session of the Peace Conference," Presentation of the Covenant of the League of Nations, February 14, 1919, in Wilson, *Public Papers,* vol. 3: *War and Peace,* 413–29.

10. For more on the two impulses—messianic and cosmopolitan—characterizing post-1919 progressivism, see Alan Dawley, *Changing the World: American Progressives in War and Revolution* (Princeton, N.J.: Princeton University Press, 2003), 335–37. Wilson clearly exhibited both impulses before the end of World War I.

11. This insight comes from Thomas Knock. For his explanation of Wilson's progressive internationalism, see especially Thomas J. Knock, *To End All Wars: Woodrow Wilson and the Quest for a New World Order* (Princeton, N.J.: Princeton University Press, 1995; originally published by Oxford University Press, 1992), vii–ix, 48–69.

12. For more on the Cold War's "chilling" impact on progressivism overall, from an author who laments that the Cold War marginalized progressivism for decades and depressed the Socialist and Communist Left in America, see Dawley, *Changing the World,* 341–52.

13. Woodrow Wilson, *Constitutional Government in the United States* (New York: Columbia University Press, 1911), 77–79.

14. Truman to Bess, September 22, 1939, and September 23, 1939, in Truman, *Dear Bess,* 419–20.

15. Address by Hon. Harry S. Truman of Missouri, at Caruthersville, Mo.,

October 8, 1939, reprinted in appendix to U.S. Congress, *Congressional Record,* vol. 85, part 2, 76th Congress, 2nd Session, pp. 202–3. Truman continued: "We virtually say to aggressor nations, 'We'll sell you arms and ammunition in peacetime and help you get ready to attack those nations who have not put on an armament race, who have tried to live peaceably with their neighbors, those nations who maintain no bunds or Silver Shirts or Communist parties to help undermine our institutions; but when war comes we'll help you by not letting our friends buy arms and munitions in our markets.' I think it is to our interest, our very selfish interests, to lift the embargo."

16. Ibid.

17. Truman quoted in the *New York Times,* June 24, 1941.

18. Bennett Clark was the son of Champ Clark, whom Truman and his father had initially preferred over Wilson in 1912.

19. Thomas Fleming, *The New Dealers' War: F.D.R. and the War within World War II* (New York: Basic Books, 2001), 101. For a detailed study of the Truman Committee, see Donald H. Riddle, *The Truman Committee: A Study in Congressional Responsibility* (New Brunswick, N.J.: Rutgers University Press). On page 11, Riddle points out that the Truman Committee was the only one of the World War II investigation bodies that made "a systematic effort to survey the entire war program on a continuing basis"; on page 142, Riddle gives information about the committee's findings over the course of its lifetime.

20. Emphasis in the original. "Billion Dollar Watchdog," *Time,* March 8, 1943, reprinted in U.S. Congress, *Congressional Record,* vol. 89, p. 1560, cited in Riddle, *Truman Committee,* 154.

21. Wilson D. Miscamble, "The Evolution of an Internationalist: Harry S. Truman and American Foreign Policy," *Australian Journal of Politics and History* (August 1977): 268–83. Truman paired off with Republican Representative Walter H. Judd from Minnesota, who also had enlisted in World War I.

22. Truman to Bess, April 30, 1942, in Truman, *Dear Bess,* 474.

23. Indeed, according to historian Robert Ferrell, Truman was Roosevelt's running mate in 1944 because of maneuvering by party leaders rather than the president's own judgment, and "it is clear that [FDR] believed that he would live out his fourth term or do even better." Ferrell adds that Roosevelt "hardly knew Truman and thereafter made little effort to know him. He would never, one must believe, have passed the presidency to Truman." For this and Ferrell's summary of how much FDR failed to tell Truman after the latter was chosen as the vice presidential candidate, see Robert H. Ferrell, *The Dying President: Franklin D. Roosevelt, 1944–1945* (Columbia: University of Missouri Press, 1998), 151–52.

24. On the last point, Dean Acheson found Truman to be a remarkable man because of his education. Acheson explained that Truman was well educated because he read so much and it became part of him. See "Oral History Interview with Dean Acheson," Washington, D.C., June 30, 1971, by Theodore A. Wilson and Richard D. McKinzie, HSTL, May 1986.

25. David McCullough, *Truman* (New York: Simon and Schuster, 1992), 399, with no original citation.

26. Chester Wilmot, *The Struggle for Europe* (New York: Harper and Brothers, 1952), 689–717. Also see Forrest C. Pogue, "The Declaration to Halt at the Elbe," in Kent Roberts Greenfield, ed., *Command Decisions* (Washington, D.C.: Department of the Army, 1960), 479–92.

27. This despite a minority opinion that was concerned about the Soviets. White House press research of June 1945, for example, referred to potential "problems" within the uneducated vote and the Catholic vote because they were anti-Soviet. 220-misc., 1945, Official File, Box 824, HSTP, HSTL.

28. For Truman's discussion of this time period, see Harry S. Truman, *Memoirs: Year of Decisions* (Garden City, N.Y.: Doubleday, 1955), 210–19. Truman was probably also influenced by discussion of an April 21, 1945, State Department memorandum that was requested by Admiral William Leahy in response to Churchill's argument. For a copy of the memorandum, see MS 90, Notebooks, from Yalta to Potsdam, James F. Byrnes Papers, Clemson University Library (hereafter, CUL). As the memo stated: "The question of the tactical deployment of American troops in Germany is largely a military question. In so far as the question has political implications, the Department believes that General Eisenhower should be given certain latitude and discretion; that where time permits, he should consult the Combined Chiefs of Staff before any major withdrawal behind our zone frontiers." Also: "The views of the US Chiefs of Staff expressed in connection with CCS 810/17 were discussed informally with the Department of State and have its concurrence." In addition, presidential advisor Harry Hopkins consistently maintained to Truman that America did not want to be misunderstood by the Soviets through failure to withdraw troops. Bernard Baruch had also prepared an April 1945 report for FDR, which he gave to Truman after FDR's death. While it cannot be known if Truman read the memo, Baruch argued that the United States could deal with the Soviets by honoring commitments and expecting the same of the Kremlin. See Folder 632, Byrnes Papers, CUL.

29. May 27, 1945, Hopkins's communication to Truman, Communications—Stalin Conference with Harry Hopkins, May 1945, Box 8, Naval Aide Files, HSTP, HSTL.

30. U.S. Department of State, *Foreign Relations of the United States, 1941–1954* (Washington, D.C.: U.S. Government Printing Office, 1958–1996) (hereafter, *FRUS*): 1945, vol. 3, 132–36.

31. Truman understood that the Soviets were causing delays on treaty agreements. See Truman to Bess, June 19, 1945, in Truman, *Dear Bess*, 516. For Potsdam, see William Leahy, Diary, June 15, 1945, Library of Congress (hereafter, LOC).

32. Churchill was quicker to understand what Stalin once said to Milovan Djilas: "This war is not as in the past; whoever occupies a territory also imposes on it his own social system. Everyone imposes his own system as far as his army can reach. It cannot be otherwise." See Milovan Djilas, *Conversations with Stalin* (New York: Harcourt, Brace and World, 1962), 114.

33. For a brilliant, though at times revisionist, account of the dilemma that Yalta produced, see Robert L. Messer, *The End of an Alliance: James F. Byrnes, Roosevelt, Truman, and the Origins of the Cold War* (Chapel Hill: University of North Carolina

Press, 1982). Messer focuses on Byrnes and the selling of Yalta as a panacea to the American public. Also see *FRUS,* 1945, vol. 5, 254, where Admiral Leahy summarized the difficulty for Truman on April 23, before the meeting with Molotov: "Admiral Leahy said that he had left Yalta with the impression that the Soviet Government had no intention of permitting a free government to operate in Poland and that he would have been surprised had the Soviet Government behaved any differently than it had. In his opinion the Yalta agreement was susceptible to two interpretations. He added that he felt that it was a serious matter to break with the Russians but that we should tell them that we stood for a free and independent Poland."

34. Truman, *Year of Decisions,* 217.

35. Truman was informed of the Katyn massacre before he left for Potsdam. While at the conference, he decided that the United States needed the USSR in order to beat the Japanese, but he determined that the Soviets should not gain control in Japan as they had in Eastern Europe. Meanwhile, Stalin was as interested in Truman and as unwilling to trust him. On June 1, 1945, Moscow ordered its New York station chief to find out everything possible about Truman, including the ways in which Harry Dexter White, Henry Morgenthau, and Henry Wallace might influence him and "to study Truman himself, his intentions, politics, etc . . . [based] on conversations with high-ranking officials, etc." See Allen Weinstein and Alexander Vassiliev, *The Haunted Wood: Soviet Espionage in America—The Stalin Era* (New York: Random House, 1999), 167–68.

36. "Address before a Joint Session of the Congress on Universal Military Training," October 23, 1945, in Truman, *Public Papers,* vol. 1, 405. Despite the obstinacy to the idea, Truman doggedly and consistently argued for universal military training during the coming years. "But above all else, we are strong because of the courage and vigor and skill of a liberty loving people who are determined that this nation will remain forever free," the president said here to a joint session of Congress. "With our strength comes grave responsibility. With it must also come a continuing source of leadership in the world for justice and peace." For evidence of Truman's dedication to this position in the months before he gave this address, see George Elsey's handwritten notes of August 22 and 24, 1945, and between August 31 and September 20, 1945, National Defense—UMT (folder 1), Box 89, George M. Elsey Papers, HSTL.

37. See, most obviously, William E. Leuchtenburg, *In the Shadow of FDR: From Harry Truman to Ronald Reagan,* rev. ed. (Ithaca, N.Y.: Cornell University Press, 1985), 1–40.

38. Truman to Eleanor Roosevelt, September 1, 1945, in Truman, *Off the Record,* 63.

39. Draft Speech (undelivered), October 1946, in Truman, *Off the Record,* 100–2.

40. Truman to Bess, December 21, 1941, in Truman, *Dear Bess,* 469–71.

41. Truman to Bess, August 18, 1944, in Truman, *Dear Bess,* 508–10. Two of the many retellings of the August 1944 lunch between FDR and Truman are found in Ferrell, *Dying President,* 88–90, and Fleming, *New Dealers' War,* 450–51.

42. Truman to Bess, June 14, 1946, in Truman, *Dear Bess,* 526.

43. Truman, *Where the Buck Stops,* 361, 366, 362, 363, 362.

44. Ibid., 362.

45. Roosevelt to Churchill, September 28, 1944, no. 624, in Franklin D. Roosevelt and Winston Churchill, *Roosevelt and Churchill: Their Secret Wartime Correspondence,* ed. Francis L. Loewenheim, Harold D. Langley, and Manfred Jonas (New York: Saturday Review Press/E. P. Dutton, 1975), 579. For more on the subject of compromise, see FDR's concession to Stalin's wishes on voting procedures in the UN Security Council as set forth in Roosevelt to Churchill, December 5, 1944, no. 666, in ibid., 615–16.

46. A good example of FDR's indebtedness to and adaptation of Wilsonianism is Roosevelt's "Address before the Woodrow Wilson Foundation—'From Now on, War by Governments Shall Be Changed to Peace by Peoples,'" December 28, 1933, in Franklin D. Roosevelt, *The Public Papers and Addresses of Franklin D. Roosevelt, 1928–1945,* vol. 2: *The Year of Crisis, 1933* (New York: Random House, 1938), 544–49.

47. Interdependence, what he also called mutual dependence, was an FDR theme since his first election for president. See "National and International Unity" in Franklin D. Roosevelt, *Looking Forward* (New York: John Day, 1933), 250. During World War II, FDR argued that interdependence was the reason U.S. foreign policy was determining domestic policy; during the Great Depression, he had said interdependence was the reason that U.S. domestic policy was determining foreign policy. For FDR's description of what postwar machinery of international economic relations would be needed, see Roosevelt to Churchill, February 23, 1944, no. 476, in Roosevelt and Churchill, *Secret Wartime Correspondence,* 451–52.

48. Historian Robert Dallek has strongly argued these points (while perhaps overstating the view that the United States would have retreated into isolationism without the United Nations). See Robert Dallek, *Franklin D. Roosevelt and American Foreign Policy, 1932–1945* (New York: Oxford University Press, 1979), 11–12, 536, 508, 536.

49. "The Annual Message to the Congress," January 6, 1941, in Roosevelt, *Public Papers and Addresses,* vol. 9: *War—and Aid to Democracies, 1940* (New York: Macmillan, 1941), 663–72.

50. Joint Statement by President Roosevelt and Prime Minister Churchill, August 14, 1941, in *FRUS,* 1941, vol. 1, 367–69.

51. "'Keep Us Strong in Our Faith That We Fight for a Better Day for Humankind'—Christmas Eve Fireside Chat on Teheran and Cairo Conferences," December 24, 1943, in Roosevelt, *Public Papers and Addresses,* vol. 12: *The Tide Turns, 1943* (New York: Harper and Brothers, 1943), 553–63.

52. "'We Cannot Fail Them Again, and Expect the World to Survive'—Address to the Congress Reporting on the Yalta Conference," March 1, 1945, in Roosevelt, *Public Papers and Addresses,* vol. 13: *Victory and the Threshold of Peace, 1944–45* (New York: Harper and Brothers, 1950), 570–86.

53. Ibid.

54. "'We Must Keep on Striking Our Enemies Wherever and Whenever We Can Meet Them'—Fireside Chat on Progress of the War," February 23, 1942, in

Roosevelt, *Public Papers and Addresses,* vol. 11: *Humanity on the Defensive, 1942* (New York: Harper and Brothers, 1950), 105–17.

55. Roosevelt to Churchill, March 29, 1945, no. 729, 689–90; Roosevelt to Churchill, April 6, 1945, no. 736, 705; Roosevelt to Churchill, April 8, 1945, no. 737, 706–7; Roosevelt to Churchill, April 10, 1945, no. 739, 707; and Roosevelt to Churchill, April 11, 1945, no. 742, 709—all in Roosevelt and Churchill, *Secret Wartime Correspondence.* The point about FDR on Poland is credited to presidential advisor Samuel Rosenman; see note on page 709.

56. *FRUS,* 1945, vol. 5, 232–33. In an August 1947 letter to Joseph Grew, Bohlen remembered similarly the president's "stiffened policy." See Charles E. Bohlen to Joseph C. Grew, August 2, 1947, Records of Charles E. Bohlen, Record Group 59, Box 1, National Archives Collection, George C. Marshall Library (hereafter, GCML).

57. Admiral William Leahy, for one, believed that the president's attitude would have a "beneficial effect on the Soviet attitude toward the rest of the world." See Leahy, Diary, April 23, 1945, LOC. Truman had also been thoroughly briefed by this point about ongoing Soviet designs in Romania. See Cortlandt V. R. Schuyler, "The View from Romania," in Thomas T. Hammond, *Witnesses to the Origins of the Cold War* (Seattle: University of Washington Press, 1982), 123–60.

58. Truman, May 23, 1945, Longhand Notes File, 1945–1952, Box 333, PSF, HSTP, HSTL.

59. "Radio Address to the American People after the Signing of the Terms of Unconditional Surrender by Japan," September 1, 1945, in Truman, *Public Papers,* vol. 1, 257.

60. "Address on Foreign Policy at the Navy Day Celebration in New York City," October 27, 1945, in Truman, *Public Papers,* vol. 1, 431–38.

61. Truman to Bess, July 25, 1945, in Truman, *Dear Bess,* 521. He wrote Bess from Berlin, "There are some things we can't agree to. Russia and Poland have gobbled up a big hunk of Germany and want Britain and us to agree. I have flatly refused. We have unalterably opposed the recognition of police governments in the Germany Axis countries. I told Stalin that until we had free access to those countries and our nationals had their property rights restored, so far as we were concerned there'd never be recognition."

62. "Address on Foreign Policy at the Navy Day Celebration in New York City," October 27, 1945, in Truman, *Public Papers,* vol. 1, 431–38.

63. Winston S. Churchill, "'Foreign Policy,' A Speech to the House of Commons, November 7, 1945," in Winston S. Churchill, *The Sinews of Peace: Post-War Speeches by Winston S. Churchill,* ed. Randolph S. Churchill (Boston: Houghton Mifflin, 1949), 26–36.

64. Ibid. A sample of Churchill's language: "If such a statement had been made in the Summer of 1914, the Kaiser would never have launched an aggresive [*sic*] war over a Balkan incident." (Thus began a litany that at every major juncture in the interwar period, a statement such as Truman's could have averted the next conflict and, ultimately, prevented World War II.)

65. Messer argues that Truman's complaint about Byrnes was unjustified and that the president only had to ask for a full report. He counts the documents that Byrnes did send to the White House. See Messer, *End of an Alliance,* 149, for example. But Truman was president and should not have had to ask for a report. In elevating process over statesmanship, Byrnes consistently depicted Truman as the essentially passive supporter of the secretary of state's foreign policy and active leadership. See James F. Byrnes, *Speaking Frankly* (New York: Harper and Brothers, 1947). Truman, while he was able to disconnect himself from being president and accept criticism, allowed no one to demean the institution of the presidency. He surrounded himself with advisors whose loyalty he could trust and whose advice was in keeping with his general opinions. By slighting the presidency, Byrnes cut himself off from being a trusted counselor. Although the position of secretary of state was increasingly important, the man who occupied it would soon become a liability.

66. Byrnes, *Speaking Frankly,* 59, 282–83.

67. The most that Truman seems to have criticized FDR publicly concerning the wartime conferences was with respect to the Yalta Conference, saying in August 1945, "The question of Poland was a most difficult one. Certain compromises about Poland had already been agreed upon at the Crimea conference. They obviously were binding upon us at Berlin." See "Radio Report to the American People on the Potsdam Conference," August 9, 1945, in Truman, *Public Papers,* vol. 1, 208–9. Indeed, before his experience at Potsdam, Truman believed that issues such as Poland and the entrenchment of Soviet troops in Eastern Europe were negotiable. The difficult, almost unacceptable, lesson of Potsdam for Truman was that he could not change the circumstances without engaging in, most likely, a protracted conflict.

68. "Message to the Congress on the State of the Union and on the Budget for 1947," January 21, 1946, in Truman, *Public Papers,* vol. 2, 36–37.

69. While debate remains as to whether Truman actually read this memo to Secretary Byrnes on January 5, 1946 (and most say Truman did not), it is agreed that he wrote it in early January. For more on similar comments by Truman regarding the Soviets, see, for example, Eben A. Ayers, diary entry, December 17, 1945, in *Truman in the White House: The Diary of Eben A. Ayers,* ed. Robert H. Ferrell (Columbia: University of Missouri Press, 1991), 104.

70. Truman, Longhand Notes File, 1945–1952, Box 333, PSF, HSTP, HSTL. Byrnes was supposed to meet with Truman on Saturday, January 5, but the meeting was postponed until January 7. Given Truman's handwritten notation of the January 7 meeting in his daily appointment sheets, this probably was the occasion on which he presented the views of the memorandum. See Presidential Appointments File, Daily Sheets, 1946 January, Box 83, PSF, HSTP, HSTL.

Some argue that Truman could not have been displeased with the secretary of state around this time because Byrnes was on the presidential yacht S.S. *Williamsburg* for New Year's Eve and joined in the singing and celebration with the president. But Byrnes was petulant about not receiving a formal invitation. He also resented that the president had wanted to vet his radio address of December 30 about his trip to Moscow. In a private two-hour conference between Byrnes and Truman on

December 29 on the yacht, Truman could have taken the opportunity to voice some of the concerns, especially about the primacy of the president in foreign policy, which he would set forth in the January 5 memorandum. For details on the yacht trip, see December 29, 1945, January 1, 2, and 5 in Diary-1945 and Diary-1946, Box 16, Eben A. Ayers Papers, HSTL.

71. For consideration of such imprisonment, including one of his own staff, see Arthur Bliss Lane, *I Saw Poland Betrayed: An American Ambassador Reports to the American People* (Indianapolis: Bobbs Merrill, 1948), 197. Throughout his account, Lane gave dates of and conversations with Truman in which he apprised the president personally of the situation in Poland from June 6, 1945, into 1947.

72. Leahy, Diary, February 20, 1946, and February 21, 1946, LOC. From these passages, Leahy agreed with the president's frequent criticism of professional diplomats and what Truman saw as their appeasement tendencies.

73. Along with Winston Churchill's Fulton address, George Kennan's Long Telegram of February 22, 1946, is considered by all scholars—for all intents and purposes and regardless of their methodologies—to be a seminal document in the development of the American strategy of containment and a policy of peace through strength. See, for example, Gaddis, *United States and the Origins of the Cold War*, 302–4, and, more recently, Hamby, *Man of the People*, 346.

74. Election Address by Joseph Stalin, February 9, 1946, in *Vital Speeches of the Day*, March 1, 1946, vol. 12, no. 10, 300–4. For an examination of Stalin's anti-Western campaign—almost a half year before Churchill's Fulton speech and almost one year before the official campaign of Zhdanovshchina, see Vladimir O. Pechatnov, "'The Allies are pressing on you to break your will . . .': Foreign Policy Correspondence between Stalin and Molotov and Other Politburo Members, September 1945–December 1946," Working Paper no. 26, Cold War International History Project, September 1999. For a detailed examination of the Soviet belief in an "inevitable Anglo-American contradiction," especially as expressed by prominent Soviet diplomats Ivan M. Maisky and Maxim Litvinov, see Vladimir O. Pechatnov, "The Big Three after World War II: New Documents on Soviet Thinking about Post War Relations with the United States and Great Britain," Working Paper no. 13, Cold War International History Project, July 1995.

75. Charles E. Bohlen, *The Transformation of American Foreign Policy* (New York: W.W. Norton, 1969), 73–75. This book, analyzing the grand transformation in American foreign policy after World War II, is closer to Truman's thought than to Kennan's. It preceded Bohlen's formal memoir by four years. It is interesting to note that Bohlen was more realist and more like Kennan in the later book. See Charles E. Bohlen, *Witness to History, 1929–1969* (New York: W.W. Norton, 1973).

76. Paul H. Nitze, *From Hiroshima to Glasnost: At the Center of Decision; A Memoir* (New York: Grove Weidenfeld, 1989), 78. In Nitze's account, varying approaches and views within the Truman administration emerge.

77. Kennan's Moscow Embassy telegram, February 22, 1946, in *FRUS, 1946*, vol. 6, 696–709.

78. Diary entry of January 2, 1946, in James V. Forrestal, *The Forrestal Diaries*,

ed. Walter Millis (New York: Viking Press, 1951), 126–128, 134. The report from Professor E. F. Willett, entitled "Dialectical Materialism," can be found in Folder 13, Box 63, Foreign Affairs—Russia, Elsey Papers, HSTL. The outside report seems to have contributed to the research for the Clifford memorandum. Forrestal also passed the report and his correspondence with Willett to Clifford. See File 4, Subject File—Russia, Box 16, Clark M. Clifford Papers, HSTL. In a January 22, 1946, memo to Forrestal, Willett explained the differences between the Communist and Christian conceptions of man, including the Communist use of Rousseau. He concluded: "The Communist therefore lowers the individual dignity of man in that he regards him as a product of the economic system whereas the Christian dignifies the role of man by regarding him as the creator of the economic system." Willett's understanding of Marxism-Leninism has been impugned by some scholars, but his report straightforwardly presents Communist doctrine. Interestingly, Willet's January 1946 report is the same report that Forrestal conveyed to Kennan in fall 1946, asking him for a response, which resulted in January 1947 in the memorandum that became the X article.

79. In his later writings, Kennan argued that he had proffered containment simply in its political—in his terms, psychological, diplomatic, and moral—sense. He disavowed a political purpose that relied on the combination of political, economic, and military strength informed by more than power or behavior. See especially George F. Kennan, *Memoirs, 1925–1950* (Boston: Little, Brown, 1967), 354–67.

80. Forrestal, *Forrestal Diaries,* 127–28.

81. Kennan, *Memoirs,* 294–95.

82. Dean Acheson, *Present at the Creation: My Years in the State Department* (New York: W.W. Norton, 1969), 151. Acheson argued that the United States responded slowly to Kennan's predictions and warnings.

83. *FRUS,* 1946, vol. 6, 700.

84. Diary entry of March 10, 1946, in Forrestal, *Forrestal Diaries,* 144.

85. In addition to Truman's speeches and press conferences on U.S.-Soviet relations, see Truman, May 23, 1945, Longhand Notes File, 1945–1952, Box 333, PSF, HSTP, HSTL.

86. *FRUS,* 1946, vol. 6, 706.

87. For development of Kennan's existentialism, which becomes nihilism at some points, see, for example, the Long Telegram chapter in his *Memoirs,* 271–97. This existentialist philosophy also seems to underpin Kennan's attitude toward democracy.

2. Framing Containment

1. Quoted in Martin Gilbert, *Winston S. Churchill,* vol. 8: *Never Despair, 1945–1965* (Boston: Houghton Mifflin, 1988), 159. After receiving Churchill's acceptance of the invitation to speak at Fulton, Truman responded: "I am most happy that you have made up your mind to spend some time in Florida, and that you are willing to deliver a speech on World Affairs at Westminster College in Missouri. I would be most pleased to introduce you." See Truman to Churchill, November 16, 1945, General File, Churchill, Winston, 1945–46, Box 115, PSF, HSTP, HSTL.

2. *New York Times,* March 6, 1946, 5.

3. Winston Churchill, "The Sinews of Peace," March 5, 1946, in Winston S. Churchill, *The Sinews of Peace: Post-War Speeches by Winston S. Churchill,* ed. Randolph S. Churchill (Boston: Houghton Mifflin, 1949), 93–105. Also see "A Speech to the General Assembly of Virginia," March 8, 1946, 106–110. Churchill elaborated three days after Fulton: "But peace will not be preserved without the virtues that make victory possible in war. Peace will not be preserved by pious sentiments expressed in terms of platitudes or by official grimaces and diplomatic correctitude, however desirable this may be from time to time. It will not be preserved by casting aside in dangerous years the panoply of warlike strength."

4. "Sinews of Peace," March 5, 1946, in Churchill, *Sinews of Peace,* 93–105.

5. Ibid.

6. William Taubman, *Stalin's American Policy: From Entente to Détente to Cold War* (New York: W.W. Norton, 1982), 166.

7. Of his trip to America, Churchill wrote Truman: "If you, as you suggest in your postscript, would like me to visit your home State and would introduce me, I should feel it my duty—and it would also be a great pleasure—to deliver an Address to the Westminster University on the world situation, under your aegis. This might possibly be advantageous from several points of view. At any rate it is the only public-speaking engagement which I have in mind and the explanation for it would be my respect for you and your wishes." As Churchill noted later in the month, Truman "proposes himself to be present and introduce me. This will obviously be a public appearance of considerable importance. . . . This is the only engagement which I propose to make at the present time." See November 8, 1945, Churchill letter to Truman, and November 22, 1945, Churchill telegram message to Colonel Frank Clarke, both in General File, Churchill, Winston, 1945–46, Box 115, PSF, HSTP, HSTL.

8. Leahy, Diary, February 10, 1946, LOC.

9. January 29, 1946, Churchill to Truman, General File, Churchill, Winston, 1945–46, Box 115, PSF, HSTP, HSTL.

10. December 10, 1945, Truman to Dr. F. L. McCluer, president of Westminster College, General File, Churchill, Winston, 1945–46, Box 115, PSF, HSTP, HSTL.

11. Cited in Gilbert, *Never Despair,* 197.

12. According to Truman's daughter, the president wrote his mother and sister on March 11: "I'm glad you enjoyed Fulton. So did I. And I think it did some good, although I am not yet ready to endorse Mr. Churchill's speech." See Margaret Truman, *Harry S. Truman* (New York: William Morrow, 1973), 312. I have been unable to locate the actual letter at the Truman Library. Even Hamby, who thoroughly culled the Truman papers, uses Margaret Truman's account. See Hamby, *Man of the People,* 348. Regardless, Truman did not disavow the speech; he said that he was not yet ready to endorse it. The evidence that runs counter to Margaret Truman's interpretation is found in Colonel Frank Clarke's March 5, 1946, message to Mrs. Churchill, no. 14, Box 12, Naval Aide Files, HSTP, HSTL, where Clarke wrote: "We are now on President Truman's special train returning via Columbus, Ohio.

Everything went well today and Winston's speech was enthusiastically received by the audience. The President is very pleased and MacKenzie King telephoned from Ottawa to congratulate Winston. I hope you heard the speech clearly. Winston is very well and quite happy over the day." For Truman's August 30, 1949, recollection of his opinion about Churchill and the Fulton address, see Jonathan Daniels's Notes, Part I, Notes for *The Man of Independence*, Jonathan Daniels Papers, HSTL, where Truman said: "I was not upset by what Churchill said at Fulton, Mo—I had not read his speech but he said what I wanted him to say—glad he said what he did—Churchill had tried to get me not to withdraw troops from Prague etc., and to go ahead and take Berlin—I told him we were bound not to do that by our agreements with the Russians—but if I had known then what I know now, I would have gon [*sic*] to the eastern boundaries of Russia."

13. Cited in Gilbert, *Never Despair*, 205.

14. See, for example, ibid., 206, and McCullough, *Truman*, 490.

15. "The President's News Conference of March 8, 1946," in Truman, *Public Papers*, vol. 2, 144–48.

16. *New York Times*, March 7, 1946, 1, 5.

17. Editorials in the *Chicago Daily News, Detroit News*, and *St. Louis Post-Dispatch* cited in U.S. Congress, *Congressional Record*, March 13, 1946, House, 79th Congress, 2nd Session, pp. A1330–31.

18. *New York Times*, March 6, 1946, 6.

19. *Hansard*, Vol. 420, Col. 760, quoted in Henry B. Ryan, "A New Look at Churchill's 'Iron Curtain' Speech," *Historical Journal*, December 1979, 911.

20. Folder 639, Notes and Memos—for book, October 1955, Byrnes Papers, CUL.

21. Diary entry of March 12, 1946, in Henry A. Wallace, *The Price of Vision: The Diary of Henry A. Wallace, 1942–1946*, ed. John Morton Blum (Boston: Houghton Mifflin, 1973), 556–58; also see March 5, 1946, entry on pages 556–57.

22. *New York Times*, March 7, 1946, 24.

23. See Fraser J. Harbutt, *The Iron Curtain: Churchill, America and the Origins of the Cold War* (New York: Oxford University Press, 1986). Harbutt rightly emphasizes Truman's "complicity" with Churchill's Fulton address but shortchanges Truman's own strategic thinking both before and after the speech. Rather than a turn from accommodation to confrontation, as Harbutt asserts, the Fulton address should be seen as the first major public (and most dramatic) manifestation of a change in policy starting before March 1946.

24. American Institute of Public Opinion (AIPO) polls of March 13, 1946, in Hadley Cantril, ed., and Mildred Strunk, prep., *Public Opinion 1935–1946* (Princeton, N.J.: Princeton University Press, 1951), 1060, 963. For an evaluation of how the iron curtain speech encouraged a shift in commercial media—such as *Collier's*, the *Saturday Evening Post*, and *Life*—from support to criticism of the Soviet Union between March and June 1946, see John Fousek, *To Lead the Free World: American Nationalism and the Cultural Roots of the Cold War* (Chapel Hill: University of North Carolina Press, 2000), 116–19.

25. The vice consul in Tabriz reported these developments to the secretary of state. See *FRUS,* 1946, vol. 7, 340. Also see Kuniholm, *Origins of the Cold War in the Near East,* 314–15, 317, 319.

26. Lane, *I Saw Poland Betrayed,* 220.

27. *New York Times,* March 7, 1. By March 11, an armed coup by Tudeh and Soviet agents was expected at any moment in Teheran. See Joseph M. Jones, *The Fifteen Weeks (February 21–June 5, 1947)* (New York: Viking Press, 1955), 53; also see Kuniholm, *Origins of the Cold War in the Near East,* 319–20.

28. Harry S. Truman, *Memoirs: Years of Trial and Hope* (Garden City, N.Y.: Doubleday, 1956), 95. For more on Stalin's anti-Western strategy during this period, see Pechatnov, "'The Allies are pressing on you.'" See page 16 for an example of Stalin chastising Commissar of Foreign Affairs Vyacheslav Molotov in May 1946: "Byrnes pushed, and you were on the defensive, while you had all the reasons to attack. . . . Byrnes told you . . . about the expansionist tendencies of the USSR and that it was necessary to prove their absence. In response, you must tell Byrnes that he seems to share the slanderous attitude that Churchill expressed in his anti-Soviet speech in the United States and that Stalin has thoroughly criticized. Under such circumstances the Soviet government may have a pretext to let the Soviet media make a series of commentaries against the imperial policy of the US government. Byrnes must be convinced that the Soviet press has no lack of appropriate materials for publication."

29. Iran was the first test case, as it were, for the United Nations, with the UN Security Council meeting for the first time in January 1946.

30. For more on this aspect of the crisis, see Natalia I. Yegorova, "The 'Iran Crisis' of 1945–1946: A View from the Soviet Archives," Working Paper no. 15, Cold War International History Project, May 1996.

31. Hamby, *Man of the People,* 349.

32. Qavam was less anti-Communist than his predecessor. In addition, he was adept at playing both sides against the middle. See Jones, *Fifteen Weeks,* 52, 56–58. Also see Melvyn P. Leffler, *A Preponderance of Power: National Security, the Truman Administration, and the Cold War* (Stanford, Calif.: Stanford University Press, 1992), 110.

33. Byrnes's reading copy, Folder 626, Speeches, 1946, Byrnes Papers, CUL. Truman attached a note to the speech: "Jim:—I've read it and like it." For discussion of the speech and Byrnes's emphasis of Truman's underlinings, see Messer, *End of an Alliance,* 188. To Truman, much as Churchill and FDR had said of the Nazis, the Soviets were pursuing a war of nerves for their own ends. In going over the speech with Byrnes, Truman also told him "to stiffen up and try for the next three months not to make any compromises"; see Ayers, diary entry, February 27, 1946, in Ayers, *Truman in the White House,* 139.

34. Cited in Arthur Hendrick Vandenberg, *The Private Papers of Senator Vandenberg,* ed. Arthur H. Vandenberg Jr. and J. A. Morris (Boston: Houghton Mifflin, 1952), 246–48. Vandenberg actually uses the phrase "destiny of the United Nations." While Vandenberg implored Truman to act in this speech, he saw Byrnes as the real problem. See page 225 for his 1945 description of Byrnes as the one "who

helped surrender at Yalta" and as someone whose "whole life has been a career of compromise."

35. Leahy, Diary, March 7, 1946, LOC.

36. Truman, *Years of Trial and Hope*, 95–96.

37. Jones, *Fifteen Weeks*, 62. According to Jones, if Byrnes had not prevailed over Forrestal, the *Missouri* would also (and again) have patrolled the Mediterranean. It seems that Truman was uninformed of this debate. Any indecision in this case was on the part of Byrnes, not Truman. It should be noted that the body of the Turkish ambassador had been interred at Arlington National Cemetery since late 1944, until it could be returned to the ambassador's homeland. See also Clark Clifford with Richard Holbrooke, *Counsel to the President: A Memoir* (New York: Anchor Books, Doubleday, 1992), 101.

38. Hamby, *Man of the People*, 349.

39. For more on NSC 68, the most important government document on the Cold War issued by the Truman administration, see chapter 8. For more on the shortage of manpower and Truman's efforts to rectify the situation through universal military training, see Norman Friedman, *The Fifty Year War: Conflict and Strategy in the Cold War* (Annapolis, Md.: Naval Institute Press, 2000), 61–62.

40. By this time in his correspondence, Truman was defending his position of strength to those who criticized him in their letters. For an example, see 220-misc., 1946, President's Official Files, Box 824, HSTP, HSTL.

41. See, for example, Robert H. Ferrell, *Harry S. Truman: A Life* (Columbia: University of Missouri Press, 1994), 249–51.

42. Rejection of Truman by Congress pertained to domestic as well as foreign policies. When the president proposed an ambitious twenty-one-point domestic program in 1946, an impasse resulted, with many southern Democrats joining with Republicans to defeat or delay proposals related to national health insurance, social security, and full employment, among other issues. On the foreign policy front, Democrats wanted the UN to take the lead. For example, while Senator Tom Connally of Texas—who chaired the Foreign Relations Committee from 1941 until 1947—supported Truman on containment policies in 1947 through the Korean War, he supported Wilsonian internationalism and a UN approach in 1945 and 1946.

43. For discussion of this point, see Alonzo L. Hamby, *Liberalism and Its Challengers: FDR to Reagan* (New York: Oxford University Press, 1985), 67–68.

44. Some in the ADA supported Truman's anti-Communist efforts in 1947 and 1948 but thought he was too quick to abandon the United Nations. For more on Truman's relationship with his party, see Sean J. Savage, *Truman and the Democratic Party* (Lexington: University Press of Kentucky, 1997).

45. See "The Price of Free World Victory," May 8, 1942, reprinted in Wallace, *Price of Vision*, 635–40.

46. For more on Wallace's views in the 1930s and 1940s, see Henry A. Wallace, *New Frontiers* (New York: Reynal and Hitchcock, 1934), and Henry A. Wallace, *Democracy Reborn*, ed. Russell Lord (New York: Reynal and Hitchcock, 1944).

47. Wallace to Truman, December 22, 1945, document with December 27 cov-

er letter, Henry A. Wallace Papers, Reel 38, reproduced from Wallace's papers at the University of Iowa Library and available at the LOC.

48. Diary entries of February 13, 1946; February 12, 1946; March 15, 1946; March 1, 1946; and March 6, 1946—all in Wallace, *Price of Vision*, 550, 547, 563, 554, 556–57. On March 5, 1946, Wallace wrote that Walter Lippmann and his wife agreed with his assessment of the Fulton address.

49. See the discussion of Wallace's breakfast meeting with Anatoly Gorsky, the Soviet Union's NKGB's Washington station chief. Gorsky's report of the meeting—which eventually reached Foreign Minister Molotov—is one of the Soviet intelligence dispatches uncovered in Weinstein and Vassiliev, *Haunted Wood*, 283–84.

50. Truman, September 17, 1946, Longhand Notes File, 1946, Box 333, PSF, HSTP, HSTL.

51. Wallace to Truman, July 23, 1946, Reel 38, Wallace Papers, LOC.

52. Henry Wallace, "The Way to Peace," September 12, 1946, reprinted in its entirety with original and edited passages, in Wallace, *Price of Vision*, 661–69. For a revisionist account that is greatly indebted to Wallace, including his views about atomic diplomacy, see Offner, *Another Such Victory.*

53. Diary entry of September 12, 1946, in Wallace, *Price of Vision*, 612.

54. "The President's News Conference of September 12, 1946," in Truman, *Public Papers,* vol. 2, 426–29.

55. Truman, September 16, 17, and 19, 1946, Longhand Notes File, 1946, Box 333, PSF, HSTP, HSTL.

56. Truman especially expected this behavior from his cabinet members, because they all knew well by this point the difficulties that he had had with Byrnes.

57. Entry of September 21, 1946, Charles G. Ross Personal Diary, 1946, Subject File II, Box 21, Charles G. Ross Papers, HSTL.

58. "The Way to Peace," in Wallace, *Price of Vision*, 668–69.

59. The public analogue to Truman's understanding of what constitutes an advisor's duty to his president—stated privately in the January 1946 memo to Byrnes—was the president's statement upon receipt of Wallace's resignation. See "The President's News Conference on Foreign Policy," September 20, 1946, in Truman, *Public Papers,* vol. 2, 431. Byrnes accepted his position as secretary of state and worked to implement the president's foreign policy. Wallace refused to accept his position as secretary of commerce, and so Truman had to ask for his resignation. Wallace's response was to issue his own statement, in an effort to defend himself, surely, but also to undercut Truman's foreign policy and presidency; see excerpt in Wallace, *Price of Vision*, 630–31.

60. Elsey's handwritten notes of meeting, July 12, 1946, Folder 3, Box 63, Elsey Papers, HSTL.

61. Clifford memorandum, printed in its entirety as an appendix, in Arthur Krock, *Memoirs: Sixty Years on the Firing Line* (New York: Funk and Wagnalls, 1968), 419–82. Here, see 425–26. (A similar approach would be taken later by Paul Nitze—who analyzed the association between the Soviet design, its intentions, and its capabilities—in NSC 68, requested by Truman in 1950.) George Elsey helped extensively to prepare

the 1946 report, as is evidenced by his own papers at the Truman Library, so much so that some scholars now refer to the document as the Clifford-Elsey memorandum. Throughout his memoir, Clifford praises Elsey.

62. Clifford with Holbrooke, *Counsel to the President,* 116. For quote, see Clifford memorandum, in Krock, *Memoirs,* 428.

63. See Elsey's handwritten notes, Genesis of Report, undated summer 1946, Box 63, Elsey Papers, HSTL. Elsey wrote that Kennan's views were expressed on a Clifford personal copy of the report but not on the copy he was given.

64. Clifford memorandum, in Krock, *Memoirs,* 431.

65. Ibid., 432–35. As will be explored in later chapters, Truman's political thought of containment deepened the Clifford memorandum on this point. By 1950, Truman and the National Security Council saw the power and influence sought and exercised by the USSR as separate factors married in service to communism.

66. Handwritten memorandum for Mr. Clifford, undated summer 1946, Box 63, Elsey Papers, HSTL.

67. Clifford memorandum, in Krock, *Memoirs,* 457.

68. Ibid., 447, 448–62.

69. Ibid., 468, 469–75.

70. Ibid., 476.

71. The State-War-Navy Coordinating Committee was already considering various overt and covert programs in 1946.

72. Clifford memorandum, in Krock, *Memoirs,* 476, 477.

73. Contrary to some charges, it did not serve as a mouthpiece for Forrestal and other hard liners. See, for example, Leffler, *Preponderance of Power,* 131–32, 137–38.

74. Clifford memorandum, in Krock, *Memoirs,* 476, 480, 482.

75. Krock, *Memoirs,* 224.

76. Clifford with Holbrooke, *Counsel to the President,* 123–24. Elsey remembered Truman's judgment much the same way: the president thought that it was much too explosive a document "because it covered so comprehensively, so many issues, and he told Clifford he did *not* think it advisable to give copies to members of his Cabinet, or to have any distribution of it. So, the President retained a limited number." See Oral History Interview with George M. Elsey, Washington, D.C., February 10 and 17, 1964; July 10 and 17, 1969; and April 9 and July 7 and 10, 1970, by Charles T. Morrissey and Jerry N. Hess, HSTL (May 1974).

3. The Truman Doctrine

1. See, especially, the publications of the Cold War International History Project. For an interesting essay on this subject that is more blunt than his *We Now Know,* see John Lewis Gaddis, "On Moral Equivalency and Cold War History," in Joel H. Rosenthal, ed., *Ethics and International Affairs: A Reader,* 2nd ed. (Washington, D.C.: Georgetown University Press, 1999), 194–217.

2. ORE first stood for the Office of Research and Evaluations (home to the

analysts in the Central Intelligence Group), which was a name change for the Central Reports Staff in July 1946. In October 1946, the name was changed to the Office of Reports and Estimates, by which it was known until it was abolished in November 1950. ORE is the name typically used for this analytical office for the whole period from 1946 through 1950. For additional details, see Woodrow J. Kuhns, ed., *Assessing the Soviet Threat: The Early Cold War Years* (Washington, D.C.: Center for the Study of Intelligence, Central Intelligence Agency, 1997), 3.

3. ORE 1, July 23, 1946, "Soviet Foreign and Military Policy," 56–66, and Weekly Summary Excerpt, August 23, 1946, "Soviet Military Policy in Eastern Europe," 74–76, both in Kuhns, *Assessing the Soviet Threat.* For development of the situation in the Near East, see Kuniholm, *Origins of the Cold War in the Near East,* 303–82.

4. Memorandum for James F. Byrnes from the President, October 20, 1945, General File, Box 115, PSF, HSTP, HSTL.

5 Howard Jones, *"A New Kind of War": America's Global Strategy and the Truman Doctrine in Greece* (New York: Oxford University Press, 1989), 8.

6. Forrestal, meeting with the president, August 15, 1946, in Forrestal, *Forrestal Diaries,* 192. Also see Jones, *Fifteen Weeks,* 62–66. For confirmation of Truman's understanding of the Middle East in *Years of Trial and Hope,* 95–101, see especially Jones, 66. The weekly ORE report to Truman backed up his decisions. See Weekly Summary Excerpt, August 16, 1946, "Soviet Proposal for Revision of Straits Convention," in Kuhns, *Assessing the Soviet Threat,* 70–71.

7. *FRUS,* 1945, vol. 5, 253; *FRUS,* Potsdam I, 1041–42.

8. Truman to Byrnes, October 20, 1945, General File, Box 115, PSF, HSTP, HSTL.

9. For elaboration of these two points, see Kuniholm, *Origins of the Cold War in the Near East,* 378–82.

10. Truman, *Years of Trial and Hope,* 100, 98. Truman's account is akin to his Truman Doctrine speech, indicating that his memoirs reflect the opinion he held at the time of events.

11. *FRUS,* 1947, vol. 5, 96–98, and Acheson, *Present at the Creation,* 219.

12. Jones, *Fifteen Weeks,* 142.

13. Diary entry of March 7, 1947, in Forrestal, *Forrestal Diaries,* 250–51.

14. Cabinet meeting, March 7, 1947, Notes on Cabinet Meetings—Post-Presidential File (Set I), January 3–December 17, 1947, Box 1, Matthew J. Connelly Papers, HSTL.

15. For Jones's description of the preparation of the Truman Doctrine speech, see Jones, *Fifteen Weeks,* 148–70. The State-War-Navy Coordinating Committee (SWNCC) report included important language, such as the theme of "two ways of life," that stayed in the drafts until the final speech. Ibid., 150–53.

16. Letter from George M. Elsey to Mr. Clifford, March 7, 1947, The Truman Doctrine, Documents, Truman Presidential Museum and Library (hereafter, TPML), available from http://www.trumanlibrary.org/whistlestop/study_collections/doctrine/large/index.php.

17. For Clifford's description of the preparation of the Truman Doctrine speech, see Clifford with Holbrooke, *Counsel to the President,* 133–37.

18. March 10, 11, and 12, 1947, Presidential Appointments File, Daily Sheets, 1947 March, Box 85, PSF, HSTP, HSTL.

19. Leahy, Diary, March 10, 1947, LOC.

20. Leahy, Diary, March 12, 1947, LOC. As Leahy recalled: "President Truman was convinced by his experiences at Potsdam that the present Government of Russia could not be expected to permit other smaller states a free choice of their own forms of government. Confirmation of this conviction by incidents in the year that has elapsed brought him to a decision to make clear to the people of the United States the difference between the philosophy of democracy and Communism."

21. Jones, *Fifteen Days,* 155. Clifford says that Kennan "wandered into the drafting process" from his position at the War College and found "a global policy that he felt was all out of proportion to the situation." See Clifford with Holbrooke, *Counsel to the President,* 134.

22. Kennan, *Memoirs,* 315–17. Considering that Kennan and most realists dismiss the domino theory when applied to Communist domination, here it seems ironic that Kennan would accept a domino theory attached to liberal democracy's influence. Also see "Comments on the National Security Problem," 3/28/47, File 28, Writings and Publications, 1938–1947, Box 16, George F. Kennan Papers (hereafter, GFKP), Seeley G. Mudd Library (hereafter, SGML), Princeton University (hereafter, PU). As Kennan said of Turkey: "Turkey's present position, while indeed an exposed one, is fundamentally different from that of Greece. Turkey is indeed in the situation of one who has nothing to fear but fear—for the moment." If the Turks "keep their nerves and their confidence," he added, there would be no serious Soviet penetration.

23. Lane, *I Saw Poland Betrayed,* 205; Weekly Summary Excerpt, January 3, 1947, "The Polish Election," 95–96, and Weekly Summary Excerpt, January 17, 1947, "Communist-Instigated Purge in Hungary," 99–100, both in Kuhns, *Assessing the Soviet Threat.*

24. Truman, *Years of Trial and Hope,* 96–98, 101.

25. "Truman's Special Message to the Congress on Greece and Turkey," March 12, 1947, in Truman, *Public Papers,* vol. 3, 176–80.

26. Ibid.

27. Ibid. Although he again did not appreciate fully the connection, Truman's founding of American postwar foreign policy followed consistently from America's founding.

28. Ibid.

29. Ibid. Also see Truman, *Years of Trial and Hope,* 105.

30. "Truman's Special Message to the Congress on Greece and Turkey."

31. Ibid.

32. For more on this background, including Truman's March 6, 1947, speech at Baylor University, see chapter 4 in this volume.

33. He failed to note that another reason for a smaller and more imperiled earth lay in the fact that ideological tyranny—such as National Socialism in the 1930s and during World War II and communism in the twentieth century—reached deeper and wider than ever before.

34. "Truman's Address at the Jefferson Day Dinner," April 5, 1947, in Truman, *Public Papers,* vol. 3, 192–96.

35. Ibid.

36. March 12, 1947, Wallace telegram to Truman, White House Messages, Traffic, 1947, Classified File, Box 3, Robert L. Dennison Papers, HSTL.

37. Wallace, NBC radio address of March 13, 1947, reprinted in appendix to U.S. Congress, *Congressional Record,* vol. 93, 80th Congress, 1st Session, pp. A1328–29. Also see Richard J. Walton, *Henry Wallace, Harry Truman, and the Cold War* (New York: Viking Press, 1976), 145–48.

38. Lippmann, *Cold War,* 58, 54.

39. Lippmann to Robert Waldo Ruhl, June 17, 1947, in Walter Lippman, *Public Philosopher: Selected Letters of Walter Lippmann,* ed. John Morton Blum (New York: Ticknor and Fields, 1985), 496.

40. McCullough, *Truman,* especially 582–83.

41. "Remarks at a Meeting with the American Society of Newspaper Editors," April 17, 1947, in Truman, *Public Papers,* vol. 3, 207–10. In taped interviews in 1959 with his close friend and literary agent, William Hillman, and his old speechwriter, David Noyes, Truman stressed that the proximate cause of the Cold War was that the Soviets would not keep their agreements, especially from Yalta. He said what he learned from Potsdam made him realize that "the only way you can get [the Soviets] to keep their agreements is to be stronger than they are." See Harry S. Truman, *Talking with Harry: Candid Conversations with President Harry S. Truman,* ed. Ralph E. Weber (Wilmington, Del.: Scholarly Resources, 2001), 68, 268.

42. "The President's Special Conference with the Association of Radio News Analysts," May 13, 1947, in Truman, *Public Papers,* vol. 3, 238–41.

43. Eleanor Roosevelt to Truman, April 17, 1947, and Truman to Mrs. Roosevelt, May 7, 1947, Correspondence between President Truman and Eleanor Roosevelt, April/May 1947, The Truman Doctrine, Documents, TPML, http://www.trumanlibrary.org/whistlestop/study_collections/doctrine/large/documents/index.php?documentdate=0000-00-00&documentid=54&studycollectionid=NATO&pagenumber=1. For more on Eleanor Roosevelt's position on the Truman Doctrine and her relationship with President Truman, see Mary Ann Glendon, *A World Made New: Eleanor Roosevelt and the Universal Declaration of Human Rights* (New York: Random House, 2001), especially 21–25, 54–55, 105–6.

44. From 220-misc, 1945, 1946, and 1947, Official File, Box 824, HSTP, HSTL. Note that the correspondence with Buck preceded Truman's reception of the Clifford-Elsey memo.

45. An important corollary to this point is that Truman maintained a healthy respect for international law, especially as a tool to be justly applied in world politics, but he recognized that the Soviet Union aimed to subvert international law; in Wilsonianism, by contrast, international law was a creed, rather than a tool, and Wilson seemed to claim that international law extrapolated from and applied the Declaration of Independence to the world community.

46. Undated Campaign Strategy Speech Data, Box 60, PSF, HSTP, HSTL. Like

the critics of Truman in the 1940s, corporatists, in particular, emphasize that Truman saw a moderation in Soviet behavior in 1947 in order to criticize the president for immoderation in the Truman Doctrine and subsequent actions of containment.

47. Lippmann, for example, thought that Truman was neither a sound nor an articulate thinker, neither an effective leader nor an administrator. See Lippmann, *Public Philosopher,* 490–91. Lippmann wrote to John J. McCloy on November 14, 1946: "The situation where Byrnes is away from Washington all the time, being his own negotiator, is very bad indeed. With Truman what he is, there is simply no one to take a general view of our interests and our policy. That's why the policies we have are made in bits and pieces—now in one department, now in another; now in one bureau, now in another. Since Truman can't conduct foreign affairs as Roosevelt did, or Wilson, Byrnes is the only man who can perform that function, but since he is his own negotiator for the details, he just can't perform the function and there is, therefore, a terrible vacuum at the central point where policies must be made."

48. One can argue that Soviet aggression and Truman's March 12 speech moved public opinion. In April 1947, just after the Truman Doctrine speech, 58 percent of Americans in a NORC survey said the United States should "stop any attempt by Russia to control the countries near her in Europe and Asia," up from 51 percent in October 1946. See Benjamin I. Page and Robert Y. Shapiro, *The Rational Public: Fifty Years of Trends in Americans' Policy Preferences* (Chicago: University of Chicago Press, 1992), 201, 200.

4. The Politics of the Marshall Plan

1. For an insightful treatment of Truman's abilities, see Gregory A. Fossedal, *Our Finest Hour: Will Clayton, the Marshall Plan, and the Triumph of Democracy* (Stanford, Calif.: Hoover Institution Press, 1993), 291–94.

2. The Department of Defense was created in July 1947 as part of the National Security Act. Forrestal officially became secretary of defense in September 1947.

3. Townsend Hoopes and Douglas Brinkley, *Driven Patriot: The Life and Times of James Forrestal* (New York: Alfred A. Knopf, 1992), 437. Louis Johnson had been campaigning aggressively to be Forrestal's replacement, even helping columnist Drew Pearson discredit the secretary of defense. Truman not only respected Forrestal and his abilities but also disliked Johnson's tactics, no matter how qualified he was for the job. In Walter Isaacson and Evan Thomas, *The Wise Men: Six Friends and the World They Made* (New York: Simon and Schuster, 1986), the authors depict a Truman with less liking and sympathy for Forrestal. On balance, Hoopes and Brinkley's account seems more convincing.

4. In an off-the-record interview in March 1947, "Marshall deplored the emotional anti-Russian attitude in the country and kept emphasizing the necessity to talk and write about Europe in terms of economics instead of ideologies." See Marshall, George C.—Interview: Memo by James B. Reston, March 1947, Box 1, Works: Memoranda, Arthur Krock Papers, SGML, PU.

5. See John Lamberton Harper, *American Visions of Europe: Franklin D.*

Roosevelt, George F. Kennan, and Dean G. Acheson (New York: Cambridge University Press, 1994), 267–68.

6. Nitze, *From Hiroshima to Glasnost,* 78.

7. Acheson, *Present at the Creation,* 219. Biographer David McLellan offers a useful comparison of the words used by Acheson to describe Soviet behavior between August 1945 and January 1947 versus those he used between January 1947 and January 1949. In the latter period, Acheson used much harsher language. See David S. McLellan, *Dean Acheson: The State Department Years* (New York: Dodd, Mead, 1976), 144.

8. For elaboration of Acheson's realpolitik, see James Chace, *Acheson: The Secretary of State Who Created the American World* (New York: Simon and Schuster, 1998).

9. Under Byrnes, who was abroad for 350 of his 562 days as secretary of state, Acheson often served as acting secretary of state. Under Marshall, who became secretary on January 20, 1947, Acheson was put in charge of working with the president on U.S. policies in the Near East. See Bruce R. Kuniholm, "Loy Henderson, Dean Acheson, and the Origins of the Truman Doctrine," in Douglas Brinkley, ed., *Dean Acheson and the Making of U.S. Foreign Policy* (New York: St. Martin's Press, 1993), 73–108.

10. Acheson, *Present at the Creation,* 219–24. Acheson's memoir, although magisterial and considered definitive by many, sometimes rewrites events and people's roles in those events. Although writing in a seemingly self-effacing manner, Acheson makes it clear that his intervention was crucial on many occasions. Especially when he recounts policies and episodes having to do with containment and the Cold War, he presents a realist rather than a prudential perspective. He suggests that Truman did not understand the true circumstances, which Acheson sees through a realist lens.

11. For an insightful analysis of the relationship between Truman and Acheson, see McLellan, *Dean Acheson,* especially 5, 28, 410–11.

12. Arthur R. Wilson, major general (ret.), to Senator Harley M. Kilgore, September 16, 1955, copy enclosed in Wilson to Marshall, September 22, 1955, Folder 1, Box 241, George C. Marshall Papers (hereafter, GCMP), GCML.

13. Presidential Appointments File, Daily Sheets, 1947 February 17–18, HSTP, HSTL.

14. Marshall was consistent. In March 1948, he declined to attend a lunch with members of the Democratic National Committee and the cabinet until Truman explained that he wanted the secretary present in order to describe the world situation; and toward the end of his tenure, Marshall continued to distinguish sharply between State Department duties and what he termed the "political considerations" of the White House. See March 11, 1948, letter to Katherine Tupper Marshall, Folder 134/23, Marshall, George C., and Katherine Tupper, and August 31, 1948, confidential memo to Robert Lovett, Folder 134/9, Lovett, Robert A., General, Life-Michael, both in Box 134, Secretary of State, 1947–1949, GCMP, GCML.

15. Leahy, Diary, January 21, 1947, LOC.

16. Robert H. Ferrell, *George C. Marshall as Secretary of State, 1947–1949,* vol. 15 in American Secretaries of State and Their Diplomacy (New York: Cooper Square,

1966), 72–73. Marshall's recollections are from a November 1950 conversation in the Pentagon.

17. Bohlen, *Transformation of American Foreign Policy,* 88. In a more realist manner, Bohlen offers a similar description in *Witness to History,* 262–63.

18. "Radio Address on Returning from Moscow Conference," April 28, 1947 (reading copy), Folder 12, Speeches and Statements, Marshall, 1947 January–1948 February, Box 157, Secretary of State, 1947–1949, GCMP, GCML. While Marshall identified Germany as the crux of the problem, the Soviet pressure on Austria seems to have been the point at which his full understanding of Soviet ambitions crystallized. In addition to praising Vandenberg and Connally, Marshall also singled out the help of John Foster Dulles.

19. "The President's Special Conference with the Association of Radio News Analysts," May 13, 1947, in Truman, *Public Papers,* vol. 3, 238–41.

20. "Statement by the President upon Signing Bill Endorsing the Truman Doctrine," May 22, 1947, in Truman, *Public Papers,* vol. 3, 254–55.

21. "The President's News Conference of June 5, 1947," in Truman, *Public Papers,* vol. 3, 262–66.

22. Stefan T. Possony, *A Century of Conflict: Communist Techniques of World Revolution* (Chicago: Henry Regnery, 1953), 288–89. Weekly Summary Excerpt, May 2, 1947, "Soviet Strategy in the CFM," 110; Weekly Summary Excerpt, May 9, 1947, "Indications of Changed Emphasis in Communist Strategy," 111–12; and Weekly Summary Excerpt, June 20, 1947, "Apparent Soviet Plans in Eastern Europe and Further Communist Moves in Hungary," 113–14—all in Kuhns, *Assessing the Soviet Threat.* Additional information can be found in Karel Bartosek, "Central and Southeastern Europe," in Stéphane Courtois, Nicolas Werth, Jean-Louis Panné, Andrzej Paczkowski, Karel Bartosek, and Jean-Louis Margolin, *The Black Book of Communism: Crimes, Terror, Repression,* ed. Mark Kramer, trans. Jonathan Murphy (Cambridge, Mass.: Harvard University Press, 1999), 399–400. Also see Eduard Mark, "Revolution by Degrees: Stalin's National-Front Strategy for Europe, 1941–1947," Working Paper no. 31, Cold War International History Project, February 2001.

23. "The Requirements of Reconstruction," U.S. Department of State, *Department of State Bulletin,* vol. 16, no. 411 (May 18, 1947): 991–94. There was a debate later by State Department figures about the significance of the Delta address and its contribution to the Marshall Plan. In July 1948, Charles Kindleberger, chief of the Division of German and Austrian Economic Affairs in the State Department, argued: "I have had a hard time seeing how the Acheson speech at Delta, Mississippi, was the midwife to the Marshall plan"; he thought that Clayton's role was more important than Acheson's and even Kennan's. See Memorandum by Mr. Charles P. Kindleberger, Origins of the Marshall Plan, July 22, 1948, in *FRUS,* 1947, vol. 3, 241–47.

24. "Address on Foreign Economic Policy, Delivered at Baylor University," March 6, 1947, in Truman, *Public Papers,* vol. 3, 167–72.

25. Truman, *Years of Trial and Hope,* 111–12. For elaboration of Will Clayton's role in the Baylor address, press coverage of the speech, and the connection between the Baylor speech and the Truman Doctrine address, see Fossedal, *Our Finest Hour,* 212–14, 319–20.

26. As Acheson recalled in a 1958 interview, "because of the death of Bilbo and the fact Truman didn't wish to become involved in the politics of Bilbo's successor, Truman sent me to make this speech. I discussed with him making a speech to draw attention to the bad fix we were in—that is, the free world, with western Europe about to go under." See Dean Acheson interview by Mrs. Ellen Garwood, Washington, D.C., November 2, 1958, Marshall Plan Project File, Box 1, Ellen Clayton Garwood Papers, HSTL.

27. "Requirements of Reconstruction," 991–94.

28. See George C. Marshall, *George C. Marshall Interviews and Reminiscences for Forrest C. Pogue*, ed. Larry I. Bland (Lexington, Va.: George C. Marshall Research Foundation, 1991), 559. As Marshall recalled, "There were only three or four people that were aware of what I was going to do—I think, two, possible [*sic*] three in the State Department and the president. No one else, because I knew if it got out and got into a debate in Congress beforehand, we would never make the move." For an alternative view, which suggests that the Marshall Plan came about after Marshall's reaction to Stalin in Moscow in spring 1947 and that Truman was essentially out of the loop, see Forrest C. Pogue, *George C. Marshall: Statesman, 1945–1959* (New York: Penguin Books, 1989), 210–11. Because of the secrecy, some have argued that Truman and Marshall did not understand the importance of the Harvard speech. Bohlen argued that nothing could be further from the truth and that Marshall thought the entire success of the venture depended on a European commitment to the Marshall Plan before any adverse publicity in the United States could taint the intentions of the European Recovery Program. See May 29, 1959, Charles E. Bohlen letter to Mrs. Ellen Clayton Garwood, Correspondence of W. L. Clayton and Mrs. Ellen Clayton Garwood, Box 1, Garwood Papers, HSTL.

29. Again, Clayton was a factor here and in sync with Truman's thought. Much of his thought went into shaping the Marshall Plan address, even more than Kennan contributed. Clayton wrote important memoranda; see, especially, one he submitted after a trip to Europe, May 31, 1947, Clayton memorandum to Marshall and Clayton January 7, 1950, letter to Ellen Garwood (his daughter), General File, Marshall Plan Memos, 1947, Box 6, William L. Clayton Papers, HSTL.

30. "European Initiative Essential to Economic Recovery," June 5, 1947, U.S. Department of State, *Department of State Bulletin*, vol. 16, no. 415 (June 15, 1947): 1159–60. Marshall would soon benefit from the help of his new undersecretary of state, Robert Lovett, who—like Marshall—was a personal friend of Vandenberg. Lovett described the period of bipartisanship as occurring largely because of Truman's "amazing leadership" and the chairmanship of the Senate Foreign Relations by Vandenberg, "with whom I was always completely frank, under the instructions of the President. I would stop by Senator Vandenberg's apartment on the way home with a sheaf of telegrams in my hand and go over what had happened during the day with him if it was a thing in which he was interested." See Oral History Interview with Robert A. Lovett, New York, N.Y., July 7, 1971, by Theodore A. Wilson and Richard D. McKinzie, HSTL (September 1981).

31. Kennan, "Current Problems of Soviet-American Relations," U.S. Naval

Academy, Annapolis, Md., May 9, 1947, File 32, Box 16, Writings and Publications, 1938–1947, GFKP, SGML, PU.

32. Kennan to Mr. Lyon, October 13, 1947, PPS files, Box 20042, Box 6, C. Ben Wright Collection, GCML.

33. Kennan, Notes on the Marshall Plan, December 15, 1947, File 50, Box 23, Writings and Publications: Official and Semi-official Memoranda, Reports, Notes, Telegrams, 1934–February 22, 1949, GFKP, SGML, PU.

34. He did not see the deployment of U.S. military power and the Marshall Plan working in combination. Walter Lippmann to Raymond Gram Swing, November 13, 1947, and Lippmann to Henry R. Luce, November 14, 1947, both in Lippmann, *Public Philosopher,* 497–99. In 1948, Lippmann vacillated between preferring an independent Europe and preferring a Europe that was part of a larger Atlantic community. In this instance, he argued for a Europe without either the United States or the Soviet Union.

35. Henry A. Wallace, *Toward World Peace* (New York: Reynal and Hitchcock, 1948), 36.

36. June 22, 1947, Byrnes to Marshall, Folder 129/18, Byrnes-Byus, Correspondence, Box 129, Secretary of State, 1947–1948, Correspondence, GCMP, GCML. Unless sanitized from the files, there was no response from Marshall, although, by August 1948, he invited Byrnes to be one of four men accompanying him to Paris for the fall Council of Foreign Ministers' meeting.

37. Truman, *Years of Trial and Hope,* 119. In understanding the interrelatedness of politics and economics, with politics as the primary partner in the relationship, and in applying that insight to the Truman Doctrine and the Marshall Plan, the president continued to construct a new liberal internationalism that fundamentally differed from that of Wilson and FDR. In his Baylor University address, for instance, he refused to separate the ideal of permanent peace from the reality of freedom and reiterated that freedom was the ground upon which peace would occur. Rather than an international organization or multilateralism in the Wilsonian sense, Truman knew that the European Recovery Program would demand American unilateralism and European cooperation at the same time.

38. "European Initiative Essential to Economic Recovery," 1159–60.

39. "Address on Foreign Economic Policy, Delivered at Baylor University," March 6, 1947, in Truman, *Public Papers,* vol. 3, 167–72.

40. This political interpretation is from Soviet Ambassador to the United States Nikolai V. Novikov's June 24 telegram to Molotov: "In this context, the main goals of U.S. foreign policy, the essence of the 'Truman doctrine,'—to check the process of democratization in European countries, to stimulate forces hostile to the Soviet Union and to create conditions for the buttressing of the positions of American capital in Europe and Asia—remain without any substantial changes. A thorough analysis of the 'Marshall Plan' shows that, in the final analysis, it is directed toward the establishment of a West European bloc as an instrument of American policy. . . . Thus, instead of the haphazard actions of the past, which were aimed at economic and political subjugation of European countries to American capital and to the establishment

of anti-Soviet groupings, the 'Marshall Plan' envisages a wider-scale action, designed to solve the problem more effectively." See Scott D. Parrish and Mikhail M. Narinsky, "New Evidence on the Soviet Rejection of the Marshall Plan, 1947: Two Reports," Working Paper no. 9, Cold War International History Project, March 1994, 43. The same day, June 24, Soviet economist Yevgeny Varga presented a report to Molotov with the economic take on the Marshall Plan: "The US economic position was of decisive importance in proposing the Marshall Plan. The Marshall Plan was meant primarily to be instrumental in resolving the imminent economic crisis, the approach of which no one in the USA denies. Thus, the USA, in its own interests, *must grant much greater credits than it has done heretofore—just to rid itself of surplus goods at home,* even it if knows in advance that part of those credits will never be repaid. . . . In this context, the Marshall Plan's aim was this: If it is necessary for the USA, in its own interests, to send abroad American goods worth billions of dollars on credit to unreliable donors, then it is necessary to try to squeeze the maximum political advantages from this." Ibid., 42–43.

41. Daily Summary Excerpt, July 18, 1947, "USSR: Soviet Reaction to Marshall Proposals," in Kuhns, *Assessing the Soviet Threat,* 122–23.

42. Weekly Summary Excerpt, June 20, 1947, "Apparent Soviet Plans in Eastern Europe and Further Communist Moves in Hungary," 113–14; Weekly Summary Excerpt, July 11, 1947, "Soviet Opposition to the Recovery Program and Effects of Non-Participation on the Satellites," 117–21; Weekly Summary Excerpt, July 25, 1947, "Strategy of Soviet Delay in Treaty Ratification," 124–26—all in Kuhns, *Assessing the Soviet Threat.* See also Bartosek, "Central and Southeastern Europe," in Courtois et al., *Black Book of Communism,* 398–402.

43. For translation of the pertinent proceedings from the May 1946 Meeting of the Central Committee of the Hungarian Communist Party, see Csaba Bekes, "Soviet Plans to Establish the COMINFORM in Early 1946: New Evidence from the Hungarian Archives," in Cold War International History Project *Bulletin,* no. 10 (March 1998): 135–36. In May and June 1946, Stalin also discussed the Cominform setup with Tito. For additional treatment of the connection between the Cominform and the Comintern, see Bartosek, "Central and Southeastern Europe," in Courtois et al., *Black Book of Communism,* 437–38.

44. Mark, "Revolution by Degrees," 6–7.

45. Special Evaluation no. 21, October 13, 1947, "Implications of the New Communist Information Bureau," in Kuhns, *Assessing the Soviet Threat,* 141–44, which quoted the Cominform's long-range objectives "to expand the organization to cover the European continent and eventually to set up similar organizations in other areas," and to do so "by expelling the non-cooperating Socialists and misguided fellow-travellers from the 'Democratic' ranks, to prepare a hard nucleus of ideologically sound Communists, capable of direct action and of reversion to underground methods if such procedure becomes necessary."

46. This Moscow peace movement grew out of Stalin's anti-Western campaign before and after Churchill's Fulton address in March 1946, as well as from the Cominform and Zhdanovschina.

47. The Cominform and Zhdanovschina outlived Zhdanov himself. But in September 1947, Zhdanov referred to "America's aspirations to world supremacy" and stated that "the new expansionist and reactionary policy of the United States envisages a struggle against the U.S.S.R., against the labour movement in all countries, including the United States, and against the emancipationist, anti-imperialist forces in all countries." Reinforcing Stalin's 1946 election address, Zhdanov added, "The frank expansionist program of the United States is therefore highly reminiscent of the reckless program, which failed so ignominiously, of the fascist aggressors, who, as we know, also made a bid for world supremacy." After asserting America's "plans for the enslavement of Europe" and "unbridled expansion of American imperialism," he attacked the "aggressive character" of the Truman Doctrine as "American assistance to all reactionary regimes which actively oppose the democratic peoples," as well as the Marshall Plan as "a scheme to create a bloc of states bound by obligations to the United States, and to grant American credits to European countries as a recompense for their renunciation of economic, and then of political, independence." See Andrei Zhdanov, Report on the International Situation at the Founding Conference of the Communist Information Bureau in Poland, September 1947, excerpted in Robert V. Daniels, ed., *A Documentary History of Communism,* vol. 2 (New York: Vintage Books, 1960), 155–60. For more on Zhdanov, see Parrish and Narinsky, "New Evidence on the Soviet Rejection," especially 35–39. For elaboration of the Cominform's efforts as they pertained to the European Recovery Program and to agitation of a third political party in the United States, see Harvey Klehr, John Earl Haynes, and Kyrill M. Anderson, *The Soviet World of American Communism* (New Haven, Conn.: Yale University Press, 1998), 261.

48. Lippmann to Henry R. Luce, November 14, 1947, in Lippmann, *Public Philosopher,* 498–99.

49. "The President's Special Conference with Editors of Business and Trade Papers," September 30, 1947, in Truman, *Public Papers,* vol. 3, 450.

50. Public perception of the Soviet Union had been deteriorating in the United States throughout 1947, with only 18 percent in a NORC survey in late 1947 saying that the Kremlin could be counted on to "meet us halfway" in working out problems together. See Page and Shapiro, *Rational Public,* 199–200.

51. "Special Message to the Congress on the First Day of the Special Session," November 17, 1947, in Truman, *Public Papers,* vol. 3, 492–98.

52. The Foreign Aid (Interim Aid) Act of 1947 was approved by Congress on December 17, 1947.

53. "Truman's Special Message to the Congress on the Marshall Plan," December 19, 1947, in Truman, *Public Papers,* vol. 3, 515–29. For further evidence that Marshall supplemented rather than supplanted or softened Truman's understanding of the ERP, civilization, political and economic freedom, and individual rights, see Report by George C. Marshall, Secretary of State, "The London Meeting of the Council of Foreign Ministers: November 25–December 15, 1947," U.S. Department of State, *Department of State Bulletin,* vol. 17, no. 443 (December 28, 1947): 1244–47, and "Soviet Disagreement on Fundamental Principles for Germany," December

15, 1947, ibid., 1247–49. Truman referred to and endorsed Marshall's statement, as well as the breakup of the London Conference, in a December 18 news conference.

54. In this regard (and also with respect to blacks), Truman was atypical of much of his generation and much of his elders' generation of midwesterners. While he abided by Bess's mother's wishes until her death about who should and should not enter her house, he socialized and worked with people of all religions and races. A Catholic and longtime advisor to Truman—including appointments secretary throughout the administration—Matthew Connelly said that Truman had no religious bigotry. See Oral History Interview with Matthew J. Connelly, New York, N.Y., 11/28 and 11/30/67 and 8/21/68 by Jerry N. Hess, HSTL (May 1969).

55. Truman's quote from the *Congressional Record* is cited in Michael T. Benson, *Harry S. Truman and the Founding of Israel* (Westport, Conn.: Praeger, 1997), 55.

56. Quote is from Truman's speech to United Rally, Chicago, April 14, 1943, cited in Hamby, *Man of the People,* 269 (where Hamby also describes the rest of Truman's commitment during his senatorial years).

57. See Clifford with Holbrooke, *Counsel to the President,* 8.

58. Clifford cited in Benson, *Harry S. Truman and the Founding of Israel,* 54.

59. Truman identified several of his favorite passages in the Bible for William Hillman, *Mr. President: The First Publication from the Personal Diaries, Private Letters, Papers and Revealing Interviews of Harry S. Truman* (New York: Farrar, Straus and Young, 1952), 105.

60. When Truman approved the papers for de jure recognition of Israel and Transjordan, he asked for twenty-four hours' notice, if possible, of the date and hour proposed for recognition because he was anxious to have a close friend of his from Kansas City with him when he made the announcement. This friend seems to have been Jewish and was perhaps Jacobson. See January 27, 1949, Acheson meeting with Truman, Memoranda of Conversations, January–July 1949, Box 64, Dean Acheson Papers, HSTL.

61. "Statement by the President Following the Adjournment of the Palestine Conference in London," October 4, 1946, 442–44, and "Message to the King of Saudi Arabia Concerning Palestine," October 28, 1946, in Truman, *Public Papers,* vol. 4, 467–69.

62. Truman to Mary Jane Truman, March 21, 1948, Letters to Mrs. John A. Truman and Sister Mary Jane Truman—January 25, 1946–November 7, 1948, Box 47, Post-Presidential Files, HSTP, HSTL.

63. Truman, longhand notes, March 21, 1948, reprinted in Truman, *Off the Record,* 127.

64. Clifford with Holbrooke, *Counsel to the President,* 13–14. For the rest of Clifford's retelling of Truman's commitment to Palestine and to the founding of Israel, as well as the infighting at home and disputes abroad, see pages 4–15 and 18–25.

65. Truman expressed this opinion as early as June 1945. He was against sectarianism and division and did not believe that God picked favorites among "race, creed or color." See Truman, June 1, 1945, Longhand Notes File, 1945–1952, Box 333, PSF, HSTP, HSTL.

66. Truman quoted his own May 1947 note to Niles in Truman, *Years of Trial and Hope,* 157.

67. Letter from President Truman to Eddie Jacobson, February 27, 1948, The Recognition of the State of Israel, Documents, TPML, available from http://www.trumanlibrary.org/whistlestop/study_collections/israel/large/docs.php

68. The coup should be seen in the context of a long-term Soviet campaign against America and the Marshall Plan, with such slogans as "Marshall aid means martial aid," which was a favorite of Henry Wallace, among others.

69. "Non-Communist" refers to the Democratic, Social Democratic, and Socialist parties.

70. For these and other details, see U.S. Congress, House Committee on Foreign Affairs, *The Strategy and Tactics of World Communism, Supplement III: The Coup d'Etat in Prague,* 81st Congress, 1st session (Washington, D.C.: U.S. Government Printing Office, 1949). See also Daily Summary Excerpt, December 23, 1947, "Czechoslovakia: Communist Drive Expected in January," 162–63; Weekly Summary Excerpt, January 30, 1948, "Soviet Policy in Eastern Europe," 168–69; Daily Summary Excerpt, February 19, 1948: "Communists May Precipitate Crisis," 171; Daily Summary Excerpt, February 24, 1948, "Czechoslovakia: Estimate of Political Crisis," 173; Weekly Summary Excerpt, February 27, 1948, "Communist Coup in Czechoslovakia," 174–75—all in Kuhns, *Assessing the Soviet Threat.* And see Bartosek, "Central and Southeastern Europe," in Courtois et al., *Black Book of Communism,* 403–7.

71. See March 21, 1948, Truman letter to Mary Jane Truman, Box 47, Letters to Mrs. John A. Truman and Sister Mary Jane Truman, January 25, 1946–November 7, 1948, Post-Presidential Files, HSTP, HSTL. As Truman wrote: "I had to appear before the Congress on Wednesday and state the Russian case. I had been thinking and working on it for six months or more. I had discussed it with all the members of the Cabinet and many others. As usual, the State Department balked. They tried by every means at their command to upset my plans."

72. The American people were in agreement with Truman and perhaps ahead of Congress. The percentage of the American public who thought that the United States was being "too soft" on the USSR reached a very high level of 84 percent in a Gallup poll of March 1948; only 3 percent felt that the United States was being "too tough." The response to a NORC question about whether the United States should "be firmer" or compromise with the Soviet Union reached 68 percent for firmer policies in April 1948. See Page and Shapiro, *Rational Public,* 200–201. Many of the polls broke down participants by their education and income levels. In the mid- to late 1940s, there was large agreement about the USSR, irrespective of the amount of education. Having said that, it is interesting to note that highly educated Americans arrived later at a firmer opinion against the Soviets than less educated Americans did. See Cantril and Strunk, *Public Opinion 1945–1946,* and Page and Shapiro, *Rational Public,* 201–5.

73. See Kennan, Notes for Seminar at Princeton University (handwritten), January 23–26, 1949, File 20, Box 17, Writing and Publications, Drafts and Reproductions of Articles, Speeches, and Lectures, Unpublished, 1948–1949, GFKP, SGML, PU. Although he psychologized Western reaction to communism, Kennan said that the

sublimated fear should be recognized as a "real phenomenon." It is interesting to note that a modern revisionist account of 1948 accords with Kennan's realist depiction. See Frank Kofsky, *Harry S. Truman and the War Scare of 1948: A Successful Campaign to Deceive the Nation* (New York: St. Martin's Press, 1993), 268. The title almost speaks for itself. Kofsky not only called the whole year of 1948 a "war scare" but also said Truman's legacy was to "mire the United States inextricably in a perpetual arms race and a permanent war economy." The author concluded that in doing so, Truman deceived the public and Congress about the intentions of the USSR and the likelihood of war, rebuffed Soviet efforts to reach accommodation, escalated the arms race, and rescued a failing aircraft industry under the guise of enhancing the nation's defenses. Apart from agreeing with Kennan on this point, Kofsky has mixed revisionism and corporatism, thanking, among others, Melvyn Leffler, Thomas McCormick, William Pemberton, and Walter LaFeber.

74. "Truman's Special Message to the Congress on the Threat to the Freedom of Europe," March 17, 1948, in Truman, *Public Papers*, vol. 4, 182–86. Although this speech did not have a formal name like the Truman Doctrine or the Marshall Plan, it was perceived as a major and pivotal policy statement by the president's advisors—much to their displeasure. Two Policy Planning Staff meetings were devoted to discussion of implementing Truman's words. At the first meeting, Acheson, in particular, spoke about how the United States "will, by appropriate means, extend to the free nations the support which the situation requires." See 144th meeting, March 25, 1948, Box 5, Folder 10, Policy Planning Staff Material, Minutes of Meetings, 1948, C. Ben Wright Kennan Biography Project, GCML.

75. When asked about the lessons of Plutarch's *Lives*, which Truman had read many times for insights, Truman responded, "But about Plutarch. It was the same with those old birds in Greece and Rome as it is now. I told you. The only thing new in the world is the history you don't know." See Merle Miller, *Plain Speaking: An Oral Biography of Harry S. Truman* (New York: G. P. Putnam's Sons, 1974), 70. Speech quotes are taken from "Truman's St. Patrick's Day Address in New York City," March 17, 1948, in Truman, *Public Papers*, vol. 4, 186–90.

76. See Letters to Mrs. John A. Truman and Sister Mary Jane Truman, January 25, 1946–November 7, 1948, Box 47, Post-Presidential Files, HSTP, HSTL.

77. "Truman's St. Patrick's Day Address in New York City," March 17, 1948, in Truman, *Public Papers*, vol. 4, 186–90.

5. Kennan's Sources of Soviet Conduct

1. Kennan began to voice these concerns in a Policy Planning Staff paper that he drafted in November and December 1949 and submitted to Acheson on January 29, 1950, as a seventy-nine-page personal paper on the subject of the international control of atomic energy. See *FRUS*, 1950, vol. 1, 22–44.

2. "Measures Short of War (Diplomatic)," September 16, 1945, National War College, File 12, Writings and Publications, 1938–1947, Box 16, GFKP, PU. In the psychological field, Kennan placed propaganda, radio, magazines, and the psycho-

logical effects of anything a modern state does in war; of economics, he said that it would work over time on a totalitarian state and its satellites; and of the third category, he described "political" in the sense of "cultivation of solidarity with like minded nations on every given issue of foreign policy." (In this last regard, he said, "I am very much impressed with the usefulness of the United Nations to us and our principles in the world; the advantages which are to be gained for us in working through it.")

3. "Comments on the General Trend of U.S. Foreign Policy," August 20, 1948, File 54, Writings and Publications: Official and Semi-official Memoranda, Reports, Notes, Dispatches, Summaries, Drafts, Remarks, Comments, Telegrams, 1934–February 22, 1949, Box 23, GFKP, PU.

4. Kennan, *Memoirs,* 119. Here and in the preceding pages, Kennan excerpts at length from an early 1940 paper that he wrote.

5. The latter is from Kennan's October 3, 1946, letter to military historian Edward Mead Earle, in which he wrote of columnist Joseph Alsop: "Allsop [*sic*] is a good writer, and has recently dealt some lusty blows at the more hypocritical aspects of left-wing thought on Russian relations." He continued, "I have the impression, however, that he takes somewhat too dramatic and tragic a view of the situation." See File 7, Correspondence: With Persons in Alphabetical Order of 1939–1949, Box 28, GFKP, SGML, PU.

6. Quote is from Kennan, "Russia—Seven Years Later," September 1944, 521, reprinted in Kennan, *Memoirs,* as Appendix A, 504–31. Kennan's pride in the paper is from Kennan, *Memoirs,* 225. As Kennan also explained on page 225, in "Russia—Seven Years Later," "I poured forth, as in nothing else I ever wrote, the essence of what I knew about Russia generally, and Stalin's Russia in particular, as a phenomenon on the horizon of American policy makers," and "it laid out my interpretation of the evolution of Soviet foreign policy over the years of the Stalin era, assessed the situation in which the Soviet leaders found themselves at the time, and forecast in general terms the lines of their reaction and behavior in the immediate postwar period."

7. Kennan, *Memoirs,* 130. Kennan had a sense of impending tragedy, as well as an almost passive resistance to the inevitable occurrences of tyranny. See George F. Kennan, *From Prague after Munich: Diplomatic Papers, 1938–1940* (Princeton, N.J.: Princeton University Press, 1968), 85–86: Kennan recorded that, on the day of the final Nazi occupation of Prague, five people—two Czech spies who had been in Germany, two German Social Democrats who were fugitives from the Reich, and a Jewish acquaintance—came to him at the American legation seeking help. After a day of skiing and an evening at the opera in March 1939, he was awakened and called to the legation. "A Jewish acquaintance came," Kennan wrote. "We told him that he was welcome to stay around there until he could calm his nerves. He paced wretchedly up and down in the anteroom, through the long morning hours. In the afternoon, he decided to face the music and went home." Kennan then recounted the incident of another "Jewish acquaintance who had worked for many years for American interests," who sought refuge in his house. Kennan would not grant him asylum, although he and his wife allowed the man to stay until the authorities demanded him. When

the man said he had not ruled out suicide, Kennan said that he and his wife pleaded with him "not to choose this way out, not because she or I had any great optimism with respect to his chances for future happiness but partly on general Anglo-Saxon principles and partly to preserve our home from this sort of an unpleasantness."

8. Kennan paper, "'Trust' as a Factor in International Relations," Yale Institute of International Affairs, October 1, 1946, File 15, Writings and Publications, 1938–1947, Box 16, GFKP, SGML, PU.

9. Kennan as discussion leader, "The Soviet Way of Thought and Its Effect on Soviet Foreign Policy," January 7, 1947, Council on Foreign Relations, File 20, Writings and Publications, 1938–1947, Box 16, GFKP, SGML, PU. Hamilton Fish Armstrong, editor of *Foreign Affairs,* the CFR's journal, asked if Kennan could work his remarks from this discussion into an article for publication.

10. Kennan, remarks, January 28, 1947, American Press Institute, Graduate School of Journalism, Columbia University, File 23, Writings and Publications, 1938–1947, Box 16, GFKP, SGML, PU.

11. Kennan, undated speech to Admiral Hill, Ladies, and Gentlemen (in same folder as a University of Virginia lecture of February 20, 1947), File 25, and Kennan as discussion leader, "The Soviet Way of Thought and Its Effect on Soviet Foreign Policy," January 7, 1947, File 20, Writings and Publications, 1938–1947, both in Box 16, GFKP, SGML, PU.

12. Kennan seems to suggest here that Moscow either did not or could not in the future direct world communism. The full passage on communism and progress, written in longhand by Kennan, reads: "The failure to distinguish what is indeed progressive social doctrine from the rivalry of a foreign political machine which has appropriated and abused the slogans of socialism. I am far from being a communist; but I recognize in the theory of Soviet communism: in the *theory,* mark you—not the practise [*sic*]—certain elements which I think are probably really the ideas of the future. I hate to see us here reject the good with the bad—throw out the baby with the bath, as they say in Europe—and place ourselves in that way on the wrong side of history." See undated speech to Admiral Hill, Ladies, and Gentlemen (in same folder as a University of Virginia lecture of February 20, 1947), File 25, Writings and Publications, Box 16, 1938–1947, GFKP, SGML, PU.

13. Since Kennan was in government when the X article would appear, and the article itself was a late January 1947 paper that he had written for Forrestal—which, in turn, came in part from Kennan's informal early January 1947 remarks to the Council on Foreign Relations—he did not want his name on the final piece in *Foreign Affairs.* When Kennan asked if anonymity was acceptable, *Foreign Affairs* editor Hamilton Fish Armstrong responded that "the interest of the projected article more than outweighs from our point of view the disadvantage of anonymity." See Armstrong letter to Kennan, March 7, 1947, File, 1947, Correspondence: With Persons in Alphabetical Order of 1939–1949, Box 28, GFKP, SGML, PU. In March 1947, Armstrong added that Kennan should go ahead and put his memo (to Forrestal, it seems) and his talk to the CFR into article form.

14. For substantiation that the X article had more influence on the academic and

professional levels of the American public, see Joseph Barber, ed., *The Containment of Soviet Expansion: A Report on the Views of Leading Citizens in Twenty-Four Cities* (New York: Council on Foreign Relations, 1951). Even at this relatively early date of 1951, Kennan's version of containment was not accepted in full.

15. At that time, "counterforce" did not carry the nuclear meaning that it did later.

16. Kennan himself saw "no inconsistency between the views I held in 1945 and those that I put forward in later years"; see Kennan to Lukacs, April 28, 1995, in George F. Kennan and John Lukacs, *George F. Kennan and the Origins of Containment, 1944–1946: The Kennan-Lukacs Correspondence* (Columbia: University of Missouri Press, 1997), 72.

17. [Kennan] X, "Sources of Soviet Conduct," 566–82.

18. At times, Kennan was inconsistent on this point, contributing to the belief of various Truman officials that Kennan was saying what they already thought. Overall, however, Kennan presented Marxism as a tool to gain power rather than as an ideology embraced by those who espoused it.

19. [Kennan] X, "Sources of Soviet Conduct," 567.

20. Ibid., 568.

21. In the same vein, which can be also seen as informing the X article, Kennan said in September 1946 that the iron curtain was suspended "from the basic backwardness of Russia; from the differentness of Russia; from its close proximity to the Orient; from its love-hate complex with respect to the West; from its fear that the West will be superior and will put something over on it; and at the same time from its basic faith that they in Russia have something way down there, behind all the . . . poverty and misery, that they could teach us, too; and they don't want to lose it." See Kennan, *Memoirs,* 303, quoting from his September 17, 1946, stenographic record for the speeches he delivered around the country that summer.

22. [Kennan] X, "Sources of Soviet Conduct," 574, 571.

23. Scholars of power politics—from Arthur Schlesinger and Hans Morgenthau to current realists—have extended this point. See especially Arthur Schlesinger Jr.'s famous 1967 article ("Origins of the Cold War") as the example on this point.

24. [Kennan] X, "Sources of Soviet Conduct," 575.

25. Ibid.

26. See chapters 1 through 4 in this volume for treatment of these themes.

27. Kennan reserved these qualities for the masses and thought that they should be preserved, if not encouraged, among them. In the case of the Soviet Union, he argued, such feelings, especially of insecurity, had permeated the highest echelon, but in the United States they should only affect the people at large. If his containment prevailed, Kennan felt that the Kremlin would retain its goals of continual expansion in name alone and that it would moderate its behavior. For all of their insecurity and fanaticism, he lauded the cleverness of the Soviets. In the X article, he disdained the "whims of democratic opinion," which would fail to discern such cleverness and would act impatiently.

28. Kennan elaborates this point in earlier and later writings. For later, see, for example, Kennan, *American Diplomacy,* and George F. Kennan, *Realities of American*

Foreign Policy (Princeton, N.J.: Princeton University Press, 1954). For earlier, see, for example, Kennan's draft chapters for a book he wanted to write advocating a form of authoritarian government for America, which would free the elite from special interest and ethnic groups as well as politicians; see "The Prerequisites: Notes on Problems of the United States in 1938," Box 25, GFKP, SGML, PU, cited and described in Wilson D. Miscamble, *George F. Kennan and the Making of American Foreign Policy, 1947–1950* (Princeton, N.J.: Princeton University Press, 1992), 17.

29. Kennan quoting from his March 14 and 28, 1947, stenographic notes for lectures at the National War College, in Kennan, *Memoirs,* 319. Kennan was again consistent. In the 1990s, he referred to the "evil genius" as the "the demonic side of human nature," a "little demon companion," and the "little troublemaker"; see George F. Kennan, *Around the Cragged Hill: A Personal and Political Philosophy* (New York: W.W. Norton, 1993), 28–29.

30. Lippmann did not take credit for coining the phrase. He said he picked it up from a phrase used in Europe in the 1930s to describe Hitler's war of nerves against the French. See Ronald Steel, *Walter Lippmann and the American Century* (Boston: Little, Brown), 445.

31. Lippmann, *Cold War,* 52–54, 55, 56, 57–59. Ironically, Lippmann misconstrued the X article. He accused Kennan of overemphasizing ideology, when, as we have seen, the role of ideology was less important to Kennan than the influence of history or the oriental mind-set.

32. Ibid., 29, 16–17, 18–20.

33. Ibid., 40, 50, 56, 54. Realists and postrevisionists find fault in the Truman Doctrine, but they depict the Marshall Plan as a temperate, logical, and precise response to the problems of Europe stemming from economic devastation rather than Communist encroachment.

34. Lippmann, *Cold War,* 20–22, 24–28, 20.

35. George F. Kennan to Walter Lippmann, April 6, 1948, File 7, Writings and Publications: Drafts and Reproductions of Articles, Speeches, and Lectures, Unpublished, 1948–1949, Box 17, GFKP, SGML, PU. Curiously, Kennan wanted Lippmann to read the paper but not retain a copy of it; he also wanted to use the letter as a basis for a public article rebuttal to Lippmann. Office Memorandum, April 7, 1948, from Kennan to Charles Bohlen, and May 11, 1948, letter from Henry S. Villard to Kennan, both in File 7, Box 17, GFKP, SGML, PU.

36. Kennan to Lippmann, April 6, 1948.

37. Ibid.

38. This was the Willett report, which had made such an impression on Forrestal in early 1946. See chapter 1 in this volume for details.

39. Kennan, *Memoirs,* 354–55, 357–58.

40. Ibid., 359.

41. Ibid., 364.

42. Ibid., 356. For two other revealing reassessments by Kennan of the X article—one on its twenty-fifth anniversary—see "Interview with George F. Kennan," *Foreign Policy,* 1972, and Eric Sevareid, "Conversation with George Kennan," 1975, in

George F. Kennan, *Interviews with George F. Kennan*, ed. T. Christopher Jespersen (Jackson: University Press of Mississippi, 2002), 131–43 and 144–61.

43. Kennan, *Memoirs*, 365–66.

44. Kennan technically stayed on as counselor to the State Department until June 1950, by which time he was associated with the Institute for Advanced Study at Princeton University. His one-year sabbatical was to begin officially in summer 1950, but he was already out of the loop and somewhat piqued about it. As he told Acheson and Nitze over lunch while visiting Washington in summer 1950, "When I left the department, it never occurred to me that you two would make foreign policy without having first consulted me." See Nitze, *From Hiroshima to Glasnost*, 86. The leave of absence ended up essentially being final. After serving briefly as U.S. ambassador to the Soviet Union in 1952, Kennan was released from the Foreign Service in 1953, with the start of the Eisenhower administration and under Secretary of State John Foster Dulles.

45. Kennan, *Memoirs*, 358.

46. Ibid., 500. Kennan added that his new post at Princeton University afforded him "with greater possibilities for creative expression than any I had ever known."

47. December 5, 1955, Kennan to Ray (no last name), Correspondence, 1955–1967, Box 31, GFKP, SGML, PU.

48. The work of the first book must have helped Gaddis forge the thesis of the latter. This fidelity to Kennan is strongest in chapters 2, 3, 4, parts of 5, and the end of 6, of which Gaddis assumed chief responsibility for chapters 2 and 4 and Etzold for chapters 3, 5, and 6. See Thomas H. Etzold and John Lewis Gaddis, eds., *Containment: Documents on American Policy and Strategy, 1945–1950* (New York: Columbia University Press, 1978), x. Gaddis, *Strategies of Containment*, is considered a modern classic and is still regularly assigned in political science and history classes.

49. The only way that Truman would have signed a Policy Planning Staff paper was if it had become a National Security Council paper. And what he would have signed often did not resemble the draft paper.

50. Kennan, *Memoirs*, 335. Kennan says that the ideas inspiring PPS 1 "came from many sources; the drafting was largely my own." On page 329, he also says that the "intellectual background" to the paper came from a speech he gave at the National War College on May 6 and from Acheson's speech of May 8, but he suggests that more of the reasoning came from him than from Acheson. In his own records, he offers that he retained a copy of his speech but not any records of the PPS discussion before the final draft of PPS 1.

51. Kennan, *Memoirs*, 336.

52. For a preview of this argument, see Kennan, "Problems of U.S. Foreign Policy after Moscow," May 6, 1947, File 31, Writings and Publications, 1938–1947, Box 16, GFKP, SGML, PU. In Kennan's words: "I don't think we have to go in with financial support everywhere. If we have given that impression in advancing the Greek and Turkish program—I say 'we' because I am associated with the State Department; I have had nothing to do with that advancing—I think we have given the wrong impression. There is a great difference in the danger of Communism in

areas which are contiguous to Soviet military power and the danger of Communism in areas remote from it, as for example, in South America." He also repeated here that Turkey should not have gotten aid because it had money of its own; if money had to go to Turkey, it should be only economic aid and not for the military.

53. Etzold and Gaddis, *Containment,* 102.

54. Refer to chapter 3 in this volume for consideration of these points.

55. Etzold and Gaddis, *Containment,* 107.

56. Again, this was a Policy Planning Staff, not a National Security Council, paper. PPS 4, in Etzold and Gaddis, *Containment,* 107–14. Gaddis and Etzold obtained the paper from the records of the Policy Planning Staff held in the State Department's Foreign Affairs Documentation and Reference Center in Washington, D.C.

57. Most likely, Kennan was the principal author of this study. Three views of Kennan's direction of the staff and its writing follow. Ware Adams explained: "And when the Planning Staff, for its own purposes, needed a paper, if it was in [Kennan's] area, he would do the first draft, very often. Most of the writing for, for [*sic*] the group was done by George himself. He was a superb draftsman. And I'd say practically all of the final writing of the work of the Planning Staff was done by George himself. He, we, would our work around about [*sic*], and then come together in the conference room to put together all the information we had from our background." Charles Burton Marshall recalled: "I think Kennan used the staff more as a try out audience. He would turn [*sic*] he would write something out and then would call us together and we would promise to listen and make suggestions and that sort of things. But I think there was a good deal more of the business of collaboration with Nitze." As Nitze summarized, Kennan would get ideas and papers from the PPS staff and then retreat to a carrel in the Library of Congress with his secretary, Dorothy Hessman, to write his paper. Once Kennan had put his ideas on paper, he became "intellectually locked into" the paper, and his analysis and "style of expression" could not be changed. Nitze went on to explain that he had a different view when he was PPS director. See Transcripts—Ware Adams, September 30, 1960, Interview, Folder 9; Transcripts—Charles Burton Marshall, October 1, 1970, Interview, Folder 17; and Transcripts—Paul H. Nitze, October 2, 1970, Folder 18—all in Box 8, Kennan Biography Project, GCML.

58. PPS 4, in Etzold and Gaddis, *Containment,* 107–9.

59. Ibid., 108.

60. Ibid., 108–9.

61. It seems that Gaddis takes his thesis about the "long peace" and the supposed stability of superpower bipolarity from this Kennan point; see John Lewis Gaddis, *The Long Peace: Inquiries into the History of the Cold War* (New York: Oxford University Press, 1987).

62. PPS 4, in Etzold and Gaddis, *Containment,* 109, 114.

63. Kennan, *Memoirs,* 352–53.

64. PPS 4, in Etzold and Gaddis, *Containment,* 107; Kennan, *Memoirs,* 352.

65. PPS 13, "Resume of World Situation," November 6, 1947, in *FRUS,* 1947, vol. 1, 772–77, reprinted in Etzold and Gaddis, *Containment,* 90–97. On page 90,

Etzold and Gaddis intimate that, since it was submitted to Marshall rather than to Forrestal, Kennan's "Resume of World Situation" reflected more coherently what Kennan conceived and wanted to implement in containment. Gaddis makes the same point about PPS 13 as a "clearer explanation" in *Russia, the Soviet Union, and the United States,* 188.

66. Kennan, *Memoirs,* 379. See pages 378–79 for discussion of the entire paper. Kennan largely paraphrases his November 1947 paper, changing the future verb tense in reference to the Czechoslovak coup to the past tense.

67. PPS 13, in Etzold and Gaddis, *Containment,* 90, 91.

68. Ibid., 92, 93.

69. Ibid., 93, 91, 93.

70. Ibid., 94.

71. Ibid., 96–97.

72. Gaddis, *Russia, the Soviet Union, and the United States,* 188.

73. This is somewhat ironic, given that Kennan was one among several who helped compose Marshall's Harvard address. See Marshall, *Interviews and Reminiscences for Forrest C. Pogue,* 559. As Marshall recalled, "The way the speech was primarily built was this. I talked it over with George Kennan in the Plans Section [i.e., the Policy Planning Staff] and Chip Bohlen, and I told them to each start out wholly independent of the other and give me what they thought. Then I got impatient and right away, and I dictated something that I thought. And when theirs came in, they were quite apart. It was not a case of one opposing the other. It was almost a totally different approach. And I cut out part of Kennan's speech and part of Bohlen's speech and part of my speech and put the three together, and that was the beginning of the talk." In *The Fifteen Weeks,* page 255, Jones remembered it a bit differently, writing that Bohlen used primarily the Kennan and Clayton memoranda, as well as Clayton's oral descriptions of the European situation, to draft the speech. The draft, he said, was gone over by Clayton and Acheson and then given to Marshall, who was not satisfied with the part about the European initiative and rewrote it. Whichever account is more accurate, they both convey that Kennan was an important, but not the most important, contributor to the Marshall Plan.

The PPS was not involved in the implementation of the Marshall Plan. In addition, William Clayton provided much of the background to and substance for the Marshall Plan, in the form of March and May 1947 memoranda. See, for example, Clayton's May 1947 memo for Marshall, with Clayton's January 7, 1950, cover letter to his daughter, Ellen Garwood, General File, Marshall Plan Memos, 1947, Box 6, Clayton Papers, HSTL. Also see Fossedal, *Our Finest Hour,* for additional consideration of Clayton's important role.

74. Unlike any other document in *Containment,* Gaddis and Etzold present excerpts from PPS 23 in four different sections of the book, intimating that this paper reinforced and saturated all of containment as it should have transpired.

75. PPS 23, "Review of Current Trends: U.S. Foreign Policy," February 24, 1948, in *FRUS,* 1948, vol. 1 (part 2), 510–28, reprinted in Etzold and Gaddis, *Containment,* 97–100, 114–25, 161–64, 226–28. Among Kennan's writings, PPS

23 made a considerable impact on Gaddis, who included reference to and discussion of it in both *Strategies of Containment* and *Russia, the Soviet Union, and the United States.*

76. PPS 23, in Etzold and Gaddis, *Containment,* 97, 98, 99.

77. Ibid., 98, 100.

78. One wonders if the sentiment expressed here explains some of Kennan's reluctance to assist Turkey in the Truman Doctrine or to include that country and Greece in the North Atlantic Alliance.

79. PPS 23, in Etzold and Gaddis, *Containment,* 98, 99.

80. Ibid.

81. Ibid., 100.

82. Kennan quoted only part of Plato's sentence. The full passage from the *Republic,* Book V, 473d–e, reads: "'Unless,' I said, 'the philosophers rule as kings or those now called kings and chiefs genuinely and adequately philosophize, and political power and philosophy coincide in the same place, while the many natures now making their way to either apart from the other are by necessity excluded, there is no rest from ills for the cities, my dear Glaucon, nor I think for human kind, nor will the regime we have now described in speech ever come forth from nature, insofar as possible, and see the light of the sun.'"

83. See Plato's *Laws,* Book IX, 875a–d, and Book IV, 711b–712a, and Aristotle's *Politics,* Book II.

6. The Beginning of the Atlantic Alliance

1. The North Atlantic Treaty did not fully become the North Atlantic Treaty Organization until 1950. The acronym NATO is used here, however, because that is how the alliance is best known to most people.

2. Memorandum of Conversation, White House, April 3, 1949, Miscellaneous White House Documents, HSTL, quoted in Hamby, *Man of the People,* 517, 524.

3. See "Special Message to the Congress Transmitting Report on Assistance to Greece and Turkey," November 10, 1947, in Truman, *Public Papers,* vol. 3, 486–87.

4. Possony, *Century of Conflict,* 288. See also Weekly Summary Excerpt, January 30, 1948, "Soviet Policy in Eastern Europe," 168–69; Daily Summary Excerpt, February 13, 1948, "Possible Soviet Plans for Poland," 170, which refers to the long-range Kremlin decision "never to let go of eastern Germany"; Intelligence Memorandum 13, March 16, 1948, "Soviet Pressure on Berlin," 180–83; and Daily Summary Excerpt, March 27, 1948, "USSR May Close Eastern Zone Border," 186—all in Kuhns, *Assessing the Soviet Threat.*

5. Marshall served as Truman's liaison with the Europeans in promoting and expanding the Brussels Treaty, while Undersecretary of State Robert Lovett was delegated to work closely with Vandenberg on drafting and promoting what became the Vandenberg Resolution.

6. Vandenberg gave a speech in October 1948 that he considered a political address and a response to some of the president's campaign remarks, but Truman,

speaking privately to the senator in the White House, described it as a "grand speech" in support of "bipartisan foreign policy." Vandenberg defined bipartisan foreign policy in the speech thus: "This common action does not mean that we cease to be 'Republicans' or 'Democrats' at home. It does not mean that we mute our criticisms of mistakes. It does not mean a fake 'unity' devoid of popular consent. It means that we strive by consultation to lift foreign policy above partisan issue. It means that we attempt to hammer out the greatest possible measure of agreement so we can speak to the world, not as 'Republicans' or 'Democrats' but as undivided Americans." See Vandenberg, *Private Papers,* 451.

7. One must distinguish Vandenberg's words from his son's interpretation. Vandenberg's message to Churchill is on page 546 of Vandenberg, *Private Papers.* The italics are the senator's. Vandenberg did not echo Truman on other matters, but for examples of his support of Truman's conception of the Truman Doctrine, Marshall Plan, Berlin, and the North Atlantic pact, see Vandenberg, *Private Papers,* especially 342, 347, 378, 390–91, 399, 402, 478, 489–91.

8. Truman, April 1948, Longhand Notes File, 1945–1952, Box 333, PSF, HSTP, HSTL. Campaign quote is from "Rear Platform and Other Informal Remarks in Nevada and California," September 22, 1948, in Truman, *Public Papers,* vol. 4, 535–44. For elaboration of Vandenberg's phrasing, see Vandenberg, *Private Papers,* 112–13.

9. For elaboration of this point, see Harold I. Gullan, *The Upset That Wasn't: Harry S Truman and the Crucial Election of 1948* (Chicago: Ivan R. Dee, 1998), 186. Gullan cites Samuel Lubell's observation that "the stay-at-homes . . . had not been primarily overconfident Republicans; instead they had been apathetic Democrats."

10. "Address at the Gilmore Stadium in Los Angeles," September 23, 1948, in Truman, *Public Papers,* vol. 4, 555–59. For contemporary analysis of the challenges facing liberals from the Progressives and Communists, see Schlesinger, *Vital Center,* 157–70.

11. "Rear Platform and Other Informal Remarks in Pennsylvania and New Jersey," October 7, 1948, and "Address in St. Paul at the Municipal Auditorium," October 13, 1948, both in Truman, *Public Papers,* vol. 4, 683–99 and 770–74.

12. "Rear Platform and Other Informal Remarks in Indiana and Ohio," October 26, 1948, in Truman, *Public Papers,* vol. 4, 854–63. Truman's indictment of Herbert Hoover was somewhat ironic, because he had developed a high opinion of the former president's abilities, relied on him to deal with food shortages in Europe between 1945 and 1947, and appointed him to head the Commission on Organization of the Executive Branch of the Government (popularly, the Hoover Commission) in 1947. But their personal relations were not warm at the time, in large part because of their partisan differences, perhaps explaining Truman's tactical, derogatory, and repeated invocation of Hoover's name in the 1948 election. For a delineation of their close professional relationship and eventual personal friendship in the 1950s until Hoover's death, see Timothy Walch and Dwight M. Miller, eds., *Herbert Hoover and Harry S. Truman: A Documentary History* (Worland, Wyo.: High Plains Publishing for the Herbert Hoover Presidential Library Association, 1992).

13. Franklin Roosevelt had used similar language in the campaign of 1944, when he accused those who opposed the revival of the New Deal of being fascists.

14. "Radio Remarks in Independence on Election Eve," November 1, 1948, in Truman, *Public Papers,* vol. 4, 939–40.

15. "Rear Platform and Other Informal Remarks in Oregon," June 11, 1948, in Truman, *Public Papers,* vol. 4, 329. This statement was not typical of Truman, although some scholars have argued otherwise. In his public papers, memoirs, and postpresidential writings, he criticized the Communist system and all of its rulers, did not praise Stalin (even where he referred to him as Uncle Joe), and hoped for freedom for all enslaved peoples. Truman's entire remark reads: "I went to Potsdam in 1945 with [peace] in mind, I went there with the kindliest feelings in the world toward Russia, and we made certain agreements. I got very well acquainted with Joe Stalin, and I like old Joe! He is a decent fellow. But Joe is a prisoner of the Politburo. He can't do what he wants to. He makes agreements, and if he could he would keep them; but the people who run the government are very specific in saying that he can't keep them. Now sometime or other that great country and this great country are going to understand that their mutual interests mean the welfare and peace of the world as a whole."

16. "Commencement Address at the University of California," June 12, 1948, in Truman, *Public Papers,* vol. 4, 336–40. After making his "I like old Joe" remark, Truman promised to explain U.S. foreign policy in this Berkeley address. Those who focus on the "old Joe" comment do not concentrate similarly on the commencement speech.

17. Cited and discussed in Walton, *Henry Wallace, Harry Truman, and the Cold War,* 216.

18. "Statement by the President Following an Exchange of Views in Moscow between the U.S. Ambassador and the Foreign Minister," May 11, 1948, in Truman, *Public Papers,* vol. 4, 252.

19. Quoted in Graham White and John Maze, *Henry A. Wallace: His Search for a New World Order* (Chapel Hill: University of North Carolina Press, 1995), 263, and Walton, *Henry Wallace, Harry Truman, and the Cold War,* 218.

20. Quoted in Walton, *Henry Wallace, Harry Truman, and the Cold War,* 219–220, and White and Maze, *Henry A. Wallace,* 263.

21. Wallace, *Toward World Peace,* 112, 47, 17. Also see Schlesinger, *Vital Center,* 117–20.

22. See Eyes Only, Clay to Chamberlin, included in Leahy, Diary, March 31, 1948, LOC. As General Lucius Clay summarized the Soviet threat in late March: "Unless we take a strong stand now, our life in Berlin will become impossible. A retreat from Berlin at this moment would, in my opinion, have serious if not disastrous political consequences in Europe. I do not believe that the Soviets mean war now. However, if they do, it seems to me that we might as well find out now as later. We cannot afford to be bluffed."

23. R. H. Hillenkoetter, Director of Central Intelligence, Memorandum to the President, December 22, 1947, Naval Aide Files, HSTP, HSTL. Also see

Intelligence Memorandum 13, March 16, 1948, Soviet Pressure on Berlin, 180–83; Daily Summary Excerpt, April 24, 1948, "Reported Soviet Plans for Eastern German Regime," 197; ORE 29–48, April 28, 1948, "Possible Program of Future Soviet Moves in Germany," 198–200; Weekly Summary Excerpt, April 30, 1948, "Deadlock over Transport Problems in Berlin," 201; Daily Summary Excerpt, May 7, 1948, "Germany: Soviet Attempt to Interrupt US Air Traffic," 202; and Weekly Summary Excerpt, July 2, 1948, "Berlin Blockade," 220–21—all in Kuhns, *Assessing the Soviet Threat.*

24. Truman, *Years of Trial and Hope,* 130–31.

25. Diary entry of June 28, 1948, in Forrestal, *Forrestal Diaries,* 454–55.

26. Entry from July 19, 1948, reprinted in Truman, *Off the Record,* 145. On July 23, 1948, Truman agreed with Clay that leaving Berlin would mean losing everything for which the United States and the West had fought. See Summary of National Security Council Discussion, July 23, 1948, Box 220, PSF, HSTP, HSTL.

27. See Oral History Interview with General Lucius D. Clay, New York, July 16, 1974, with Richard D. McKinzie, HSTL. With benefit of hindsight, Clay praised Truman's statesmanship. When he made his second trip to Washington regarding the Berlin airlift, he asked for more DC-4s. He recalled that after the National Security Council meeting over which Truman presided and during which most rejected additional air support, the president called him and Secretary of the Army Ken Royall into his office and told Clay, "Don't worry, you're going to get your airplanes." Clay asked if he could tell reporters, and Truman said yes. Clay assessed: "Truman realized that the Berlin crisis was a political war, not a physical military war. I am not being critical of the Joint Chiefs of Staff, because I think they visualized it as a military operation; in that sense of the word they were correct. Truman's a man of great courage and he didn't hesitate to make his own decisions."

28. Since Truman's approach worked, we do not know if more strength would have been needed. As it was, the Berlin airlift wore the Soviets down and showed to them for about a year the superior capabilities of the West in the air. The United States outperformed the Communists in terms of commitment and technology. For an account that is good on the details of the airlift, see Thomas Parrish, *Berlin in the Balance, 1945–1949: The Blockade, the Airlift, the First Major Battle of the Cold War* (Reading, Mass.: Addison-Wesley, 1998).

29. Hamby, *Man of the People,* 399.

30. For a helpful examination of the concern by both Presidents Truman and Eisenhower about deficit-fed inflation, see Aaron L. Friedberg, *In the Shadow of the Garrison State: America's Anti-Statism and Its Cold War Grand Strategy* (Princeton, N.J.: Princeton University Press, 2000), 94–95.

31. According to Aaron Friedberg, Congress chose a return to the draft over universal military training (UMT) in Truman's package, especially since education, labor, and farm leaders in spring 1948 remained strongly opposed to UMT and were willing to accept the draft as an alternative to universal conscription. Truman, for his part, was unhappy about the draft because of the inequities involved in its application; see Friedberg, *In the Shadow of the Garrison State,* 175, 174.

32. Truman's satisfaction was qualified (hence part of his renewed request for universal military training and a draft) because some armed forces were tied to occupation duties in Germany and Japan.

33. Economic background is drawn from Hamby, *Man of the People*, 398–99; Gaddis, *Strategies of Containment*, 359; and Jack M. Holl and Terrence Fehner, "Military Spending," in *The Harry S. Truman Encyclopedia*, ed. Richard S. Kirkendall (Boston: G. K. Hall, 1989), 237–39. See Forrestal, *Forrestal Diaries*, 382–450, for diary entries that describe his frustration with Truman and the service secretaries.

34. For an alternative representation from a corporatist, see Hogan, *A Cross of Iron*, 91–118, 161–84. For an analysis that examines the economic burden of fighting the Cold War, and often deems it too high, see Derek Leebaert, *The Fifty-Year Wound: The True Price of America's Cold War Victory* (Boston: Little, Brown, 2002), 67, 80–83.

35. See Ayers diary entries, October 9 and 12, 1948, Diary-1948, Box 16, Eben A. Ayers Papers, HSTL. Ayers wrote on October 12 that he and others thought David Noyes, an old friend of Truman's, came up with the idea for the mission. Vandenberg believed that Truman already had dropped the idea as of October 5, 1948. Vandenberg, Senator Tom Connally, and Truman were in private conversation in the White House. When Truman mentioned the possibility that he might "call Stalin on the phone," Vandenberg said that the president "was *not* announcing his purpose to do so. He was quite casually exploring the idea." In reference to the Vinson mission, Vandenberg said, "Connally and I left at the end of perhaps an hour. The fact that he said *nothing* to us about the Vinson Mission leads me to believe that he had totally dismissed the matter from his mind when he found that Marshall disagreed, and that he had *no intention at any time* of going ahead with the idea except with Marshall's approval." See Vandenberg, diary entry, October 5, 1948, in Vandenberg, *Private Papers*, 458. For a summary of the briefly considered Vinson mission, and its proposal to Truman by two temporary speechwriters, one of them Noyes, see Hamby, *Man of the People*, 460–61. For a somewhat different view, see Ferrell, *Harry S. Truman: A Life*, 262–64.

36. Initial NATO members were the United States, Canada, Great Britain, France, Belgium, the Netherlands, Luxembourg, Iceland, Norway, Denmark, Portugal, and Italy.

37. For elaboration of Acheson's frustration with and occasional admiration of Vandenberg especially, see Acheson, *Present at the Creation*, 64, 72, 224, 309–312, 317–18.

38. See "Annual Message to the Congress on the State of the Union," January 5, 1949, and "Inaugural Address," January 20, 1949, both in Truman, *Public Papers*, vol. 5, 1–7 and 112–16.

39. Truman, *Years of Trial and Hope*, 240.

40. The North Atlantic Treaty is fully reprinted in Lawrence S. Kaplan, *The United States and NATO: The Formative Years* (Lexington: University Press of Kentucky, 1984), 227–30.

41. "Address on the Occasion of the Signing of the North Atlantic Treaty," April 4, 1949, in Truman, *Public Papers*, vol. 5, 196–98.

42. Memorandum of Conversation, White House, April 3, 1949, quoted in and paraphrased from Hamby, *Man of the People,* 517, 524.

43. "Address in Chicago before the Imperial Council Session of the Shrine of North America," July 19, 1949, in Truman, *Public Papers,* vol. 5, 385–89. For another typical example, see "Address in Little Rock at the Dedication of the World War Memorial Park," June 11, 1949, in ibid., 286–91.

44. "The President's Special Conference with the Association of Radio News Analysts," October 19, 1949, in Truman, *Public Papers,* vol. 5, 517–21.

45. "Address at the Unveiling of a Memorial Carillon in Arlington National Cemetery," December 21, 1949, in Truman, *Public Papers,* vol. 5, 582–83.

46. Kennan, Notes for Seminar at Princeton University (handwritten), January 23–26, 1949, GFKP, SGML, PU; also see Kennan, *Memoirs,* 412.

47. Gaddis, for example, makes this argument throughout his writings, especially in *Strategies of Containment.* For another example, see *Russia, the Soviet Union, and the United States,* 193. Once more, he intertwines this perspective with his defense of Kennan.

48. Kennan, "Where Do We Stand?" December 21, 1949, National War College, File 30, Box 17, GFKP, SGML, PU.

49. Wallace remarks reprinted in U.S. Congress, *Congressional Record,* 81st Congress, 1st Session, March 14–May 19, 1949, p. A1866.

50. U.S. Congress, *North Atlantic Treaty: Hearings before the Senate Committee on Foreign Relations,* 81st Congress, 1st session, April 27–May 3, 1949 (Washington, D.C.: Government Printing Office, 1949), 463 ff, cited in Coral Bell, *Negotiation from Strength: A Study in the Politics of Power* (New York: Alfred A. Knopf, 1963), 40. Wallace's testimony of May 5, 1949, cited in Walton, *Henry Wallace, Harry Truman, and the Cold War,* 345–46.

51. Lippmann to Quincy A. Wright, February 14, 1949; Lippmann to Sumner Welles, January 28, 1949; and Lippmann to Russell C. Leffingwell, March 1, 1949—all in Lippmann, *Public Philosopher,* 531–32, 527, 532–33. Also see Lippmann to Bernard Berenson, March 1, 1949, in ibid., 533–34, in which he wrote: "[W]e face the extraordinarily difficult task of developing military power sufficient enough to deter the Russians from aggression, sufficient to exert pressure which will in the end cause them to retire from Europe, and yet not of a kind which would provoke a war of desperation on the part of the Soviet Union."

52. Etzold and Gaddis, *Containment,* 135. PPS 37, "Policy Questions Concerning a Possible German Settlement," August 12, 1948, in *FRUS,* 1948, vol. 2, 1288–96, reprinted in Etzold and Gaddis, *Containment,* 135–44.

53. PPS 37, in Etzold and Gaddis, *Containment,* 144.

54. Ibid., 135–37.

55. Later in his memoirs, Kennan argued against the connection with the blockade. In accord with revisionism and corporatism, he recalled the Berlin blockade as a defensive action on the part of the Soviets to bring the United States, Britain, and France back to the negotiating table after they had begun the London Conference. See Kennan, *Memoirs,* 419. Realism, like the subsequent three schools of thought, discounts Communist ideology and portrays the Soviets as defensive in much of their

behavior. Kennan made the same point about Korea, arguing that the Communists acted defensively there in response to the Japanese peace settlement.

56. PPS 37, in Etzold and Gaddis, *Containment,* 138–39.

57. Ibid., 140, 141, 143. In a curious love-hate relationship with Germany and its people, Kennan admired that the Germans had achieved greatness yet worried that they again could disrupt the stability of the continent. In his memoir reminiscence on PPS 37, he placed the responsibility for this German duality on American shoulders, blaming the United States for materialistic exploitation and occupation of Germany, when it should have given needed spiritual and intellectual guidance to that country. See Kennan, *Memoirs,* 428–29. For analysis of how eastern Germany was already being shaped as a Communist police state, see Norman M. Naimark, "'To Know Everything and to Report Everything Worth Knowing': Building the East German Police State, 1945–1949," Working Paper no. 10, Cold War International History Project, August 1994.

58. PPS 37, in Etzold and Gaddis, *Containment,* 143–44.

59. Kennan, *Memoirs,* 428. Gaddis emphasized this same point in *Strategies of Containment,* especially 89–126.

60. Kennan's memoir discussion of PPS 37 segues into a defense of what he called "Plan A," his formal alternative to the London Program and the Western allied plan for Germany. While other contemporary memoirs did not deem this plan as crucial or even allude to it, Kennan and then Gaddis and Etzold regarded Plan A as the indispensable link between PPS 37 and PPS 43 in Kennan containment.

61. See Kennan, *Memoirs,* 418–48; Gaddis, *Strategies of Containment,* 75; and Etzold and Gaddis, *Containment,* 144, 153. See also PPS 43, "Considerations Affecting the Conclusion of a North Atlantic Security Pact," November 23, 1948, in *FRUS, 1948,* vol. 3, 284–88, reprinted in Etzold and Gaddis, *Containment,* 153–58.

62. Etzold and Gaddis, *Containment,* 158. Gaddis and Etzold did not talk about those on the Policy Planning Staff who disagreed with Kennan. Elsewhere, Gaddis attributed sole authorship of PPS 43 to Kennan, directly quoting the paper as Kennan's words and opinion. See Gaddis, *Strategies of Containment,* 73 and 375 n. 51.

63. PPS 43, in Etzold and Gaddis, *Containment,* 154; Kennan, "What Is Policy?" December 18, 1947, National War College, File 40, Writings and Publications, 1938–1947, Box 16, GFKP, SGML, PU.

64. PPS 43, in Etzold and Gaddis, *Containment,* 154.

65. Ibid., 155.

66. Ibid., 156–57.

67. Kennan, *Memoirs,* 411.

68. Gaddis, *Russia, the Soviet Union, and the United States,* 197.

69. Kennan, *Memoirs,* 412.

7. The Purpose and Structure of National Security

1. In describing what he considered Truman's great administrative ability, Matthew Connelly said, "He listened and he had judgment, and he wanted to know

all the answers before he made a final decision." See Oral History Interview with Matthew J. Connelly, New York, N.Y., November 28 and 30, 1967, and August 21, 1968, by Jerry N. Hess, HSTL (May 1969). Elsey praised Truman's thoroughness in a related way: "Those of us on the staff were frequently dumbfounded to have a messenger arriving a moment or two after we did at the office in the morning with longhand notes from the President that he'd written during the night, asking questions or saying please do this or can you see me on such and such, and most of us have sizeable collections of these longhand memoranda from the President." See Oral History Interview with George M. Elsey by William D. Stilley and Jerald L. Hill, Washington, D.C., March 17, 1976, HSTL (July 1986).

2. "Remarks of the President to the Final Session of the C.I.A.'s Eighth Training Orientation Course for Representatives of Various Government Agencies," November 21, 1952, reprinted in Michael Warner, ed., *CIA Cold War Records: The CIA under Harry Truman* (Washington, D.C.: Center for the Study of Intelligence, Central Intelligence Agency, 1994), 471–73.

3. Although the National Security Council was profiled in the press at its inception and referred to on occasion by Truman in his news conferences, its daily classified papers obviously did not receive coverage. As a result, criticism of Truman and the NSC comes mostly from modern historians and political scientists, who have had recent access to papers and archives, and from people such as Kennan, who explained his view in his later memoir. Wallace's criticism applied to the National Security Act overall; see Wallace, *Toward World Peace*, 85–86.

4. See the National Security Act of July 26, 1947, PL 253, 80th Congress, 61 Stat. (part 1), 495–97.

5. For development of this latter point, see Anna Kasten Nelson's excellent article, "President Truman and the Evolution of the National Security Council," *Journal of American History* 72 (September 1985): 360–78.

6. Memorandum by the Secretary of State to the President, February 7, 1947, in "General; The United Nations," *FRUS,* 1947, vol. 1, 712–15. Marshall asked Kennan in late April to head up the Policy Planning Staff; he must have set up the PPS for a variety of reasons, but the timing suggests that the two most important proximate reasons were his disillusion with Stalin in spring 1947 (described in chapter 4 in this volume) and his wish to have a State Department structure established before passage of the National Security Act.

7. Diary entry of September 26, 1947, in Forrestal, *Forrestal Diaries,* 320.

8. Nelson, "President Truman and the Evolution of the National Security Council," 377. Nelson obtained Truman's quote from "Minutes of NSC Meeting, April 2, 1949," declassified, Freedom of Information Act request, National Security Council. In July 1949, Truman again emphasized that "he is chairman of the council and makes the decisions himself"; see Ayers, diary entry, July 28, 1949, in Ayers, *Truman in the White House,* 319.

9. Comment, written in Truman's hand and initialed by him, on first page of transcripts of Souers interview, December 15, 1954, PPF Memoirs File (Associates), Souers, Sidney, Dec. 15–16, 1954, HSTL, cited in Rhodri Jeffreys-Jones, *The CIA*

and American Democracy, 2nd ed. (New Haven, Conn.: Yale University Press, 1998), 35.

10. When Truman signed a document or letter, he meant it to bestow his approval. The president refused to delegate the right to sign his name and would not use a mechanical pen. See Truman, *Autobiography of Harry S. Truman,* 104, 136.

11. "Commencement Address at Princeton University," June 17, 1947, in Truman, *Public Papers,* vol. 3, 281–85.

12. "Address in Miami at the Golden Jubilee Convention of the Veterans of Foreign Wars," August 22, 1949, in Truman, *Public Papers,* vol. 5, 431–34.

13. Of this sentiment, Gaddis footnoted: "Truman for years carried in his wallet a copy of the portion of Tennyson's poem, 'Locksley Hall,' that predicted a 'Parliament of Man, the Federation of the world.' 'We're going to have that someday,' he insisted, 'I guess that's what I've really been working for ever since I first put that poetry in my pocket.' (John Hersey, 'Mr. President,' *New Yorker,* vol. XXVII [April 7, 1951], 49–50.)" For this reference, see Gaddis, *Strategies of Containment,* 56. For additional discussion of this exchange, see Hamby, *Liberalism and Its Challengers,* 72.

14. In addition to discussion and references from the preceding chapter, see Daily Summary Excerpt, March 16, 1948, "Czechoslovaks Believe USSR Willing to Risk War," 179; Daily Summary Excerpt, March 17, 1948, "Turks Fear War May Be Imminent," 185; ORE 22–48 Excerpt, April 2, 1948, "Possibility of Direct Soviet Military Action during 1948," 187; and Weekly Summary Excerpt, April 23, 1948, "Prospective Communist Strategy Following the Italian Elections," 194–96—all in Kuhns, *Assessing the Soviet Threat.* On top of these actions, the Soviets pursued a massive military buildup in 1948.

15. April 17(?) 1948, Draft Speech (undelivered), in Truman, *Off the Record,* 131–33. For representative public statements by Truman in March 1948, see discussion in chapter 4 in this volume of Truman's "Special Message to the Congress on the Threat to the Freedom of Europe."

16. Truman to Eleanor Roosevelt, March 16, 1948, in Truman, *Off the Record,* 125–26.

17. Truman to Margaret Truman, March 3, 1948, in Margaret Truman, ed., *Letters from Father: The Truman Family's Personal Correspondence* (New York: Arbor House, 1981), 103–8.

18. Diary entry of March 31, 1948, in Forrestal, *Forrestal Diaries,* 408.

19. Truman, handwritten notes, May 17–30, 1948, President's Appointment File, Daily Sheets, 1948 April 12–July, Box 89, PSF, HSTP, HSTL. His language ended up verbatim in "Remarks in Philadelphia in the Girard College Chapel," May 20, 1948, in Truman, *Public Papers,* vol. 4, 264–66.

20. Milovan Djilas, *The New Class: An Analysis of the Communist System* (New York: Frederick A. Praeger, 1957), especially 53. Also see Michael B. Petrovich, "The View from Yugoslavia," in Hammond, *Witnesses to the Origins of the Cold War,* 34–59.

21. Report of Milovan Djilas about a secret Soviet-Bulgarian-Yugoslav meeting, February 10, 1948, translated by Vladislav Zubok (National Security Archive), reprinted in Cold War International History Project *Bulletin,* no. 10 (March 1998):

128–34. As the translator points out, Djilas had recounted this meeting in great detail in *Conversations with Stalin*, without the above cited written report, and "Djilas' memory retained with remarkable precision some pivotal moments of the conversation."

22. Elsey believed that Yugoslavia was able to assert its independence to an extent because Greece and Turkey had not fallen to the Soviets. See Oral History Interview with George M. Elsey, Washington, D.C., February 10 and 17, 1964; March 9, 1965; July 10 and 17, 1969; April 9 and July 7 and 10, 1970, by Charles T. Morrissey and Jerry N. Hess, HSTL (May 1974).

23. Nikita Kruschchev, *Khrushchev Remembers: The Last Testament*, trans. and ed. Strobe Talbott (Boston: Little, Brown, 1974), 181, where Khrushchev maintained, "I'm absolutely sure that if the Soviet Union had a common border with Yugoslavia, Stalin would have intervened militarily. As it was, though, he would have had to go through Bulgaria, and Stalin knew we weren't strong enough to get away with that. He was afraid the American imperialists would have actively supported Yugoslavia—not out of sympathy with the Yugoslav form of socialism, but in order to split and demoralize the socialist camp."

24. The question should not be one of nationalist independence, as realists and postrevisionists have asserted. This view of nationalism is a theme in Kennan's *Memoirs* and, to a lesser extent, in Bohlen's *Witness to History*. Within a defense of Kennan, Gaddis pressed the point to the utmost in postrevisionism. For an example of Gaddis's agreement with realism's view of nationalism, see *Strategies of Containment*, 41–49. This theme is present in most of Gaddis's writings of the 1970s and 1980s. In *The United States and the End of the Cold War: Implications, Reconsiderations, Provocations* (Oxford: Oxford University Press, 1992), Gaddis addresses nationalism as a force for destructive fragmentation after the Cold War.

25. Truman to Bess, September 30, 1947, in Truman, *Dear Bess*, 550–51. Truman said publicly almost the same thing on the same day. See "The President's Special Conference with Editors of Business and Trade Papers," September 30, 1947, in Truman, *Public Papers*, vol. 3, 449–50.

26. Truman to Winston Churchill, July 10, 1948, in M. Truman, *Letters from Father*, 110. In quoting Churchill's famous words and hoping to avoid "blood and tears," Truman implied that much toil and sweat—the rest of the famous litany—would be necessary in facing the Communist challenge.

27. Gaddis, *Strategies of Containment*, 68, 65.

28. Ibid., 68.

29. Such action was anticipated by ORE 49–48 Excerpt, November 18, 1948, "The Trend of Soviet-Yugoslav Relations," 260, and then detailed by the U.S. intelligence in Weekly Summary Excerpt, April 8, 1949, "Communist Deviation in Bulgaria," 302; Weekly Summary Excerpt, April 22, 1949, "Satellite Communist Purges," 305–6; Weekly Summary Excerpt, June 24, 1949, "Eastern Europe: Purges," 322–24; Weekly Summary Excerpt, July 29, 1949, "Nationalism in the Satellites," 328–29; Weekly Summary Excerpt, September 23, 1949, "Eastern Europe: Communist Deviation and Hungary: Treason Trial," 332–33; and Intelligence

Memorandum 248 Excerpt, November 7, 1949, "Satellite Relations with the USSR and the West," 338–40—all in Kuhns, *Assessing the Soviet Threat.*

30. Daniel Yergin, *Shattered Peace: The Origins of the Cold War,* rev. ed. (New York: Penguin Books, 1990), 402, 401. But he also writes that the imperial bent of the American regime determines its foreign policy. On this occasion, revisionism espouses the seeming amorality of realism in foreign affairs.

31. Etzold and Gaddis, *Containment,* 203. For NSC 20/1, see 173–203. For NSC 20/4, see 203–11. Gaddis's presentation of NSC documents found in the containment volume is discussed in detail in chapter 5 in this volume. Although Etzold and Gaddis noted that the series was initiated by Secretary of Defense James Forrestal, they did not reproduce the original memo from Forrestal to the National Security Council, which tied any reassessment of U.S. military preparedness to the nature of the Cold War conflict and Communist aggression and which reminded the council of its charge to integrate domestic, foreign, and military policies relating to national security. Gaddis and Etzold also published Kennan's draft NSC 20/1 rather than, or in juxtaposition with, the official, shortened version of NSC 20/1 that appeared in *FRUS.* In their preface, Gaddis and Etzold expressed satisfaction at unearthing little-known documents, such as Kennan's NSC 20/1, and publishing them for the first time; such Kennan papers, to them, were official government policy. See Etzold and Gaddis, *Containment,* ix–x.

32. Gaddis altered his view for the same end in *Strategies of Containment,* 50, 57, 61. He subtly links NSC 20/4 with NSC 7, in March 1948, giving them as examples of symmetry and universalism in American policy. NSC 7 is mentioned only in an endnote. He praises NSC 20/1 over NSC 20/4 in *Strategies of Containment,* in support of Kennan's containment.

33. The entire text of NSC 20/1 is not in *FRUS* but is available from the records of the National Security Council on deposit in the Modern Military Records Branch at the National Archives. Also see Kennan's complete NSC 20/1, "U.S. Objectives with Respect to Russia," August 18, 1948, in Etzold and Gaddis, *Containment,* 173–203. The shortened version of NSC 20/1 which is accessible to all is in *FRUS,* 1948, vol. 1 (part 2), 609–11. With a few word changes, it presents only Kennan's conclusions from the first NSC 20/1 draft, a fifty-two-page paper known as PPS 38, according to a *FRUS* footnote on page 609.

34. NSC 20/2, "Factors Affecting the Nature of the U.S. Defense Arrangements in the Light of Soviet Policies," in *FRUS,* 1948, vol. 1 (part 2), 615–24, excerpts of which are printed in Etzold and Gaddis, *Containment,* 297–301.

35. Memo, Kennan to Lovett, 10–20–48, in NSC 20 file, Box 54, RG 59, General Records of the Department of State, Records of the Policy Planning Staff, 1947–1953, National Archives II, quoted in Gregory Mitrovich, *Undermining the Kremlin: America's Strategy to Subvert the Soviet Bloc, 1947–1956* (Ithaca, N.Y.: Cornell University Press, 2000), 34.

36. Memo, George Butler to Kennan, 10/11/48, in NSC 20 file, Box 54, RG 59, General Records of the Department of State, Records of the Policy Planning Staff, 1947–1953, National Archives II, quoted in Mitrovich, *Undermining the Kremlin,* 35.

37. Mitrovich, *Undermining the Kremlin*, 35.

38. NSC 20/4, "U.S. Objectives with Respect to the USSR to Counter Soviet Threats to U.S. Security," November 23, 1948, in *FRUS*, 1948, vol. 1 (part 2), 663–69.

39. Like the long form of NSC 20/1, NSC 20/2, also by Kennan, was part of the NSC 20 series that was largely discarded. NSC 20/4 accepted only particular points of NSC 20/2. NSC 20/2 previously was PPS 33 of July 23, 1948, "Factors Affecting the Nature of the U.S. Defense Arrangements in Light of Soviet Policies." See *FRUS*, 1948, vol. 1 (part 2), 615–24. NSC 20/4 did not view Kremlin policies through the prism of Soviet intentions and attitudes, as PPS 33–NSC 20/2 did, although it did use some of Kennan's practical analysis. As for NSC 20/3, this document was not printed in *FRUS* but is available at the Truman Library. It is almost the same document as NSC 20/4. See Minutes of the 27th Meeting of the National Security Council, November 23, 1948, NSC files-meetings, Box 204, PSF, HSTP, HSTL. A November 2 draft, NSC 20/3 came to the meeting under this title and left the meeting as NSC 20/4 to be sent to the president. The NSC meeting note explained: "Adopted NSC 20/3 subject to an amendment of paragraph 22-*d* thereof" and "NSC 20/3 as amended subsequently circulated as NSC 20/4 and submitted to the President for consideration." Paragraph 22-*d* dealt with ensuring, in the event of war, that any Communist regime left in part of the Soviet Union "does not control enough of the military-industrial potential of the Soviet Union to enable it to wage war on comparable terms with any other regime or regimes which may exist on traditional Russian territory." The Joint Chiefs of Staff, not the State Department, were responsible for this amendment, which makes more precise Kennan's language.

40. NSC 20/4, in *FRUS*, 1948, vol. 1 (part 2), 663–64.

41. Ibid., 663–66.

42. Ibid., 668. For development of Kennan's view, see chapter 5 in this volume.

43. NSC 20/4, in *FRUS*, 1948, vol. 1 (part 2), 668. The quote in this paragraph differs from NSC 20/1, in which "for what it is" is used rather than "true nature," and in which there is no mention of the Soviet-directed world Communist Party.

44. NSC 20/4, in *FRUS*, 1948, vol. 1 (part 2), 666.

45. Nitze, *From Hiroshima to Glasnost*, 97. Nitze consistently aimed to give credit where due. Here, he thought Kennan deserved the credit; regarding the Marshall Plan speech, he disagreed with Kennan's recollection and bestowed more credit on Bohlen (see page 53).

46. See chapter 5 in this volume for consideration of PPS 43.

47. See PPS 39/1, "United States Policy toward China," November 23, 1948, in Etzold and Gaddis, *Containment*, 247–51, reprinted from *FRUS*, 1948, vol. 8, 208–11.

48. See PPS 43, "Considerations Affecting the Conclusion of a North Atlantic Security Pact," November 23, 1948, in Etzold and Gaddis, *Containment*, 153–58, reprinted from *FRUS*, 1948, vol. 3, 284–88. Gaddis and Etzold's view of PPS 43, regarding Kennan's begrudging acceptance, is on page 153.

49. NSC 7, "The Position of the United States with Respect to Soviet-Directed World Communism," March 30, 1948, in *FRUS*, 1948, vol. 1 (part 2), 545–50, re-

printed in Etzold and Gaddis, *Containment,* 161–64. Postrevisionism, seeking to validate Kennan's influence, tends to deprecate or overlook this document; in *Strategies
of Containment,* for example, Gaddis put NSC 7 in an endnote, seemingly to criticize
the universalism of those who did not listen to Kennan. Yet just because a universal threat was recognized, it did not mean that Truman (or the National Security
Council) was incapable of prudent American actions. Nor did it mean that the president and the council succumbed to uncritical universalism. NSC 7, in fact, warned of
the deficiency of a defensive policy that "by attempting to be strong everywhere runs
the risk of being weak everywhere." Such a policy, said the document, would cede the
initiative to the Kremlin, enabling it to strike or withdraw at the time and place of its
choosing (see page 547).

50. See chapter 4 in this volume for discussion of these two speeches.

51. Two memoranda in April 1948 reveal that diplomatists and strategists split
on the merits of NSC 7. These memos also show that Truman drew from his top
advisors without being mired in their disagreements. See "Memorandum by the
Acting Director of the Policy Planning Staff (Butler) to the Under Secretary of State
(Lovett)," April 9, 1948, in *FRUS,* 1948, vol. 1 (part 2), 560–61. Kennan was ill at
the time but obviously attentive to the matter. Butler crafted a memo which omitted by name those on the PPS who supported NSC 7 and mentioned that Bohlen,
Rusk, Henderson, Hickerson, and Butterworth found it too general. Of Kennan, he
wrote, "Mr. Kennan feels very strongly that the Secretary and he should have an opportunity to study and comment on the paper before the National Security Council
members consider it. Mr. Bohlen concurs in this view. The Planning Staff so recom-
mends." In the margin, Lovett handwrote, "I think the paper is inadequate and will
give a false impression if not revised—as an *initial* study it may have value." Then
see "Memorandum by the Secretary of Defense (Forrestal) to the National Security
Council," April 17, 1948, in *FRUS,* 1948, vol. 1 (part 2), 561–64. Here, the Joint
Chiefs of Staff concurred in all but one of NSC 7's conclusions with military implications. In their exception, the Joint Chiefs of Staff were concerned that, if machine
tools were supplied to non-Communist nations, the exportation of tools not interfere
with U.S. needs and that they not fall into Soviet hands.

52. The NSC staff structure bothered Kennan, because it was dominated by
military personnel and was active in preparing papers, and this was part of his disagreement with papers like NSC 7. The NSC staff structure was reorganized in July
1950 so that high-level representatives from all related departments were represented.
But what Kennan had friction with during his tenure as Policy Planning Staff director—and even when he was temporarily acting as PPS director at the outbreak of the
Korean War in June 1950 when Nitze was on vacation—was an NSC staff structure
he disliked intensely and whose influence on policymaking he deplored. For more on
the composition of the National Security Council staff, see Mitrovich, *Undermining
the Kremlin,* 24 and 24 n. 49.

53. NSC 7, in *FRUS,* 1948, vol. 1 (part 2), 546.

54. Ibid., 547.

55. Ibid., 547, 548.

56. Cited and paraphrased from *FRUS, 1945–1950, Emergence of the Intelligence Establishment* (Washington, D.C.: U.S. Government Printing Office, 1996), 616.

57. NSC 7, in *FRUS*, 1948, vol. 1 (part 2), 549.

58. NSC 4-A, "Memorandum from the Executive Secretary of the National Security Council (Souers) to Director of Central Intelligence Hillenkoetter," December 14, 1947, in *FRUS, Intelligence,* 650.

59. "Memorandum for the President of Discussion at the 9th Meeting of the National Security Council," April 2, 1948, in *FRUS, Intelligence,* 664; "Memorandum from the Assistant Secretary of State for Public Affairs (Allen) to Acting Secretary of State Lovett," March 31, 1948, in ibid., 661–62; "Memorandum from the Director of the Office of Information and Educational Exchange (Stone) to Acting Secretary of State Lovett, April 1, 1948, in ibid., 663; and Policy Planning Staff Memorandum, May 4, 1948, in ibid., 668–72.

60. Cited and paraphrased from NSC 10/2, "National Security Council Directive on Office of Special Projects," June 18, 1948, in *FRUS, Intelligence,* 713–15.

61. Policy Planning Staff Memorandum, May 4, 1948, in *FRUS, Intelligence,* 668–72. See also William M. Leary, ed., *The Central Intelligence Agency: History and Documents* (Tuscaloosa: University of Alabama Press, 1984), 41.

62. See the series of documents after September 1947 and leading up to and including the Policy Planning Staff memorandum of May 1948 that are collected in *FRUS, Intelligence,* in the chapter entitled "Psychological and Political Warfare," 622–745.

63. Deputy Chief of CIA History Staff Michael Warner points out that a "recently declassified CIA study of the Office of the Policy Coordination called NS 10/2 a treaty between the Secretaries of State and Defense that gave the office two, competing masters." See Michael Warner, "The CIA's Office of Policy Coordination: From NSC 10/2 to NSC 68," *Intelligence and Counterintelligence,* vol. 11, no. 2, 211–19. The study is by Gerald Miller, "Office of Policy Coordination, 1948–1952," no date, and its declassified sections are accessible on the CIA's Web site.

64. "Memorandum from the Director of the Policy Planning Staff (Kennan) to the Under Secretary of State (Lovett)," June 8, 1949, in *FRUS, Intelligence,* 702; "Memorandum from the Director of the Policy Planning Staff (Kennan) to the Under Secretary of State (Lovett) and Secretary of State Marshall," in ibid., 709.

65. Kennan's October 28, 1975, testimony, cited in Leary, *Central Intelligence Agency,* 43. Two recent books—one academic and one popular—have examined NSC 10/2 and argued that Kennan was the mastermind behind the document and U.S. covert actions. "When the diplomatic archives were finally unsealed," writes Peter Grose, "they revealed the architect and champion of American covert action against east European communism to be 'Mr. X' himself, George F. Kennan." See Peter Grose, *Operation Rollback: America's Secret War behind the Iron Curtain* (Boston: Houghton Mifflin, 2000), 6. See also the author's argument about Kennan's role on pages 94–99, in which the author sometimes confuses dates from 1947 and 1948. Gregory Mitrovich finds Kennan's contribution to the NSC 20 series to be paramount (see chapter 6 in this volume) but also details Kennan's involvement in NSC 10/2. In

describing Kennan's efforts to secure primary authority for the State Department—not the Defense Department or CIA—in the Office of Special Projects, Mitrovich is closer to the truth than Grose is. See Mitrovich, *Undermining the Kremlin,* 19; see also pages 18, 28–29. Not a recent discovery, NSC 10/2 had been published in 1978; see Etzold and Gaddis, *Containment,* 125–128.

66. Truman, June 7, 1945, Longhand Notes File, 1945, Box 333, PSF, HSTP, HSTL.

67. Allen Weinstein, *Perjury: The Hiss-Chambers Case* (New York: Alfred A. Knopf, 1978), 4.

68. Clifford with Holbrooke, *Counsel to the President,* 180–81. For Clifford's take on the loyalty program, see pages 175–84, which include a scorching indictment of Hoover.

69. Truman, *Years of Trial and Hope,* 270. It should be emphasized that this memoir opinion was written after the phenomenon of McCarthyism.

70. Acheson, *Present at the Creation,* 360.

71. For additional information on Hiss, see Sam Tanenhaus, *Whittaker Chambers: A Biography* (New York: Random House, 1997), 385–86, 225–26.

72. "The President's News Conference of August 5, 1948," in Truman, *Public Papers,* vol. 4, 431–35. For consideration of the "red herring" statement in later years, see Tanenhaus, *Whittaker Chambers,* 479. As Tanenhaus writes of 1953: "The 'conspiracy on a scale so immense as to dwarf any previous such venture in the history of man'—in McCarthy's words—had indeed been formidable. But the most important agents had been flushed out years before. Critics still harped on Truman's 'red herring' statement. They ignored the thrust of his remarks. . . . So things had stood in 1948. Five years later the pickings were even slimmer, as almost everyone knew but was afraid to say, for fear of inciting McCarthy, whose grip had become paralyzing."

73. "The President's News Conference of August 19, 1948," in Truman, *Public Papers,* vol. 4, 452–55.

74. Truman did not define Hiss as a top advisor. Again, we do not have Truman's opinion of what breaches he inherited from the Roosevelt administration. In *Harry S. Truman,* page 301, Ferrell offers a breakdown of the loyalty program's efforts through mid-1952: out of the more than 4 million people—actual or prospective employees—who had gone through the check, 9,077 were charged by loyalty program boards, 2,961 were brought to hearings, and 378 were dismissed or denied employment. According to Ferrell, none of the discharged cases led to discovery of espionage.

75. Truman to the Attorney General, December 16, 1948, reproduced as document 22 in Robert Louis Benson and Michael Warner, eds., *Venona: Soviet Espionage and the American Response 1939–1957* (Washington, D.C.: National Security Agency, Central Intelligence Agency, 1996), 119.

76. Benson and Warner, *Venona,* vii–xxx. See especially, Cecil James Phillips, "What Made Venona Possible?" xv. Also see Richard Gid Powers's introduction to Daniel Patrick Moynihan, *Secrecy: The American Experience* (New Haven, Conn.: Yale University Press, 1998), 54.

77. Moynihan, *Secrecy,* 71. Also see *SECRECY: Report of the Commission on*

Protecting and Reducing Government Secrecy (Washington, D.C.: U.S. Government Printing Office, 1997), appendix, pp. A33-A34, cited in Weinstein and Vassiliev, *Haunted Wood,* 291.

78. Moynihan, *Secrecy,* 70–73. Moynihan here reprints an October 18, 1949, memorandum by FBI agent Howard B. Fletcher, describing a recent conference between General Carter W. Clarke, then chief of the Army Security Agency; Admiral Earl E. Stone, head of the Armed Forces Security Agency; and Bradley in regard to the "dissemination of [Venona] material to the Central Intelligence Agency." From context, it appears that the Army Security Agency had withheld Venona information from the CIA and, perhaps, the FBI until this time. For more on this episode, see John Earl Haynes and Harvey Klehr, *Venona: Decoding Soviet Espionage in America* (New Haven, Conn.: Yale University Press, 1999), 14–19.

8. The Culmination of Truman's Containment

1. Acheson, *Present at the Creation,* 374–75. For instance, Acheson biographer James Chace builds his chapter on the Truman Doctrine around the "clearer than truth" phrase. See Chace, *Acheson,* especially 168. Even in April 1950, Acheson wanted no action yet on NSC 68 and seems to have found it an exaggeration. See Memorandum for the President, April 21, 1950, Student Research Files, Folder 10, Box 1, PSF, HSTP, HSTL. In March 1950, Acheson said that the dynamic American steps of 1947 through 1949 had "lost their momentum and we seem to have slowed down to a point where we are on the defensive while the Soviets are apparently showing more confidence. We could not hold our position defensively, we would slip backward. It was, therefore, necessary to find some new idea or new step which would regain the initiative." Although the timing is right for NSC 68 and Nitze was present in this conversation, Acheson appears to have been talking about the need for a bold new public initiative, perhaps the Campaign of Truth of 1950. See March 7, 1950, Memorandum of Conversation, File: March 1950, January–July 1950, Box 66, Acheson Papers, HSTL. Acheson eventually committed to NSC 68 and did everything he could to assure its implementation after Truman approved the document. See, for example, Acheson's October 10, 1950, conversation with Lovett, File: October 1950, August–December 1950, Box 67, Acheson Papers, HSTL.

2. For details on the Sino-Soviet relationship, see David Wolff, "'One Finger's Worth of Historical Events': New Russian and Chinese Evidence on the Sino-Soviet Alliance and Split, 1948–1959," Working Paper no. 30, Cold War International History Project, August 2000, especially 2–10 and Documents 1–7. Document 6, a December 1, 1949, entry from the diary of USSR Ambassador to the PRC N. V. Roshchin, describes Soviet and Chinese plans (discussed on November 15, 1949) to attack Tibet after the "liberation" of Sichuan and Xinjiang and preparations for an operation on Formosa in 1950.

3. For analysis that was given to Truman of the repercussions of the Soviet acquisition of an atomic capability, see Weekly Summary Excerpt, September 30, 1949, "Soviet Union: Atomic Explosion," in Kuhns, *Assessing the Soviet Threat,* 334–35.

4. Nitze, *From Hiroshima to Glasnost,* 87, 91. Nitze received this account directly from Acheson. As Acheson's delegate to a working group to advise the special committee of the National Security Council, Nitze was present at other meetings and had been advising Acheson along the way on the feasibility of the H-bomb.

5. Nitze later commended Truman for his decision and pointed out that, unknown to the United States at the time, Stalin had approved Soviet pursuit of the H-bomb around November 1, 1949—a full three months before Truman made his decision. Since the Soviets used a different technique from the United States, they succeeded in producing usable thermonuclear weapons much earlier than the United States did. As Nitze concluded: "There can now be little doubt that had Mr. Truman not acted when he did, the Soviets would have achieved unchallengeable nuclear superiority by the late 1950s." See Nitze, *From Hiroshima to Glasnost,* 91–92.

6. "Remarks at the Armed Forces Dinner," May 19, 1950, in Truman, *Public Papers,* vol. 6, 423–25. Truman had public opinion on his side. In March 1950, 74 percent of people in a NORC survey were for firmer policies against the Soviet Union; by April 1950, 89 percent of Americans in NORC surveys said they considered "stopping the world spread of communism" to be "very important." See Page and Shapiro, *Rational Public,* 201.

7. NSC 68, April 1950, in *FRUS,* 1950, vol. 1, 263, where Nitze and his coauthors wrote: "The Kremlin design seeks to impose order among nations by means which would destroy our free and democratic system. The Kremlin's possession of atomic weapons puts new power behind its design, and increases the jeopardy to our system. It adds new strains to the uneasy equilibrium-without-order which exists in the world and raises new doubts in men's minds whether the world will long tolerate this tension without moving toward some kind of order, on somebody's terms."

8. Above all, see Kennan's personal paper to Acheson, "International Control of Atomic Energy," January 20, 1950, in *FRUS,* 1950, vol. 1, 22–44, also excerpted in Etzold and Gaddis, *Containment,* 373–81.Gaddis and Etzold explain that no one would go along with Kennan when this paper began as a PPS analysis, so Kennan submitted it by himself to Acheson. See Etzold and Gaddis, *Containment,* 373. Kennan himself considered this paper to be the most important one he ever wrote.

9. Truman had not liked Chiang from the time he (Truman) became president, and Marshall's 1947 opinions, developed during his mission to China (that Chiang was as bad as Mao in some respects and that no plausible solution was possible for a non-Communist China through American efforts), reinforced the president's view. In this regard, China was written off as early as 1947.

10. See November 1945 memorandum, in Truman, *Off the Record,* 74, and Truman's letter to Byrnes, January 5, 1946, Longhand Notes File, 1945–1952, Box 333, PSF, HSTP, HSTL. For more on the letter to Byrnes, see chapter 1 in this volume.

11. Harry S. Truman, interview by Jonathan Daniels, November 12, 1949, Notes for *The Man of Independence,* Daniels Papers, HSTL.

12. "Dear Bill," Truman to William O. Douglas, September 13, 1951, in Truman, *Off the Record,* 217–18. As Truman concluded his letter, "I am being very frank with you Bill because fundamentally I am very fond of you but you have missed

the boat on three different occasions if you really wanted to get into politics. Since you are on the highest Court in the land it seems to me that the best thing you can possibly do would be to give your best effort to that Court and let the President of the United States run the political end of foreign and domestic affairs." The "three different occasions" referred to the fact that Truman had twice asked Douglas to be secretary of the interior, in 1946 and 1948, and had asked him to join the 1948 ticket as his vice-presidential candidate.

13. According to Steven Rearden, Truman received a preliminary copy of NSC 68 on March 31, and it was officially submitted to him on April 11. See Steven L. Rearden, *The Evolution of American Strategic Doctrine: Paul H. Nitze and the Soviet Challenge* (Boulder, Colo.: Westview Press, 1984), 83 n. 34. But at the Truman Library, the NSC files document Truman's request for NSC 68 on April 7. Whichever date is correct, the president took the initiative well ahead of the National Security Council's meeting as a group. See also letter from Truman to Lay, April 12, 1950, National Security Council Meeting 55, April 20, 1950, Box 207, PSF, HSTP, HSTL.

14. For more on the latter point, see Isaacson and Thomas, *Wise Men,* 504.

15. See Minutes to 68th Meeting of the National Security Council, September 29, 1950, National Security Council Meeting 68, Box 209, PSF, HSTP, HSTL. Also see *FRUS,* 1950, vol. 1, 400, 466–69.

16. Memo to the President, July 27, 1950, subject: Discussion at 62nd Meeting NSC, July 27, 1950, RG 273, Records of the NSC, NARA, cited in Samuel R. Williamson Jr. and Steven L. Rearden, *The Origins of U.S. Nuclear Strategy, 1945–1953* (New York: St. Martin's Press, 1993), 139.

17. Bell, *Negotiation from Strength,* 6. Also Steven L. Rearden, "Frustrating the Kremlin Design," in Douglas Brinkley, ed., *Dean Acheson and the Making of U.S. Foreign Policy* (New York: St. Martin's Press, 1993), 168.

18. See Nelson, "President Truman and the Evolution of the National Security Council," 372. Nelson makes this point persuasively and adds that James Lay "was either unwilling or unable to assume the tasks of coordinating information and soothing relationships that were performed by Souers." In addition, Souers became a White House counsel and offered his services intermittently to Truman.

19. Truman had never been happy with Johnson as secretary of defense. But Johnson's fund-raising efforts had been crucial to Truman's election in 1948, and Johnson subsequently demanded the DOD post. Johnson's behavior about NSC 68 was the final straw in a long list of rudeness and ego. Truman worked behind the scenes to get a new secretary of defense, too. He wanted George Marshall and got him to take the job in late September 1950. For examples of Truman's displeasure with Johnson, see August 3, 1950, memorandum from Louis Johnson, with handwritten note to Sidney Souers on it, File: Souers—White House Counsel, 1950–1953, Box 1, Sidney Souers Papers, HSTL; and Truman's September 11, 1950, longhand personal memo on Louis Johnson, Longhand Notes File, 1945–1952, Box 333, PSF, HSTP, HSTL. In the latter, Truman referred to Johnson's egotism and said that the secretary of defense suffered from some sort of complex.

20. Souers, memorandum for file, June 8, 1950, Box 1, Souers Papers, HSTL;

Oral History Interview: The Truman White House, by Hugh Heclo and Anna K. Nelson, February 20, 1980, HSTL, 75–77, quoted in Nelson, "President Truman and the Evolution of the National Security Council," 376.

21. NSC 68, in *FRUS*, 1950, vol. 1, 234–92. An original hard copy of the document with the date of April 14 can be found in Meeting 55, April 20, 1950, Box 207, Records of the National Security Council, HSTL.

22. For more consideration of this point, see chapter 1 in this volume.

23. NSC 68, in *FRUS*, 1950, vol. 1, 237–38.

24. Ibid., 238.

25. Truman, *Years of Trial and Hope*, 108. Truman quotes from his own Jefferson Day speech in this passage.

26. NSC 68, in *FRUS*, 1950, vol. 1, 238.

27. Ibid., 239.

28. Ibid., 240, 239, 240.

29. Ibid., 240.

30. Ibid., 241–42.

31. Ibid., 243–44. According to the authors, "Practical and ideological considerations therefore both impel us to the conclusion that we have no choice but to demonstrate the superiority of the idea of freedom by its constructive application, and to attempt to change the world situation by means short of war in such a way as to frustrate the Kremlin design and hasten the decay of the Soviet system."

32. Ibid., 246, 245. The previous two sentences of the paragraph paraphrase from "Study Prepared by the Director of the Policy Planning Staff (Nitze), February 8, 1950," in *FRUS*, 1950, vol. 1, 145–47. In key respects, Nitze's study reads as an advance précis of NSC 68.

33. Gaddis, *Strategies of Containment*, 34. Gaddis has mostly supported Kennan's contention that ideology justified retroactively rather than guided Soviet behavior. In his latest writings, Gaddis acknowledges more of a role for Communist ideology.

34. "Study Prepared by the Director of the Policy Planning Staff (Nitze)," in *FRUS*, 1950, vol. 1, 145–47.

35. Gaddis sustained the emphasis on intentions in *Strategies of Containment*, in order to criticize what he termed Truman's distortion of Kennan.

36. The distinction is critical. While realists saw nationalism as a possible challenge to communism, they accented the downside of nationalism. NSC 68, by contrast, focused on the positive qualities of different peoples' nationalities. If given the opportunity, according to NSC 68's reasoning, free peoples would set up free nations with free institutions.

37. NSC 68, in *FRUS*, 1950, vol. 1, 247.

38. Ibid., 252–53.

39. Ibid., 284.

40. Ibid., 264–65.

41. Ibid., 263, 291.

42. Nitze, *From Hiroshima to Glasnost*, 98, regarding the fact that NSC 68's conclusions already undergirded American foreign policy. Despite his support of NSC 68

at the time (total) and over the following decades (near total), Nitze altered his view for certain academic audiences. See John Lewis Gaddis, "NSC 68 and the Problem of Ends and Means," and Paul Nitze, "The Development of NSC 68," both in "NSC 68 and the Soviet Threat Reconsidered," *International Security* 4, no. 4 (Spring 1980): 164–76. Gaddis accented alleged false perceptions, while Nitze downplayed NSC 68 as a product of its time. But then Nitze somewhat revised his view of NSC 68 for his memoir, in contrast to the 1980 *International Security* article.

43. For Kennan's own explanation of how he has been consistent since the 1940s, see Kennan to John Lukacs, April 28, 1995, in Kennan and Lukacs, *George F. Kennan and the Origins of Containment,* 63–72.

44. George F. Kennan, *American Diplomacy,* foreword. I deliberately use the original 1951 edition here, rather than Kennan's later and expanded version of *American Diplomacy.*

45. Ibid.

46. Kennan, *American Diplomacy,* 9–10.

47. As Kennan said in 1975, "Sometimes I've been charged with being an elitist. Well, of course, I am. What do people expect? God forbid that we should be without an elite. Is everything to be done by gray mediocrity? After all, our whole system is based on the selection of people for different functions in our life. When you talk about selection, you're talking about an elite." See Eric Sevareid, "Conversation with George Kennan," 1975, in George F. Kennan, *Interviews with George F. Kennan,* ed. T. Christopher Jespersen (Jackson: University Press of Mississippi, 2002), 153–54.

48. Kennan, *American Diplomacy,* 11, 12.

49. The New Left overviews of twentieth-century American diplomacy have used the same periodization and chronology of events. See the work of William Appleman Williams (*Tragedy of American Diplomacy*) and Walter LaFeber (*America, Russia, and the Cold War, 1945–1966* [New York: John Wiley and Sons, 1967]) for two standard examples.

50. Kennan, *American Diplomacy,* 20. The rest of the sentence carries on in the same vein.

51. Ibid., 51.

52. Ibid., 71.

53. Ibid., 77.

54. Ibid., 77–79.

55. Ibid., 89–106, 106–27. "America and the Russian Future" is reprinted from George Kennan, same title, in *Foreign Affairs* 29, no. 3 (April 1951): 351–70. In this article, Kennan argued that America should never expect Russia to resemble the United States in its principles or institutions. He awaited a more moderate Russia and said that totalitarianism was a disease to which all humanity was vulnerable. He concluded that the Soviet Union could not last forever and that the best course for America was to set its own house in order and, as Thoreau put it, hold out a taper of light. Kennan interpreted this taper and its rays as the example of the United States. He thought it sufficient if America "shed the shackles of disunity, confusion and doubt" and took a "new lease of hope and determination, and was setting about her tasks with enthusiasm and clarity of purpose."

56. Kennan was not unkind to his predecessors, but he bestowed a backhanded compliment; see Kennan, *American Diplomacy,* 80, 81. Kennan seemed to find the gap wider because of the existence of atomic weapons and modern technology, rather than because of a totalitarian possession or use of them. Refer to chapter 5 in this volume for further discussion of this point.

57. Kennan, *American Diplomacy,* 82, 81.

58. Ibid., 85.

59. Ibid., 56.

60. Kennan, *Memoirs,* 358, and November 23, 1950, Kennan letter to Nathan Leites, author of "The Operational Code of the Politburo," File 1, 1950, Correspondence, 1950–1956, Box 29, GFKP, SGML, PU.

61. Kennan, *Memoirs,* 358, 250–51, 367.

62. Truman, *Years of Trial and Hope,* 290.

9. History, Faith, and Peace in Truman's Thought

1. Truman, January 27, 1952, Longhand Notes File, 1945–1952, Box 333, PSF, HSTP, HSTL.

2. Truman, May 18, 1952, Longhand Notes File, 1945–1952, Box 333, PSF, HSTP, HSTL.

3. Ibid.

4. Truman, July 16, 1945, from Potsdam, in Truman, *Off the Record,* 50–53.

5. Truman, May 23, 1945, Longhand Notes File, Box 333, PSF, HSTP, HSTL.

6. In an October 8, 1939, address in Caruthersville, Missouri, Truman showed the opposing ways that technology could be used, deploring the three dictators—Russian, German, and Italian—who have "used this magnificent machine age of ours to destroy our vaulted civilization" and his unshakable belief, here and in other places, that America could and should develop advanced capabilities so as to be prepared for war. See his address, read into the appendix to U.S. Congress, *Congressional Record,* October 9, 1939, vol. 85, part 2, 76th Congress, 2nd Session, pp. 202–3. On the subject of human nature, Truman was definitely concerned about the development of weapons of mass destruction. In September 1946, he wrote, "The human animal and his emotions change not much from age to age. He must change now or he faces absolute and complete destruction and maybe the insect age or an atmosphereless planet will succeed him." See Truman, Longhand Notes File, 1946, Box 333, PSF, HSTP, HSTL.

7. Harry S. Truman, *Mr. Citizen* (New York: Popular Library, 1961), 160.

8. Truman, January 1 and 2, 1952, Longhand Notes File, 1952, Box 333, PSF, HSTP, HSTL.

9. Truman, *Mr. Citizen,* 204.

10. Truman to Edward Harris, July 19, 1950, in Truman, *Off the Record,* 186–87.

11. This eight-volume set of books is, formally, *Great Men and Famous Women:*

A Series of Pen and Pencil Sketches of the Lives of More Than 200 of the Most Prominent Personages in History. The individuals are divided into three categories: soldiers and sailors, statesmen and sages, and artists and authors. The section on statesmen and sages—which runs from Moses, King David, and Pericles to Peter the Great, George Washington, and Abraham Lincoln—begins with this passage from Longfellow: "Lives of great men all remind us, / We can make our lives sublime, / And departing, leave behind us / Footprints on the sands of time." The books were published in 1894 by Selmar Hess Publisher of New York.

12. Truman, *Mr. Citizen,* 111.

13. It is pertinent to note here that Marcus Aurelius's *Meditations* reinforced Truman's opinion. Of this work, he said, "Some people think they're old-fashioned, but I don't. What he wrote in his *Meditations,* he said that the four greatest virtues are moderation, wisdom, justice, and fortitude, and if a man is able to cultivate those, that's all he needs to live a happy and successful life. That's the way I look at it anyway." For a description of the lines Truman underlined in his copy of the *Meditations,* see Miller, *Plain Speaking,* 26–27. For illumination of Truman's thought about history and religion, this book is of use when cross-referenced with other sources.

14. In this context, it is interesting to note that George Washington's favorite play was *Cato.* Memorandum, July 8, 1953, in Truman, *Off the Record,* 294–95. Truman used Washington and Cincinnatus as personal models. Beginning in April 1950, he started to write in longhand of why he would not be a candidate for president in 1952, specifically citing Washington and Cincinnatus. See April 16, 1950, Longhand Note Files, 1950, Box 333, PSF, HSTP, HSTL. Although he was elected only once to the presidency, it is clear from many of his notes that Truman believed that by the end of 1952 he would have served nearly the equivalent of the precedent set by the first president and should not run again. When he started to write notes to himself about not running, his poll ratings were little different from 1948's; he seems to have been moved primarily by Washington's precedent.

15. For a depiction of Truman's view of history as old-fashioned and simple, see, for example, McCullough, *Truman,* 463–64.

16. Address by Hon. Harry S. Truman before the National Aviation Forum, February 20, 1939, read into the U.S. Congress, *Congressional Record,* February 21, 1939, vol. 84, part 11, 76th Congress, 1st Session, Jan. 3–Mar. 28, 1939, pp. 642–43.

17. Truman, *Mr. Citizen,* 196–97.

18. In this chapter, the terms "faith" and "religion" are used interchangeably.

19. Ferrell, *Harry S. Truman: A Life,* 49, 134.

20. McCullough, *Truman,* 83.

21. Hamby, *Man of the People,* 21, 474.

22. George Elsey, who worked with Truman on many presidential speeches, recalled that Truman believed in the spiritual and moral statements he had made in his speeches and that "[m]any of these phrases and sentences were added by him in longhand very near the final draft of a speech." See Oral History Interview with George M. Elsey, Washington, D.C., February 10 and 17, 1964; March 9, 1965; July

10 and 17, 1969; and July 7 and 10, 1970 by Charles T. Morrissey and Jerry N. Hess, HSTL (May 1974).

23. Truman, Autobiographical Sketch, Biographical File, Box 298, PSF, HSTP, HSTL. From the context, it appears that Truman wrote this sketch some time after January 20, 1945.

24. Ferrell, *Harry S. Truman: A Life,* 49; Truman, *Where the Buck Stops,* 341–43. In 1906, Truman upheld his civic duties of citizenship by serving as a Democratic election clerk in Jackson County, Missouri.

25. Truman to Bess, February 7, 1911, in Truman, *Dear Bess,* 22–23.

26. This letter was also most probably the first missive from Truman to Bess in which he signed his first name rather than his full name.

27. Truman to Bess, February 7, 1911, in Truman, *Dear Bess,* 22–23.

28. Truman to Bess, March 19, 1911, in Truman, *Dear Bess,* 24–25.

29. Truman, *Mr. Citizen,* 95. Truman credited this to his grandfather: "When a man spends Saturday night and Sunday doing too much howling and praying, you had better go home and lock your smoke house."

30. Truman, Autobiographical Sketch, Biographical File, Box 298, PSF, HSTP, HSTL.

31. This sentiment was one he learned from both of his grandfathers. See Truman, *Mr. Citizen,* 95.

32. Truman to Bess, July 31, 1918, in Truman, *Dear Bess,* 268.

33. Truman to Bess, June 22, 1936, in Truman, *Dear Bess,* 388.

34. Truman, June 1, 1952, in Truman, *Off the Record,* 251–52.

35. Truman, *Mr. Citizen,* 95.

36. Truman, June 1, 1945, Longhand Notes File, 1945–1952, Box 333, PSF, HSTP, HSTL. Truman maintained that God picked no "priorities," in the context of writing that Jews were not picked out for special privilege by God. See also Truman, *Talking with Harry,* 289; speaking of religious divisions, Truman said, "There isn't any sense in it at all, because when you get right down to brass tacks, they all believe in honor and the welfare of the individual, and some time or other, we'll come to the conclusion where we can sit down side by side and let the other fellow do as he pleases."

37. "Address on Foreign Policy at a Luncheon of the American Society of Newspaper Editors," April 20, 1950, in Truman, *Public Papers,* vol. 6, 260–64. The expansion of Voice of America involved not only additional and improved information and educational services but also new technology to overcome Soviet jamming of the broadcasts.

38. Edward W. Barrett testimony, "Voice of America," July 27, 1950, U.S. Senate Committee on Foreign Relations, Subcommittee on Public Affairs, Executive Session, SFRC Selected Documents, Box 10, HSTL, cited in Walter L. Hixson, *Parting the Curtain: Propaganda, Culture, and the Cold War, 1945–1961* (New York: St. Martin's Griffin, 1998), 14.

39. Quoted in Hixson, *Parting the Curtain,* 15.

40. See, for example, "Letter to Senator Flanders on the Appropriation for the

Campaign of Truth," August 30, 1950, in Truman, *Public Papers,* vol. 6, 602–3. Truman aide Mark Etheridge recalled that Dean Acheson was not enthusiastic about the overseas program: "He didn't think information ought to be mixed with policy." See Hixson, *Parting the Curtain,* 241 n. 49.

41. The American Committee for Freedom for the Peoples of the USSR was started in 1951, and its broadcast station became known as Radio Liberty. For more on Voice of America during this period, see David F. Krugler, *The Voice of America and the Domestic Propaganda Battles, 1945–1953* (Columbia: University of Missouri Press, 2000); for more on Radio Free Europe and Radio Liberty, see Arch Puddington, *Broadcasting Freedom: The Cold War Triumph of Radio Free Europe and Radio Liberty* (Lexington: University Press of Kentucky), 2000. When most historians and political scientists evaluate these bodies, they view them primarily in psychological terms. They assert that a change in the perception of the U.S.-Soviet relationship caused a sense of weakness in the West and an American unwillingness to approach negotiations with the Kremlin. In this view, Chinese communism and the Soviet atomic bomb were psychological shocks rather than political realities. See, for example, Gaddis, *Strategies of Containment,* 85. Corporatism, too, places emphasis on perceptions over reality.

42. "Address in Columbus at a Conference of the Federal Council of Churches," March 6, 1946, in Truman, *Public Papers,* vol. 2, 141–44. The main thrust of this speech concerns rebuilding America in the aftermath of World War II, as well as the new challenge of atomic energy. Secondarily, Truman seems to be referring to the threat from communism.

43. Truman to Bess, October 2, 1947, in Truman, *Dear Bess,* 551–52. Particularly in 1946 and 1947, Truman met constant objections from Protestants, including from leaders of his own Baptist faith, about Taylor's ongoing mission in Rome.

44. "Address in Spokane at Gonzaga University," May 11, 1950, in Truman, *Public Papers,* vol. 6, 374–77.

45. Roman Catholics were the largest minority population in the United States at the time. For the connection between the Catholic Church and larger anti-Communist efforts and this particular speech, see File on Foreign Relations—Mission to Vatican, Box 65, Elsey Papers, HSTL. Elsey was active in helping Truman with the Gonzaga University speech.

46. "Exchange of Messages with Pope Pius XII," December 23, 1949, in Truman, *Public Papers,* vol. 5, 587–88.

47. "Address in Spokane at Gonzaga University," May 11, 1950, in Truman, *Public Papers,* vol. 6, 374–77.

48. On this point see Merlin Gustafson, "Harry Truman as a Man of Faith," *Christian Century* 90 (January 17, 1973): 75–77. In the 1970s, Gustafson wrote this and another article on Truman's religion; in each, he misread Truman as a Calvinist determinist.

49. Truman to Rev. Johnson, president of the Baptist World Alliance, July 15, 1950, File 220, 1949–53, Box 823, HSTP, HSTL.

50. "Address before the Midcentury White House Conference on Children and Youth," December 5, 1950, in Truman, *Public Papers,* vol. 6, 733–37.

51. "Address in Philadelphia at the Dedication of the Chapel of the Four Chaplains," February 3, 1951, in Truman, *Public Papers,* vol. 7, 139–41.

52. "Address at the Cornerstone Laying at the New York Avenue Presbyterian Church," April 3, 1951, in Truman, *Public Papers,* vol. 7, 210–13.

53. Ibid. Truman was wont to say that the United States had rejected its responsibility as a global leader in the aftermath of World War I.

54. "Address to the Washington Pilgrimage of American Churchmen," September 28, 1951, in Truman, *Public Papers,* vol. 7, 547–50.

55. Ibid.

56. Ibid.

57. Acheson, *Present at the Creation,* 574–75. As Acheson recalled, "At one of our meetings early in October the President observed that I was an even greater practitioner of the delaying tactic than Fabius Maximus Cunctator himself and that, if left to me, no appropriate time would come."

58. Footnote explanation in "The President's News Conference of October 25, 1951," in Truman, *Public Papers,* vol. 7, 601.

59. Donald R. McCoy, *The Presidency of Harry S. Truman* (Lawrence: University Press of Kansas, 1984), 277. Clark himself was a Protestant, as was Myron Taylor.

60. Truman, February 26, 1952, Longhand Notes File, 1952 (longhand personal memos, folder 1), PSF, HSTP, HSTL.

61. As Truman recalled in 1959, "I wanted the moral forces of the world to make a common front against the unmoral forces, and we got pretty well along with it. It made quite an impression on a great many of the countries and the leaders of the religious sects in various countries. The people who were most violently opposed to it were the Protestants right here in the United States." See Truman, *Talking with Harry,* 290.

62. "Address at the Cornerstone Laying at the New York Avenue Presbyterian Church," April 3, 1951, in Truman, *Public Papers,* vol. 7, 210–13.

63. "Inaugural Address," January 20, 1949, in Truman, *Public Papers,* vol. 5, 112–16.

64. "Address at the Unveiling of a Memorial Carillon in Arlington National Cemetery," December 21, 1949, in Truman, *Public Papers,* vol. 5, 582–83. The connection between what Truman said here and his consistent request for additional funding for Voice of America and, eventually, Radio Free Europe and Radio Liberty seems strong.

65. Truman, *Mr. Citizen,* 101. Truman described his earliest exposure to the Bible: "My mother, married in 1881 to my father, had a great big gold-back Bible with the first part of the Revised Version. One column represented the Bible as it should be, the other side was the Revised Version. And I got a chance to read them both. If I wanted to find out anything in either Testament, I didn't read the Revised Version. I read the translation that was made under King James of Great Britain. That was the greatest thing he ever did in his life, and the reason for that, in my opinion, is the fact that that, along with Shakespeare, established the English language as we know it." Truman said of his inauguration: "I was presented with a Vulgate and a copy

of the Gutenberg Bible, and I was sworn in on that Latin Book. And as you know, I had them turn to the twentieth chapter of Exodus." As was common of those of his generation, Truman had studied Latin in school. He seemed to be quite proficient, for he did extra drilling with Bess as a schoolboy since poor vision prevented him from joining in neighborhood sports. While president, he corrected Chief Justice Fred Vinson's Latin. For this last point, see Ferrell, *Harry S. Truman: A Life*, 19.

66. Truman, *Mr. Citizen*, 102.

67. Ibid., 103.

68. "Address on Foreign Policy at the Navy Day Celebration in New York City," October 27, 1945, in Truman, *Public Papers*, vol. 1, 431–38. Truman often invoked the golden rule in speeches and press conferences.

69. Truman, Longhand Notes File, 1952 (longhand personal memos, folder 1), Box 333, PSF, HSTP, HSTL.

70. Truman, *Mr. Citizen*, 104. "'Do you know where the Good Neighbor Policy of the United State originated?' Truman continued. 'It originated in the tenth chapter of St. Luke. If you will read this tenth chapter of Luke, you will find out exactly what a good neighbor means. It means treat your neighbor as you yourself would like to be treated. . . . Luke gives us the best definition of it, and you don't have to go anywhere else to find it.'" See Truman, *Mr. Citizen*, 105.

71. Ibid., 105.

72. Truman, August 15, 1950, Longhand Notes File, 1945–1952, Box 333, PSF, HSTP, HSTL.

73. Truman, *Mr. Citizen*, 98.

74. Truman, Longhand Notes File, 1952 (longhand personal memos, folder 1), Box 333, PSF, HSTP, HSTL. Truman singled out Marx, Lenin, Trotsky, and Stalin as those who "upset morals and intellectual honesty."

Conclusion

1. "Truman's Special Message to the Congress on Greece and Turkey," March 12, 1947, in Truman, *Public Papers*, vol. 3, 176–80.

2. Ibid.

3. Truman, Longhand Notes File, 1945–1952, Box 333, PSF, HSTP, HSTL.

4. NSC 68, April 1950, in *FRUS*, 1950, vol. 1, 234–92.

5. "Truman's Special Message to the Congress on Greece and Turkey," March 12, 1947, in Truman, *Public Papers*, vol. 3, 176–80. In a March 13, 1946, AIPO (American Institute of Public Opinion) survey, 60 percent of Americans said that the United States was being "too soft" in its policy toward the USSR. For the same day, AIPO reported that 71 percent of Americans disapproved of the policy the USSR was following in world affairs, and the disapproval percentage was the same in July 1946. In a May 15, 1946, AIPO survey, 58 percent said that the Soviet Union was trying to build itself up to be the "ruling power" of the world, while 29 percent said the USSR was just building up "protection" against being attacked in another war. In September 1946, 62 percent of Americans told AIPO they felt "less friendly" toward

the Soviet Union than they were a year ago, and in December 1946, 48 percent said they felt the same toward the USSR as they had six months before. See Cantril and Strunk, *Public Opinion*, 963, 1060, and 962.

6. Just after the Truman Doctrine speech, 58 percent of Americans in a NORC survey said we should "stop any attempt by Russia to control the countries near her in Europe and Asia," up from 51 percent in October 1947. Responses to a NORC question about whether the United States should "be firmer" or compromise with the USSR were more toward the former than the latter: 68 percent for firmer policies in April 1948, shortly after the Czechoslovak coup; 60 percent for firmer policies in June; and 74 percent in March 1950, after the Communist victory in China and the Soviet detonation of an atomic bomb. By April 1950, 89 percent of Americans said they considered "stopping the world spread of communism" to be "very important." For more on these and other surveys of the period, see Page and Shapiro, *Rational Public*, 199–202.

7. In October 1952, a Gallup poll found that 32 percent of Americans approved and 55 percent disapproved of the way Truman was handling his job as president. It should be remembered that Truman never enjoyed high approval for long when he was president. See Jeffrey M. Jones, "In Election Year 2000, Americans Generally Happy with State of the Nation," Gallup News Service, November 7, 2000, www.gallup.com/poll/releases/pr990401.asp.

8. Alfred Steinberg, *The Man from Missouri: The Life and Times of Harry S. Truman* (New York: G. P. Putnam's Sons, 1962), 11–12, gives this account from Roger Tubby, Truman's assistant press secretary. Truman biographer David McCullough wrote that this account was recorded by press secretary Joe Short, who was on board the *Williamsburg,* as well as being paraphrased in Tubby's diary. See McCullough, *Truman,* 1050 n. 874. *FRUS* accounts by Secretary of State Dean Acheson and Joint Chiefs of Staff Chairman Omar Bradley accented Churchill's praise of Truman with respect to Korea; see *FRUS, 1952–1954,* vol. 6, 730–41. For Acheson's account, also see January 6, 1952, Acheson Memorandum of Dinner Meeting on S.S. *Williamsburg,* January 5, 1952, between President Truman and Prime Minister Churchill, File: January 1952, Box 70, January–June 1952, Acheson Papers, HSTL.

9. In less eloquent terms, the president agreed with Churchill. See Truman, May 15, 1952, Longhand Notes File, 1952 (longhand personal memos, folder 1), PSF, HSTP, HSTL. "Let us define Trumanism," wrote Truman. "One, we have found by hard earned experience that the Soviet [*sic*] respect only force. So we have built up our armed forces. We have saved Greece, Turkey, Italy, France from invasion by Russia." And he went on, "Four, we prevented Tito from taking Trieste right after the German foldup, we forced Stalin out of Iran, we saved Greece and Turkey, we stayed in Berlin, and we knocked the socks off the communists in Korea."

10. See John Lewis Gaddis, *We Now Know: Rethinking Cold War History* (Oxford: Clarendon Press, 1997), 37, 38–39, 20–21, 47. For an earlier take on themes related to ideology, see John Lewis Gaddis, "The Tragedy of Cold War History," *Diplomatic History* 17 (Winter 1993): 1–16. For his most recent work in the same vein, see John Lewis Gaddis, *The Cold War: A New History* (New York: Penguin Press, 2005).

11. John Lewis Gaddis, *Surprise, Security, and the American Experience* (Cambridge, Mass.: Harvard University Press, 2004), 59–66.

12. John Lewis Gaddis, "After Containment: The Legacy of George Kennan in the Age of Terrorism," *New Republic*, April 25, 2005, 27–31.

13. Ibid.

14. Ibid.

Bibliography

Primary Sources

Manuscript Collections

Clemson University Library (CUL), Clemson, South Carolina

James F. Byrnes Papers

Library of Congress (LOC), Washington, D.C.

W. Averell Harriman Papers
William Leahy Diary
Paul H. Nitze Papers
Henry A. Wallace Papers

George C. Marshall Library (GCML), Lexington, Virginia

George C. Marshall Papers (GCMP)
National Archives Collection
C. Ben Wright Collection
C. Ben Wright Kennan Biography Project

Seeley G. Mudd Library (SGML), Princeton University (PU), Princeton, New Jersey

James Forrestal Papers
George F. Kennan Papers (GFKP)
Arthur Krock Papers

Harry S. Truman Library (HSTL), Independence, Missouri

Dean Acheson Papers
Eben A. Ayers Papers
William L. Clayton Papers
Clark M. Clifford Papers
Matthew J. Connelly Papers
Jonathan Daniels Papers
Robert L. Dennison Papers

George M. Elsey Papers
Ellen Clayton Garwood Papers
Oral History Interviews
    Dean Acheson
    Lucius D. Clay
    Matthew J. Connelly
    George M. Elsey
    Robert A. Lovett
Charles G. Ross Papers
Sidney Souers Papers
Harry S. Truman Papers (HSTP)
    Naval Aide Files
    Official File
    Post-Presidential Files
    President's Official Files
    President's Secretary's Files (PSF)
        Presidential Appointments File
    Records of the National Security Council
Project Whistlestop. Truman Presidential Museum and Library (TPML). Available from http://www.trumanlibrary.org

Documents

Benson, Robert Louis, and Michael Warner, eds. *Venona: Soviet Espionage and the American Response, 1939–1957.* Washington, D.C.: National Security Agency, Central Intelligence Agency, 1996.

Daniels, Robert V., ed. *A Documentary History of Communism.* Vol. 2. New York: Vintage Books, 1960.

Etzold, Thomas H., and John Lewis Gaddis, eds. *Containment: Documents on American Policy and Strategy, 1945–1950.* New York: Columbia University Press, 1978.

Kuhns, Woodrow J., ed. *Assessing the Soviet Threat: The Early Cold War Years.* Washington, D.C.: Center for the Study of Intelligence, Central Intelligence Agency, 1997.

Roosevelt, Franklin D. *The Public Papers and Addresses of Franklin D. Roosevelt, 1928–1945.* 13 vols. Vol. 1: *The Genesis of the New Deal, 1928–1932.* Vol. 2: *The Year of Crisis, 1933.* Vol. 3: *The Advance of Recovery and Reform, 1934.* Vol. 4: *The Court Disapproves, 1935.* Vol. 5: *The People Approve, 1936.* Vol. 6: *The Constitution Prevails, 1937.* Vol. 7: *The Continuing Struggle for Liberalism, 1938.* Vol. 8: *War—and Neutrality, 1939.* Vol. 9: *War—and Aid to Democracies, 1940.* Vol. 10: *The Call to Battle Stations, 1941.* Vol. 11: *Humanity on the Defensive, 1942.* Vol. 12: *The Tide Turns, 1943.* Vol. 13: *Victory and the Threshold of Peace, 1944–45.* New York: Random House, 1938–1950 (vols. 6–9, Macmillan imprint; vols. 10–13, Harper and Brothers imprint).

Truman, Harry S. *Public Papers of the Presidents of the United States: Harry S. Truman— Containing the Public Messages, Speeches, and Statements of the President, April 12,*

1945, to January 20, 1953. 8 vols. Vol. 1: *1945.* Vol. 2: *1946.* Vol. 3: *1947.* Vol. 4: *1948.* Vol. 5: *1949.* Vol. 6: *1950.* Vol. 7: *1951.* Vol. 8: *1952–53.* Washington, D.C.: U.S. Government Printing Office, 1961–1966.

U.S. Congress. *Congressional Record.* Washington, D.C.: U.S. Government Printing Office, 1939–1949.

U.S. Congress. House Committee on Foreign Affairs. *The Strategy and Tactics of World Communism, Supplement III: The Coup d'Etat in Prague.* 81st Congress, 1st Session. Washington, D.C.: U.S. Government Printing Office, 1949.

U.S. Congress. Joint Committee on Printing. *Memorial Services in the Congress of the United States and Tributes in Eulogy of Harry S Truman, Late a President of the United States.* 93rd Congress, 1st Session, House document no. 93–131. Washington, D.C.: U.S. Government Printing Office, 1973.

U.S. Department of State. *Department of State Bulletin.* Vols. 16 and 17. Washington, D.C.: U.S. Government Printing Office, 1947.

U.S. Department of State. *Foreign Relations of the United States, 1941–1954.* Washington, D.C.: U.S. Government Printing Office, 1958–1996. (*FRUS*)

Warner, Michael, ed. *CIA Cold War Records: The CIA under Harry Truman.* Washington, D.C.: Center for the Study of Intelligence, Central Intelligence Agency, 1994.

Wilson, Woodrow. *The Public Papers of Woodrow Wilson.* Vol. 1: *College and State: Educational, Literary, and Political Papers (1875–1913).* Vol. 2: *The New Democracy: Presidential Messages, Addresses, and Other Papers (1913–1917).* Vol. 3: *War and Peace: Presidential Messages, Addresses, and Public Papers (1917–1924).* Authorized ed. Ed. Ray Stannard Baker and William E. Dodd. New York: Harper and Brothers, 1925–1927.

Published Memoirs and Papers

Acheson, Dean. *Present at the Creation: My Years in the State Department.* New York: W.W. Norton, 1969.

Ayers, Eben A. *Truman in the White House: The Diary of Eben A. Ayers.* Ed. Robert H. Ferrell. Columbia: University of Missouri Press, 1991.

Barber, Joseph, ed. *The Containment of Soviet Expansion: A Report on the Views of Leading Citizens in Twenty-Four Cities.* New York: Council on Foreign Relations, 1951.

Bohlen, Charles E. *The Transformation of American Foreign Policy.* New York: W.W. Norton, 1969.

———. *Witness to History, 1929–1969.* New York: W.W. Norton, 1973.

Byrnes, James F. *Speaking Frankly.* New York: Harper and Brothers, 1947.

Churchill, Winston S. *The Sinews of Peace: Post-War Speeches by Winston S. Churchill.* Ed. Randolph S. Churchill. Boston: Houghton Mifflin, 1949.

Clifford, Clark, with Richard Holbrooke. *Counsel to the President: A Memoir.* New York: Anchor Books, Doubleday, 1992.

Djilas, Milovan. *Conversations with Stalin.* New York: Harcourt, Brace and World, 1962.

Forrestal, James V. *The Forrestal Diaries.* Ed. Walter Millis. New York: Viking Press, 1951.

Hillman, William. *Mr. President: The First Publication from the Personal Diaries, Private Letters, Papers and Revealing Interviews of Harry S. Truman.* New York: Farrar, Straus and Young, 1952.

Jones, Joseph M. *The Fifteen Weeks (February 21–June 5, 1947).* New York: Viking Press, 1955.

Kennan, George F. *American Diplomacy: 1900–1950.* New York: New American Library, 1951. Originally published 1951 by University of Chicago Press.

———. *Around the Cragged Hill: A Personal and Political Philosophy.* New York: W.W. Norton, 1993.

———. *From Prague after Munich: Diplomatic Papers, 1938–1940.* Princeton, N.J.: Princeton University Press, 1968.

———. *Interviews with George F. Kennan.* Ed. T. Christopher Jespersen. Jackson: University Press of Mississippi, 2002.

———. *Memoirs, 1925–1950.* Boston: Little, Brown, 1967.

———. *Realities of American Foreign Policy.* Princeton, N.J.: Princeton University Press, 1954.

———. *Sketches from a Life.* New York: Pantheon Books, 1989.

[George F. Kennan] X, "The Sources of Soviet Conduct," *Foreign Affairs* 25, no. 4 (July 1947), 566–82.

Kennan, George F., and John Lukacs. *George F. Kennan and the Origins of Containment, 1944–1946: The Kennan-Lukacs Correspondence.* Columbia: University of Missouri Press, 1997.

Khrushchev, Nikita. *Khrushchev Remembers: The Last Testament.* Trans. and ed. Strobe Talbott. Boston: Little, Brown, 1974.

Krock, Arthur. *Memoirs: Sixty Years on the Firing Line.* New York: Funk and Wagnalls, 1968.

Lane, Arthur Bliss. *I Saw Poland Betrayed: An American Ambassador Reports to the American People.* Indianapolis: Bobbs Merrill, 1948.

Lippmann, Walter. *The Cold War: A Study in U.S. Foreign Policy.* New York: Harper and Brothers, 1947.

———. *Public Philosopher: Selected Letters of Walter Lippmann.* Ed. John Morton Blum. New York: Ticknor and Fields, 1985.

Marshall, George C. *George C. Marshall Interviews and Reminiscences for Forrest C. Pogue.* Ed. Larry I. Bland. Lexington, Va.: George C. Marshall Research Foundation, 1991.

Nitze, Paul H. *From Hiroshima to Glasnost: At the Center of Decision; A Memoir.* New York: Grove Weidenfeld, 1989.

Roosevelt, Franklin D. *Looking Forward.* New York: John Day, 1933.

Roosevelt, Franklin D., and Winston Churchill. *Roosevelt and Churchill: Their Secret Wartime Correspondence.* Ed. Francis L. Loewenheim, Harold D. Langley, and Manfred Jonas. New York: Saturday Review Press/E. P. Dutton, 1975.

Stalin, Josef. *The Great Patriotic War of the Soviet Union.* New York: International Publishers, 1945.

Truman, Harry S. *The Autobiography of Harry S. Truman.* Ed. Robert H. Ferrell. Boulder: Colorado Associated University Press, 1980.

———. *Dear Bess: The Letters from Harry to Bess Truman, 1910–1959.* Ed. Robert H. Ferrell. New York: W.W. Norton, 1983.

———. *Memoirs: Year of Decisions.* Garden City, N.Y.: Doubleday, 1955.

———. *Memoirs: Years of Trial and Hope.* Garden City, N.Y.: Doubleday, 1956.

———. *Mr. Citizen.* New York: Popular Library, 1961.

———. *Off the Record: The Private Papers of Harry S. Truman.* Ed. Robert H. Ferrell. New York: Harper and Row, 1980.

———. *Talking with Harry: Candid Conversations with President Harry S. Truman.* Ed. Ralph E. Weber. Wilmington, Del.: Scholarly Resources, 2001.

———. *Where the Buck Stops: The Personal and Private Writings of Harry S. Truman.* Ed. Margaret Truman. New York: Warner Books, 1989.

Truman, Margaret, ed. *Letters from Father: The Truman Family's Personal Correspondence.* New York: Arbor House, 1981.

Vandenberg, Arthur Hendrick. *The Private Papers of Senator Vandenberg.* Ed. Arthur H. Vandenberg Jr. and J. A. Morris. Boston: Houghton Mifflin, 1952.

Walch, Timothy, and Dwight M. Miller, eds. *Herbert Hoover and Harry S. Truman: A Documentary History.* Worland, Wyo.: High Plains Publishing for the Herbert Hoover Presidential Library Association, 1992.

Wallace, Henry A. *Democracy Reborn.* Ed. Russell Lord. New York: Reynal and Hitchcock, 1944.

———. *New Frontiers.* New York: Reynal and Hitchcock, 1934.

———. *The Price of Vision: The Diary of Henry A. Wallace, 1942–1946.* Ed. John Morton Blum. Boston: Houghton Mifflin, 1973.

———. *Toward World Peace.* New York: Reynal and Hitchcock, 1948.

Wilson, Woodrow. *Constitutional Government in the United States.* New York: Columbia University Press, 1911.

Secondary Sources

Alperovitz, Gar. *Atomic Diplomacy: Hiroshima and Potsdam.* New York: Vintage Books, 1967.

Bekes, Csaba. "Soviet Plans to Establish the COMINFORM in Early 1946: New Evidence from the Hungarian Archives." Cold War International History Project *Bulletin* 10 (March 1998): 135–36.

Bell, Coral. *Negotiation from Strength: A Study in the Politics of Power.* New York: Alfred A. Knopf, 1963.

Benson, Michael T. *Harry S. Truman and the Founding of Israel.* Westport, Conn.: Praeger, 1997.

Bernstein, Barton, ed. *Politics and Policies of the Truman Administration.* Chicago: Quadrangle Books, 1970.

Brinkley, Douglas, ed. *Dean Acheson and the Making of U.S. Foreign Policy.* New York: St. Martin's Press, 1993.

Cantril, Hadley, ed., and Mildred Strunk, prep. *Public Opinion 1935–1946.* Princeton, N.J.: Princeton University Press, 1951.

Chace, James. *Acheson: The Secretary of State Who Created the American World.* New York: Simon and Schuster, 1998.

Courtois, Stéphane, Nicolas Werth, Jean-Louis Panné, Andrzej Paczkowski, Karel Bartosek, and Jean-Louis Margolin. *The Black Book of Communism: Crimes, Terror, Repression.* Ed. Mark Kramer. Trans. Jonathan Murphy. Cambridge, Mass.: Harvard University Press, 1999.

Dallek, Robert. *Franklin D. Roosevelt and American Foreign Policy, 1932–1945.* New York: Oxford University Press, 1979.

Dawley, Alan. *Changing the World: American Progressives in War and Revolution.* Princeton, N.J.: Princeton University Press, 2003.

Djilas, Milovan. *The New Class: An Analysis of the Communist System.* New York: Frederick A. Praeger, 1957.

Ferrell, Robert H. *The Dying President: Franklin D. Roosevelt, 1944–1945.* Columbia: University of Missouri Press, 1998.

———. *George C. Marshall as Secretary of State, 1947–1949.* Vol. 15 in American Secretaries of State and Their Diplomacy. New York: Cooper Square, 1966.

———. *Harry S. Truman: A Life.* Columbia: University of Missouri Press, 1994.

Fleming, D. F. *The Cold War and Its Origins.* Vol. 1: *1917–1950.* Garden City, N.Y.: Doubleday, 1961.

Fleming, Thomas. *The New Dealers' War: F.D.R. and the War within World War II.* New York: Basic Books, 2001.

Fossedal, Gregory A. *Our Finest Hour: Will Clayton, the Marshall Plan, and the Triumph of Democracy.* Stanford, Calif.: Hoover Institution Press, 1993.

Fousek, John. *To Lead the Free World: American Nationalism and the Cultural Roots of the Cold War.* Chapel Hill: University of North Carolina Press, 2000.

Fowler, Robert Booth. *Believing Skeptics: American Political Intellectuals, 1945–1964.* Westport, Conn.: Greenwood Press, 1978.

Friedberg, Aaron L. *In the Shadow of the Garrison State: America's Anti-Statism and Its Cold War Grand Strategy.* Princeton, N.J.: Princeton University Press, 2000.

Friedman, Norman. *The Fifty Year War: Conflict and Strategy in the Cold War.* Annapolis, Md.: Naval Institute Press, 2000.

Gaddis, John Lewis. "After Containment: The Legacy of George Kennan in the Age of Terrorism." *New Republic,* April 25, 2005, 27–31.

———. *The Cold War: A New History.* New York : Penguin Press, 2005.

———. "The Emerging Post-Revisionist Synthesis on the Origins of the Cold War." *Diplomatic History* 7 (Summer 1983): 171–90.

———. *The Long Peace: Inquiries into the History of the Cold War.* New York: Oxford University Press, 1987.

———. "NSC 68 and the Problem of Ends and Means" in "NSC 68 and the Soviet Threat Reconsidered." *International Security* 4, no. 4 (Spring 1980): 164–76.

———. *Russia, the Soviet Union, and the United States: An Interpretive History.* New York: Alfred A. Knopf, 1978.

———. *Strategies of Containment: A Critical Appraisal of Postwar American National Security Policy.* Oxford: Oxford University Press, 1982.

———. *Surprise, Security, and the American Experience.* Cambridge, Mass.: Harvard University Press, 2004.

———. "The Tragedy of Cold War History." *Diplomatic History* 17 (Winter 1993): 1–16.

———. *The United States and the End of the Cold War: Implications, Reconsiderations, Provocations.* Oxford: Oxford University Press, 1992.

———. *The United States and the Origins of the Cold War, 1941–1947.* New York: Columbia University Press, 1972.

———. *We Now Know: Rethinking Cold War History.* Oxford: Clarendon Press, 1997.

Gardner, Lloyd C., Arthur Schlesinger Jr., and Hans J. Morgenthau. *The Origins of the Cold War.* Waltham, Mass.: Ginn, 1970.

Gilbert, Martin. *Winston S. Churchill.* Vol. 8: *Never Despair, 1945–1965.* Boston: Houghton Mifflin, 1988.

Glendon, Mary Ann. *A World Made New: Eleanor Roosevelt and the Universal Declaration of Human Rights.* New York: Random House, 2001.

Graebner, Norman A. *Cold War Diplomacy: American Foreign Policy, 1945–1960.* Princeton, N.J.: D. Van Nostrand, 1962.

Greenfield, Kent Roberts, ed. *Command Decisions.* Washington, D.C.: Department of the Army, 1960.

Grose, Peter. *Operation Rollback: America's Secret War behind the Iron Curtain.* Boston: Houghton Mifflin, 2000.

Gullan, Harold I. *The Upset That Wasn't: Harry S Truman and the Crucial Election of 1948.* Chicago: Ivan R. Dee, 1998.

Gustafson, Merlin. "Harry Truman as a Man of Faith." *Christian Century* 90 (January 17, 1973): 75–77.

Halle, Louis J. *The Cold War as History.* New York: Harper Torchbooks, 1975. Originally published 1967 by Harper and Row.

Hamby, Alonzo L. *Liberalism and Its Challengers: FDR to Reagan.* New York: Oxford University Press, 1985.

———. *Man of the People: A Life of Harry S. Truman.* New York: Oxford University Press, 1995.

Hammond, Thomas T., ed. *Witnesses to the Origins of the Cold War.* Seattle: University of Washington Press, 1982.

Harbutt, Fraser J. *The Iron Curtain: Churchill, America and the Origins of the Cold War.* New York: Oxford University Press, 1986.

Harper, John Lamberton. *American Visions of Europe: Franklin D. Roosevelt, George F. Kennan, and Dean G. Acheson.* New York: Cambridge University Press, 1994.

Haynes, John Earl, and Harvey Klehr. *In Denial: Historians, Communism and Espionage.* San Francisco: Encounter Books, 2003.

———. *Venona: Decoding Soviet Espionage in America.* New Haven, Conn.: Yale University Press, 1999.

Herz, Martin F., ed. *Decline of the West? George Kennan and His Critics.* Washington, D.C.: Ethics and Public Policy Center, 1978.

Hixson, Walter L. *Parting the Curtain: Propaganda, Culture, and the Cold War, 1945–1961.* New York: St. Martin's Griffin, 1998.

Hogan, Michael J. *A Cross of Iron: Harry S. Truman and the Origins of the National Security State, 1945–1954.* Cambridge: Cambridge University Press, 1998.

———. *The Marshall Plan: America, Britain, and the Reconstruction of Western Europe, 1947–1952.* Cambridge: Cambridge University Press, 1987.

Hogan, Michael J., and Thomas G. Paterson, eds. *Explaining the History of American Foreign Relations.* Cambridge: Cambridge University Press, 1991.

Hoopes, Townsend, and Douglas Brinkley. *Driven Patriot: The Life and Times of James Forrestal.* New York: Alfred A. Knopf, 1992.

Horowitz, David. *The Free World Colossus: A Critique of American Foreign Policy in the Cold War.* New York: Hill and Wang, 1965.

Isaacson, Walter, and Evan Thomas. *The Wise Men: Six Friends and the World They Made.* New York: Touchstone, 1988.

Jeffreys-Jones, Rhodri. *The CIA and American Democracy.* 2nd ed. New Haven, Conn.: Yale University Press, 1998.

Jones, Howard. *"A New Kind of War": America's Global Strategy and the Truman Doctrine in Greece.* New York: Oxford University Press, 1989.

Kaplan, Lawrence S. *The United States and NATO: The Formative Years.* Lexington: University Press of Kentucky, 1984.

Kirkendall, Richard S., ed. *Harry's Farewell: Interpreting and Teaching the Truman Presidency.* Columbia: University of Missouri Press, 2004.

———, ed. *The Harry S. Truman Encyclopedia.* Boston: G. K. Hall, 1989.

Klehr, Harvey, John Earl Haynes, and Kyrill M. Anderson. *The Soviet World of American Communism.* New Haven, Conn.: Yale University Press, 1998.

Knock, Thomas J. *To End All Wars: Woodrow Wilson and the Quest for a New World Order.* Princeton, N.J.: Princeton University Press, 1995.

Kofsky, Frank. *Harry S. Truman and the War Scare of 1948: A Successful Campaign to Deceive the Nation.* New York: St. Martin's Press, 1993.

Krugler, David F. *The Voice of America and the Domestic Propaganda Battles, 1945–1953.* Columbia: University of Missouri Press, 2000.

Kuniholm, Bruce Robellet. *The Origins of the Cold War in the Near East: Great Power Conflict and Diplomacy in Iran, Turkey, and Greece.* Princeton, N.J.: Princeton University Press, 1994, with epilogue; originally published 1980 by Princeton University Press.

Kupchan, Charles A. *The End of the American Era: U.S. Foreign Policy and the Geopolitics of the Twenty-First Century.* New York: Alfred A. Knopf, 2002.

LaFeber, Walter. *America, Russia, and the Cold War, 1945–1966.* New York: John Wiley and Sons, 1967.

Leary, William M., ed. *The Central Intelligence Agency: History and Documents.* Tuscaloosa: University of Alabama Press, 1984.

Leebaert, Derek. *The Fifty-Year Wound: The True Price of America's Cold War Victory.* Boston: Little, Brown, 2002.

Leffler, Melvyn P. "The American Conception of National Security and the Beginnings of the Cold War, 1945–48." *American Historical Review* 89 (April 1984): 346–81.

————. *A Preponderance of Power: National Security, the Truman Administration, and the Cold War.* Stanford, Calif.: Stanford University Press, 1992.

Leuchtenburg, William E. *In the Shadow of FDR: From Harry Truman to Ronald Reagan.* Rev. ed. Ithaca, N.Y.: Cornell University Press, 1985.

Liebovich, Louis. *The Press and the Origins of the Cold War, 1944–1947.* New York: Praeger, 1988.

Maddox, Robert James. *The New Left and the Origins of the Cold War.* Princeton, N.J.: Princeton University Press, 1973.

Maier, Charles S. "Revisionism and the Interpretation of Cold War Origins." *Perspectives in American History* 4 (1970): 313–47.

Mark, Eduard. "Revolution by Degrees: Stalin's National-Front Strategy for Europe, 1941–1947." Cold War International History Project. Working Paper no. 31 (February 2001).

Mastny, Vojtech. *Russia's Road to the Cold War: Diplomacy, Warfare and the Politics of Communism, 1941–1945.* New York: Columbia University Press, 1979.

McCormick, Thomas J. "Drift or Mastery? A Corporatist Synthesis for American Diplomatic History." *Reviews in American History* 10 (December 1982): 318–30.

McCoy, Donald R. *The Presidency of Harry S. Truman.* Lawrence: University Press of Kansas, 1984.

McCullough, David. *Truman.* New York: Simon and Schuster, 1992.

McLellan, David S. *Dean Acheson: The State Department Years.* New York: Dodd, Mead, 1976.

Messer, Robert L. *The End of an Alliance: James F. Byrnes, Roosevelt, Truman and the Origins of the Cold War.* Chapel Hill: University of North Carolina Press, 1982.

Miller, Merle. *Plain Speaking: An Oral Biography of Harry S. Truman.* New York: G. P. Putnam's Sons, 1974.

Milward, Alan S. "Was the Marshall Plan Necessary?" *Diplomatic History* 13 (Spring 1989): 231–53.

Miscamble, Wilson D. "The Evolution of an Internationalist: Harry S. Truman and American Foreign Policy." *Australian Journal of Politics and History* (August 1977): 268–83.

————. *George F. Kennan and the Making of American Foreign Policy, 1947–1950.* Princeton, N.J.: Princeton University Press, 1992.

Mitchell, Franklin D. *Harry S. Truman and the News Media: Contentious Relations, Belated Respect.* Columbia: University of Missouri Press, 1998.

Mitrovich, Gregory. *Undermining the Kremlin: America's Strategy to Subvert the Soviet Bloc, 1947–1956.* Ithaca, N.Y.: Cornell University Press, 2000.

Morgenthau, Hans J. *In Defense of the National Interest: A Critical Examination of American Foreign Policy.* New York: Alfred A. Knopf, 1951.

Moynihan, Daniel Patrick. *Secrecy: The American Experience.* New Haven, Conn.: Yale University Press, 1998.

Naimark, Norman M. "'To Know Everything and to Report Everything Worth Knowing': Building the East German Police State, 1945–1949." Cold War International History Project. Working Paper no. 10 (August 1994).

Nelson, Anna Kasten. "President Truman and the Evolution of the National Security Council." *Journal of American History* 72 (September 1985): 360–78.

Nitze, Paul. "The Development of NSC 68" in "NSC 68 and the Soviet Threat Reconsidered." *International Security* 4, no. 4 (Spring 1980): 164–76.

Offner, Arnold A. *Another Such Victory: President Truman and the Cold War, 1945–1953.* Stanford, Calif.: Stanford University Press, 2002.

Page, Benjamin I., and Robert Y. Shapiro. *The Rational Public: Fifty Years of Trends in Americans' Policy Preferences.* Chicago: University of Chicago Press, 1992.

Parrish, Scott D., and Mikhail M. Narinsky. "New Evidence on the Soviet Rejection of the Marshall Plan, 1947: Two Reports." Cold War International History Project. Working Paper no. 9 (March 1994).

Parrish, Thomas. *Berlin in the Balance, 1945–1949: The Blockade, the Airlift, the First Major Battle of the Cold War.* Reading, Mass.: Addison-Wesley, 1998.

Paterson, Thomas G., ed. *Cold War Critics: Alternatives to American Foreign Policy in the Truman Years.* Chicago: Quadrangle Books, 1971.

———. *Meeting the Communist Threat: Truman to Reagan.* New York: Oxford University Press, 1988.

Pechatnov, Vladimir O. "'The Allies are pressing on you to break your will . . .': Foreign Policy Correspondence between Stalin and Molotov and Other Politburo Members, September 1945–December 1946." Cold War International History Project. Working Paper no. 26 (September 1999).

———. "The Big Three after World War II: New Documents on Soviet Thinking about Post War Relations with the United States and Great Britain." Cold War International History Project. Working Paper no. 13 (July 1995).

Pierce, Anne R. *Woodrow Wilson and Harry Truman: Mission and Power in American Foreign Policy.* Westport, Conn.: Praeger, 2003.

Pogue, Forrest C. *George C. Marshall: Statesman, 1945–1959.* New York: Penguin Books, 1989.

Possony, Stefan T. *A Century of Conflict: Communist Techniques of World Revolution.* Chicago: Henry Regnery, 1953.

Puddington, Arch. *Broadcasting Freedom: The Cold War Triumph of Radio Free Europe and Radio Liberty.* Lexington: University Press of Kentucky, 2000.

Rearden, Steven L. *The Evolution of American Strategic Doctrine: Paul H. Nitze and the Soviet Challenge.* Boulder, Colo.: Westview Press, 1984.

Riddle, Donald H. *The Truman Committee: A Study in Congressional Responsibility.* New Brunswick, N.J.: Rutgers University Press.

Rosenthal, Joel H., ed. *Ethics and International Affairs: A Reader.* 2nd ed. Washington, D.C.: Georgetown University Press, 1999.

Ryan, Henry B. "A New Look at Churchill's 'Iron Curtain' Speech." *Historical Journal,* December 1979, 911.

Savage, Sean J. *Truman and the Democratic Party.* Lexington: University Press of Kentucky, 1997.

Schlesinger Jr., Arthur. "Origins of the Cold War." *Foreign Affairs* 46 (October 1967): 23–52.

————. *The Vital Center: The Politics of Freedom.* Cambridge, Mass.: Riverside Press, 1949.

Scott, Andrew M. *The Revolution in Statecraft: Informal Penetration.* New York: Random House, 1965.

Smith, Joseph, ed. *The Origins of NATO.* Exeter, U.K.: University of Exeter Press, 1990.

Steel, Ronald. *Walter Lippmann and the American Century.* Boston: Little, Brown, 1980.

Steinberg, Alfred. *The Man from Missouri: The Life and Times of Harry S. Truman.* New York: G. P. Putnam's Sons, 1962.

Tanenhaus, Sam. *Whittaker Chambers: A Biography.* New York: Random House, 1997.

Taubman, William. *Stalin's American Foreign Policy: From Entente to Détente to Cold War.* New York: W.W. Norton, 1982.

Theoharis, Athan G. *Seeds of Repression: Harry S. Truman and the Origins of McCarthyism.* Chicago: Quadrangle Books, 1971.

Truman, Margaret. *Harry S. Truman.* New York: William Morrow, 1973.

Walton, Richard J. *Henry Wallace, Harry Truman, and the Cold War.* New York: Viking Press, 1976.

Warner, Michael. "The CIA's Office of Policy Coordination: From NSC 10/2 to NSC 68." *Intelligence and Counterintelligence* 11, no. 2: 211–19.

Weinstein, Allen. *Perjury: The Hiss-Chambers Case.* New York: Alfred A. Knopf, 1978.

Weinstein, Allen, and Alexander Vassiliev. *The Haunted Wood: Soviet Espionage in America—The Stalin Era.* New York: Random House, 1999.

Wellborn, Charles. *Twentieth Century Pilgrimage: Walter Lippmann and the Public Philosophy.* Baton Rouge: Louisiana State University Press, 1969.

White, Graham, and John Maze. *Henry A. Wallace: His Search for a New World Order.* Chapel Hill: University of North Carolina Press, 1995.

Williams, William Appleman. *The Tragedy of American Diplomacy.* New York: Delta, 1959; revised 1962.

Williamson Jr., Samuel R., and Steven L. Rearden. *The Origins of U.S. Nuclear Strategy, 1945–1953.* New York: St. Martin's Press, 1993.

Wilmot, Chester. *The Struggle for Europe.* New York: Harper and Brothers, 1952.

Wolff, David. "'One Finger's Worth of Historical Events': New Russian and Chinese Evidence on the Sino-Soviet Alliance and Split, 1948–1959." Cold War International History Project. Working Paper no. 30 (August 2000).

Woods, Randall B., and Howard Jones. *Dawning of the Cold War: The United States' Quest for World Order.* Chicago: Ivan R. Dee, 1994. Originally published 1991 by University of Georgia Press.

Yegorova, Natalia I. "The 'Iran Crisis' of 1945–1946: A View from the Soviet Archives." Cold War International History Project. Working Paper no. 15 (May 1996).

Yergin, Daniel. *Shattered Peace: The Origins of the Cold War.* Rev. ed. New York: Penguin Books, 1990.

Index

Catholic Church, 146; in America,
294n45; against Communism,
210–12, 216–17
Central Intelligence Agency (CIA), 8,
154; director of, 171; OPC in, 172
China, 56, 83; Communist revolution in, 178, 225; Marshall on,
83; Open Door in, 193; Treaty
of Friendship, Alliance, and
Mutual Assistance with USSR,
178; Truman on, 16, 30, 180–81,
287n9
Christianity: Forrestal on, 243n78;
Truman on, 206–7, 211
Churchill, Winston, 16, 21, 37, 193,
228; American response to Fulton
address by, 41–42; British response
to Fulton address by, 42; Fulton
address by, 6, 40, 245–46n12,
246n23; Fulton, Missouri speech
of, 38–43; Navy Day speech responded to by, 27–28; on peace,
245n3; on Soviet Union, 38–39;
Truman praised by, 228; Truman's
meeting with (1946), 39–40
CIA. See Central Intelligence Agency
Clark, Bennett, 15, 237n16
Clark, Champ, 10, 237n16
Clark, Mark, 216
Clark, Tom, 173
Clay, Henry, 69
Clay, Lucius, 138, 274n27
Clayton, Will, 118, 256n25, 257n29
Clifford, Clark, 48, 108, 132, 135,
182; memorandum of, 53–60; on
Truman and Palestine, 97–98
Clifford memorandum, 6, 38, 53–60;
creation of, 55; Elsey's involvement
in, 54–56, 249n62; Long Telegram
and, 54–55; new Soviet policy
proposed by, 57–58; reasons for,
54; Soviet violations catalogued by,
56–57; theoretical sections of, 56;
Truman on, 59–60, 250n76

Cold War, 24, 66, 209–18; academic
views of, 4; as battle of ideas, 122;
beginning, 1; golden age of bipartisanship and, 2–3, 9, 78, 131,
226; hot war scare of, 159–63;
Kennan on, 108; military strength
in, 150–51; Nitze on, 185; progressivism, effect on, 236n12;
public opinion of, 41–43, 76,
262n72, 296n5, 297n6; Truman
on cause of, 253n41; Truman's,
223; Truman's mastery of, 231; war
on terrorism's similarities to, 7–8,
229–30. See also Acheson, Dean;
Churchill, Winston; Communism;
containment; Kennan, George
F.; Lippmann, Walter; Marshall,
George C.; Marshall Plan; Truman,
Harry S.; Union of Soviet Socialist
Republics; Wallace, Henry A.
The Cold War (Lippmann), 112
Comecon. See Council of Mutual
Economic Assistance
Cominform, 93, 260n47; Stalin/Tito
discussions of, 259n43
Comintern, 93
Commission on Protecting and
Reducing Government Secrecy. See
Moynihan, Daniel Patrick
communism, 4, 52, 79, 105; Catholic
Church against, 210–11; in China,
178, 225; in Czechoslovakia,
99–100, 124, 130–31; Forrestal
on, 243–44n78; in Greece, 64–65;
hegemony and, 106; NSC 20 series
and, 165–66; Truman on, 4, 101–
2, 142, 213; in Turkey, 64–65. See
also Marxism; Stalin, Josef; Union
of Soviet Socialist Republics
Communist Information Bureau. See
Cominform
Communist International. See
Comintern
conference(s): Crimea, 22–23; London,

order, 4, 11, 12, 13, 77, 78, 125, 126,
128, 135, 159, 186, 204–5, 222,
224, 287n7
ORE. *See* Office of Research and Evaluation

Paine, Thomas, 214
Palestine, 95–99
Paris Peace Conference, 53–54, 62
particularism, 74
peace, 16, 74; Churchill on, 245n3;
global, 159; Moscow and, 140;
Paris, conference, 53–54, 62;
Truman's desire for, 16, 76–77;
Truman on faith/freedom and,
218–22; Truman on history, faith
and, 199–222; USSR peace move-
ment, 93–94, 210, 225, 259n46;
Wilson's call for, 11
Pearson, Drew, 51, 254n3
Pepper, Claude, 42, 43
Persian Gulf, 63, 182
Petkov, Nikola, 93
Philby, Kim, 176
Philippines: aid for, 144
Policy Planning Staff (PPS), 32, 103;
PPS 1, 118–19, 268n50; PPS 4,
120–22; PPS 13, 123; PPS 23, 126
Postdam, 18, 27, 30, 77, 162, 224,
252n20
postrevisionism, 5, 6, 115, 155, 163–
64, 229
power, 4–5, 12, 110, 169–70, 183–85
PPS. *See* Policy Planning Staff
practical idealism, 28–29
Present at the Creation (Acheson),
255n10
Progressive Citizens for America, 49
progressive internationalism, 3, 13,
223–24
Progressive Party, 133–34
progressivism: Cold War's impact on,
236n12
propaganda, 51, 57, 94, 170, 178,
209–10, 225–26, 263n2

prudence, 41, 138, 154, 155, 196, 220,
224–25
public opinion, 225; on Cold War, 41,
43, 76, 296n5, 297n6

Qavam, Ahmad, 45

Radio Free Europe (RFE), 58, 154, 167,
171, 172, 210, 226
Radio Liberty (RL), 154, 167, 171,
210, 226, 294n41
realism, 2, 4, 13, 20, 74, 276n55; of
Acheson, 83–84, 119; of Kennan,
5, 104, 115, 122, 126–28, 191–92,
194–96; of Lippmann, 5, 146;
NSC 68 and, 224
religion(s), 205–9, 211–14, 221; disagreements among different, 217;
false, 194; unity for, 216
revisionism, 5, 35, 49, 51–52, 73, 104,
107, 146, 155, 156, 163, 238n33
RFE. *See* Radio Free Europe
RL. *See* Radio Liberty
Romania, 67, 68, 92, 93, 199
Roosevelt, Eleanor, 18, 43, 49, 75, 160;
on post-WWII, 21
Roosevelt, Franklin Delano (FDR),
2–3, 9, 19, 24, 49, 143, 174, 228;
on containment, 23; interdependence and, 240n46; liberal internationalism of, 19–20, 84, 129, 224;
mourning of, 43; pragmatism of,
20, 22, 231; Truman under shadow
of, 18–24; Truman's criticism of,
11, 19, 242n67; Truman's differences with, 26–27, 29–30, 78–79;
Truman's relationship to, 15, 16,
237n23
Royall, Ken, 274n27

secretary of defense: Johnson as,
288n19. *See also* Forrestal, James
secretary of state: Acheson as, 255n9.
See also Marshall, George C.